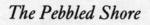

The Pebbled Shore

The Pebbled Shore

· *The Memoirs of* ·

ELIZABETH LONGFORD

Weidenfeld and Nicolson • *London*

To

Frank, our children and grandchildren

First published in Great Britain by
George Weidenfeld & Nicolson Limited
91 Clapham High Street, London SW4 7TA

ISBN 0 297 78863 9

Printed and bound by
Butler & Tanner, Frome and London

Like as the waves make towards the pebbled shore,
So do our minutes hasten to their end,
Each changing place with that which goes before,
In sequent toil all forwards do contend.

SHAKESPEARE, Sonnet 60

Contents

Illustrations

Author's Thanks

I would like to express my thanks to all who have helped me with this book. To my children for having preserved and lent to me their Record Books, which I wrote up from the day of each one's birth until I handed them over when they reached their late teens. (Antonia says these books were my first essays in biography.) I am also grateful to them for not having excised any pages and for allowing me freedom of quotation.

My thanks are due to everyone who has read the manuscript, whether to jog my memory or to make suggestions and corrections: again all my children, and my sister-in-law Mary Clive. Violet Powell, another of Frank's sisters, and Mary have each written wonderfully entertaining memoirs of their own (*Five Out of Six* and *Brought Up and Brought Out*), which taught me a lot about the Pakenhams and also about how and what to remember. Indeed I have learnt from the whole of Frank's family, all of whom were or are writers: beside Mary, Violet and Frank himself, his brother Edward and sister-in-law Christine Longford, his sisters Pansy Lamb and Julia Mount.

Julia's son Ferdinand Mount is a writer in the third generation who, incidentally, first told me the meaning of the name Pakenham, or rather of the Suffolk village from which the family took its name. 'It means "Pacca's homestead" ', wrote Ferdy, ' – but who Pacca was no one knows. I see him as rather a second-rate packman or pedlar of shoddy goods. On the other hand, he may have been a Saxon prince renowned through East Anglia for his valour & purity of heart – or then again he may not.' As a member of the family by marriage I prefer the idea of the pure prince to that of the trashy pedlar.

My brother-in-law Anthony Powell has recently written his memoirs, as well as being master of the comedy of manners. I was once sent to interview him for an American paper. It was like a fascinating day-long tutorial, eked out with the delicious food and wine that Violet had made. Tony had many wise things to say, among them, 'Writing a book is a question of instinct, against contrivance. You must try hard but if you try too hard it will be sham, cardboard.'

Four of my children – Antonia, Thomas, Judith and Rachel – are writers and so are two of my grandchildren, Rebecca and Flora. There is always a great deal of manuscript bartering in our family – 'I'll read yours if you read and criticize mine' – for which I am grateful.

To Harold Pinter, my son-in-law, I am deeply indebted for holidays in the sun, especially one last year when I was midway through this book and needed a second wind. It was an exhilarating experience to listen to the Pinters' and Billingtons' play-reading sessions, interlaced with passionate talk about Amnesty and Star Wars under the stars.

I must thank my cousins Margaret Godfrey and Margy Kinmonth for records of the Chamberlain family to which my mother belonged, my cousin Michael Hope for letters of the 1930s, and my sister Kitty McLachlan for jogging my memory and correcting inaccuracies. My brothers John and Michael Harman reminisced about our childhood, while my cousins Lola and Peter Cameron made available their researches on our Harman forebears.

I thank George Weidenfeld for his encouraging belief that there was a memoir inside me trying to get out, despite the placidity of my life story – no earthquakes or revolutions. Linda Osband and John Curtis of Weidenfeld and Michael Shaw, my agent, have made invaluable suggestions. Agnes Fenner has typed all my books from *Victoria R.I.* onwards and I am most grateful for her stamina and judgement. Frank Dunn has skilfully compiled my index.

One needs to write this kind of book in the right atmsophere. It seemed that our home in Sussex would never be the same again after Mrs Pope and Alice, a devoted mother and daughter – to each other and to us – died. I cannot thank their successors – Gwen Brown and Ellen Grinter – enough for carrying on in the best tradition and making Bernhurst a paradise for writers. Our family doctors, Eardley Davidson and 'Mac' McMichael, who made life so secure for us, both lived, thankfully, into old age, the one to ninety and the other to eighty-six. On the subject of health, I must also thank my son-in-law Alec Kazantzis for introducing me to the perfect diet during a critical time in the writing of this book.

I end by thanking Frank for everything, including the many letters he wrote during our fifty-five years of married life; an agony to read and write, but infinitely worth it. I must also thank him for having kept only a handful of mine ('I am not a man of property'), otherwise I should have been overwhelmed with material. For we wrote to each other almost every day we were apart, particularly during the war. Today, when we are both eighty, thank God that is less and less necessary.

Sussex
Chelsea
January 1986

The Harmans of Harley Street
· *1906–16* ·

My first memory is of Nurse Robins' arrival. I was just three and I see myself standing at the top of the sixty-four stairs to our floor, on the watch. Suddenly a small stout figure appeared, built like Mrs Tiggy Winkle but puffing like a toy steam-engine. She wore a bottle-green cape and bonnet with a lacquered brim and crown. Her shiny black domed trunk preceded her up to the nursery landing, and was carried into our day nursery and set down between the fireplace and the treadle sewing-machine.

My two-year-old brother John and I stared at it with avid curiosity. Our chance to investigate came when Mother took Nurse into the night nursery where she would sleep with the new baby. We two fell upon the unlocked trunk, rummaging among the corsets and buttoned boots until we found, in the top tray, a silver napkin ring and tin of talcum powder. After closing the dome we sprinkled it thickly with powder and then rolled the ring backwards and forwards over the rounded top, making deep tracks in the powder. Nurse suddenly returned and flew into the first of her monumental rages.

But for my lasting alliance with John, I suppose Nurse Robins' obvious lack of enthusiasm for the tiresome elder children in the nursery might have given me a grievance. 'You're not the only pebble on the beach,' was her constant warning to me. She once settled an argument by hitting me over the head with a saucepan. When a bump came up, she assuaged it with a scented paper sachet, after I had promised not to tell Mother. Looking back I can see that Nurse's character defects did me no harm, while I probably owe what imagination I have to her amazing talents. She had been born a Cockney sparrow but with the plumage of a bird of Paradise, frizzy orange hair and brilliant blue eyes, not quite straight. She could do the 'splits' for she had been connected with the music-hall stage as a child. On being asked for a demonstration she would leap into the air, shaking the whole room as she crash-landed on the nursery lino with both legs 'split' in opposite directions. Her excuse for refusing to perform was always the same: 'I've got a bone in my leg. . . .'

Another of her magical gifts was to make our toys come alive. They were kept in a mahogany toy cupboard, into which they were bundled before we left, reluctantly, for our afternoon walk in Regent's Park or the Botanical Gardens. 'Unless you go,' Nurse used to threaten, 'the toys won't be able to come out to play.' One day I returned to see the toys scampering back into their cupboard as I opened the nursery door – all except Frederick, the dare-devil doll, who had delayed too long and got caught half in and half out. Nurse had set up the scene before we left and imagination did the rest. She easily convinced me that Herne Hill and Brixton where she spent her days off were far more exciting places than Harley Street, where we lived.

I was born in 1906 at 108 Harley Street and it was my home until I married twenty-five years later. In some ways it has changed little. It is still the street of the doctors; probably more of them than ever, for when my father bought our house on a 999-year lease he was allowed to put up only two other brass plates beside his own, whereas today I see that some of the houses have seven. Our block of Georgian houses is near the northern end, the last block but one before Marylebone Road. From the outside our house still looks the same as it always did, and the same as those near it: wide front doors with pretty fanlights surmounted by carved stone arches each with a classical head for a keystone. The face over our door always seemed to have a peculiarly nasty sneer.

On the ground floor facing the street are the two large windows of what was our dining-room; of the three smaller windows on the second floor, two belonged to the bedroom shared by my sister and me and the third to Father's dressing-room. I occasionally had to sleep there and hated it. Once when I was undressing a mysterious gust of wind suddenly stirred the curtains and out of the corner of my eye I saw in Father's mirror that my hair had risen an inch from my head. The third floor was given up to children and servants. At the back of the house at this level, looking out on the mews, was our night nursery; below it my parents' bedroom and the only bathroom; on the ground floor back two rented-out consulting rooms, one of them later taken back as our morning-room; in the basement a large kitchen with coal range and skylight, our luncheon-room and various gloomy 'offices' that we rarely visited.

While sleeping in the night nursery I was often woken up by a concert of tom-cats on the mews' roofs. Suddenly Father's sash window would be thrown up and he would hurl a jugful of cold water at the serenaders, or rush downstairs and turn on the roof-garden hose. Splash. Squeals and snarls. Silence for about three minutes. Then the cats would creep stealthily back and the mewing in the mews would start again. On our nursery window-sill we kept creeping jenny and a box of silkworms. One day the silkworms fell to their death on the drawing-room balcony below and I was horrified to find that their 'blood' was not red but yellow.

Today John and his family live on the top two floors, his present drawing-room having been the bedroom in which he and I and all of us were born.

My parents were technically both doctors, though only Father practised. Katherine Chamberlain, my mother, had left her Birmingham home to qualify as a doctor at the Royal Free Hospital in London. She earned only one private fee of £3 for extracting a wisdom tooth before marrying my father. She never practised again. She was already thirty-three when I was born in 1906 and forty-one when the last of her five children arrived. We were all brought into the world at 108 Harley Street by gynaecologists, a Mrs Florence Willey for the second batch and a Lady Barrett for the first. As a schoolgirl, I vaguely thought of the latter as one of the 'Barretts of [nearby] Wimpole Street'. Mrs Willey was the first person I had heard of who had been deserted by her husband, which gave her a romantic interest.

I can never visualize my mother as a doctor, despite her great intelligence, exceptional memory and unsleeping sympathies. There must have been ambition for her to become the only one of seven sisters, most of them clever, to train for a profession. Marriage to my father suppressed the assertive side of her character. I saw that side as a child only when she coached us for Christmas plays or read aloud to us classical poetry and novels. She was a brilliant mimic with a low expressive voice and high colour, one of those unbelievably modest people who suddenly open up on a stage.

Nathaniel Bishop Harman was strikingly unlike his wife in every way. Where she was small and dark, with flashing brown eyes and long, almost black hair that hardly greyed even in old age, he was over 6 foot 2, lanky and fair. He was not a genial parent. I cannot remember his actually roaring with laughter on any family occasion except one. This was when he fell into the River Medway fully clothed, while trying to step from a loaded rowing-boat on to the bank. The boat floated away before his second foot was on land and he sank in stately fashion into the widening chasm of water. We children in the boat watched the drama in utter silence and in an agony of tightly corked emotion. Suddenly he began to smile. The tension broke and we all rocked and screamed with laughter.

John and I normally baited him both for his severities (Mother had to argue second helpings of beef out of him for us every Sunday) and for his sentimentalities. He once picked up a stray terrier bitch on the doorstep of 108 which he kept and called Pippa (a character from 'Pippa Passes' by

Robert Browning). We objected that she had *not* passed, and suggested she should be called Buntle Cruttenden instead, the two most unsentimental names we could think of. The 'Buntle' came from an earlier argument over names. To save butter during the Great War my mother ordered the cook to concoct a mixture of lentils and dripping, which Father said we would call by the attractive name of 'Drintle'. When John and I discovered it was made of lentils and *butter*, not dripping, we gave it the ugly label of 'Buntle', much to Father's displeasure.

There was no doubt about his distinction as a surgeon, an ophthalmic surgeon. He had wonderfully gentle, steady hands, as I realized when he sat me on a stool in his consulting-room and pricked a pimple in my adolescent face. He believed that women could never make the very best doctors because they were unable to detach themselves from their patients but went on worrying about them during the hours they should have been resting. He took his work with profound seriousness. Years later my mother told me that he never made love to her the night before a cataract operation.

His consulting-room was something of a dragon's den to us children when young, for we were supposed always to walk past it in dead silence on our way upstairs, in case he had a patient with him. If we occasionally forgot and passed his door in a spate of chatter he would bounce out in a rage and roar at us to be quiet. He must have frightened his patients far more than his children. Sometimes I would secretly enter his den when he was absent, mostly in search of new books to read. Only once did I find something that looked really promising – the majority of his volumes having titles like *The Conjunctiva in Health and Disease* – and I began to read *Staying the Plague* by N. Bishop Harman in high excitement. It was a scientific account of how to combat venereal diseases.

He was inventive with design as well as ideas, being responsible for several new instruments used in cataract and other eye operations which are now called after him. For our instruction he dissected my dead budgerigar in the 'dirty room', a sinister part of the Harley Street basement, eviscerated it, embalmed it and presented me with my stuffed pet. Unfortunately it did not last. He was also an outstanding draftsman and skilful water-colourist, teaching me many tricks about landscape, such as leaving a faint mist in the folds of the hills that I was forever sketching from our holiday house in Kent. John and I drew and painted every day, he amusingly, I romantically. I remember his very first picture: a teapot out of which the steam was trying to escape with the words LET ME GO in a balloon from the spout. John had drawn them in looking-glass writing as OG EM TEL, but each letter printed backwards. Father was delighted at such naïve ingenuity. He liked my paintings of tree roots inspired by Arthur Rackham, as he had played cricket with Rackham at Cambridge. (He idolized St John's College, Cambridge, and sent all three of his sons there; Oxford was good enough for his daughters.)

My father was not at his best with children. He repressed his natural conviviality in their supposed interest and became deeply irritable when they did not make equal sacrifices for his sake. His nephew, the Revd Arthur Barnes, wrote of him after his death: 'Nat, the elder of my mother's brothers, was not very easy with children and adopted a teasing and rather superior attitude. You needed to stand up to him and argue the point; then he began to thaw.' With his own children, however, standing up to him hardly ever paid. We regarded our mother as perfection, him as a spoilsport. Indeed there was only one hour in the whole week when he let himself go and played with us. This was on Sunday evenings. After a romp called 'The Lion Game' that ended in a race up and down the hall, he would get out his Stylo pen and offer to draw a picture for each of us in turn. He never used fresh paper; always the back of some medical document. After the birth of our youngest brother, when I was eight, my choice of subject was always the same: How Babies Are Born. My father as regularly cheated. He produced a series of storks, chimneys and doctors' bags, finally surpassing himself with a sketch of tadpoles emerging from frogspawn. When I protested that this was no answer to my question, he said, 'But they *are* babies being born.'

Strangely enough my parents, though both doctors with advanced views on certain subjects, never told any of us children the facts of life. It was John who correctly speculated about them to me, after observing the mating of our silkworm moths. Even so, I knew nothing about menstruation until it happened to me at boarding-school, aged fourteen. Two years earlier my mother had casually remarked: 'If you see a mark on your combinations one day, come and tell me.' For a time I used to examine every tiny speck on my clothes meticulously in case it turned out to be the mysterious 'mark'; then gave up. My sister remembers having the same experience. I was almost grown up before I knew the purpose of the menstrual flow. My best friend at school, also the daughter of a doctor, confidently assured me, 'It's really mother's milk gone bad.'

The reason why I did not try to breach my parents' reticence on sex, after my early attempts, is not far to seek. On a summer holiday, having run out of the sea to get dressed, I blundered by mistake into my parents' bathing-machine instead of my own. My father's voice, full of menace, bellowed 'Get out!' I retreated in terror and confusion, feeling that I had only just missed seeing something extremely nasty in the marine woodshed.

I was not born, apparently, with the keen appetite for living that I was later to acquire. 'She is doing her best to grow,' wrote my mother of me at two months. 'She is a little minx and refuses to take more of her bottle than she thinks she wants. There is no opportunity for overfilling her! However, she grows in strength if not in size and is very lively when awake.' A few years later I would be standing impatiently beside Nurse waiting to drain the remains of my delicate brother Roger's bottle of Mellin's Food and raw beef juice.

My only sister Kitty was three years younger than me and like Mother to look at. I can remember nothing about her birth, though I made a dreadful scene when she was weaned and left Mother's bedroom for what I considered my domain, the nursery. This is how my mother described it in a letter to her father, my Grandpapa Chamberlain. (I was called by my full and only name, Elizabeth, until a year old, when my mother began referring to me as Betty.)

Betty, about whom I was most anxious, has not given Baby that welcome to the nursery which she extended to her before! She is quite jealous of Nurse taking Baby & had such storms of sobs & tears that . . . she was left with a racking headache . . . more cheerful today, though she hopes I shan't keep Baby very long.

My mother had to take Kitty back for two nights and was worn out between her two daughters.

During those early days Nurse Robins was allowed to introduce a religious ritual into the nursery which my parents did not themselves practise: grace at meals. When John was nearly three our current nursemaid Grace was replaced by Nellie. On the day of the change Nurse said as usual, 'John, say your grace.' John rattled off, 'Nellie, thank-the-Lord-for-my-good-tea-please-may-I-get-down-Nurse?' 'John, you're not to say "Nellie",' corrected Nurse; 'begin "Thank the Lord". . . .' 'You told me to say Grace,' argued John aggrieved, 'but this isn't Grace any more – this is Nellie now.' John possessed an obstinate realism even as a baby.

After Kitty came Roger, whose birth I remember vividly, being nearly six at the time. A few days before his arrival I noticed that Nurse was running up a baby's nightgown on the sewing-machine. 'Whose baby is it for?' I asked. 'It's not for a baby,' she replied, 'it's for your birthday doll.' (I was already counting the days to my birthday.) 'But the sleeves are too big for a doll's arms,' I objected. 'They're not sleeves,' lied Nurse, loyally keeping my mother's secret, 'they're just trimmings to hang down like this', and she cleverly arranged the baby's sleeves in a way that completely took me in. In fact my new brother was doll-size, being premature.

My father woke me on the night Roger was born to tell me the news. I demanded to see him but was told to wait till morning. Whereupon I had a self-flattering dream of an angelic little child dressed all in pale blue who ran into my arms and refused to go to anyone else. With the morning came bitter disappointment. Roger turned out to be a tiny wizened yellow face with moist black hair lying motionless on a white pillow. Nevertheless the dream showed that one day I might develop maternal feeling.

As a child I was an alarmingly capricious mother to my dolls. My two favourites were Mary, a stately flaxen beauty resembling the Queen, and Verona, called after a girl in my dancing-class. They were mostly kept high up in our wardrobe and brought down to be played with only intermittently. While the enthusiasm lasted, I would begin sewing new outfits for them and making elaborate plans for their welfare. Suddenly, with nothing completed, the craze would vanish, and John and I would amuse ourselves hurling Mary, Verona and all their belongings back into the wardrobe for another month of total neglect.

Despite his angelic appearance – golden hair and large light blue eyes – John was always mischievous and sceptical. I think he egged me on in my anti-doll excesses, which was not difficult, as I much preferred my paint-box and notebooks to any doll. I felt he went too far, however, one day in the Botanical Gardens. Having organized a gang of brothers to kidnap all the dolls from their sisters' dolls' prams, he tied them by their necks to a long string until they were, he assured me, stone dead. The moral of that story must be that the child is not always father to the man or mother to the woman. John is exceptionally good with small children and a doting grandfather, while I could never have enough babies – far more (eight) than I ever had dolls.

My youngest brother, Michael, was born in 1914. I admired his dark curls and slanting black eyes, and felt sure of a family triumph when Nurse decided to enter him for the 'Decorated Baby-and-Pram' at the Botanical Gardens Rose Show. (My mother was above such things and left them to Nurse.) But when we reached the Gardens (half-an-hour's hot trudge from Harley Street), the sweet peas trailing around the hood of his pram had all withered, and in any case looked sparse and meagre compared with some of the lavish entries. This was my first experience of an all-too-common syndrome: setting forth for a party well satisfied with one's turn-out, only to find it mortifyingly inadequate. However, Nurse, with Cockney spirit, pushed Michael's pram right under Queen Alexandra's nose, thus forcing a compliment from HM. We children noticed with interest that her face did not crack though made, we understood from

Nurse, of enamel. My disappointment over the pram was fully compensated for by the sight of a ravishing girl dressed all in roses with golden curls and a pink hat, stationed with the judges on the grandstand. I shall always believe it was my first glimpse of Barbara Cartland.

'The Gardens', as we called that fee-paying playground for the children of fee-paid parents – now Queen Mary's Gardens, a public part of Regent's Park – was the almost daily pilgrimage of Nurse, nursemaid, pram, mailcart, baby, toddlers, John and me. Many of my earliest meditations took place either in the Gardens or on the way there. It was while crossing the bridge over Regent's Park lake, clinging to one handlebar of the big green double pram, that a puzzling thought entered my head: suppose everything that's happening now – the walk, the bridge, the water, Nurse, John, Kitty, me, everyone – is all in a dream? How am I to know? I couldn't know, could I, unless I woke up? But if I went on dreaming? . . . Years later when reading philosophy at Oxford I was glad to find my childish thoughts had found a place in more magisterial minds.

Actually dreams were one of my great interests, and many was the breakfast-time when John and Kitty had to howl me down as I began, 'I had such a funny dream last night. . . .' I always dreamt in colour, my most memorable dream being of flying over an oriental garden carpeted with a tapestry of brilliant flower-beds. The sensation of flying was delicious, as I circled among birds and over domes and minarets.

From my worst nightmare I always awoke screaming that the wolves were after me and had set the house on fire. The awakening was almost as frightening as the dream, for in order to find Mother I had to rush down the dark well of our high London house, Father having insisted on 'lights off' everywhere except on the very top landing and in the hall. As I grew older my nightmares changed into sleepwalking. Mother once found me in her bedroom sitting at a chest of drawers that I thought was a piano on which I was practising my scales. A more alarming experience was when I had been married a few years and Frank and I were attending a conference at Bouffémont outside Paris. We were lodged in a girls' finishing-school, several storeys up, each twin room having French windows and a low balcony. The first night I woke up standing on the balcony in my nightdress, about to step out into what I thought was a moonlit garden. I awoke just in time to see the concrete far below. Next night Frank pushed his bed across the window but was awakened by me clambering over his feet towards my imagined garden. After that we had to lock ourselves in.

There was a lake in the Botanical Gardens that I sketched lusciously with Windsor & Newton pastels, smudging in the autumn tints and getting an effect with no effort. I also collected frogspawn from the shallows and brought two newts from the country to keep in a bowl in Harley Street. I was besotted by their little faces and delicate hands and the bubbles they blew; until one day I found the bowl empty and a tiny dried-up corpse on the stairs, another under the mat at the front door. I had not realized they sometimes needed dry land and was overwhelmed by the pathos of their long, fatal search for the Harley Street countryside.

It was in the Gardens that I remember asking myself tearfully whether I would ever in my life get through a whole day without once crying. I decided probably not. Yet with all the boredom, which caused teasing, which in turn caused tears, there were occasional small dramas in the Gardens that would make my day. One afternoon a swan from the lake strode hissing towards us with spread wings and Mother, intrepidly seizing it by its long outstretched neck, marched it back into the water. We all laughed hysterically as it twisted its neck about and about, as if wondering whether it had been wrung. Afterwards Mother explained that a swan's wings could break a man's leg.

Another time a gentleman took a photograph of me by the lakeside, saying he wanted a poetic-looking child (I was rather pale with greenish blue eyes and light brown wispy hair) to illustrate a book he was writing. Mother was contemptuous. She was no less so when a red-haired boy from the Gardens sent me by post a silver box. It was returned to him forthwith and I, mourning the loss of my admirer and my box, was informed that it was not silver but only antimony.

I treasured incidents like this because the sight of my pale face in the mirror convinced me I would never be pretty. This made me feel shy. However, I greatly underestimated my powers of getting what I wanted, shy or not. I can recall one example of this push (probably the special gift of eldest children) and the surprise it caused me. I had been taken to a Christmas party at our cousins the Debenhams in Addison Road. I knew hardly anyone there and felt left out. The Debenham children acted 'The Frog Prince', red-haired Alison taking the part of the princess. As soon as it was over there was a rush by the audience of children to seize one of the lovely princess's hands and lead her in to tea. To my amazement I found myself in the forefront of the mob and in triumphant possession of a hand.

I loved wet days in my childhood. If we were in the Gardens when it came on to rain, we were allowed to shelter in the vast humid conservatory among writhing tropical plants instead of playing eternal hide-and-seek in the shrubberies. If we were in Regent's Park we would dash for one of the sooty Victorian summerhouses. From here, with luck, we could see the very pillar-box in which, Nurse told us, the suffragettes had posted dynamite instead of letters. If it was too wet to leave our nursery, there were great rejoicings and the paint-boxes were immediately brought out.

A London pea-souper or even black fog was the best of all, when Nurse admitted she couldn't see the lamppost outside Number 108. So we had to stay indoors. By bedtime, however, plenty of smuts had seeped into the nursery through the two large sash windows and we would beg Nurse to show us the *black* face flannel with which she had just cleaned our noses and ears.

When I was four I learnt to read from a set of cards. My mother was put out to find that she had wasted her money, since I only used each card once. I can still hear John's imaginative attempts to read 'The Cat is on the Mat'. Obediently he would spell out the sounds of 'c-a-t' and then triumphantly pronounce it 'apple'. As there were only eleven months between us in age we were put into the same class at our first kindergarten. I soon had to be moved up, being hard-working and attentive, whereas John's attention could not be commanded. Yet at university he beat us all with a first.

Our kindergarten was run by a Miss Newth in Baker Street. Two of the small boys I got to know in those days are still friends. One is David Eccles. His father, Dr McAdam Eccles, lived in the next block to ours. David did not attend Miss Newth's but escorted us and his own younger brother Peter to the threshold of Miss Newth's before going off to his own prep school. I regarded David with awe, partly because he never walked with us small fry but always a few paces in front. Our march to school was conducted with military precision. David would halt us at each crossing, make us look both ways and only then give us the order to advance. This was long before schoolchildren were taught kerb drill.

My other friend from Miss Newth's was the future newspaper and magazine proprietor, Edward Hulton. Younger than me, Teddy arrived as a terrified small boy who was bullied by the student teacher. When at first he was too shy to co-operate she penned him into a corner behind the desks. 'All right, if you won't join in you can stay there!' I managed to distract her so that he escaped.

When it was time for me to move on to a girls' day school, my parents made their first and only attempt to give me an 'ideological' education. It was a total failure. They chose a small school in Frognal with a Nonconformist connection, to suit their own beliefs. The atmosphere was cheerless, and as a new girl of ten I made the conceited mistake of always learning more of the set verses for poetry prep than anyone else, and reciting them at length. For this I was regularly punished with a prick in the neck from a pair of compasses by the girl sitting behind me. I hated making hopeless swipes with my hockey stick on autumnal Hampstead Heath.

I am not a natural rebel; in fact I am temperamentally adapted to putting up with things. After one term, however, I rebelled against Frognal, inventing to satisfy my parents a story that the journey from Harley Street to Frognal was too tiring and that I was always falling asleep on the No. 2 bus and overshooting my stop. (I did it once.) I realized that there would be religious objections to the school I wanted to attend instead, but decided to make a rare fight for it.

The school of my choice was the Francis Holland Church of England School for Girls in Baker Street. 'All my friends go there,' I said, meaning the various doctors' daughters who lived in or near Harley Street and went to the Gardens and Miss Bretell's dancing and gym classes in Nottingham Place. But before describing what Francis Holland School meant to me, I should perhaps say something about my early religious upbringing.

It was simple in content and serious in tone. No frills like cribs at Christmas. I never heard the expression 'baby Jesus' until I had left my own babyhood far behind. Mother taught me the Lord's Prayer beside the lake in the Gardens, changing the word 'trespasses' as being too hard for a child, into 'debts' – 'Forgive us our debts as we forgive our debtors.' Every evening she sat, first on my bed and then on John's, to hear our prayers. They were monotonously the same: 'Please God bless me and keep me safe this night. Bless Mother and Father, John [or Betty], Kitty, Roger and Michael and all my friends. Make me a good girl [or boy]. Amen.' There was an enjoyable occasion when John accidentally began reciting the alphabet, 'ABCD . . .', and then changed to counting, 'One Two Three Four . . .'; such was the effect of endless repetition.

On Sunday mornings we walked to church with our parents, the first we attended being the King's Weigh House, an imposing terracotta Congregational Church in Duke Street. (Today it is the Ukrainian Catholic Cathedral.) I enjoyed the hymns, when I would rock furiously from side to side, having observed that adults swayed while singing. Later we transferred to Essex Church near Notting Hill, a plain brick Unitarian building which was free from the pacifist preaching and high church practices that I was told had begun to infiltrate the Weigh House. After the service we walked all the way home across Hyde Park to Sunday dinner of invariable roast sirloin of beef and apple pie. My father's conversation on these weekly walks was consciously instructive. He announced to us the Russian Revolution – 'a terrible event but good to be rid of the Tsars'; the Amritsar massacre – 'unavoidable'; and the arrival of Epstein's *Rima* in the bird sanctuary – 'a disgusting parody of a woman, breasts stuck on like postage stamps'. I was rather thrilled at my father mentioning breasts and realized he was unusually angry.

I was not religiously moved at Essex Church, except by a few of the hymns, such as 'Lord of all being throned afar' and a gloomy prayer that began 'The harvest is done, the summer is over and we are not saved'. John told me years later that this prayer affected him too. During the sermons I would while away the time by twisting up rubber bands and making them jump on to the backs of the family sitting in front of us, the Leonard Huxleys. I can remember being only once deeply stirred in church during the whole of my childhood. This was on Armistice Day, 1918, when all the Nonconformist sects gathered together in the beautiful Austin Friars church in the City to give thanks. I had never heard a massed choir before or seen a great church at night with the traceries of the tall Gothic windows shining against the blackness outside. I was twelve, the age to burst one's lungs singing, 'Now thank we all our God'.

But if we were not generally responsive church-goers, John and I had fits of secret religious enthusiasm at a very early age. Our place of worship was hidden under the dark branches of a yew tree. We used an oblong biscuit tin as an altar, decorated it with tiny home-made candles of wax moulded around wicks of darning wool and filled it with small green apples. At the end of the ceremony the tin was opened and the apples eaten. Kitty and I developed a rather more sophisticated religious game. We sewed together little paper books of texts, my favourite being 'Judge not that ye be not judged'.

After Sunday dinner and before the muffin man began ringing his bell for tea, bringing the uniformed parlourmaids up from their basements to buy, Mother would read us passages from the New Testament. More than once she insisted that Jesus was a very good man, not God, and gave us her proof. 'Well, Jesus was not perfect, was he? You remember, don't you, that he ran away from his parents in Jerusalem and gave Mary and Joseph a very unhappy time looking for him?' Her low, serious and beautiful voice made me feel that everything she said must be true. More than sixty years later, when I came to read my father's love-letters to my mother, I discovered that he had given way on the divinity of Christ, in which he really believed, in order to win her. He also agreed that she should teach us the basic tenets of Unitarianism.

I have sketched my religious upbringing until about the age of ten. But how to convey all the conflicting ingredients of our family atmosphere? Austerity and undemonstrativeness along with powerful affection; puritanism with all the comforts of a middle-class Edwardian home; the status conferred by a house in Harley Street offset by the minority creed of outsiders. I must go back to my mother's and my father's families from which the mixture evolved, remembering that the head of the Chamberlain clan was offered a tomb in Westminster Abbey, while the grave of Grandfather Harman remains difficult to find in Old Highgate Cemetery.

2

'Dear Miss Chamberlain'
· 1842–1906 ·

The two sides of my family – Chamberlains and Harmans – had some things in common. Both began as yeomen farmers and could be traced back in personal detail to the eighteenth century but no further. They were both dissenters, the Chamberlains being Unitarians, the Harmans Strict Baptists. And they were both in trade: 'the higher sort of tradesmen' as the Chamberlains were to be called, 'plain, honest and sincere', originally Wiltshire yeomen farmers who had arrived via Sussex at the City of London where they ran a successful shoe business in Milk Street. Three of them rose to be Masters of the Worshipful Company of Cordwainers.

My grandfather, Arthur Chamberlain, born in 1842 in Camberwell Grove, London, was the second son of Joseph Chamberlain and Caroline Harben of East Sussex. Arthur's parents had married at St Olave's in the City. Beneath them, as they plighted their troth, lay Samuel Pepys and his wife. The bridegroom, being a Unitarian, could not follow the Anglican marriage service and had to be prompted by the impatient clergyman: 'Kneel, sir, kneel!' Their eldest son Joseph, the future statesman, was Arthur's senior by six years. Family stories about young 'Joey' made him out to be combative: at four he stamped his mother's silver thimble flat, at nine he and the minister's son blew up a snail with gunpowder. It should have been Arthur who committed this act of war for my grandfather was to manufacture cordite.

Arthur's mother aspired to be an elegant hostess. The family moved in 1846 to 25 Highbury Place, Islington, where Arthur's aunt Charlotte Bailey described a dinner of champagne and hock, salmon and 'a pretty little forequarter' in honour of their relative Dr James Martineau, the formidable divine. The ladies were soon engaging the doctor in a discussion of Auguste Comte's philosophy, a subject with which Unitarians felt quite at home. A year later Aunt Charlotte was to move in even more exalted circles. Her year-old son Edward had just been vaccinated against smallpox. She travelled with Edward and his nurse to

13

Windsor Castle, where first Prince Bertie and then both Queen Victoria and Prince Albert were vaccinated 'from the pus' on baby Edward's arm. His nurse was afterwards tipped £5 by Sir James Clark, the Queen's doctor, on HM's behalf.

It was through John Nettlefold of Birmingham, Arthur's uncle by marriage, that the Chamberlains were eventually uprooted from London. The Nettlefolds had stepped into the industrial limelight when they bought the patent of a nail-making machine from America in 1786. I remember my mother repeating to us children a favourite rhyme of her own youth:

> For want of a nail the shoe was lost,
> For want of a shoe the horse was lost,
> For want of a horse the battle was lost,
> And all through the want of a horse-shoe nail.

The Nettlefolds of Birmingham were not going to be caught that way, and again in the next century the firm proposed to buy for £30,000 another American patent for mass-produced wood screws. John Nettlefold had seen the new screw at the Great Exhibition of 1851. Three years later his brother-in-law Joseph Chamberlain agreed to contribute most of the new capital and also his eighteen-year-old son Joe as supervisor. The Birmingham screw factory soon eclipsed the London shoe factory. It was to grow into the industrial colossus of Guest, Keen & Nettlefold. My grandfather saw the shop in Milk Street closed down in 1863 and with his family he followed his brother Joe to Birmingham.

I like to imagine the Chamberlain family's entry into Birmingham in terms of Mr Pickwick's famous arrival in 'the great working town' a generation earlier. Coming from the neat lawns and raked gravel of quiet Islington, the Chamberlains would have been blinded by the same sullen glare, choked by the same dense smoke pouring from 'high, toppling chimneys', deafened by the same 'din of hammers, the rushing of steam, and the dead heavy clanking of the engines'. Above all it was still the same town of 'earnest occupation', of thronging workers that had so much amazed the easygoing Mr Pickwick.

My grandfather Arthur was now twenty-one and he joined his father in a firm of Birmingham brassfounders, to be known as Smith & Chamberlain. Their new home, Moor Green Hall, was something of a rural paradise. There were conservatories, squirrels playing in a wheel and the largest snapdragons I have ever seen, bedded out in front of the grey mansion. Their musty scent still carries me back to hot summers before the Great War. I ate my first bonfire potatoes somewhere in the woods between Moor Green and the Lickey hills, which I saw through my mother's eyes carpeted in springtime with primroses and wild daffodils – except for one sinister spot where a landlord had installed a spring gun to scare poachers.

Every morning Arthur would go with his father on foot across the fields and by pony trap or omnibus to the brass foundry in Moseley. His father was to enjoy eleven years of life in Birmingham, a Victorian paterfamilias of the benignly dominant kind. In 1874, the year after my mother was born, he lay on his death-bed, peaceful after the 'struggle' and supported by his wife and two elder sons, Joe and Arthur. No need for death-bed repentance. He knew where he was going. And they after him. Raising his hands and pointing upwards he spoke his last word, 'Higher'. Next year his wife Caroline duly set out to join him in a 'higher' place.

Meanwhile the younger Chamberlains were helping other like-minded spirits to break the mould of politics in their adopted city. A powerful new entity had emerged, radical, public-spirited, well-endowed and inter-related, which they themselves called the 'cousinship'. Their illiterate political enemies called them 'the Click'. Cliquish they may have been, but it seemed to them a matter for congratulation, not shame. When the cousins gathered to eat roast sucking-pig and toast themselves at Christmas, it was with general laughter that they drank 'the Click's' health.

Joe had enjoyed a very healthy mayoralty of Birmingham and was systematically knocking the backwoodsmen off the City Council. He had made a fortune out of the new screws. In 1874 he sold the Chamberlain share of the business to Nettlefolds for over half a million and was able to retire into politics with a personal capital of £120,000.

Arthur was also advancing along the route of municipal reform. He was appointed chairman of the Birmingham Licensing Committee, from which commanding height he was to wage lifelong war against the brewers, whom he regarded as the Tory Party not at prayer but in their cups. My mother once told me that before Grandpapa launched his crusade to withhold licences there was a pub at each end and in the middle of even the shortest street. Arthur could see the effect of intemperate drinking on his own workers.

By the 1880s 'his workers' – for he was a paternalist – had grown into a far more significant work-force than the one which had cast the brass for Smith & Chamberlain twenty years before. He reached his zenith as a director and then chairman of Birmingham's world-famous firm, Kynoch's. I was once taken by my mother to see the portentous descent and ascent of Kynoch's huge steam hammer. 'When we were young,' said my mother, 'Papa used to demonstrate the absolute control of this monster by telling us that we could lay a little finger on the slab and the hammer would come down within an inch of the finger – not the slightest danger of crushing it.' 'And did you lay your finger there?' I asked breathlessly. 'No, Papa always demonstrated with a ring.'

My grandfather was to become not only a pioneer of 'shareholders' rights' in efficient takeovers but also a champion of directors' authority. There is a story of Chairman Chamberlain and a persistent heckler at a shareholders' meeting. The chairman was suddenly observed to lean over and whisper to the company secretary, 'What's his holding?' 'Ten pounds.' The chairman drew a £10 note from his wallet. 'There's your holding,' he addressed the heckler, 'now leave the room.'

Politically he was an uncompromising Liberal. After years of intense loyalty to his brother Joe, he split over Liberal Free Trade versus Tory Protection. Joe had become a Tory.

The extent of Arthur Chamberlain's revulsion from his brother's politics was startlingly revealed towards the end of his life. My grandfather distributed a kind of 'Farewell to Politics' letter to each of his children. The letter was composed after the Liberal election drama of 1910, in which Arthur was proud to have been given a speaking part. (He took the chair for Mr Asquith, the Liberal Prime Minister, in Birmingham.) The last paragraph ran:

In addition . . . there is the fact, remaining for ever, that I have done something for the family inheritance in that I have saved our name from the shame (as I think it) of being altogether bound up with re-action & wrong-doing. Your Uncle Joe is so big a man that there was a danger that we should all, in public estimation, be tarred with his brush!

From my position as a lifelong supporter of the Labour Party, I find myself both critical and sympathetic towards my grandfather. His ardent belief in 'freedom' from all interference led him to tackle trade unions with the same sharpness that he used on tiresome shareholders. He broke a strike in 1891 by sending a dictatorial letter to every striker:

You had absolutely no grievance of any kind sufficient to justify a strike. But you placed yourselves in the hands of political partizans [*sic*] and you imported paid agitators from outside to slander the company which for years had been paying you better wages than the majority are ever likely to get again in your lives.

The tone makes me wince.

On the other hand, he was among the first employers to introduce an eight-hour day, and he actively welcomed Lloyd George's left-wing budget of 1909 as an alternative to the 'workhouse and infirmary'. If King George V had had to support his Prime Minister Mr Asquith with a mass creation of Liberal peers, Grandpapa would have been one of them – perhaps the first Baron Birmingham. A witty talker, he was also said to be hot-tempered and quarrelsome, not one to suffer fools gladly. This last trait he shared with his brother Joe and both probably inherited it from generations of humble but opinionated forefathers. At a temperance meeting in 1904 Arthur did not hesitate to rap his Tory colleagues over the knuckles: 'I cannot help thinking', he said, 'that some people will pay a heavy price in the next world for having been Magistrates in this.' He himself was prepared to pay the price in this world of unpopularity.

I can just remember him as an awe-inspiring figure with drooping eyelids, slit eyes, a grey frock-coat and watch-chain. His complexion was somewhat yellow (he may already have been suffering from the cancer of which he died in 1913), so what with the eyes and skin, I had the vague idea that Grandpapa Chamberlain was a mysterious oriental. The mystery was enhanced by his arrival for a moment each morning in our midst. We grandchildren were assembled in the great hall. Suddenly the door of a lift at the far end of the hall would open and the Expected One would step out. 'Good morning, Grandpapa!' we would all scream together – or not quite together, for the ritual was to see who could salute him first. I was always last. And a further humiliation awaited me at Sunday lunch. Before the dessert when the long white tablecloth was removed, every child had to recite a poem to Grandpapa. My cousin Margaret Godfrey (formerly Hope) can still recall the burst of merriment that greeted my shrill, near-Cockney drawl:

> *I* would be a yellow primrose
> Growing on a shady bank . . .

I longed for any bank, the shadier the better, behind which to hide from that ironical applause.

The Harmans of Highgate were Strict Baptists. My grandfather Walter John Harman, born in 1829 east of the City, was only eight when his mother died and he and all his younger brothers and sisters were handed over to the care of their old family nurse. A Baptist herself of the Strict variety, this nurse promptly converted her charges from the conventional Anglicanism of their dead mother to her own eclectic creed. Baptists in general were not the most relaxed of Nonconformists and the Strict sect outshone all others in the rigours of their ethic. They were Calvinists believing in predestined salvation by faith; they expressed that faith by total immersion in adult baptism; and they spread that faith by exceptional emphasis on missions. All these things were to affect my father.

My grandfather's temperament leapt to meet this imported puritanism. The inherent self-reliance that the new creed encouraged was further developed by the death of his father. At only seventeen he registered his father's death from 'disease of the lungs' at his home, 23 Lucas Street (now Lukin Street), Stepney, made arrangements for the education of his two brothers and generally became a youthful but authoritarian head of the family.

For many years it was a hard struggle and at first his way of life had to be extremely modest compared with his parents'. His father Edward Harman had been a banker and was registered at death as 'Quality: Gentleman'. Despite the bleak outlook my grandfather Walter Harman resolved to work his way back to prosperity equal to his father's. He was soon running the business for a Major Lambert, silversmith and jeweller of Coventry Street, Piccadilly. Though Walter was never offered a partnership, he developed a keen eye for antique silver and a charm that made him a good salesman. The charm, however, was left behind at work instead of being brought home to his family, who saw the dark side of his Calvinism.

After living in various places including Vicars Road, Kentish Town, where my father was born, Walter's family were finally ensconced in a fine new house built to his requirements at 5 Dartmouth Park Road on Highgate Hill. He named it Balcombe House after his mother, the 'Belle of Balcombe' in Sussex. It had a long garden, a dining-, drawing- and morning-room, seven bedrooms and one of the first bathrooms in the district with h and c and a flush lavatory. He saved enough to buy house property in North London. Every Saturday morning he would inspect it and collect the rents. Long after Grandfather's death I can remember some of those same tenants, silent and unexplained people, bringing their rents to Father in Harley Street.

Grandfather Harman was immensely proud of all his possessions: house, wife, children and religious faith. The house still stands, divided into flats; the religion was carried on by only one of his seven surviving children. So proud was he of the Harmans of Highgate that he managed to trace them back to a Clerk of the Crown in the reign of Henry VII. My father, emulating him, claimed a certain Edward Harman, barber-surgeon (doctor) to Henry VIII, as an ancestor. In fact the line goes back with certainty only to Elizabeth I's reign – generation after generation of Sussex yeomen all buried in East Grinstead churchyard.

A few personal impressions of Walter John remain: of a Victorian papa whose family fell into immediate silence when he began to speak and did not resume conversation until he had finished; a model of suburban gentility who always ate his bread and butter with a small knife and fork; a tyrant who dragged his daughter Gertie to Highgate Cemetery when she said she was afraid of ghosts (she was afraid of *him* and hated him); a harsh puritan who drove his talented fifteen-year-old son Sydney away from home for saying 'damn'; a believer in primogeniture who allowed 'Mr Nat' (my father), the elder son, to do almost anything, even to tease Clara, their old servant, by calling her 'Methuselah'; an advocate of girls' education who sent all his clever daughters to Camden School under the pioneering Miss Beale; a patriarch with glittering eyes and long white beard that parted in the wind as he strode up Highgate Hill; a fallible human being who ran down the Hill once too often to catch his usual bus and died of heart failure. In order to save a few guineas he had made his own will, thereby causing his family much confusion and embarrass- ment. He managed notwithstanding to leave his widow £700 a year for life. He and the Victorian era ended appropriately in the same year, 1901.

His widow, Hannah Bellamy, my grandmother, lived on until 1912. Tall and of a florid beauty, she was descended from a long line of rope-makers, first in Bristol (1680s) and then London, where her father and grandfather owned a rope-walk in Southwark. She and Caroline Harben (my great-grandmother on the Chamberlain side) were the partners who brought artistic feeling into homes otherwise dedicated to commerce and industry. I remember being taken to tea at the age of four with Grandmama Harman. I did not like her dark drawing-room at Muswell Hill where she moved after 'Mr Nat' married – Harley Street had Georgian lightness – but I did admire her wavy white hair that had once been red-gold and her lavishly-trimmed dress that I later equated with 'black bombazine'. She gave me a child's wooden chair on the seat of which was carved 'FOR MY PET'. In our undemonstrative family those sentimental words struck me as a strange and wonderful outpouring.

The Chamberlains were unsentimental, reserved and unorthodox to the marrow of their bones; the Harmans could gush and their noncon- formity was an accident. My parents' uneasy courtship was to illustrate the conflicting elements in our heredity.

My father fell in love with my mother in the Belgrave Hospital for Children, Clapham Road, London. Today it is derelict. Architecturally, though, it still looks like some ornate sorcerer's palace, the gold mosaics from the ceiling and walls of the entrance hall lying winking on the floor. As a surgeon my mother was wearing her white coat against which her cheeks looked as red as apples and her lashes as black as ebony. In her arms she held tenderly a 'dirty squalling' slum baby whose eyes she had called Father in to examine. He hardly noticed the baby's running eyes or snotty nose. He was enslaved.

Now thirty-five, my father had already experienced several meta-morphoses in his life. After leaving the City of London School at sixteen (where he got bad marks for rebellious behaviour), he went to work on the Baltic Exchange in Liverpool. Here the Baptist missions to seamen took him up and soon had him training for the ministry at the Regent's Park College. But this first 'call' was soon to be overlaid by a more insistent one – to become a *medical* missionary. As he said many years later while driving past the Regent's Park College with his doctor son, John, 'I thought if I was going to be a missionary, I might as well be a useful one.'

That meant a step hitherto unheard of in his family: going to university for a medical degree. His father cannot have approved, for Nat's brother Sydney had to lend him the money for his fees. (Sydney was working as a silversmith in Lambert's, which was to become Harman & Lambert.) Nat obtained a double first at Cambridge and was unlucky not to become an anatomy fellow of St John's College. Dashed by this failure he served in the Boer War as a civilian consultant to the army. In 1902 he became an 'eye-man', examining and prescribing for the eyes of London County Council schoolchildren and teaching in hospitals. He also set up in private practice at an address in Queen Anne Street, off Harley Street. His female companionship consisted of 'Methuselah', the old servant at Queen Anne Street, and his mother and sisters at Balcombe House, where he still lived. True, he had been engaged to be married for a few months, but to a woman who turned out not to be 'my match'. After this set-back he gave up hope of ever meeting 'my ideal woman'. Then in the summer of 1904 he met Miss Chamberlain.

Katherine (Katie) Chamberlain's family were originally larger than the Harmans by only two – nine surviving children against seven – but socially they were ten times the size, being augmented by the enormous 'cousinship', now in the second generation. The Kenrick cousins were especially close, Arthur's wife Louisa and Joe's second wife Florence Kenrick being twins, while Joe's first wife Harriet Kenrick had been the twins' first cousin. And the Kenricks were already related to the Chamberlains through the marriage of Mary, sister of Joe and Arthur, to Sir William Kenrick of The Grove, Harborne. A formidable family to marry into.

It was from the Welsh Kenricks that Katie got her very dark hair and eyes, with perhaps a contribution from her maternal grandmother, Maria Paget, whose family came from the Auvergne in France.

Katie was in Dresden learning German when the engagement was announced in 1890 of her sister Maggie to a Nettlefold cousin. 'I wish you were here to make us merry,' wrote Maggie. 'I'm sure I never made fun of my Professoresses as you invariably do. Get along with you, do! I'm ashamed of your levity.'

Most of my mother's 'levity' vanished after she married. To her sister she had been 'Kittywitz', 'Kay', 'Kathleen Mavourneen', 'Katherine the Minx'. That all came to an end. I never heard either of my parents use a nickname or indeed their Christian names to each other; they both became impersonally 'My dear'.

Her Mama's letters to Katie in Dresden gave a human picture of life in Birmingham while the cousinship was growing up. Unlike the Harmans, culture rather than religion dominated the Chamberlains. There were no family prayers at Moor Green or Highbury, though all did their stint teaching at Sunday School. Nellie was reading Maths at Newnham College, Cambridge, where another sister, Lottie, was to follow her. Their mother, Louisa Chamberlain, was not altogether in love with Newnham for her lively daughters. 'I saw all the girls dancing together one evening,' she wrote in February 1890, 'a funny-looking lot! but don't tell Nellie so.' A year later Mama was writing to Katie, 'I don't want you to go off to Cambridge. I want to keep you *here*; where you can have a very nice course of reading.'

In fact Katie did not go to Cambridge, for Mama was taken seriously ill with rheumatoid arthritis in spring 1890. She consulted a Mrs Atkins (a lady doctor) in London. 'I shall probably toddle off to Bath and "take the waters", which will cure me; but who will entertain me at the Pump Room like it is in "Northanger Abbey" and talk scandal over the spotted and tamboured muslins?'

During Katie's last months in Dresden Mama had kept her posted on Papa's little foibles. They went to Bellan, their Welsh shooting lodge, for Papa to speak at the Eisteddfod – 'he is so musical, you know!' (Katie inherited her father's absolute tunelessness.) There was a family visit to Elmley Castle at the foot of Bredon Hill. 'Papa insisted on going in his frock-coat and high hat and tight boots.' He considered it the correct dress for visiting a country house unless one were shooting, which he was not. His brother kindly lent him 'a blue serge loose suit & socks & boots' so that he was able to take one walk up Bredon Hill.

The other male, besides Papa, in whom Katie felt deep interest was her first cousin Neville Chamberlain, the future Prime Minister and younger son of her Uncle Joe. (Years later she told my sister Kitty that Neville had asked her to marry him, to which she replied, 'Don't be silly'; he had met no one as yet outside the family circle.) She received an account of

Neville's twenty-first birthday party, a 'Cousinly dinner', after which they played a children's game called 'Blowing the Feather'.

These young people of the 1890s were expected to behave one moment like conventional adults, the next like children – paying calls and interviewing servants interspersed with blowing the feather. Was this perhaps characteristic of all the well-heeled young who had not yet tasted a great war? Queen Alexandra gave a children's party for her daughter Louise's nineteenth birthday.

It was only seven months after Neville's twenty-first birthday that the cousinship suffered an unexpected blow. 'Uncle Joe has sent for Neville to go out to America to inspect a possible business,' wrote Mama to Katie, still in Dresden. 'We all think it horrid, the idea of a business out there for Neville is too gloomy; and even if it comes to nothing more, very disturbing to a young man who is doing good work now in an accountant's office.' (The project, to grow a cash crop of sisal in the Bahamas, did come to nothing, but not before Uncle Joe had suffered the huge loss of £50,000 and Neville utter and undeserved humiliation.) Before he departed Neville asked for a photograph of the absent Katie.

The 'Highburys' always had romance for the 'Moor Greens', the 'Highburys' being the Joe Chamberlains and the 'Moor Greens' the Arthur Chamberlains; and similarly the William Kenricks were the 'Groves'. The cousinship significantly called each other by the names of their mansions. How right Galsworthy was in his choice of a favourite biblical text for the Forsytes: 'In my Father's house are many mansions.' It was the text for 'nouveaux' who could not aspire to large landed estates but could build themselves big houses.

As a famous statesman in the 1890s Joe entertained more big names than Arthur did. For instance, Katie's sister Nellie wrote of a dinner at Highbury in honour of the Duke and Duchess of Devonshire: 'I was glad to stare at the Duke and Duchess . . . both ate potato chips with their fingers.' And Mama wrote to Katie when wondering how to amuse an elderly guest: 'I thought of walking her round Highbury – that unfailing entertainment of visitors.' I can just remember being walked around Highbury and seeing Great-Uncle Joe, then smitten with a stroke, sitting in his wheelchair, his imposing colourless head looking strangely larger than his diminished frame.

Katie's charming and literary mother died early in 1892, leaving Katie, now the eldest daughter at home, to look after Papa and her younger brothers John and Arthur, take Sunday School, attend lectures with Kenrick cousins, lunch with Kenrick aunts and interview cooks. About this time she had a fearful riding accident which prevented her from doing anything for a year. When recovered, she must have decided to take the 'London Matric' with a view to becoming a doctor. I can find no record of her reasons. It may have been that her next sister Bertha was now old enough to take over at home. (Each of the unmarried sisters in turn, except the backward Mary, did their filial duty, the youngest, Lottie, returning to home duties after going up to Newnham, and so missing her chance, like many home-bound girls, of marrying. Again, Katie's prolonged stay abroad may have given her a taste for change. Though she was the only one of the sisters to marry outside the circle, there were already rumbles at its restrictions. Four months before her engagement to John Nettlefold, Maggie was describing a dance at his home: 'There seemed to be very much the same gentlemen there as I've seen since my earliest infancy, but I suppose that can't be helped. Still I do think a new lot ought to be imported!' Katie was to export herself, though not for matrimony, and incidentally to find a very different type of gentleman.

What of Katie's choice of medicine as a career? There was much ladylike feminism among the cousins. In 1905 Mrs Osler, a member of the circle, was chairman of the Birmingham Society for Women's Suffrage, and medicine was one of the professions in which women were tepidly welcome. Louisa Chamberlain, my grandmother, consulted a lady doctor and Arthur Chamberlain would 'talk hospitals' with any dinner partner who was involved, like himself, in the new Birmingham Hospital for Women. One of the Moor Green horses was called Lady Doctor in Katie's honour.

The little I know about my mother's medical training comes from her letters to Grandpapa. She lived in various hostels around the Royal Free Hospital, then the Women's Medical School of London University. The January exam results of 1896 listed her second in Class II biology. She was overjoyed – until she realized that the order was alphabetical. In July she wrote, 'I was plunged in melancholy last week & most of this & am recovering now.' Though she had passed well in botany she had failed in chemistry and physics, despite a new chemistry class for girls only, to ensure them extra attention. Two years later she was thanking her father for a cheque. 'You, at any rate, are helping to give women equal chances with men. There are plenty of misapprehensions still about women medicals I fancy – Lord Dufferin, the president of the Royal Free Hospital, thought that a number of students were "lady convalescents of the hospital"! (this has not made him popular) . . . .'

Three years pass and things are improving. Katie has got her degree. At the Royal Free two women Residents are at last to be appointed, and there is news of a recently qualified woman who is assistant to a country doctor: *she* does the surgery and *he* only gives the anaesthetic. 'An excellent arrangement!' Katie stays voluntarily in hospital over Easter since the nurses are 'indulging in a perfect orgy of Church-going'. She is very happy to work in casualty even though 'the drunks are now beginning to come in!'. She will deal on her own at the Royal Free with a fractured skull, convulsions and a stroke, and perform a successful tracheotomy.

Her indomitable will to succeed did not conceal from her sisters in Birmingham the loneliness of London. 'I am afraid it must all be pretty horrid & dull,' wrote Nellie in 1898, 'until you get home again.' Her chief social life revolved around Prince's Gate, the London house of Joe Chamberlain and his third wife Mary, daughter of the American Judge Endicott. Katie kept special invitation cards: 'To have the honour of meeting HRH the Prince of Wales', 'To meet the Chiefs of Bechuana-land'.

Every Sunday Katie would lunch at Prince's Gate, a pleasure that presented its problems. If Uncle Joe had a speech in the near future nobody was allowed to say a word to him or to each other. On political matters relations between the Highburys and Moor Greens were becoming abrasive. At the annual meeting of his company, Kynoch's, in 1898, Arthur had attacked the Government (in which Joe was Colonial Secretary) for keeping British merchants out of Turkey and Persia and so giving the ammunition trade to Germany. 'We think it will make Uncle Joe furious with Papa,' wrote Nellie gleefully from the safety of Kynoch's office in Birmingham where she worked, 'and Papa is secretly pleased because Uncle Joe was very offensive to Papa about the cordite contract.' Secret pleasure was all very well in Kynoch's, but Katie had to face the music at Prince's Gate. Nevertheless she always stood up for her father.

Six more years were to pass in London before Katie met Nat at the Belgrave Hospital for Children as described. She had qualified in 1901 and by now was a woman of thirty-one, strong-minded though deceptively gentle, small and neat in figure. The love-letters from Nat begin on 13 November 1904 and end on 2 September 1905. Katie's to him are missing.

Two painful hold-ups punctuated the course of their true love, the first while Katie was on holiday in Egypt with her father. Both she and Nat had spent the summer working in London. Every Thursday he would visit the Belgrave professionally, and after he and Miss Chamberlain had done their rounds she would summon him to her room and bewitch him over tea. All went well until the autumn when Nat put to her a fatal question. What exactly were Unitarians? Katie replied, 'Some think us heathen!' Nat did not at first reveal the shock to his system of the word 'heathen', except by rushing around various Unitarian chapels and reading books by

Unitarian writers like the American Ralph Waldo Emerson to find out what his beloved really believed. The results were disastrous. They all said different things.

However, he and she seemed to have one thing in common: their *reason* told each of them to reject 'the divinity of Christ' – hers by upbringing, his after studying science at Cambridge. If belief in Christ's divinity was the hallmark of a Christian, he was a heathen too. Reason told him he was. And yet . . . and yet . . .

By the beginning of December 1904 he had reconciled to his own satisfaction the theological differences between Baptists and Unitarians. Unwisely he set it all out in a twelve-page letter to Katie in Egypt, adding for good measure the analysis that he himself as an amateur graphologist had made of her handwriting. The salient point in the analysis was that Miss Chamberlain, while loyal to early teaching, would now be capable of freeing herself from these 'initial constraints'.

Back came a rocket from Egypt. Mr Harman had been imputing thoughts to Miss Chamberlain which she did not hold, she wrote; nor did she like what he said about his faith. She demanded a clean sweep in their relationship.

Nat immediately began to back-peddle furiously, realizing that his lucid exposition had been a total mistake. 'Dear Miss Chamberlain, Your letter was a shock to me. . . . Truly I do not know what I believe. . . .' (Surely even a Unitarian could not object to that?) He had not worshipped with the Strict Baptists for half a dozen years, except for funerals. His father had not liked it, 'but later he understood'. Could a Unitarian like her ever understand the dogmatism of his upbringing? 'I was brought up, as one [student] in the Regent's Park College said after a particularly acrimonious debate, "in the strictest sect of the pharisees", a conjoined Scottish-Calvinist-Presbyterian-Baptist influence – can you appreciate! I doubt it!' Again he protested: 'I scarcely know where I stand as regards "doctrine" and not at all where you stand.'

She suggested 'agreeing to differ on vital points', but he could not see this working. Go to a separate church from her? No, he would stay at home. And it would not be fair on the children.

When he formally asked for her hand in 1905 he was told to wait six months. At the same time Arthur Chamberlain tactfully explained his daughter's social and economic 'position'. It was far above Nat's. She could well afford a carriage of her own if she wanted it. Nat had not fully understood this and it daunted him.

Three weeks later the waiting period had evaporated and they were engaged. Letters began 'My dearest Katherine' instead of 'Dear Miss Chamberlain' as hitherto, and ended 'Your own boy Nat'. In April he was talking of 'hot and cold in bath and basin on the best bedroom floor' of their new home; but also of 'the long enthralling, bewildering Kiss'. 'Oh, my Katherine you have much to teach me. You are very gentle and calm, and "sober", and I am sadly rough and boisterous. You must give me some of your gentle calmness.' She gave him instead the poet Browning to read and he loved best the quotation: 'THE BEST IS YET TO BE'.

But the 'best' was suddenly to recede again into a problematic future.

It was true that lyrical happiness seemed to intoxicate him all through the merry month of May, at least as reflected in his letters to Katie.

May 14th, 1905. You are very dear to me, my Dearest. There is no one, no thing, and no thought that is dearer to me than you are, and I know I am right in counting you the dearest of all things. And you have brought me happiness and rest more than you know, so now I love you more and with a greater happiness than I did at first.

He recalled to her their frank talk on Easter Sunday at Glanhonndu in Wales, sitting by that great tree stump, when she gave him a scarab, saying that years ago men had held it to be the symbol of immortality. Before that magical day, he reminded her, their religious differences had taken shape as a barrier between them.

But now . . . I need not fear as I did at first 'Must I always go through this life one hand in my Katherine's and the other fighting off these doubts about the meaning of things?'

Four days later his happiness was expressed by practising the accompaniment to his songs on the family piano. (I can remember his singing 'Nazareth' in a full-bodied bass-baritone that made the show-case of china in the drawing-room vibrate.) When he looked at 'the piles of bricks in Harley Street', he told her, he felt almost guilty at dragging her away from her beautiful home with its lawns, flowers and trees. Even Harley Street at its best – 'its parquet floors & marble fittings & Adam's ceiling' – would be no attraction to him without her; 'it is as a frame to you & your beauty I think of it & am glad of it all'.

On her thirty-second birthday, 23 May, he busied himself with her future career, visiting the education office of the London County Council and obtaining an application form for one of the new posts of women medical inspectors. She must apply quickly. There were 420 candidates for four or five places.

Exactly a month later the bomb dropped on his poor Katherine at Moor

Green Hall, as she put in her last stint of housekeeping for Papa before the wedding.

23.vi. '05. My dearest Katherine, I shall send you a telegram at the same time as I post this asking you not to come tomorrow.

(Katie kept the telegram among this packet of letters. It ran: 'Cannot come unwell Nat'.) Nat's letter continued:

I have been having a bad week of it – a mental conflict that I don't think I could explain to you & may be you would not understand if I could. . . . Things theological I thought I had cleared in my mind . . . that sort of habit of mind made by long training in youth has risen up & I can't choke it down. And to meet the woman I love with these uncertainties uncleared I cannot . . . but whether or no I ought to fight this battle out alone I don't know – if I cannot win it myself I am scarcely man enough for you . . . such a hold have these thoughts just now that everything else seems as nothing . . . Goodbye from Nat.

Next day and on the two following days he wrote again in the same mood of confused despair. First he tried lying down in a darkened room, then a walk over the fields after the 'bewildering' bright sun had set; he still could not allow her to visit him and receive from him 'an unreal kiss'. Nor could he visit her – 'a lame duck among your strong fit circle would have been out of it altogether'. He had come to believe that he could only gain peace of mind by letting her go: '& it was bitter indeed. I cannot tell you how bitter.' Sleeping-draughts helped but as soon as he awoke, 'then began the churn and turn through my cracked brain again'. To add to their woes, Katherine was thrown from her horse, and he felt guilty. Surely it was the shock of his breakdown that had caused her to lose her grip when the horse shied.

Did he see dimly in his darkened room that *he* had shied at marriage and thrown her?

A medical friend had persuaded him that his trouble was 'nerves' due to overwork; 'so the brain runs riot'. A week's solitary cruise was planned, beginning on 30 June. Meanwhile he kept trying, incoherently, to explain to her his crisis: 'My early impressions have been so essentially religious . . . a habit of mind that cannot be altered now. . . . I don't care for creeds and dogmas but there is an atmosphere I do care for, for in that alone do I feel really comfortable and natural.' He meant an atmosphere of evangelical piety, not conspicuous at Moor Green Hall.

On the 28th in response to a more cheerful if still disordered telegraphic message – 'Fit as flea please stay haste dear flea please Nat' –

she met him at the LCC offices before her interview. There is no record of success or failure, but it must have been the latter. Small wonder considering her present trials. His last letter before the cruise contained a joke and a sketch – good signs. 'This letter is going to Katherine and I am going to St Katherine's Dock. I wish it were the other way about.' The sketch shows a tiny boy-porter shouldering the tall invalid's portmanteau.

My father's cruise around the coast of Britain, picking up fishes' heads on quays to examine their eyes, improved his health. Yet he continued trying sporadically to analyse his breakdown in letters written between his home-coming and wedding-day. By August he was daring to defend 'healthy sentiment' in religion against pure logic – his past against his present. Even if the rationalist creed was 'the only provable one', it was 'insipid and lifeless' like distilled water. In thus pitting the 'sentiment' of Baptists against the 'logic' of Unitarians, my father was allowing a last fling to the mysteries of Christianity on which he had been raised. He reminded my mother that her forbears had once felt the same way as he did, and begged her to think kindly of those who still did. At least they had taught him to reject those 'bugbears of humanity – the cult of priestcraft & forms & ceremonies'. Would she not perhaps consent to 'shared sentiment' expressed in some form of piety such as family prayers? She would not.

Indeed he had already surrendered too completely for any last-minute terms to be made. If they had children, he had written on 14 July 1905, he would give their teaching with absolute confidence 'to their Mother – you'.

No doubt there were other causes of his 'terrible' breakdown beside the emotional clinging to a divine Christ. The fear of marriage after long years as a bachelor; the great fear of that 'strong circle', the rich, famous Chamberlains. But the tug-of-religion was the fiercest and he had lost it.

And so, having renounced his own father's 'faith' for the sake of the woman he loved, he was doubly resolved to preserve his father's 'works' when he himself became a father – the insistence on Victorian standards of obedience, sobriety, law and order within the family. We children were to feel the severities without knowing the reason for them.

Meanwhile, he was preparing to 'housekeep' with his darling: buying a genuine Chippendale bookcase for £4, tuning his own piano, counting the sacks of coal before the coalman shot them through a round hole in the pavement into the cellar. All this he recounted in order to show his 'sweetheart' that he had truly recovered his senses.

On 2 September the men came at 6 a.m. to Balcombe House with two vans to remove his possessions, and he rode in state to 108 Harley Street seated in an armchair far above the horses. 'I had a coachman and four footmen all powdered – with dirt.' The Chamberlains themselves could do no better.

They were married at the Old Meeting House in Birmingham on 4 September 1905.

I was born just under a year later, on 30 August 1906. When my mother asked him about his 'wants' before their wedding, he had replied: 'I want a Little One – and that that Little One is good!' I was the best she could do for a start.

That year was not a bad one to be born in, except for the sizzling August heat-wave. *The Times* described it on my birthday as 'an intense anticyclone'. As usual there was a news heading, 'The Russian Crisis', and as usual it was reported from Melbourne that the Victoria Legislative Council had rejected Women's Suffrage – for the fourteenth time. No less predictably, HM King Edward VII was in Marienbad, where he held 'an animated conversation on the Kreuzbrunnen with Sir Henry Campbell-Bannerman', the Prime Minister. Plays by Shakespeare, Pinero and Baroness Orczy were running in London. There was an advertisement for a weekend cottage in Sussex with three sitting-rooms and eight bedrooms, price £70 freehold; and a telegram to 'Mayfairing' would obtain for you a governess, companion, secretary, nurse, house-keeper, cook and 'all maids'.

It was true that one third of all women workers existed as domestic servants, many as slaveys or skivvies. Mrs Hunt's Domestic Agency in London, to which I was to accompany my mother on many a dreary pilgrimage, had drawn up a list of crimes for which the 'lady' could dismiss her maid without notice: neglect, stealing, immorality, drunkenness, 'utter incapability' – but it was usually wise, advised Mrs Hunt's office, to pay a month's wages.

Among the educated classes opportunities for women were steadily increasing. There were 378 women on the Medical Register in England and Wales, among them K. Chamberlain, MB, BSc London (1901); Mrs Florence Willey, ditto, who brought me into the world; Elizabeth Blackwell, USA (1849), the first woman to qualify and still a consultant in Hastings; Maud Chadburn, London (1898), who was to bring my eldest child into the world.

Careers recommended for women by *The Englishwomen's Year Book 1906* included indexing, which required the alleged female characteristics of conscientiousness, quickness, versatility and common sense; the Civil Service, where some women could 'rise to the top' (that is, become clerks); and interior decoration. Both the latter occupations, however, needed 'superb health'. The stage was 'alarmingly overcrowded';

contrariwise, the demand for governesses now exceeded the supply. Women fiction writers were said to belong to two classes: born writers, and those who had had a memorable love experience. The typical woman journalist was considered 'aggressive' in her mannish tailor-mades. (My father admitted to my mother that he had thought all women doctors 'hard' until he met her.)

In sport there were two Lady Masters of Foxhounds and nine Lady Masters of Harriers; several aristocratic ladies owned their own grouse moors; a few owned racehorses, like Mrs Langtry, the Jersey Lily, under the name of 'Mr Jersey'. Women cyclists (whom my aunt Nellie Chamberlain had considered 'vulgar' in their 1899 bloomers) were warned in 1906 'to avoid as much as possible the use of the voice when passing foot passengers'. Women's societies were on the increase. Twenty-five societies were dedicated to obtaining the suffrage and one to abolishing the double standard in sex: the White Cross League for Purity in Men. And there was a total of forty-three social clubs in London available to women. Yet, despite her professional training, my mother belonged to none of the clubs through which women were striving to establish their separate identity. As a wife she worked for a medical charity. As a mother she joined the Parents' National Educational Union, the better to develop her skills as her children's first teacher. She never became a medical inspector of London schools, as my father had clearly hoped she would. Nor did she put up her own brass plate at 108 Harley Street, though Nat had set aside one room as '*our* workroom'.

A professional career for my mother run from the home would have been rare but not unique among our neighbours. In fact an amusing little girl with whom I used to go for walks had a psychiatrist for a mother. One day she noticed that I was stepping over the lines in the pavement as I hurried to reach the next lamppost before an oncoming car did so. 'My mother says', she warned me, 'that if you try not to tread on the lines, or try to get to a lamppost before something else does, it means you'll go mad.' I felt happy at that moment to think that *my* mother was not a practising doctor.

3

'Take Your Pleasures Moderately'
· *1916–26* ·

Here I was in 1916 at my chosen London day school, the Francis Holland Church of England School for Girls, Clarence Gate. I felt a fine sense of justification as I stood with a group of my friends on the first day of term, waiting for the school doors to open. As I was ten, I would be in IIIb with them, my friends told me. In fact I was in IIIa; but any satisfaction at such promotion was speedily wiped out by my mother's having forgotten to send me with the required Health Certificate designed to guarantee my freedom from any contagion. I was whisked away from all humankind, an untouchable. I suspected that nothing short of expulsion would fit my case. The sight of the headmistress confirmed my fears. She seemed as tall as my father but bosomy, in a man's tie and high-necked shirt blouse rattling with gold chains. She allowed me to stay; but by the end of our interview I had experienced all the feelings of a prisoner in the dock, an outcast, a patient being interrogated about a disgraceful disease. I also learnt thus early that to be innocent of a crime does not prevent one feeling guilty.

During my years at this school the formidable head was to graduate in my eyes into a mystery figure. The mystery was attached to morning prayers. I had been strictly admonished by my parents to abstain from joining with the rest of the school in saying the Creed. This I did; but while staring fixedly ahead each morning I gradually became aware of a curious phenomenon on the platform. Day after day the headmistress, who turned sideways to face the east for the Creed, would take the opportunity at precisely the same moment apparently to straighten her tie. I asked my mother about this trick; she had no clue. It was only much later that I realized the figure in profile had been crossing herself. This was my first absurd experience of a symbol that has since become part of my life.

I remained hard-working and therefore successful throughout my four years at day school. Drawing was supposed to be my talent. Actually I never achieved any real freedom with my pencil, though a strong decorative sense carried me some way. The most traumatic episode of my youth occurred before a public drawing exam to which I was passionately looking forward. There was a maths lesson first. I could do maths only by the most intense concentration. Suddenly I found that I could neither concentrate nor read the figures on the blackboard, since each was cut in half down the middle, and when I stood up beside my desk to answer a question, the words either stuck or came out in a nonsense jumble. The mistress sized up the situation with mathematical precision, marched me downstairs and telephoned my parents. Meanwhile my vision was full of beautiful coloured cogwheels revolving slowly across the landscape from left to right. By the afternoon I was sufficiently recovered to attempt the drawing exam, with poor results. And my father had told the school secretary, 'Don't worry. It's just a migraine. I have them myself. Let her rest. She'll be all right.'

When I got home and enquired about my terrifying experience, he played it down. No mention of a possible recurrence. Not even an admission that he had migraines too and could advise me how to deal with them. Perhaps he was right to keep our secret dark. Certainly I had no more migraines for fifteen years, until I was pregnant – and then at first just one thumping great migraine to celebrate the quickening of each baby. My brother John devised some sodium choleate capsules that controlled the enemy for almost another decade. After that all remedies ceased to work and for nearly forty years I have lived with migraines: to begin with every fortnight and gradually dwindling to about ten attacks a year. For most of my life medical opinion has held that the spasm can cause intense pain without permanently injuring the brain. Now I read of new research suggesting that the brain *is* permanently damaged. However, at eighty I can afford to be stoical.

Several of my school years were enlivened by the zeppelin raids on London. We were too young to be more than pleasantly startled by the assorted thumps that we could hear from our refuge in the wine cellar. If bombs actually fell – as they did for instance on nearby Bolsover Street – Father would immediately say, 'That's the Regent's Park *gun*!' Of course we were not taken in as the sounds were quite different. At one period the raids or alerts came so regularly that I used to leave my homework to do in the cellar. Sometimes Mother read aloud to us and once Kitty sang a touching lullaby in a small sleepy voice. We all applauded.

I was lifted out of bed one night to see a zeppelin caught in searchlights. My father gave us no hint of his vengeful feelings on such occasions, but he wrote to my mother in September 1915 after the German bombs had broken all the glass in the hospital windows around Bloomsbury: 'People who could do such a thing should be exterminated.' It was the idea of an indiscriminate attack from the *air* that in those days shocked so deeply.

Apart from the apparently flaming airship I can remember being woken to see two other fires: the huge conflagration of Madame Tussaud's exhibition and the tiny green light of a glow-worm in the garden.

My most dramatic and sinister memory of the First World War was purely imaginary. A schoolfriend lived in a street next door to the British Museum in Bloomsbury. She would sometimes ask me to tea on winter evenings, when our great thrill was to hide behind the window curtains and watch the shadow of a German spy signalling from inside the museum to his accomplice outside. To be sure, all we could really see was the reflection on a blind of someone moving in the room opposite, but that was enough. We revelled in eerie speculations, in which German spies and Egyptian mummies were horrifically mingled.

Two other genuine events of the war remain with me: the deaths of Lord Kitchener and the Lord Mayor of Cork. Kitchener's drowning we first saw announced on a poster as we walked to the Park. 'He's not dead,' declared Nurse obstinately as she pushed the heavy pram up York Gate, nodding her bonnet and squaring her elbows defiantly under her green cape. 'We'd lose the war without him. He's swum to an island and he'll be back. You'll see.' She was wrong, of course.

The same lesson on a higher level was presented by the Lord Mayor of Cork's hunger strike. One morning at breakfast Father unexpectedly came up to the nursery. By way of conversation Nurse said something about Terence MacSwiney's end being near. 'Don't you believe it,' my father said irritably. 'They'll never let him die – they're feeding him on holy wafers. You'll see.' A few days later, amazingly to me and despite my father's admired omniscience, MacSwiney was dead. I felt myself slipping on to the Irish side of the argument. Father had been wrong. The underdog it was that died.

It was more serious when both my mother and John were against me. Mother read the *Iliad* aloud to us in Pope's verse translation. I was instinctively on the side of the losers, the Trojans. 'You can't support that hopeless crew,' John said derisively. 'You *must* be Greek, the Trojans are no good.' But I stood firm by the hopeless Trojans and they rewarded me with an early insight into the point of view of a lost cause. *Victrix causa deis placuit, sed victa Catoni.* The cause of the victor pleased the gods, but Cato chose the cause of the conquered.

I kept a diary during my last period at Francis Holland. The actual diary must have been sent to my father as a medical advertisement and passed on to me, for it was a small black leather book advocating Robin's Peptonate for 'nervous irritability in women and girls, neuropathic disorders in women and children'. I did not venture to ask what these mysterious disorders were, perhaps because John and I had both developed various 'ticks' as very small children for which we were severely scolded. We enjoyed twitching, blinking, grimacing. Mother would say, 'That's the way imbeciles behave in asylums.' Nurse would say, 'When the wind changes your faces will stick.'

My diary was begun at the suggestion of a schoolfriend. When I asked her what to put in it on the days when nothing happened, she replied: 'What ho!' There are many 'What hos!' through the winter of 1919–20, but in the spring I substituted weather reports, no more or less dull than those of George v who was keeping a diary at the same time. Dull diaries were considered a perfectly worthwhile occupation during my youth. For a few weeks, indeed, my weather reports were not only pointless but pompous. My father brought home an illustrated book on clouds, and from then on I was able to fill blank pages with descriptions of stratocumulus and cirrus formations.

It was during the school holidays that my diary really flourished. Ever since 1913 we had spent Christmas, Easter and summer in a small rented house at Detling, near Maidstone in Kent. Its name was Lynchfield, the 'lynch' being the steep grass bank behind our house on the North Downs. If I had to nominate one thing in the world that accounted for the happiness of my childhood, I would say Lynchfield. I find I have reproduced, whether consciously or not, certain favourite features from Lynchfield in our Sussex home. Bernhurst now has its brick paths, its yellow banksia rose on the house, its orange crown imperials and white Japanese anemones in the borders, its golden yew at the westernmost point. And luck has also given us a Wellingtonia on the lawn; I have added the missing cedar of Lebanon.

On our first day at Lynchfield we were driven up from Maidstone station in Boakes's brougham. We tumbled out into the soaking garden and rushed from feature to feature through the unmown grass: the pergola, the dell, the cave beside the croquet lawn built of flints and concealed by a curtain of ivy, the barn at the back, the summerhouse behind the cave with its carved Gothic windows stolen from some Pilgrim's Rest. Lynchfield was on the old Pilgrim's Way to Canterbury. At eleven and twelve, John and I followed the route on our bicycles from Detling. I often ran into ploughed fields so that I fell off my machine and tore my stockings. We tottered into the Cathedral. A verger shouted at us: 'Get out! Clean yourselves!' I doubt whether modern child pilgrims would receive such a frosty welcome.

Life was altogether freer at Lynchfield. Nurses and nursemaids, sometimes even the parents, joined with children in games of 'Rescue' and 'Go Home!'. Father, however, made it his business to see that joy was never completely unconfined. When John wished to bring a gramophone on a river picnic, Father objected in the memorable words: 'Always take your pleasures moderately, children.'

Our 'moderate' pleasures included the making of bows and arrows from the yew wood behind the house; the painting and sewing of wigwams and collecting and dyeing of feathers for Indian head-dresses; performing *Rumpelstiltskin*, *Snow White and Rose Red* in the village school; walking along the Downs to the dolmen called Kit's Coty House; picking out the blue-grey British battleships through Father's field-glasses (bought for the South African war) as they lay huddled together like translucent insects in the Thames estuary; eyeing the bearded tramp who lived rough in the chalk-pit, my first example of a dropout: he had been a county cricketer. Our picnic food was 'moderately' pleasant: slices of bread, cold meat, chocolate and hard-boiled eggs. One day we children had the idea of putting the slippery eggs into our mouths whole – until Father told us he had once had to cut a friend's throat with the bread knife to get the egg out and save him from choking to death.

Unpleasant conflicts could also take place at Lynchfield that would never have happened in London – our family life was not at close enough quarters there. One evening at supper my mother and father broke into an argument on some academic subject. I had hardly ever heard them disagree, never quarrel, but now there was a terrible edge to both voices.

'I learnt anatomy at *Cambridge*', said my father with disdainful emphasis, 'and I *think* we knew what we were talking about.'

'Oh, of course, at *Cambrrridge* – and at *Oxforrrrd*', parodied my mother sarcastically, 'you understood things *so* much better than we at *mere London*. . . .'

Suddenly I knew they were going to be divorced. People could not be so bitter and stay married. I fled from the room, crushed like our mongrel Tinker when he saw the packed trunks and realized that our holidays were over and we were going to leave him. My mother followed me to my bedroom. She did not try to explain but somehow convinced me that *Cambrrridge* would never raise its horrid head again.

Another episode involved my own pride, not my mother's. Our parents did not go in for regular slapping or smacking. Occasionally I would see my father fetch the clothes brush for John, but Michael says he, the youngest, was never hit. Nor was I; until the day when my father lost his temper at some piece of mockery and dealt me a sharp blow. I rushed out into the garden and flung myself weeping on the grass beside the lily pond where a mother hedgehog and her six babies had recently been drowned. Again it was my mother who became peacemaker, persuading my father to apologize. Afterwards I realized to my shame that my reaction had been mainly melodrama. That does not make me any more in favour of corporal punishment; indeed the whole scene was a good example of how human relations lose their reality when force is introduced.

It was at tranquil Lynchfield, strangely enough, that I had the most horrible nightmare of my life. My mother for a time suffered from palpitations. They were relatively harmless and due to the change of life, though of course I did not know it. I dreamt that I saw her standing on the sunlit lawn with something odd strapped round her waist and hanging down on one side like a sword on a belt. Suddenly I realized it was a small coffin, the size to fit a doll, with a white skeleton painted on the black lid. With the awful certainty of a dream, I knew it was my mother's coffin and she was dead inside, though at the same time walking on the grass in her long white summer skirt and floppy straw hat with its black ribbon.

On a brilliant autumn day, my fifty-third wedding anniversary, our son Paddy drove me over to Lynchfield from Bernhurst to see what had become of it in the fifty-odd years since I lived there. The sixteenth-century church of St Martin of Tours was unchanged. I showed Paddy the spot where the vicar's daughter was killed by a runaway lorry while on her voluntary milk-round during the war – 'and the blood ran all the way down the village street from top to bottom', as our cook Mrs Cheeseman told us. The steep village street has since become a cul-de-sac, so that such gruesome accidents can no longer happen, and the new A249 dual carriageway now slices through the bottom of the beech woods and our garden. As I stood beside the remains of Lynchfield – the tattered Wellingtonia and horse chestnut beside the vanished front gate, the moulting cedar on the former lawn – I could not help remembering Kipling's poem, 'The Way Through the Woods'.

> They shut the way through the woods
> Seventy years ago . . .

But in the poem you could still hear ghostly riders 'steadily cantering through . . .'. In my case it was the footsteps of runners that I could still hear – children racing headlong from top to bottom of the path through the woods, using a beech trunk as a bollard to stop themselves running out on to the main road.

The little black diary ended with my first term at boarding-school. As a diary it had degenerated into reading lists and lists of my paintings: 'Studies of Smoke from the Train', 'Lucy Manette', 'Snowballing', 'A Group of Trees', 'Meditation', 'Sheep Feeding from a Trough' (which won a public prize for schoolchildren). My reading veered from Stanley Weyman and L. M. Alcott to Walter de la Mare, Milton, Mark Twain and

Nathaniel Hawthorne, but with the French Revolution predominating. Mother was reading *A Tale of Two Cities* aloud to us. As a result, at thirteen I wrote my only novel, 'On the Stroke of Twelve', in which the villainous Michel le Meunier was himself executed for keeping prisoners in his own château instead of handing them over to the guillotine. My mother's comment was, 'Too much talk, not enough action.'

New Year's Day 1920 seems to have provoked in me some Good Resolutions of a mawkish kind. 'I believe my chief fault is TEASING,' I wrote. 'I am determined to conquer this fault by keeping a list of quarrels.' There followed twenty-seven listed family quarrels in six days, and in addition our new nurse, Lee, whom I adored, was highly critical. 'Lee says I am very dilitry [*sic*] and lazy and shall never get on in the world. I am afraid this is true.'

My boarding-school was just outside Oxford. Headington School for Girls was relatively raw, having been founded only a few years before with an eye on the daughters of dons. It was supposed to be inexpensive, as befitted professional people. I was never homesick at Headington, despite the fierce chilblains and weak gaslight. 'I can hardly see what books to get out, far less to read,' I complained to my parents. I was carried along by new stimuli. Friendships in a boarding-school were more absorbing than in a day school. I was romantically in love with the French mistress, who made me learn 'The Hound of Heaven' by heart, for which I am grateful. I was in turn courted by the daughter of a film-star. Her father used to kiss her goodbye on the eyelids. I would watch spellbound from a discreet distance on Paddington station. One of my closest friends was the sister of Christopher Wood, the painter. I stayed with her in Huyton and heard how her mother had virtually brought Christopher back to life from polio. When he later threw himself under a train on Salisbury station I began to understand the meaning of tragedy. Another schoolfriend, Ursula Gilbert, who was later to support a People's Peace Camp, joined me in writing plays for the house to act, for which I also painted the scenery. 'The Serf' was set in the reign of Richard II. Boarding-school had changed my hostile feelings towards the French Revolution and filled me with radical zeal. Conrad the Serf carried off the lovely Lady Isobel while the Black Death carried off her lordly lover.

In another house and therefore less easy to get to know well was Mollie Sparrow, later Mrs Barrow. Her brilliant black eyes and glowing skin at first seemed out of tune with her withdrawn, diffident temperament. But I soon came to realize that her character was as sparkling as her face. She stayed with me one holiday at Lynchfield. I was deeply impressed by her brother John Sparrow, who while still at Winchester had edited Donne's poetry. I was as much dazzled by John's elegant manners as by his genius. At family meals he would stand behind my chair until I was seated and then do the same for his mother. Such courtliness surprised me almost as much as, at a later date, I was amazed by my husband's rising when I came into a room. Mollie was to practise as a doctor in Birmingham and to marry a Quaker. My path crossed hers again upon the heady uplands of Birmingham socialism. John, however, was to become the famous ultra-conservative Warden of All Souls.

At Headington my reading list at last began to grow up. I make no boast of never having enjoyed 'trash', though I never did. It was due to our upbringing. Part of the philosophy of 'taking your pleasures moderately' involved reading the minimum of comics: one copy of *Rainbow* for each train journey to and from Kent. Even when we were young that meant no more than six *Rainbows* a year. I never got the comic habit, and at fourteen was deep in Richard Jefferies, R. L. Stevenson and Leigh Hunt. Hazlitt's language was 'so beautiful that it seems to be in blank verse'.

I began to grow up socially as well. At sixteen I went to my first dance, one of those well-meant but always futile attempts by parents to bring together children of the same religion and background. My mother bought me a shell-pink taffeta dress from Harrods. It was entirely her own choice; I neither tried it on nor even set eyes on it before the parcel arrived at Harley Street. I suppose it fitted because I remember no embarrassment over the dress; only over my white silk mittens and fan. I found nothing better to do than tease my most attentive partner. Next morning I went down with raging flu, for the first time.

At school I had become appallingly ambitious. I wrote a twelve-page history essay on the medieval parliaments entirely in Latin – a *tour de force* that tortured my teacher and earned me an exceptionally low mark instead of the star billing I expected. Summer term 1923 saw the apex of my school career in the shape of what my brother John called 'disgusting pot-hunting'. I won the school Essay Prize, the prizes for Architectural Drawing, Original Work (painting the scenery for *Dr Faustus*) and History, for which I chose Lytton Strachey's *Queen Victoria*. This subtle and entertaining book had been published only the year before and was to have a profound impact on my ideas of biography. Hitherto I had been nurtured on the staid *English Men of Letters* series; after Strachey I demanded at least the fun of Carlyle or the romance of John Buchan. And thanks to Strachey I never had to demolish a mental image of Queen Victoria as the frumpish mistress of a royal 'we' who was neither amused nor amusing.

During this year and the next, the reading and writing of poetry became an absorbing passion. Before I had learnt to write I used to dictate interminable rhymes to my long-suffering mother: hymns and ballads and, when the war broke out, marching songs, verses called 'The End of the War (when it comes)', more verses on food rationing ('Buy it with thought / Cook it with care / Eat it when bought / Don't hoard in a lair') and yet more on the Defence of the Realm Act. Versifying was the one activity that John and I did not share. As far as I know the only poem he ever wrote consisted of the line 'Osiris god of the sun' repeated twenty times.

I had played with words as soon as I could talk. From 1923, however, poetry became my private life, my secret world. I kept a fat hard-covered exercise book marked PRIVATE, in which I transcribed extracts from the masters, my own imitative efforts, reviews of all the plays I saw and many of the books I read. A wonderful and satisfying private world it was. I would meditate on single lines and phrases, mostly unaware that millions had picked them out before me: 'Told by an idiot', 'The dust of antique time', 'A bracelet of bright hair about the bone', 'Our revels now are ended'. The fact that my favourites had a melancholy undertone was not incompatible with my own innate cheerfulness.

There were long quotations from those who then represented 'modern poetry': Yeats, Flecker, Gibson, Masefield, Drinkwater, Brooke, Bliss Carman's translations of Sappho. The only poet I had actually seen was John Masefield, who had judged a national verse-speaking competition for schoolgirls at Oxford. I had been put in for it by Miss Plowden, who made a great drama of music and elocution lessons, sweeping up from Oxford in a black cloak lined with scarlet. I got through the first stage, which was to recite Blake's lyric, 'Tiger, tiger, burning bright'; but I noticed at once that Masefield's huge swimming blue eyes were fixed upon the girls from the Edinburgh Academy who were not only beautiful but chanted their poems exquisitely on one high celestial note, a technique I had never heard before. Disaster overtook me at the second stage: as I hurried to the platform to give my rendering of Keats' sonnet, 'Bright Star', I tripped at the top step and fell sprawling at the judge's feet, a calamity which left me in no state to do justice to the 'soft fall and swell' of Fanny Brawne's breast. In any case the Scots girls would have won, for their expressionless singsong was the perfect way for schoolgirls to deal with the sensuous eroticism of Keats.

James Elroy Flecker's translation of 'Hialmar speaks to the Raven' by Leconte de Lisle provided me with a humbling but delightful exercise. I read Flecker's version of the French poem only *after* I had tried my hand at translating it myself. This was my comment:

It was absolutely thrilling reading his after mine was done. I really did know then what was good (of his) and what was ordinary. I could see exactly the way his brain worked all along. I could *feel* distinctly where he was stumped for a word . . . 'On a poet's lips I slept' . . . Oh, it was great!

The climax of my first euphoric travels through 'the realms of gold' took place at Lynchfield during the winter holidays of 1923. I remember sitting in one of the hard basket chairs in the drawing-room, the paraffin lamp at my elbow throwing its small circle of light on the ceiling. Silence reigned, though there must have been at least four other people in the room. Father did not allow conversation after supper when he was reading. We resented this. Nevertheless it created the idyllic conditions in which I read straight through for the first time *Hamlet* and *Prometheus Unbound*. After that I knew what Keats felt on first looking into Chapman's Homer.

Next year I entered a popular lyrical competition open to all British Girl Guides and judged by the poet Alfred Noyes. He placed me sixth among the first ten names published, all of them high-ranking officers except me, a fact that I proudly recorded. I never knew which of the two lyrics I submitted took his fancy: the faintly humorous one about the 'Canterbury Weavers', or the impassioned celebration of the birth of a new poet on a night 'when the dog-star foams / And madness runs in the blood . . .'. I guess that my thinly-disguised appeal for poetic status was brushed aside by Noyes in favour of workaday Canterbury, hydrophobic dog-stars notwithstanding.

Even dizzier heights were to be reached when the entries of both my father and myself were printed in the *Spectator* competition for 6 June 1925: '£5 for a Warning in six lines of verse'. 'NBH's sestet on the leper's cry of "Unclean" ' was praised for its lack of ornament and for straightforwardness. The judge went on to note that 'Mr [*sic*] E. Harman' sent in the best verses written in a vein that had perhaps been overworked. They were called 'The Moving Staircase' and described the fate of John who failed to step off the escalator with his right foot first: 'The stairs were badly out of gear all day; / John reappeared at intervals they say . . .'.

Our purring art mistress at Headington, Miss Aubrey Moore, had a mesmeric personality capable of making her four cats walk on a tightrope and me aspire to the Slade School of Art. In the end, however, Miss Plowden beat Miss Moore on the small battlefield of my future. I decided to study poetry and it went without saying, or so it seemed, that I would study it at Oxford. I was steeped in the Oxford ethos. Every Sunday of term I walked in a school crocodile to attend evensong in the Cathedral or a college chapel. I had won a prize for sketching a buttress at Magdalen and was familiar with the Reynolds window at New College; I knew the

Oxford Playhouse and the Bach Choir; I was well acquainted with the various tea-rooms of Cornmarket Street, outside one of which I was shaken to recognize a spotty Gyles Isham, the dazzling 'Hamlet' of an Oxford University Dramatic Society (OUDS) production, stripped of his black tights and wearing billowy 'Oxford bags'.

There were only three of us in the sixth form at Headington. Eng. Lit. was to be my subject – the Elizabethans. But though I had the advantage of individual tuition with the senior English mistress, she was disadvantaged by never having seen a college exam paper and by having forgotten most of what she knew about Shakespeare's contemporaries. She would breeze into my classroom twice a week, pretty, plump, smiling, with her Pekinese under her arm. 'Well, Betty, what do we make of Webster?' I would proceed to give the Pekinese a lecturette on *The Duchess of Malfi*, he would begin barking madly and then dog and mistress would withdraw. I think the school was astonished when one of their allegedly brightest products failed to obtain even an interview at Lady Margaret Hall; certainly I was stunned.

For eighteen months I abandoned all academic dreams, going abroad instead, attending medical parties with my parents and falling in love with a handsome young Irish doctor at Maidstone eye hospital. The effects on the school of my débâcle (and others like it) were more positive. During the subsequent years it expanded and acquired a fully qualified staff.

It was in the pilotless months after I left school that my Chamberlain aunts and cousins rallied round. Part of my happiness at Headington had been contributed by two cousins, Marian Beesly and Valerie Nettlefold, and Val's lifelong Irish friend Mabel Shillington. We four would be swept off every half-term to the Queen Anne Manor House of grey Cotswold stone at Bampton, the home of Val's mother, my Aunt Maggie. She at least did not believe in 'taking pleasures moderately'. She loved her food and ordered delicate Rhine wines when she took us to Germany. At home she whirled us around Cotswold churches and invited the Morris dancers into her garden. We climbed about on the roof and slept out in hammocks. At Bampton I first heard 'the sound of doves in immemorial elms', and in the sewing-room and kitchen quarters first learnt that vicars have immemorially eloped with their housemaids.

After my parents rented Lynchfield they never visited the seaside for more than a day; but thanks to other families of cousins I would stay in Wales or Devon. At Lynchfield we were self-sufficient and resented visitors; with my hive of cousins I met new people. One of these was Sydney Courtauld, future wife of Rab Butler. I remember cowering on the edge of the Atlantic rollers until Sydney, with a look of fine scorn, drove me into the deep water: 'Don't be a little coward. Get right in!'

Years later when I told Sydney I was going to be a Labour candidate, she looked at me in the same way again. I nearly found myself being sucked into the Tory rollers this time as she said generously, 'If all you want is to get into Parliament, I'll help you find a Conservative seat.'

In my eighteenth year, my maiden aunt Mary Chamberlain took me and her friend Miss Doughty as her guests to the Haute Savoie. Miss Doughty was the sister of Charles Doughty, author of *Arabia Deserta*, explorer and poet. On the false assumption that his sister had the same aptitude for travel, Miss Doughty was our courier. 'We got into glorious messes,' I wrote home, 'accused French porters of robbing us when they were only buying our tickets.' We had no francs left after Miss Doughty appeased them with extravagant tips. Aunt Mary would give me tips on the ways of the world. 'Always put your *best* dress on the first evening in a hotel,' she said. 'Shouldn't I save the best till later?' I asked from the depths of my puritan upbringing. 'Certainly not. You must make a good impression *at once*.' At any rate I made a good impression on a young painter who used to come sketching with us and on returning home to England, I learnt afterwards, asked Father for my hand. He too taught me one useful thing – about colour: 'The colours of flowers cannot clash.'

In the autumn of 1924 I returned to France for a six-month university course at Grenoble. I must have been homesick at last, like the man in the fairy-tale who learnt to shiver, for I wrote to my parents: 'You can't think what pleasure I derive from having my well-known self here.' The pension I was staying in was run by two stout sisters, war widows. Always swathed in black, they doted on a pair of huge poodles that were bathed once a week in eau-de-Cologne. The mixed perfumes were unforgettable. My chief pleasure – a moderate one – consisted in wandering round Grenoble on my own, but this was soon forbidden by my nervous parents. 'I always wear my oldest clothes and look a perfect hag,' I protested, 'but of course I won't do it any more. A pity because I really learnt something during my strolls and there is no one else interested in that sort of thing.'

It turned out, however, that a Dutch student in the pension with liquid brown eyes and a humpy nose *was* interested in that sort of thing. Some time after the end of his poignantly innocent courtship we arranged to meet at dawn on the Golden Arrow or some such train, with Aunt Maggie and Val Nettlefold as chaperones. Suddenly the memories of all our self-analytical letters were as if they had never been, when submitted to ordeal by continental breakfast. He had travelled all night from Utrecht to join us. But the arrow was no longer of gold. We never met or wrote again. I imagine him today as a stalwart burgher with what Queen Victoria would have called '*une nombreuse famille*'.

A fellow student at Grenoble who intrigued me was Robert Mathew.

He attended no lectures and in very cold weather did not get up. Much admired by his foreign colleagues for his role of eccentric Englishman, he was of interest to me as being my first living Roman Catholic. I was still in the phase of regaling my parents with derogatory remarks about papists. 'A black beetle has got on my tram,' I would scribble when a priest scuttled aboard. Wayside shrines were always ludicrous: 'The end of St Germain's nose is missing and his book of hours is covered with the pencilled initials of tourists. Most inspiring.' But somehow Robert Mathew's embodiment of this strange religion seemed neither creepy nor silly.

Meanwhile, I was glad to be back in England again. Grenoble University had generously presented me with three certificates: one for passing the exam, a second for honourable mention in composition, a third for 'assiduité' – attending the courses. It all seemed too simple. I felt dissatisfied with what little I had learnt and longed for more knowledge.

In writing French essays [I complained] one has to get rid of at least half one's English ideals. All the *impressionism* which I like so much is out of the question. Imagination is allowed to a certain extent but it has to be kept under one's thumb. . . . The French don't like being pleasantly puzzled or intrigued. G. K. Chesterton would be anathema to them. Everything has to be cut and dried, very precise. They have rather a ripping vocabulary of strenuous adjectives but they are all barred to *jeunes filles* who want to pass exams.

Grenoble at least had stimulated me to try again for Oxford, this time after private tuition. My tutor, a tiny white-haired graduate whose throat was always swathed in scarves (she was dying of cancer though I did not then know it), submitted the Romantics to an exhaustive analysis with overspills into the pre-Raphaelites, the Oxford Movement and Scientific History. I attended lectures at museums and galleries, especially Philip Hendy's *tours de force* on French painting and furniture at the Wallace Collection. I even prepared a passage from Ruskin's *Stones of Venice* for my general essay. Ruskin is comparing the fall of Tyre to that of Venice:

Her successor, like her in perfection of beauty, though less in endurance of dominion, is still left for our beholding in the final period of her decline: a ghost upon the sands of the sea, so weak – so quiet – so bereft of all but her loveliness, that we might well doubt, as we watched her faint reflection in the mirage of the lagoon, which was the City and which the Shadow.

I was to bequeath this wonderful passage, still in my estimation among the most perfect examples of English prose, to my daughter Antonia when she was trying for Lady Margaret Hall, with the same happy result. The college was kind enough to say they could not believe I was the same candidate who had failed so dismally before.

> *The Times*, 18 December 1925.
>
> *Announcement of scholarship awards at Oxford.*
> Lady Margaret Hall, in order of merit:
>
> **A. M. White**, Edinburgh University, Old Students'
>   Scholarship – English;
> **E. Harman**, Headington School for Girls and
>   private tuition – English . . .

It was to be Eng. Lit. for me after all. Or so I thought.

4

Oxford: A Turning-Point
· 1926–8 ·

I had arrived, or so it seemed, in both senses. My taxi left Oxford station, crossed the canal bridge and slowed down at the top of Beaumont Street between the classical Ashmolean Museum and the Victorian-Gothic Randolph Hotel. At that precise moment I had one of the rare intuitions of my life. 'This is a turning-point.' I was alone without the company of parent or friend; nothing to interrupt the flow of my conviction. 'Everything will be different from now on. The beginning of the real thing.'

My highest ambition, however, sounded pathetically limited as rehearsed to myself while we were turning the corner into St Giles', though the jejune thought showed an equally balanced interest in knowledge and people: 'I want to meet a *scholar*.' I have always been an academic snob.

The first high-flyer I met was Hugh Gaitskell, though actually he had missed his scholarship to Oxford from Winchester. But there were to be many experiences for me nearer home before Hugh made his appearance. As my taxi entered the spacious north Oxford cul-de-sac called Norham Gardens, I saw facing me the dignified Georgian-type front of my college, Lady Margaret Hall, with its pillared portico. On my right lurked (for I did not notice it at first) the hideous original Victorian building known as Old Hall, which I was to occupy on the ground floor for a year. There was no central heating, but a good scuttle of coal was allowed per day and in icy weather the maids could be persuaded to replenish it.

I remember this coal fire for an eccentric reason. One spring day I decided to make the experiment of starving myself completely for the inside of a week. I was surprised to find that I did not suffer so much from hunger as from miserable, devitalizing cold. I kept my fire roaring all day but never got warm or was able to work.

There was a traditional way of making our beds. We rolled up the quilt into a sausage and placed it at one end of the bed to look like the arm of a sofa; then we covered the whole thing with a bedspread and arranged as

45

many cushions as we possessed along the back wall. None of this made it feel like a real couch.

I went shopping to buy some personal furniture. In Baker's of Broad Street Corner (as it advertised itself) I found a wooden armchair with flat arms and a sliding seat, which was surprisingly comfortable. It has been my working chair ever since. I also bought from Alden's nearby a print of the Sheldonian Theatre in which I was shortly to be dubbed an alumna of the University. But the picture had to be removed after I read a message something like this in an undergraduate magazine: 'Advice to Freshers. Only the most naïve will decorate their walls with prints of Oxford when they are actually surrounded by the place. Hang up your Oxford prints at home and your home prints in Oxford.'

My first-year friends and I were extremely naïve. The closest of these was Audrey Townsend, a History scholar from Bournemouth High School. Neither of us used any make-up to speak of. With finely cut features and magnolia skin, Audrey needed no more than a fingertip of vanishing cream on her nose. I would smooth mine with a tiny hard puff but did not own a lipstick – this in 1926 when hair-styling and make-up were strident: hair set in tight crinkles that would have suited a sphinx, and lips harshly outlined in scarlet. In fact my dark brown hair was 'water-waved' once a week, which meant having it pinched into loose waves while wet and then put under a net and dryer. This, and animation, were my best features, as I had a neat nape and was 'dolichocephalic' or long-headed, a fact which my father had pointed out to me with pleasure since I had inherited it from him. I was also proud of my eyebrows after my friend Kenneth Diplock told me that they were arched like Waterloo Bridge. My other features – grey-blue eyes and small mouth – were not brilliant or wide enough for beauty though I expect they suited a small, round face.

Audrey Townsend and I had much in common beside our scholar's gowns. We were each the eldest of a sizeable family, both families being intimately woven into an ever larger web of cousins. I went to stay with the Townsends in Dorset and thought I had never set eyes on such handsome children. Audrey's sister was as pretty as Audrey herself; her brother Philip had Ruritanian good looks and was jokingly nicknamed 'Prince Philip' (Prince Philip of Greece was five at the time and had not yet entered British history); as for the superlatively attractive Peter, like Dick Diver in *Tender Is the Night*, he was awaiting 'an intricate destiny' in the orbit of the Royal Family.

Male cousins at university were a convenient halfway house between strangers and brothers. Audrey and I each had a first cousin up at Oxford.

Mine was Michael Hope, black-eyed, black-haired, reading Greats (Classics) at Christ Church.

Michael was the son of Bertha Chamberlain – fourth of the seven sisters – and Donald Hope, manufacturer of casements in Birmingham. If anyone symbolizes in a unique fashion the transformation of nineteenth-century 'Brummagem' industrial society into a fine distillation of twentieth-century culture, Michael Hope is that man. As children he and I had wept together when one of our more aggressive young cousins marched through a bluebell wood picking out the rare white flowers and chopping off their heads. Twenty-five years later, at the beginning of the war, Michael's colonel was to send him into Oxford to buy a tea-service for the mess. 'You know about that sort of thing.' He was not pleased when Michael returned with some elegant bone china instead of the cheap white cups and saucers he had expected. 'I couldn't have drunk out of them, Sir,' said my fastidious cousin. He managed to raise the aesthetic tone of the mess, at least at tea-time.

Hugh Gaitskell was Audrey's cousin, reading Modern Greats at New College. Today his name evokes a nostalgic golden age of the Labour Party when politics were moderate and spirits fighting. He was to miss being Prime Minister in October 1964 only through the lethal action of a mysterious virus that had killed him in 1963.

The Hugh Gaitskell to whom I was introduced during my second term at Oxford was a far more fluid character than the politician of twenty or thirty years later. That may have been partly why the young Hugh was so eager to fix his own identity through instructing others in what he saw as the certainties of life.

'Would you like to meet my brainy cousin Hugh Gaitskell?'

Audrey and I were still finding our feet and our friends. A letter to my mother ended with the good news that the insertion of a bronze hairpin into the light-switch enabled me to use my reading lamp and ceiling light at the same time, but – 'If only I had some fizz & a reek of cigar from someone. . . .'

Hugh and Audrey had not yet got together at Oxford but she remembered him as a spirited child clinging to the pillion of his brother Arthur's motorbike and eluding his nanny when she called, "Ugh! 'Ugh!' by pretending she was shouting for someone else. 'You! You!'

I found that Hugh at twenty had great charm but had not yet acquired those aphrodisiac qualities which the possession of worldly power confers. Jolly rather than bookish at first sight, he had curly bracken-coloured hair and a rosy face with an exceptionally winning smile, a sharp, enquiring nose, lively blue eyes that were rather prominent though not large, and not quite enough chin for masculine beauty. Not that Hugh ever hungered for anything so trite. At this period he was cultivating two things above all: his own analytical intellect and the ability to influence other people. I was one of those who was to benefit beyond words from the latter. His almost objective interest in my development seemed part cousinly, part professorial; not really loverlike, except occasionally in letters and during a few weeks of my second year.

Our pact of friendship was entered upon solemnly on an Oxford hillside under a haystack between Cumnor and Boars Hill in the very early spring of 1927. Hugh was in his last year and working for a first in Philosophy, Politics and Economics. I was still faintly bemused by the multitude of Oxford myths that brushed against one like cobwebs on a ghost train. Were we indeed living in the 'home of lost causes'? And what were Matthew Arnold's 'dreaming spires' dreaming about? It could equally well be of things to come as of things past and lost.

But Hugh had not brought me this far to discuss Matthew Arnold. Suddenly he began speaking very seriously.

'What do you think of Oscar Wilde and all that?'

'Oscar Wilde? Oh, I think that's quite all right.'

I spoke with the assurance of one who had not really thought much about it. Indeed my only knowledge of sexual irregularities had come from books. I had read *The Picture of Dorian Gray* and possessed an elegant copy of *The Golden Asse of Lucius Apuleius* presented to me by a former well-wisher.

'I'm so glad,' said Hugh fervently. 'If you hadn't thought that way we couldn't have gone on.'

Though I did not realize it until afterwards, I had just passed my entrance exam for that charmed circle of Oxford aesthetes into which Hugh planned my introduction. It was one of the crucial five minutes of my life. If I had wrinkled my nose at the idea of homosexuality I should have been returned to my college by Hugh with a curt 'No thanks'. For there were quite a few genuine homosexuals among the so-called aesthetes, and many more who affected the style while up at Oxford.

Hugh's next move in my education was to present me with the unique phenomenon of Maurice Bowra. I do not want to exaggerate Hugh's preoccupation with *my* progress. He liked to do the same for all his friends. Nevertheless, he invested a generous amount of capital in me by taking me to lunch with Maurice. I cannot recall who was there that first time beside Hugh; the approach to Maurice's presence and the stunning impact of Maurice's personality have obliterated everything else.

He was Dean of Wadham College. After passing through the porter's lodge into a small, beautiful quadrangle, we turned right and were almost at once opposite a door marked 'The Dean'. A good deal of noise floated down to us from above, but there was a respectful and terrifying silence as Maurice introduced me to each of his guests around the room, always in stentorian tones: 'MISS HARMAN' . . . He had received us first at the top of the staircase, tiny feet and short legs apart, miraculously supporting an ever-increasing weight of rotundity until one reached his deep chest, broad shoulders and massive head. To me, in the first moment of excitement at meeting this renowned figure, his was the noble forehead, the smooth cap of hair, the small, penetrating eyes, straight nose, flushed cheek, square jaw and jowl of a Roman emperor.

One effect of knowing Maurice was immediate. I decided to change my 'school' and read Greats, officially known as *Literae Humaniores* and combining ancient history with ancient and modern philosophy. I was already thoroughly dissatisfied with my English school. I found no pleasure in Anglo-Saxon. Worse still, I had irritated my English tutor, Miss Janet Spens, a pinched, grey scholar of high repute who regarded all past literature with protective veneration and present students with distrust. When I wrote a carping essay on Wordsworth, she blue-pencilled the whole thing. 'It is your business to interpret, not to criticize. Who are you to set yourself up against these great ones?'

Apart from Miss Spens, there were other reasons for wanting to do classics. My cousin Michael Hope and his Wykehamist friends at New College whom I knew or knew of and admired – John Willis, George Harwood, William Hayter, Dick Crossman, Douglas Jay, Richard Wilberforce – were all classicists. English was for women. I was the only girl at Maurice's parties and felt an urge to tackle a 'man's' subject, particularly as Maurice's own devotion to the classics had irradiated the scene for me with a kind of glory.

Would my college allow me to change? Unfortunately, like Shakespeare I had 'less Greek' than Latin, in fact no Greek at all. I should have to spend extra time at Oxford learning the language – and, even if this worked out, what about my scholarship? The college pointed out that their next-to-top scholar should be running for a first. I might get one in English. But in Greats? Nevertheless they saw my point or the points which I thought it wise to reveal and courageously gave me permission to change – if my parents agreed to the extra year. I wrote an impassioned letter **home**.

Friday 11 March, 1927

Dear Mother,

This is a most important letter so, like Horatio in Hamlet, pray absent yourself from human society awhile & draw your breath in pain. I am definitely changing my school. English has proved a wash-out. I am going to read Greats. Greats, as you know, is THE school at Oxford. . . . Being the best school, any kind of degree is valuable, 1st, 2nd, or 3rd even. 1st of course imposs. . . . Will you answer by return, please, to give your consent as everything must be settled before the end of term. I am so thrilled, as classics have always been my delight & I never knew till this week that it was allowable to read Greats without having been brought up on Greek. . . .

Please answer at once per P.C. as I am burning to get on. . . .

Goodbye. Much love, & don't think of suggesting that I should *not* read Greats because I am determined. I have always done the most difficult work going, & I will continue.

Veni Vidi Vici.

Love Betty M.A. Oxon.

P.S. *Please* don't think I am changing merely out of pique because I don't like English. It is not a negative change . . . & there is apparently every chance of my turning out fairly competent.

It was lucky that my new mentor Hugh Gaitskell did not see this outpouring of mingled braggadocio and self-doubt, since it epitomized what he abhorred most in human behaviour. He called it 'dramatizing the situation'. The opposite to 'dramatizing' was cool analysis, deliberation, a steady attempt to see things as they truly were. 'Never dramatize the situation' was a slogan that I heard from him more times than I can remember.

In fact he was pleased with me for changing from English to Greats. It would help, he thought, to detach me from the world of women, which he regarded as quintessentially 'stuffy'. For the same reason he encouraged me to put in for the part of Miranda in the OUDS forthcoming production of *The Tempest*. My main competitor was Dulcie Martin, who was backed by Hugh's handsome, enigmatic friend Charles Plumb, himself a member of OUDS. Early in May Hugh wrote to me from his digs at 2 Isis Street:

I spent the evening drunkenly, during the course of which I tried, though quite in vain, to find out the result of the Women's OUDS final. . . . I hope you won, though Charles tells me that (this also drunk) he has been using all his influence for Dulcie – this probably stimulated by the rivalry of you & me, as it were.

I think, honestly, it would be a useful experience, though on no account must the OUDS (atmosphere & members) be taken seriously – it fits in with the general theory that to advance here in Oxford an undergraduette must first break away from the high school atmosphere of college & secondly from the high school atmosphere of her girl friends. This sounds unpleasant but I think it's true. . . . At the same time this is not to mean that one should have as many men friends as one can. Really it is necessary to be as alone as possible. The destructive action of breaking away is where the effort is required: the rest works itself.

While Hugh was in the midst of propounding this programme of 'Strength through Misery', there was a ring at the front-door bell of his digs and the inter-college messenger handed him a note from me. I had 'failed' – beaten by Dulcie Martin *and* Mollie Bissett, who were to play Miranda at alternate performances. Both were at Somerville College and both reading *English*.

Hugh added a word of encouragement to his hitherto severe letter.

As a matter of fact the 'failure', as *you* put it, is utterly unimportant – If we do accept the theory [of breaking away] – you evidently agree more or less – the OUDS was only one way & there are a million others & better ones too – in fact there was always the danger that the OUDS would be out of the frying pan into the fire: as 'atmospheres' go, it is not much better than that of 'the women'.

All the same I was disappointed, not only because Michael Hope was going to appear as Francisco in *The Tempest*, Osbert Lancaster (an *habitué* of Maurice's circle and of most other amusing circles too) as Sebastian and Peter Fleming (elder brother of Ian) as Antonio, but also because I longed to act somewhere, somehow. At the age of twelve I had told my mother that I was going to be an actress. She punctured my hopes for ever. 'I was much better at acting than you are, dear, but I was not good enough to be a professional.' (Did she make the attempt, I wonder?) For me college theatricals seemed to be the answer.

The Lady Margaret Hall Dramatic Society put on three plays during my first three years and I acted in all of them. The cast was, of course, entirely female and *The Fritillary*, the magazine of the combined women's colleges, gave us an indulgent review for our production of *The Way of the World* in 1927. They commented favourably on Lady Wishfort's eyebrow, 'played by Miss E. Harman in a manner almost acrobatic. . . . She raised her voice, her eyes and her hands to such heights that the play became almost rollicking.' Rollicking for us players, perhaps. But when I sneaked a glance at the fifth row of the audience, where Maurice Bowra, Michael

Hope and Hugh Gaitskell sat with glazed faces, I realized that only extreme loyalty had brought them there and kept them there until the end of the performance. (Maurice hardly ever went to plays or concerts as they interrupted the purpose of living – talk.) In my maturer years I would no more have dreamt of inviting Maurice to such college theatricals than of asking him to be my partner at a college 'hop'.

On the other hand I never really took to heart Hugh's advice on avoiding 'the women'. I chose a course halfway between being a dedicated member of my college – aiming perhaps at becoming President of the Junior Common Room – and playing no part at all in college life. I swam for my college in a boarded-off bend of the River Cherwell called Dame's Delight, but did not once enter college chapel; I hardly put my nose inside the JCR or attended 'Hall' (formal dinner), preferring to bolt my supper, when not out, at a meal lasting ten minutes that was pushed through the hatch by Emily, the enormous parlourmaid – but I applied for a part in every dramatic production that was going.

Our most successful play was *The Yellow Jacket*. I had seen it in London during the vacation and realized that its combination of rich Chinese costumes with no scenery whatever would ideally suit our college exigencies. The press were uniformly flattering. 'Weird charm . . . extremely clever but simple stage devices . . . language amusing and often poetic . . . "august" and admirable production.' Most productions, wrote the *Isis* critic, when entirely undertaken by women, were handicapped: 'But this charming little extravaganza was, on the contrary, aided by the acting of male characters by women.' As the play's producer, I had assembled a notable twenty-eight-strong cast, of whom Armorel Heron-Allen, a ravishing zoologist, was the star, doubling the parts of the villainous father and son. I managed to assign myself the other plum part and a reviewer wrote, 'Miss Harman fulfilled the role of heroine capably.'

The only criticism of the play was levelled against the producer – me. 'It was a good joke carried a little too far,' wrote the same reviewer. 'Quite a lot of pruning would not have been amiss.' I never learnt the lesson. Never in my life have I managed to write a book, article or speech that was the right length first go. For me, production and pruning, creation and cutting are wearisome inseparables.

Looking back on my obsession with theatricals I have to ask, where was the real talent? To play a heroine's part 'capably' is not the highest praise. But I was a good organizer with a decided overdose of enthusiasm for the project in hand. It was the same enthusiasm plus the ability to whip it up in others that had made me captain of my netball team at school. My athletic skills were no more than average.

The last word on my acting was said to me by myself, in dreams. For many years my recurrent nightmare was set on a darkened stage of which I held the centre. Suddenly the lights would go up and the curtains swish apart to disclose a packed audience. Only then did I realize that I knew not one single word of my part and indeed had not the faintest notion what play was being put on.

In all my intimate discussions with Hugh we hardly touched upon any subject but our own personal relations. I can remember his once telling me that he travelled by train first class in order to avoid the horrid feeling of being among the workers but not one of them; on no other occasion did he touch on his political sensibilities. This seems strange, since I knew perfectly well that Hugh had become an ardent socialist while at Oxford and had supported the workers during the General Strike of 1926. However, it fits with what Hugh himself was to write much later about Oxford undergraduates in the mid 1920s, just before the strike. 'Politics, to tell the truth, were rather at a discount. We were in revolt all right against Victorianism, Puritanism, stuffiness of any kind, but most of us weren't sufficiently bitter – or perhaps sufficiently serious – to be angry young men.' For Hugh and his friends 'the heavenly freedom of Oxford' became a freedom from dogma and sentimentality, dislike of over-emotional prejudices, general scepticism. 'We professed the happiness of the individual to be the only acceptable social aim.' This seems to relate so closely to what Peter Levi wrote about an Oxford of a much later date – 'One got so drunk with the experience of freedom and individuality' – that I wonder whether freedom and individuality are not the timeless gifts of a universal Oxford, or indeed of all universities.

In my own case politics simply did not exist during most of my time at Oxford. Two of my lifelong friends, the writers Rosalie (Grylls) Mander and Georgina (Harwood) Battiscombe, tried to make me join the Liberal Club. I resisted their blandishments. It was during the vacations rather than in termtime that the political spark would occasionally ignite, usually through an argument with my father about one of the current Shavian plays. On the way home in the underground after seeing *John Bull's Other Island*, my father was in a fury with Ireland and the Irish. 'The whole place ought to be sunk to the bottom of the sea.' For that evening at any rate I was an Irish nationalist. He was open-minded enough, however, to take me also to see Shaw's *The Doctor's Dilemma*, in which the heroine was played by Margaret Rawlings, the most romantic undergraduate at Lady Margaret Hall in my day. The play confirmed my growing suspicion that the professional face of Britain was pockmarked with humbug.

Religion at Oxford touched me even less strongly than politics. I had written a poem when I was seventeen which marked a borderline state between belief and scepticism. It was called 'Fragment of a Conversation between J.B.H. and myself when sleeping out'. In the first two verses my brother John put his point of view: that death is falling into endless sleep in which no trace of ourselves survives. In the third verse I expressed my own hopes and fears:

> 'Death is a great awakening,' I would cry,
> 'When secrets of the universe will out,
> And friend seek friend again, unerringly.'
> This would I make my faith; therefore I doubt.

My doubts increased during the next years until at Oxford they became complete scepticism. I prepared to enter Hertford College chapel for a service, but that was to be a Black Mass organized by my versatile friend Arthur Calder-Marshall and celebrated by a sinister visitor to Oxford, Aleister Crowley, known as The Beast. We had bought the black drapes and candles when the proctors got wind of it. Appropriately, it was blacked. I once entered Manchester College chapel, but that was only to see the Burne-Jones stained glass. I went to tiny Binsey church in West Oxford for Margaret Rawlings's wedding, but spent my time throwing silver sixpences into the wishing-well in the churchyard.

I also had a social link with the Roman Catholics of Balliol College through an emotional friendship with Desmond Ryan. I would meet his fellow-Catholics there, and my introduction to the Revd Martin D'Arcy, SJ, took place at a Balliol lunch party. His elegant figure, dark wavy hair, aristocratic features, intent eyes and air of subtle sophistication immediately made me think of Mephistopheles – a character who in any case I tended to equate with all but the untidiest priests. But when, at the end of lunch, Father d'Arcy politely offered me my coat back to front so that I could not get into the sleeves, I realized I had got him wrong.

I did know one genuinely but eccentrically religious undergraduate, the writer Humphrey House who was to become chaplain of Wadham. As he was courting a friend of mine he invited me to tea to talk about her. Suddenly he flopped on to his knees dragging me down with him. I took it as a joke.

Yet for all my scepticism I believe there was not total indifference. The other day I turned up some elaborate notes I had made for a play on the changing nature of God, beginning with Osiris and working through Zeus, Jaweh and Thor to the Christian deity, who is clearly on the defensive. The date must be about 1926 and shows my fascination with comparative religions, based on my reading of Frazer's *The Golden Bough*. At one point in my projected play God regrets his banishment of Satan. 'I only feel at my godliest', he laments, 'when the Devil is at close quarters.'

The thought of summer balls had begun to occupy my waking dreams and by May I had every night of Commemoration week booked up with a different ball and a different partner. Hugh Gaitskell and I were to go to the New College ball together. But there was a final page or two in the long letter from Hugh, already quoted, that had alerted me to possible complications on our night. It showed me a frivolous side of Hugh which I admired as much as his didactic side, though I found it slightly unnerving. He had just been invited, he told me, to join a party for two Commem balls, including the one at New College. A woman he had met at a dance two years ago would be in the party. 'I was very attracted by her looks and indecent conversation – needless to say I was not very sober. . . . She's married and appears to treat her husband with due contempt.' The suggestion was not, of course, that Hugh and I should scrap our own party (which incidentally was a foursome, including Hugh's brother Arthur), but that if we got bored with 'Arthur & his woman', we should go and investigate the other party. The men were, he thought, nice and anyway were 'thoroughly immoral and good-looking'. Hugh's letter then changed to a somewhat apologetic note.

I suppose my excitement about this other woman is not tactful – but you see she's just the other kind – I imagine utterly sensual – in fact with drink & everything else, perfect for an evening. I'm cooling down & see too that eventually I will probably only dance once with her at each ball, but a two years' old thrill must be forgiven.

This passage shows that Hugh was indirectly instructing me on how to grow up, to grow away from 'stuffy' heterosexual conventions, just as he had interviewed me, so to speak, on my attitude to homosexuals during our earlier meeting. That Hugh would not have approved of my college activities is clear from another paragraph in his letter.

Now shall we return to your troubles? Don't become President of anything. The only way, I'm sure, for you is to get away from all that sort of false existence – you ought to apply your intelligence not to organizing indoor games for other women but to developing your 'prostitute powers'. This is the way, first to disillusionment, secondly to knowledge, thirdly to freedom from inferiorities & fourthly to anything that may be worthwhile.

Though I did not realize it at the time, Hugh had already given me an opportunity to 'develop my prostitute powers', a chance which I had failed to seize. When visiting him one day during the vacation in his mother's London home, I was surprised by his suggestion that we should become engaged. 'Of course it won't mean anything,' he added hastily. 'Just so that we should be free to see each other without people interfering.' I could not see it as an extension of my freedom and declined. This was the nearest Hugh and I ever came to a physical relationship. 'Of course in trying to force on the physical side quickly', he was to comment a week later, 'I at least was trying to be older. . . .'

Hugh brought his May letter to a conclusion with a gallant effort to raise my spirits:

Here is an incident to be recorded – On the way home on Saturday night I met [John] Betjeman drunk who having discovered where I had been asked me if I had met a beautiful girl called Elizabeth Harman. You have such a lot on your side – you ought to make more of it. Love Hugh.

P.S. This letter appears sinister. Consciously it isn't but you never know.

When the great day of the New College ball came at last, things turned out rather differently from what either Hugh or I expected. True, I vaguely remember seeing him with 'the other kind of woman' in his arms, coat-tails flying in a waltz. He was a supple and energetic dancer. Years later I read in Philip Williams' biography of Hugh that his favourite break from work was 'relaxing with a light lady on a sofa'. A dance floor was almost as good. But if Hugh's programme for me had been eventual boredom with his brother Arthur and fun instead with Mrs X's 'thoroughly immoral' escorts, I was far from carrying it out. I found Arthur Gaitskell intoxicating.

Taller and more debonair than Hugh, he had all the novelty of an up-and-coming civil servant home on leave from the Near East and determined to enjoy every minute of it. Next day Arthur and I drove around Wytham Woods, he mildly surprised at my chewing the petals of primroses – an expression of euphoria picked up from my studies of D. H. Lawrence. Arthur afterwards came to dinner with me and my parents in Harley Street. There was little to drink though Father changed, as always, into his bow tie. At the end of a stilted but blissful evening I decided, for once, to ask my mother what she thought of my charming new friend. To my amazement she was distinctly noncommittal and, for once, influenced me in the direction of what Hugh had called 'cooling down'.

I think she felt that this summer fever might result in my leaving Oxford prematurely. When Arthur returned to the Sudan we exchanged nostalgic letters. I can still see his large tidy sloping handwriting on sheet after sheet of thin blue paper. Gradually the gaps between our letters lengthened until it was all a painless gap.

Apart from Arthur Gaitskell, there is another episode that made the night of the New College ball memorable. To explain it I must go back to the night before when the Magdalen College ball was celebrated to the fashionable wailing of Ambrose's band. About midnight, on my way back from the cloakroom to the dance floor, I was astonished to see a large sleeping figure draped over a garden chair in the middle of a wide canvas corridor. As I approached the figure on tiptoe I saw that it was wearing a 'Bullingdon' uniform, the last word in social glamour: yellow waistcoat and navy blue tailcoat with white facings and brass buttons. The face was of monumental beauty, as if some Graeco-Roman statue – the Sleeping Student maybe – had been dressed up in modern clothes by some group of jokers. I stood for a moment admiring but puzzled. 'What sort of girl', I asked myself, 'could have allowed such a magnificent partner to spend the best part of the night alone and asleep?' Years later I discovered that the girl had been Alice Buchan, daughter of John Buchan, the novelist. If the Buchan charm could not keep Frank Pakenham awake, it was clear that nothing and nobody ever would.

After a good day's sleep myself, I awoke refreshed for the New College ball on the following night, 28 June 1927. For the first and only time I wore my most poetic dance frock of lavender taffeta printed with bunches of little flowers floating in four petal-shaped panels, with a chiffon underskirt and knickers to match. Next morning I found that I had been literally (but not metaphorically) deflowered: one of the petals had floated away or been torn off. Though today it has faded to a twilight grey like my hair, I have kept it because of what happened that night; and I have never worn it again because of the missing petal.

Some time well after midnight Hugh took me along to the room in Garden Quad that Ken Mckinnon, a third-year Australian scholar, had hired for the occasion. At that point 'Provvy', as Jeremy Bentham used to call Providence, began to show her hand. There, extended on Ken's sofa, lay my vision of the night before, again deeply and serenely asleep. This time I did not hesitate. A performance of the Sleeping Beauty act was clearly called for in reverse. Bending over his mop of classical brown curls I kissed him on the forehead. His brown (as I now saw they were) eyes opened wide. 'I'd like to kiss you but I can't. . . .' As he fell back into slumber he heard the gnomic words of Ken Mckinnon uttered solemnly and with careful precision. 'Elizabeth-has-got-a-wizard-face. The-word-wizard-has-come-into-its-own-tonight.' Frank was to remember Ken's words as part of a haunting dream.

He shared digs with Hugh at 2 Isis Street. Fired by his experience of 28 June, he decided to find out more from their landlady.

'Mrs Benwell, do you know anything about that girl who sometimes comes round to see Mr Gaitskell?'

'She's a French lady I think.'

'Why do you think that?'

'I judge by the shoes.'

I had recently bought myself a flattering pair of scarlet court shoes and perhaps as a warning my cousin Michael Hope presented me with the Nonesuch edition of Hans Andersen's *Red Shoes*.

Three weeks after the New College ball Frank and Hugh received their prepaid telegrams from the Clerk of the Examination Schools. Both of them had got firsts in Philosophy, Politics and Economics. Frank had obtained some kind of *alpha* (A) in every paper except Economic Theory, his best subject. He was staying with a stockbroker friend, Alec Spearman, later a Conservative MP, and had confided his fears to Alec that his atrocious handwriting might cause the examiners to plough him. His mother, Lady Longford, had a somewhat similar anxiety. She saw the results in a newspaper while travelling up to London with Lady Birkenhead, wife of the Lord Chancellor. Beginning with the second class and proceeding downwards through the third to the fourth, to the very bottom, Lady Longford at last turned resignedly to Lady Birkenhead.

'I'm afraid Frank's failed. His name is nowhere in the list.'

Lady Birkenhead took the paper from her friend's hand and began reading from the top.

'He's got a first.'

Frank decided to give a celebration dinner at the Café Royal in London, followed by a theatre. He invited among others his sister Pansy Pakenham, Henry Lamb the painter to whom she was secretly engaged, John Maxse her admirer, Hugh and his 'French lady'. After the dinner Frank pirouetted on one of the seats in the Café Royal, passed out and was not seen again. Pansy went off with Henry; and John Maxse, who was leaving in the small hours for an extended spell with the army in India and had hoped that Pansy would see him off from Waterloo, was left to the ministrations of Hugh and me. We drove with him in a taxi to Waterloo station and walked about those eerie solitudes until it was time to wave him off in the boat train. The long wait allowed us time to manufacture a spurious concern for each other – neither Hugh nor I had met Maxse before – and I hope we gave him the feeling of a warm send-off. If Evelyn Waugh had been there too, as he well might have been a year later, I think that weird evening would have found its way into an early novel.

Next day I rang up Hugh to enquire after Frank. Should I call? 'Certainly not.' Hugh was emphatic. 'His sister Pansy is holding his head.' Though disappointed I respected Hugh's flicker of jealousy, if jealousy it was. I deliberately kept my feelings about Frank Pakenham in abeyance, particularly as I heard no more of him until the middle of next term, when I received a message that he would like to meet another of Hugh's cousins, Evelyn Martelli, who was reading History at LMH. Perhaps I would organize a tea-party in college? I did so, in high hopes, but the college atmosphere was deadening and there was no sequel.

I greatly admired Evelyn's polished short dark hair, smartly tailored coats and skirts and generally sophisticated appearance. Hugh had used her as an example of how women should dress. Strongly deprecating my fancy styles – I had designed for myself a grey satin afternoon frock trimmed with deep rows of lemon silk fringe – he insisted that women should dress quietly and in good taste. This in spite of his own gaudy ties and baggy trousers. While he was still at Oxford I tried to please by moderating my experiments in colour and design. After he went down, however, I turned to flamboyant adventures in 'bad taste'. I remember in particular an ebony cane presented to me by Armorel's father, the bibliophile Edward Heron-Allen. The cane had an ivory top and black silk tassel. I felt it needed an outfit to match and ordered a dark blue silk shirt and tie, slim blue-grey suit and striking cape, about the length of a matador's.

Meanwhile, Frank had stayed up for an extra year to read Law. We did not meet except for the college tea-party. In the spring he got severe concussion so that the Law was driven out of his head. Riding in an Oxford point-to-point on a thoroughly inadequate horse, he was thrown about halfway round the course but spiritedly remounted and careered off again – back towards the start instead of forwards to the winning post. Bill Astor, on a very adequate steed, met Frank galloping towards him and shouting, 'Wrong way, Bill! Turn round!' Bill ignored the advice of his concussed friend and went on to win.

All my intellectual interests were concentrating on the classics, poetry and my 'aesthete' friends for whom Maurice's rooms in Wadham were the unchallenged focal point. The opposite to 'aesthetes' were supposed to be 'hearties', but in fact there was no hard and fast division. The popular idea of hearties – huge Philistine brutes with an infinite capacity for beer – had evolved in an earlier generation thanks to Kipling's lines about 'the flannelled fools at the wicket or the muddied oafs at the goals'. There was a time, however, when Hugh liked nothing better than a round of golf, while Maurice himself had played a tough game of rugger while a schoolboy at Cheltenham. Frank never stopped being a devotee of rugger.

He hunted and was a member, as I observed the first time I saw him, of the Bullingdon. Yet no one thought of him as a hearty. Before I met him, Hugh had summed him up to me as 'very clever – a bit of a Philistine'.

'The county families of England baying for broken glass' – these plangent words from Evelyn Waugh's first novel, *Decline and Fall*, published in 1928, stood for the Bullingdon and Loders of Christ Church, both in their relatively harmless and in their dangerous moods. No one took much notice of the regular window-smashing that occurred after every club dinner. Someone would sweep up the glass and stones next morning, the bill for fresh glazing would be presented and paid. Persecution of individuals, often though not always aesthetes, was vicious but rare. I was told that H. W. B. Joseph of New College, whose philosophy lectures I attended, was once 'crucified' on his college lawn, held down with croquet hoops. But I read in my *Isis* for 22 June 1927: 'The other night, the first time for months, we heard the noble cry: "Come on, chaps, let's go and beat up some bl..dy aesthetes!" ' According to legend, bloody aesthetes sometimes succeeded in beating up the attacking parties. Both Oscar Wilde at Magdalen and Maurice Bowra at New College were said to have repulsed their attackers with heavy losses to the enemy.

The loosening of my ties with Hugh Gaitskell, especially our pupil– master relationship, will bring this chapter of my life to an end. Though Hugh, unlike Frank, went down after taking his degree, the magic of Oxford still drew him – until he actually went back for a weekend at the beginning of February 1928. On the 15th he wrote to me from Nottingham, where he was lecturing on economics at the university, about the Oxford visit. His letter was a typical post-mortem of our meeting, and incidentally of all that Oxford no longer meant to him and increasingly meant to me.

I had written first, regretting that the party at Maurice's had been a muddle in the sense that Hugh and I had not got a chance to talk. 'It was extremely nice to see you again,' replied Hugh magnanimously, 'and I enjoyed very much our conversation at the Randolph. However I noticed various things.' These things included the fact that I had become *more* part of Oxford society while he, as I myself noticed, was more 'serious'. He cited Maurice's conversation and Betjeman's jokes. 'I felt faintly bored. How can Maurice endure it?' Hugh then referred to a 'row' we had had the year before when I had brought some hearties to his London home. He felt I mocked his seriousness and in part his taste. (I fancy my unwelcome friends were from Balliol, Edward Stanley and Patrick de Laszlo. They were not hearties but neither were they aesthetes.) Hugh thought his own taste might be a mixture of 'highbrowness' and objection to my spending any time with hearties – 'You see they *do* have a deteriorating effect on you because you're so unshaped in some ways.' Hugh's letter ended with a plea to keep in touch, though he saw no way out of our impasse.

I think probably the whole way I treat our relations must annoy you – it does absorb me – I analyse it as though it were the Theory of Rent, but then that does not alter at all your great attraction for me . . . but there are differences between us & just now I think they are accentuated because you are in Oxford & I am not. Will you answer this? & to relieve me accuse me of everything horrible but answer.

Hugh's last attempt to end the 'differences between us' was a drastic one, though at the time it passed completely over my head. All I remember is a party in Paris at which Maurice Bowra and Hugh were both present, Maurice in uproarious spirits, pretending he was going to look up various 'light ladies' of his acquaintance later in the evening. The delicious meal I remember for my first taste of kebabs. Some fifty years later Hugh's biographer was to throw an unexpected light on what to me at the time was hardly more than an impulsive dash abroad for twenty-four hours.

In July 1928 [writes Philip Williams], after a year's separation [an inaccuracy; we had met in February], Hugh had the bizarre idea of a dinner-party for six people in Paris at which he hoped to propose to her, but it was not a success and he never did.

If the first stage of my relationship with Hugh Gaitskell ended in a cul-de-sac, the earlier part of our year together had been remarkably positive and invaluable to me. It is only looking back that I see what an extraordinarily cerebral relationship it was. He was a born teacher with a rare gift for pushing people forward at the right speed and usually in the direction best for them. Only once did he set me an impossible target, and that was when he urged me to read through the whole of Proust *in French*. Such was the force of his personality that I did it; to discover at the end that though I understood each separate word I had no idea what Proust was saying.

Hugh's friends on the whole were what he would have called 'highbrow' and he passed them on to me. When his clever cousin George Martelli, brother of Evelyn, decided to resign from the navy and become a writer – an act that Hugh loudly applauded – he immediately introduced George to Oxford society, thus initiating a lifelong friendship with me and my family. Without Hugh's intervention I should not have met Maurice Bowra or John Betjeman or the rest of that scintillating world. The meeting with Frank Pakenham was perhaps due as much to chance as to Hugh. But then, who knows what we mean by chance?

5

Oxford: The Young Lions
· 1927–9 ·

At first my meetings with Maurice Bowra were always at his parties, whether for lunch or dinner in his white-panelled room at Wadham. My memories are of incessant thunderous noise and laughter, above which Maurice's voice would rise in a volley of puns and paradoxes, interrupted only by his suddenly pushing back his chair, springing to his feet and marching purposefully around the table to fill our glasses yet again.

Maurice roared and shouted and his face got red and then purple, but I cannot remember it ever dissolving in smiles. It was his pleasure to make his friends helpless with laughter, his own expression meanwhile remaining stern and his speech loud, vehement, emphatic, sometimes menacing. He was entirely without the changing inflexions and modulations of the professional humorist or the confidential smiles that signal a joke ahead. Instead of playing on us subtly he beat us as if we were drums.

I was perfectly happy just to be present at his court. To me Maurice Bowra at thirty was Voltaire and the Sun King rolled into one.

At his table I would hear tales of past heroes like Kenneth Clark (later Lord of Civilization), Cyril Connolly, L. P. Hartley and Robert Boothby, or meet beautiful creatures like Christopher Fremantle, the future painter and philosopher. Christopher was the only friend of Maurice's who to my knowledge was magnetized away by a golden girl. He got engaged to Anne Huth-Jackson of Lady Margaret Hall, and to Maurice's indignation slipped out of orbit.

Maurice's two closest friends while I was up (and for the rest of his life) were John Sparrow and Isaiah Berlin. Sparrow's matchless epitaph on his friend, first published in the *Times Literary Supplement*, seemed to speak with Maurice's own voice, booming puns and all. Sparrow imagines Bowra in Heaven, planting himself in the judgement seat:

> He'll seize the sceptre and annexe the throne,
> Claim the Almighty's thunder for his own,
> Trump the Last Trump and the Last Post postpone . . .

I did not succeed in meeting 'Shaiah' Berlin, as he was called in those days, until after we had both gone down, when I remember sending him a letter but not knowing how to spell his name. Finally I settled for 'Dear Shyer'. 'Shyer than who?' he replied. Isaiah was and is a superb mimic. He once gave an entire lecture to an Oxford club in the voice and manner of a fellow academic. He could imitate Maurice better than anyone and like so many others (Lancaster, Sparrow) still has the characteristic Bowra 'attack'. I have always been able to spot that tell-tale emphasis in strangers and mark them down as people who had known Maurice in their youth.

In his memorial address, Isaiah was to say of Maurice: 'He admired genius, splendour, eloquence, the grand style, and had no fear of orchestral colour; the chamber music of Bloomsbury was not for him.' Not only was it not for him, but he made it unacceptable to me also.

I was once taken by my great friend David Cecil to a party in Cambridge where a number of 'Bloomsburys' were present, among them Virginia and Leonard Woolf. Never having met any of them before, I was excited and keyed up for the new experience. It was a disaster. The lowest of low keys was called for. Expecting to join a gathering of mobile figures packed in from wall to wall and creating a pleasant uproar beneath bright lights, I found myself in what seemed at first to be a dark, silent, empty room. Gradually I distinguished small knots of people – not more than three or four together – seated at separate tables and drinking tea or coffee. I began to hear the low whispering that was coming from the tables, and to see the spots of dim light that fell from shaded lamps on to the bowed, mumbling heads. In the half darkness someone rose and welcomed David affectionately but quietly to a place at a table. I followed him. On the way home David and I had a hilarious time elaborating the differences between Oxford and Cambridge. I decided that Oxford was flippant, Cambridge humourless.

Through Maurice I first met David, who had taught History at Wadham since 1925. I have never known a more brilliant conversational-ist. 'Last night I dined with David Cecil,' I wrote to my mother at the end of my third year, 'who was so funny that I laughed the complexion off my face.' He was never a monologuist and his wit was just as sparkling whether we were discussing Victorian authors or our own contemporaries – particularly Maurice, with whom we were both obsessed. I saw a great deal of David and every conversation eventually came round to Maurice. Was he a homosexual or not? Was his genius for talk as great as Oscar Wilde's? Was he a committed academic or would he some day enter the world outside Oxford?

David talked extremely fast and breathlessly, at a run, his face as mobile as Maurice's was static. Malice was unknown to him and his most irresistible stories were often told against himself. My favourite was of his visit to a pre-war Berlin night-club. (Others have since laid claim to this story but I have given my allegiance to David's version.) He had arrived in Germany feeling slightly unwell. His temperature, however, was only ninety-nine degrees and he decided to go out for the evening as arranged. On arriving at the night-club a young man accosted him with the words, 'Sind Sie normal?' To which David, surprised at the youth's perspicacity, replied: 'Well, actually it *is* a bit up, but I think I'm all right really.'

During one of our many conversations about people I asked David whether he had ever been loved by someone for whom he felt nothing.

'Yes, once, a most unpleasant experience; it was like suddenly opening the door of a furnace.' I saw so much of David that I think my mother began to hope I was going to settle down at last with someone glamorous and suitable. For the only time in her life she began to question me uninvited. 'You seem to have a great many friends, dear. Isn't there one among them . . . one who is . . . er . . . special . . . like Lord David Cecil?' Utterly taken aback I could only stammer, 'Oh, no, it's nothing like that.'

Looking back, I realize that my Victorian mother, as she insisted she was, had begun to worry about my unendingly festive life at Oxford. But at the time she never criticized and, except for that one instance, never questioned me unless I put a question to her first. During my second year I went in for some slimming and dropped to seven stone from my normal and lifelong eight and a half; as a result I had no periods for several months. When I mentioned this to my mother she began to look extremely anxious. 'I suppose you've not, not been, that you're not, not started a . . .' Again I was staggered. 'No, of course it's not that. That's impossible.' My mother then appealed to my father in his consulting-room next door. The laconic message came back: 'Betty must eat more.'

I had changed my name to Elizabeth soon after reaching Oxford but my father clung to the old diminutive. I was grateful to the rest of my family for successfully making the effort to remember me as a new woman.

Another young don whom I first met at a Bowra party was Roy Harrod. His smooth black hair and dark eyes, and the occasional theatrical gesture or phrase (he was a nephew of the actor Sir Johnston Forbes-Robertson), made a dramatic impression. I knew he was exceptionally clever – a first in Greats *and* in History and finally an inspired switch to Economics – but to me his cleverest trick was to punt a canoe. After a fortifying lunch he took me on board and deftly poled our canoe up and down the Cherwell. One of my rare visits to a church was to hear Roy reading the lesson in the Cathedral of Christ Church, of which college he was a Student (Fellow).

He professed to be an unbeliever. Nevertheless he gloried in the music of the Bible as it was thrown up into the Gothic heights by his voice and echoed back to us, sitting in the pews below.

A few days after listening to Roy's elocution I happened to be lunching alone with Maurice. Assuming, perhaps wrongly, that Maurice shared Roy's unbelief, I asked whether he could ever imagine himself spouting scripture for the sound of the words alone. Maurice immediately burst into a ringing recitation of the gospel according to St John, chapter 1, verse 1: 'In the beginning was the Word; and the Word was with God: and the Word was God. . . .' His sonorous declamation might have been before an audience of thousands instead of only one.

There was more of Maurice's ecclesiastical inventiveness at a dinner-party in the summer of 1928, when he was assistant adviser to the OUDS production of Aristophanes' *Clouds*. Michael Hope and I were both present, Michael at that time being leader of the Greek chorus. Instead of giving a toast, Maurice suddenly delivered an extempore 'Collect for a Chorus' based on the *Book of Common Prayer*. It began something like this: 'O God, for as much as thy heavenly Chorus praises thee with Faith and Charity, grant that here below the Chorus of thy servant Hope may. . .' Maurice's prayer seems to have been answered in an unexpected way for Dick Crossman, the classical scholar and future statesman, was removed from the star role of Socrates, to be replaced by Michael.

Maurice's friends have rescued from oblivion many of his verbal acrobatics. Francis King, the novelist, a contributor to *Maurice Bowra: A Celebration* (1974), remembers his denouncing Evelyn Waugh's *Men at Arms* trilogy as 'The Waugh to end Waugh'; King adds, 'There is also that story, perhaps apocryphal, of Maurice's decision to get married. When he announced that he had at last chosen a girl, a friend remonstrated: "But you can't marry anyone as plain as that." Maurice answered: "My dear fellow, buggers can't be choosers." ' That Maurice could not resist witticism even at the expense of a close friend is also pointed out by Francis King. Though devoted to Raymond Mortimer, the critic, he nicknamed him 'Old Mortality', and a less close friend would get the full treatment – 'I like him, he smells.' Coining funny phrases came almost too easily to him: 'giving the warm shoulder', 'making good blood', having 'a long and interesting silence' with a Japanese professor who could not speak English, saying of an academic rival who had fallen ill, 'While there's death there's hope.'

Perhaps in order to perpetuate his own horrifying yet stimulating memories of the Great War, Maurice had a habit of addressing the most unlikely people with the title of 'Colonel'. Noel Annan became 'Colonel Annan', Cyril Connolly was 'Colonel Connolly'; Mr Kolkhorst, who taught Spanish at Exeter College and whose salon in Beaumont Street rivalled Maurice's, became 'Colonel Kolkhorst' or sometimes 'Colonel Gug', to which Kolkhorst retorted by referring to Maurice as 'Mr Borer'. John Betjeman, however, was nicknamed 'Bishop Betjeman' and I have kept a note from the *Cherwell* that reports John's movements in 1930: 'The Right Rev. Bishop Betjeman conducted a confirmation service at All Gugs, Beaumont Street, last Sunday. . . . the service was fully choral.'

Girls were not admitted to Gug's 'Sunday mornings', so I relied on John Betjeman, a regular attender, for news of the alternative establishment. First they would drink sherry and then play a game of sticking stamps on to the Colonel's ceiling by throwing up pennies with the licked stamps balanced upon them. John wrote a ballad on the Colonel about a heaven for homosexuals, sung to the tune of the hymn, 'There's a home for little children'.

> There's a home for Colonel Kolkhorst
>   With stamps stuck on the sky
> Where the sward is strewn with pansies
>   And the services are high.
>
> And there is Walter Pater
>   And there is Oscar Wilde,
> All quaffing Empire Sherry,
>   With the Deans and Maurice Child.

One of 'the Deans' was, of course, Maurice Bowra.

It was through Bowra that I first set eyes on Betjeman. We were having one of our usual *tête-à-tête* lunches when there was a knock and a grinning face peered round the door. 'Come in, then,' roared Maurice. 'Go and help yourself.' As the visitor darted into Maurice's bedroom I saw that he was slight, not very tall and had amazingly deep brown eyes and pale skin, giving him the look of a fawn. In a moment he was back again with one of Maurice's worn suits over his arm. I could hear the extraordinary 'yaffle' of his laughter as he disappeared down the stairs.

'Who is he? Why did he want your suit?'

'That's *Betjeman*,' said Maurice, savouring the unusual name with characteristic gusto. 'He likes old things. He needs second-hand things. His father's rich.'

This was a typical Bowra paradox invented to mock the stingy rich and in fact not true of Ernest Betjeman, John's father. When I questioned John half a century later about that suit, he could not remember why he had borrowed it; perhaps for acting or a funeral. He added, 'But I *do* like old things.'

Another of the 'old things' that John liked was Lord Alfred Douglas, the beloved 'Bosie' of Oscar Wilde's heyday. John gave a party for Bosie in Wilde's old rooms in Chaplin's Yard at Magdalen College, which were then inhabited by Harford Montgomery-Hyde, later Oscar Wilde's biographer. Handsome old Bosie made an attractive picture dressed in dove grey, as I remember, and leaning on a long slender cane while he held court in the embrasure of a window.

'How did I get to that particular party,' I asked John many years later.

'Oh, you were one of the aesthetes' molls – you and Margaret Lane and Margaret Rawlings.' Lane, the future writer, was at St Hugh's; Rawlings the actress at Lady Margaret Hall.

Towards the end of John's Oxford career I met him in the High, opposite St Mary's Church. He was carrying a copy of the undergraduate magazine, *Oxford University Review*, and showed me his own contribution: a sketch of two lifesize shirt cuffs on which were written out all the facts and dates necessary for passing the forthcoming divinity exam known as 'Divvers'. You had to cut along the dotted lines, pin the paper cuffs over your own, put on your jacket so that you could refer to the facts and dates without being seen by the invigilator – and hey presto! you would pass the absurd exam. John, however, managed to fail as many times as he was allowed to enter and was duly sent down. I was to see a great deal more of him after I too had left Oxford.

The *Oxford University Review*, to which John Betjeman made his practical contribution, was edited at the time by two young peers, Freddy Birkenhead and Basil Dufferin. It had been founded by Frank Pakenham, its first editor, with his friend Robert (Quixano) Henriques as assistant editor. Frank wrote to Bernard Shaw requesting a goodwill message for the first number. He received by return a postcard signed 'Blanche Patch' (Shaw's secretary) on behalf of the great man. It ran: 'Anyone who fills up his first number with messages that no one wants to read, will fail and will deserve to. Even young Oxford should know better than that.' Frank successfully advertised his magazine with posters bearing Shaw's message. Later the paper was denounced for its 'tasteless vivisection of a well-known club' – the OUDS.

I was something of a Cinderella at Maurice's dinner-parties, for I had to be inside the gates of my college by eleven o'clock. I think this rule suited Maurice; he always saw off his undergraduate guests at 10.30 sharp. I would stay till the last minute and then gallop up Parks Road and down Norham Gardens on my high heels, arriving at the porter's lodge with a supplicating expression if a fraction late. Fundamentally I did not really resent the rule – the time limit could be extended on occasion by prepayment of a fine – as it saved me from hangovers.

One night I had a new experience. A flasher sprang out at me from behind a hedge in Norham Gardens. Surprised to find myself perfectly composed, I gave him a prim little lecture, after which, like an obedient dog, he carried out my command to 'Go home!' I found myself feeling sorry for him. Later we heard that someone calling himself Mr Hyde Parker had been caught trying to enter our college. Such an event must have been rare, for there was much clucking at the idea of a fox in the hen-run.

The growing number of times that I lunched alone with Maurice showed our relationship was gradually changing. Yet he never told me any coherent story of his life, merely dropping hints now and then which I could either pick up or leave to lie, so to speak, on the table. I knew he lived at Ightham in Kent; indeed Ightham was so near Detling that he and Michael Hope once called on me there without warning, and finding me out left a cross note. But I knew nothing of his family history. One day while he was holding forth with his feet up after lunch, I commented on his elegant socks. 'You mean the elegant *ankles*,' he corrected me. 'They're a sign of the aristocratic Bowra blood.' I laughed, not knowing what he meant and being too much in awe to question him. Afterwards I heard that he could claim illegitimate descent from Lord Cornwallis, a Viceroy of India who earlier had surrendered the British Army at Yorktown. Maurice would boast of his 'American' great-great-grandfather, which the apostles of 'stuffiness' might have considered doubly discreditable, while lecturing in the United States.

Though I seldom interrogated Maurice on personal matters, I was always questioning him about classical literature, history and life in general. As Hugh Trevor-Roper (now Lord Dacre) has written, 'the purpose of Oxford is to lead the young towards "sound learning" and "the taste of life" ' and I think Maurice enjoyed guiding me as much as Hugh Gaitskell had done, though in a diametrically opposite way. Whereas all I learnt in conversation with Gaitskell depended on personal analysis of himself and myself, with Maurice I learnt through general ideas. Underneath, however, Maurice must have begun to wonder if my 'taste of life' did not include a permanent sharing of the repast with him.

We reached the climax of our relationship on a sunny afternoon, I think in the spring of 1929. I began as usual to probe Maurice about the classics, but this time my questions seemed to be asking for a more fundamental response. Finally I said, 'Maurice, what is it about the Greeks? Why do we read them and read about them? What's it all for?'

Maurice had translated jointly with H. T. Wade-Gery, the year before, Pindar's *Pythian Odes*, a seductive little white volume from the Nonesuch Press. He had presented me with a copy. Now he gave me a review of his thoughts about Pindar by way of answering my queries in the most stimulating manner possible. At the courts of the Sicilian tyrants, he said, it was possible to see encapsulated in a brief time and restricted space a way of life that inspired a great poet, Pindar, to his loveliest verse. 'A world of religion, song, noble breeds, the gods,' as Maurice wrote in his Introduction to the book. Hieron of Syracuse in Sicily had created a rare splendour that was fit to stand in the human record of achievement with the glories of Athens, Florence and Elizabethan London. Pindar's idea of 'greatness' was ultimately the purest kind of hedonism – a hedonism that Maurice himself shared – whereas Athens bred up the rebels and reformers. They were to sweep away Pindar's world, replacing it with democracy, an orderly system that would bring out the best in every citizen.

I doubt whether Maurice would have written quite as he did about Pindar and the Sicilian tyrants after Hitler arrived in 1933. But the point in 1928 was: the Greeks showed us ways of living, all different, all honourable and worth thinking about. No doubt the tyrants' rule quickly degenerated. Nevertheless, for that short moment of their greatness, life seemed to be holding up a mirror to the ideal.

As Maurice uncovered for me this evanescent but glowing corner of the past, giving it vitality through his own vehemence and clarity of outline through his own emphasis, he must have felt that his spellbound listener was someone with a quite insatiable appetite for *his* ideas, for *him*. Speaking more gently and in blurred instead of sharp phrases, he asked me to marry him.

A year earlier the idea of Maurice's proposing to anyone would have struck me as ludicrous. But there had been one or two developments recently which showed me such a thing could happen, though I never dreamt of it happening to me. I remember his returning from a visit to Ireland all lit up by the poetry of Yeats – and the beauty of Aline Craig, daughter of the first Prime Minister of Northern Ireland. After I had got over my initial surprise I became rather bored with hearing about the charms of this unknown Irish woman, though his lyrical praise of Maud Gonne and the long-dead Countess Markievicz, two romantic Irish patriots who belonged to history, seemed to me exciting and admirable.

In March Maurice had bought for me from Blackwell's bookshop *The Tower* by Yeats, where I found posed the fascinating philosophical problem, 'How shall we know the dancer from the dance?' It was to be joined on my bookshelf by Pindar, with Maurice's austere inscription, 'E. H. d.d. C. M. B. 20.vii.28', and Robert Bridges' *Testament of Beauty* with another chaste dedication. During the vacations occasional short poems would come through the post, written in the style of Yeats.

None of this seemed to me like part of a courtship. And so when the moment came I was taken completely by surprise, a surprise at first so overwhelming that I could say nothing, but which swiftly changed into a feeling of exhilaration and joy.

It never occurred to me to say yes. I stammered some vague sentences of thanks and fled through the quad to my bicycle parked outside the porter's lodge. I can remember vividly taking a joyride around Oxford in the bright sunshine and repeating deliriously to myself, as I swayed and swooped from one side of the road to the other, '*Maurice* has asked me to marry him. . . .'

The sequel to Maurice's proposal was not nearly so nice for him as it was for me. I basked for months in the glow of the incredible event; he took my ambiguous thanks for a refusal – as indeed would have been the result had he ever repeated the offer. In fact it was never mentioned between us again.

Our friendship inevitably lost much of its luminosity. Writing in *Maurice Bowra: A Celebration*, Anthony Powell remembered Maurice once describing his own character defect as 'a skin too few' – a painfully true piece of insight. I was well aware of this hypersensitivity and usually took care not to hurt him. But having failed to think of him as a marrying man, I did not realize how wounding such a situation as ours could be. Though I continued to see a good deal of him and was, for instance, selected to proofread one of his later books, it was never 'glad confident morning again'.

Another girl, Audrey Beauchamp, to whom Maurice proposed later seems to have had more or less the same sensations as I did. 'I feel as if I were on a roundabout,' she said to Bob Boothby, 'whirling faster and faster and I don't know what to do.' Bob replied, 'Get off.'

I would think that Noel Annan and Cyril Connolly have together said the last word on Maurice and marriage. 'He was an immensely masculine bisexual,' wrote Annan. 'He had thought of marrying,' wrote Connolly, 'but I think his genius demanded an inner privacy which would never have tolerated the wear and tear of proximity.'

My own postscript would be that he liked to think of sex as earthy, funny, absurd, while love had to be romantic, tender, poetic. Marriage was not the state for him in which these two incongruous ideals could live happily together.

*   *   *

Though I kept no diary during my Oxford years, I did write nearly every week to my parents and I even dated my letters in full, thus showing, I like to think, the beginnings of historical aptitude. My mother kept some of them. Looking through these letters after nearly sixty years, I am struck by the incoherence of my activities and friendships. Most of them belonged to separate worlds with few if any linking bridges.

At home I had been presented with a surfeit of certainties. All I wanted now was liberation through Oxford, the exploring of possibilities, experiment. Relativism and its fashionable offshoots, stemming from Einstein's physical discoveries, suited my mood perfectly. And if I had known how Maurice was to define Oxford – 'a pause between one kind of life and another' – I should have disagreed with him. I felt that Oxford must be progress, not pause, though in what direction I was neither sure nor wanted to be sure. All I could say for certain was, in the words of Rosamond Lehmann's heroine when a fresher at Cambridge: 'This is Life' (*Dusty Answer*, 1927).

So I kept as many glittering balls in the air as I could manage. There was the Poetry Club, of which I was secretary. Stephen Spender was our wild-haired prophet. His rather crooning voice sounded to me exactly like a poet's; but far from taking advantage of the poet's conventional right to be selfish and difficult, he was extraordinarily kind and gentle. Indeed I regarded him as a species of modern Shelley, only better grown. (He was at University College, where an epicene Shelley lay under a dome in marble nakedness.) It was a shock when Stephen told me that he was reading *Economics* with Douglas Cole, the leading socialist academic. I stared at Stephen, totally unable to equate the Theory of Rent with that fly-away hair and Promethean profile. I was again amazed when the *Cherwell* spoke of Spender's 'ruddy and warlike look'. I suppose they were thinking of his strong features and formidable height. There was certainly something fierce about him, but not that kind of fierceness.

I also belonged to the English Club. Our most impressive visitor, as I remember, was Harold Acton, though David Cecil gave the funniest talk on 'The Bad Poetry of Good Poets'. Harold Acton stood above us on the platform like the king of aesthetes he undoubtedly was. Towards his worshipping audience he was exquisitely good-mannered, turning to this side and that with polite smiles, gesticulating with his white hands. He was tall and elegant as an aesthete ought to be, dressed in black to set off his black hair and waxy white skin. What was my astonishment to learn later that he too had read Economics.

My head was a rag-bag of jumbled quotations and this was a period when you could always call up rhymes to help you construct a poem, though the disciplines of meter and regular lines were ignored. The

Cherwell printed my 'Topers' Matins 6 a.m.', and I quote part of it here because it gives a feeling of the atmosphere in which I throve. A cynical tone was essential and though I myself never had a hangover, I knew all about them from my helpless or boastful friends. The rather precious title of my verses meant nothing more than 'The Morning After'.

> Fifteen men on the dead man's chest,
>   with a hey and a ho nonnie no.
> Flights of angels have drunk the rest,
>   A bottle of rum: Yo! Ho!
>
>   . . . . .
>
> It was a lover and his lass,
>   Wrapped round in earth's diurnal course,
>   Who gave their kingdom for a horse
> And brought to birth an ass.
>   It was his lass
>   Whose flesh was grass
> A million million years e'er he was born.
>   Yet Adam digs
>   And still the figs
> Flower in their millions on the single thorn,
>   Forlorn!
> These very twain the millionth milestone pass,
> And the last corner whence there's no return
>   They turn
> Down like an empty glass.

Nearly fifty years after 'Topers' Matins' appeared in print, Noel Annan contributed several of Maurice Bowra's comic verses of a later date to the *Celebration*. Neither his nor mine were particularly good but they were remarkably alike in their addiction to puns and dreamlike quotations. Yet I did not set eyes on Maurice's comic verse until 1974. I can only suppose that that is the way people of our age wrote. I have selected a few lines of his to make the point:

> An evzone with harmonica
> In a ginshop once I saw
>
>   . . . . .
>
> Lead blindly light amid the revolving room:
> I'm tight and stark, and fed up, far from home.

. . . . .

Poor Tom's a-cold.
Prevent us, O Lord, in all our wooings . . .

I suppose Wystan Auden was the greatest of the poets up at Oxford in my day. My connection with him was unusual and indirect. It all began with my cousin Michael Hope, whose rooms were in the same quad as Auden's at Christ Church. Michael in his second year got to know Wystan, an English scholar, well when he was in his third year; there had been a Birmingham connection between the Hope and Auden families. Michael's mother, my Aunt Bertha, was on the City Council. A day came when Dr Auden, Wystan's father, had to make his annual report as Medical Officer of Health on the children's progress. He began: 'Everyone knows that the teeth of our children have greatly deteriorated in recent times. The incidence of caries . . .' Aunt Bertha interrupted him, outraged. 'Surely Dr Auden must know that there has been a great *improvement* in our children's teeth. All that free milk. . . .' Dr Auden resumed blandly, 'I was referring of course to the deterioration since the Roman Occupation of Britain.'

Up at Christ Church, reading English like Auden, was a close friend of Michael's named Gabriel Carritt. His family lived on Boars Hill, his father being a don much respected in the University for his writings on aesthetics. Gabriel reminded me a little of another great charmer, Goronwy Rees, though Goronwy was dark in a picaresque Welsh way and Gabriel blond with tousled hair, a boyish snub nose, blue eyes with curious drooping lids and a gurgling laugh. Both, in fact, had a special laugh which sometimes seemed as if it were going to change into a girlish giggle; yet each in his own way was tough. Gabriel had been to school at Sedbergh. He was fond of regaling his friends with self-mocking stories of his sufferings on cross-country runs, than which nothing, it appeared, was more excruciating except being taken for a brisk winter walk over the White Horse Hill and on to Wayland Smith's cave by Dick Crossman.

Michael brought me and Gabriel together and for a time Gabriel, my admirer, became almost a part of the Chamberlain tribe. He came with us to Switzerland for winter sports – my brother John, my three cousins Michael Hope, Valerie Nettlefold and Alan Napier, the actor; an American ice-hockey champion up at Christ Church called Rufus Bush who once drove me at a hundred miles an hour in a red Bugatti to Cambridge and handed me the wheel on a clear stretch – no driving tests in those days; Armorel Heron-Allen and her friend Vyvyan Holland, the son of Oscar Wilde, though Vyvyan seemed to have nothing of Wilde except the wit. Gabriel would also join us on cousinly parties at Bampton, the Nettlefolds' home in Oxfordshire. My sister Kitty had meanwhile come up to St Hugh's, so there was yet another member of the family to which Gabriel seemed more and more to belong. Indeed, after I went down he became deeply devoted to my cousin Valerie.

Wystan Auden, however, could see no good in these family connections which bonded Gabriel to a life that he could not share. He wanted Gabriel for himself. A tremendous manager in those days, Auden loved to organize people's lives and to rescue them from predicaments into which he himself had plunged them. He was longing to dominate his friends, particularly those with whom he was in love. One day he asked Gabriel if he could see this Harman girl who had stolen Gabriel's affections. He did not want to meet me – heaven forbid. But just to have a look, a squint at the obstacle to his hopes. Perhaps he thought that if once he had a mental picture of what I looked like he would know how to break the spell.

So it was arranged that Gabriel should lead me to the foot of Auden's staircase in the north-west corner of Peckwater quad. There we should stand for a few minutes and conduct a stagey conversation while Auden watched the actors in the scene from his landing on the third floor. All would have gone according to plan but for one fatal flaw. Gabriel, with much joking and laughter, had urged me to look as nice as I possibly could. That meant wearing my pale grey flannel suit and grey felt hat with its sharp black quill feather slanting downward on one side. And, of course, the black cane. Unfortunately for the success of Auden's scenario, the fashionable cloche hat of those days concealed the wearer's face as effectively as if it had been a German steel helmet. Possibly a touch of chin could be seen as we approached the stairwell, but nothing whatever as I stood with Gabriel directly underneath Auden, making inane conversation. The whole thing was an Oxford charade.

At the beginning of my third year (November 1928) I was still floundering about happily in an experimental, unfocused way.

No work is being done [I wrote to my mother], but essays are still rather successful purely owing to the fact that I have at last mastered the 'historical' literary style. It has involved a good deal of unpleasantness, & the rejection of oh so many nice little flowery thoughts; but a grunted 'very well put' from the dogmatic Pro-Provost of Queen's College [the Revd Dr E. M. Walker, my Greek history tutor] comforts the sorrow of my lost rhetoric. (Not too good a sentence, this, either!)

Why I called E. M. Walker dogmatic I cannot imagine, except that he always insisted upon my using the word 'suzerain' instead of 'overlord'. I was still enough in thrall to G. K. Chesterton's prejudices to believe that any word with an English root was better than its Latin counterpart.

The Pro-Provost would sit in his darkened room beside a softly hissing gas fire, his arthritic knees wrapped in a Black Watch plaid rug. Considering his ill-health, it was generous of him to take on me and my companion from Lady Margaret Hall. Girls had to be tutored by males in pairs, to prevent extra-curricular relationships from developing; though naturally they did. The only relationship I remember developing with my tutorial 'twin' was one of considerable spikiness. While writing my essay for the Revd E. M. Walker one day, I suddenly saw the possibility of a new and better interpretation for a certain disputed Greek text. Rushing along to my tutorial twin's room I expounded my theory. She seemed impressed. Next day we read our essays aloud to Dr Walker, she first. When she reached the debatable text, Dr Walker looked up and said, 'Very interesting.' To my chagrin I realized that she had pinched my idea. I reproached her afterwards. 'How could you produce it as if it were your own?' She replied calmly, 'It *was* my own. Your emendation was not the same as mine.' This little episode taught me something useful about plagiarism in the field of scholarship. Plagiarists need to make only the smallest change in their copy to convince themselves that their work is fresh as a field of daisies.

Work seldom featured in my letters home. But there was as much gaiety and party-going as I felt my mother could stand or needed to know about. 'You may not be too pleased to hear', I wrote, 'that I have bought a (very) expensive evening cloak.' I can still remember that velvet cloak, its slippery lining and plumage of peach-coloured ostrich feathers, the kind of exoticism that would have made Hugh Gaitskell squirm. 'But you will be enchanted to see it,' I continued bracingly. 'After all, I *am* getting old, & it will be a pity for the cloak days to go by without there ever having been a cloak.' My sister Kitty I reported as glowing in crimson satin and 'splendid carbuncle ear-rings'.

I went on to describe 'an immense Proctorial Rag', when Duncan Sandys (later Commonwealth Secretary and a peer) sent out hundreds of fake Proctorial summonses to junior members of the University, who all converged on the Sheldonian Theatre at the same moment. Wondering which of their crimes had been detected, the mob milled about in the Broad blocking Balliol, Trinity and Blackwell's bookshop until dispersed by the police. 'I used to know the instigator of the Rag,' I told my mother; then, lest she should fear this would turn out to be an unsuitable suitor, added, 'but he was, though charming and virile, too keen on "runs" to Eton and town. I could not spare the time.' A smug fib. The truth was that dashing red-headed Duncan had chased me playfully round his dining-table at Magdalen and I felt I might not be able to hold my lead if there were many next times.

A number of my friends had taken their exams and were going down, so that June 1929 was the last fling for many of us, though not me. Michael Hope had a forty-minute viva for a first in Greats but settled for a second. (For me there was to be something special about that syndrome.) At the same time Maurice Green, a brilliant, enigmatic personality and future editor of the *Daily Telegraph*, clinched his double first in Mods and Greats. Pale-faced, with light hair and eyes, he spoke in rather measured tones until a sudden wave of laughter would convulse him. His father was a colonel and Maurice had been brought up in East Anglia, loving country pursuits, shooting and fishing. Partly because of this side of his character, and partly because he was never seen to work yet was believed never to go to bed either, a legend grew up that he was a werewolf, prowling over the college roofs by night like Aubrey Herbert in an older generation.

During one of our many dinners at the George, we discussed Aristotle's theory of *eudaimonia*, or happiness, throughout the lobster *Americaine* and beyond. I thought perfect happiness must be continual development and never-ending progress – perpetual motion in an upward direction. Maurice knew better. 'Happiness is the attainment of perfection,' he said, 'and the continuation in that state forever without change.' For a brief while he was to experience this state of true happiness by marrying Pearl Oko, one of my two great friends at St Hugh's College (the other being Margaret Lane). Pearl was an American graduate reading English. Her long dark hair, worn in an elegant knot, ivory skin and exquisite feet proclaimed an un-Englishness which she emphasized by never appearing in anything but silk dresses; coats and skirts were absurdities. Yet her extreme fastidiousness in no way precluded the capacity for friendship – and for marrying a man who was thoroughly English. She had a sophisticating effect on both Maurice and me. Her father, a scholar, was a friend of Jacob Epstein and through Pearl's American ambience my horizons were extended. Alas, she died while still in her early twenties. Her funeral was in the Jewish chapel of a large crematorium. It was my first experience of such places and in my grief I failed to make full enquiries about the service that was already under way. At the end I found I had been weeping for the wrong person. Pearl would have laughed, but I have ever since felt uneasy in the cool impersonality of crematoria. (Maurice was to find *eudaimonia* again with his second wife Janet.)

Another increasingly close friend who went down in 1929 was Christine Willans, a History scholar of Lady Margaret Hall. Christine combined beauty and a wit that seemed physically to sparkle: her sallies were not made with a straight face like Maurice Bowra's but with a mocking gleam in her eye as she intently watched one's reaction. I brought her and Michael Hope together at a Chinese restaurant in Piccadilly Circus that autumn, and became Christine's confidante while Michael was in America learning how to make and market Hope's Casements.

Christine was a first cousin of Naomi Mitchison, the novelist, whose mother, Mrs Haldane, lived in a mansion not far from Lady Margaret Hall. Naomi and her husband Dick, a barrister and politician, would come down regularly from London to visit her. The old lady was as deeply diehard as Dick and Naomi were advanced Left. When, therefore, Mrs Haldane was running one of her Conservative summer events – say the annual garden-party for the Victoria League – Naomi would send for Christine and Christine would send for me to help handle the true-blue belles.

I first met Naomi's ferociously intellectual brother Jack (J. B. S.) Haldane during one of these Oxford visits. He was a distinguished physicist like his famous father J. S. Haldane, and though perhaps not yet a Communist, he was already well to the Left. I described our meeting to my mother:

Naomi and I had a long conversation yesterday interrupted by Professor Haldane with an amusing though very vindictive account of the idiocy of the newspapers, Winston Churchill and the War Office generally over the poisoned gas business. Apparently Winston Churchill got as far as confusing bacteriology with respiration. He said Pasteur had been busy on respirators!!

Naomi and Dick gave parties at Rivercourt on the Thames, to which Christine took me. Here I met the Bloomsburys in more human shape than at Cambridge; indeed I remember once sitting under the supper-table with Dr Adrian Stephen, brother of Virginia Woolf and Vanessa Bell, discussing Freudian psychology. 'He's a shy creature,' said Naomi, 'not often seen above ground.'

At the end of this same evening I was led along the Embankment by A. P. Herbert, the 'water gypsy' poet and later MP for Oxford University, to his favourite shrine, an electrical generating plant. Built largely of glass, one could see its whole inside glinting in the moonlight as if it were a huge metal intestine under an X-ray: the vast flywheel, the smaller cogs and the giant piston. Alan Herbert's game was to move one's hand up and down just, but only just, in advance of the piston's own movement, so that an illusion was created of actually moving the piston oneself. It made us both

Caricature of Osbert Lancaster by Angus Malcolm, 1929

laugh hysterically. We must have looked a pair of loonies, 'conducting' the mysterious machinery as if it were some strange silent orchestra.

My third year ended with the social whirligig spinning faster and faster into Commem Week. I waltzed with John Maud at Christ Church, with whom I began falling in love – until he kindly told me that he was engaged to a brilliant professional pianist, Jean Hamilton. John was the only man to shine in the Bowra circle and at the same time become President of the Student Christian Movement. At the OUDS ball I partnered Osbert Lancaster, one of the great 'originals' of this period, whose genius was always witty, never morose. He designed for me an eighteenth-century dress of daffodil-yellow silk to complement his own elegant braid, jabot and ruffles. There I saw Peter Fleming looking the world's most 'in' outlaw, as Robin Hood. He had written a play for the OUDS Smoker in which his was the only part. I sat transfixed as the curtain rose on a pitch-dark stage which remained dark and empty for a full minute, when a slim but growing pencil of light showed that a door back-stage was very slowly opening. It opened enough to allow Peter's head to be poked round it, to remain for a minute and then to withdraw; the door as slowly and silently closing again before the curtain fell. Tumultuous applause. Peter was to get a first in English.

An exhibition of drawings and paintings by Osbert Lancaster and Angus Malcolm (grandson of Lillie Langtry and Prince Louis of Battenberg) was held opposite the George and described as 'Caricature and Fantasy' by the *Cherwell* reviewer, Betjeman, who called himself 'Sir John Matterhorn'. 'All the pictures were being bought up very quickly,' wrote the reviewer. 'The social "Snakes & Ladders" was bought, I see, by my friend Miss Harman, whose poem appears in this week's issue. Altogether a great show – yes, a great show.' The wonderful game of social 'Snakes & Ladders' ('Dine with Bowra' – up a ladder; 'Gated for 3 weeks' – down a snake) has unaccountably disappeared but I still possess two pictures I also bought at the exhibition – a black-and-white caricature of Osbert in hussar uniform by Angus and a watercolour by Osbert of the imaginary 'Hoheit *Ernst August Hippolit* Kronprinz von Pumpstadt-Schrumpfheim'.

As I grandly wrote to my mother on 12 June 1929: 'Only one more week of term – in fact, only one more week of Oxford life at all. With the vac begins that regime of *ardua ad astra* which continues till this time next year, & I *hope* will reach the stars.'

6

Oxford: All Change
· 1929–30 ·

The change to 'hard labour' that I had promised myself from July 1928 onwards was slow in coming. Instead of *ardua*, there was Armorel's twenty-first birthday party at her home in Selsey, West Sussex, followed by my first visit to Harry d'Avigdor-Goldsmid in Kent.

Armorel's doting father did his daughter proud. Nothing seemed too good for such beauty and brains: curling chestnut hair, dark violet eyes, an olive skin and the figure of an athlete. She was confidently backed for a first next year. The menus for the birthday dinner, I recorded, were written in Greek and hand-painted by Rutherston. As Armorel's friend I too received some imaginative favours from her father, in the shape of three little leather volumes printed and published by the famous Elzevirs of Amsterdam, of which one was the *Colloquia* of Erasmus, dated 1655. This book was to inspire my later interest in Erasmus and his friend Thomas More.

It was a weekend of lyrical pleasures, when we moved as in a delightful dream from the lovely market cross of Chichester to Selsey Bill's gulls and pebbled shore. The speckled pebbles might have been gulls' eggs. Everything seemed to augur well for Armorel's future; but I woke up on the last day feeling my bed being shaken by an earth tremor.

The d'Avigdor-Goldsmids lived at Somerhill, an estate that the 1st Duke of Wellington had thought of accepting from the nation after Waterloo. He decided it was too near the town of Tonbridge for the best sport. The d'Avigdor-Goldsmid family, however, had splendid weekend shoots, one of which I was invited to attend. I followed Harry round in another happy dream until I learned that I had disgraced myself and him. Ignorant of protocol, I had gone to my favourite dress shop, Fenwicks of Bond Street, and provided myself with a smart black coat and skirt for my foray into the Kentish woods. I came in covered with mud and leaves. Mrs d'Avigdor-Goldsmid drew me aside at the end of the visit and explained the need for tweed. Next time it was tweed indeed. Oddly enough I was soon to encounter someone who regularly committed a similar social gaffe, but in him it was regarded as an amusing eccentricity. 'Prof' Lindemann (later Lord Cherwell) chose always to appear on the golf course dressed in a black city suit and bowler hat.

The next time I found myself being drawn aside at Somerhill for a word in my ear was by Harry's father Osmond d'Avigdor-Goldsmid, soon to be created a baronet. With great delicacy and gentleness he said he hoped I was not falling in love with Harry, since his future duties as head of a great Jewish house would necessitate his marrying one of his own faith. Mr d'Avigdor-Goldsmid and I were closeted together, as I remember, in a tiny sanctum somewhere behind the great hall. I had just witnessed a moving scene in the mock Jacobean hall itself, for it was one of the days when large numbers of family and friends – Jews from many different places – would assemble at Somerhill to discuss plans for Zionism or for individual help. Mr d'Avigdor-Goldsmid had tactfully asked me whether or not I would like to listen in on this gathering. I was thrilled to be accepted, so to speak, in this way, being already half in love with the family *en bloc* – patriarch, matriarch, Harry and his younger brother Jackie, aunts, cousins, the lot. I loved Harry's sad Jewish eyes, his original and sharp mind, his mixture of worldly wisdom and innocence, his wit, irony and high spirits. But when his father spoke of marriage I realized that Osmond d'Avigdor-Goldsmid and I were not on the same wavelength.

Harry was part of the glamour of Oxford at that particular moment and was not associated, in my mind, with hopes of marriage or the Jewish faith or Jewish charity, for that matter, much as I admired it. However, I could not begin to explain all this to Harry's father, so I simply smiled my agreement and was released from the sanctum to re-enter the enchanted world outside. I was not to realize the paradox of the situation until a great many years had passed when Harry told me that it was my very empathy with his father, mother and family that had prevented him from giving more substance to our romance. He needed to cut loose, to learn to stand on his own feet (he was several years younger than me) without, of course, severing the ancestral bonds; and this his wife Rosie, in whom beauty and strength of character were combined, enabled him to do.

Looking back, I can trace to this friendship two changes in my general awareness. I gained an insight into a world outside Oxford that had all the attraction of seriousness and novelty: the world of the Jewish community before the war, with its splendid solidarity as well as the emotional complexities of its leadership in a country like England. But inside the world of Oxford there were changes too which more or less coincided with Harry's first year there, and I remember Harry expressing a sudden wish to meet Diana Churchill. Amazed, I asked why. 'Because she's the daughter of Winston Churchill.' Politics had entered my closed world.

Randolph Churchill, Diana's only brother, had just come up and I 'enjoyed' – if that is the right word – his friendship for a few months. Though he was nearly five years younger than me, he established a spirited relationship that was equally balanced between flirtation and rudeness. I tended to patronize him, though secretly dazzled by his extraordinary youthful beauty: thick golden hair, enormous blue eyes and a sugar-pink complexion. When he made his maiden speech at the Union they gave him the nickname of 'Pink-and-White'. It did not catch on. In fact Randolph's political ambitions passed from those of a boy to a man in a few weeks. I remember standing talking to him outside Christ Church on one sunny morning and thinking he looked like a Botticelli angel. He broke the spell. 'I'm going to America to lecture.' 'What on?' 'Politics.' I gasped. This was the world outside Oxford and no mistake. To think of Randolph, so much my junior, embarking on such an enterprise . . . The walls of Oxford continued to expand.

The spring of 1929 had marked the onset of economic storms that were to be swept away only in the greater deluge of the Second World War. A shadow began to creep over our carefree Oxford existence, a shadow that deepened as financial difficulties culminated in the Wall Street crash of that autumn. We began to talk about unemployment, hunger. Even our between-wars generation could no longer remain completely encapsulated in academic hedonism. The *Fritillary* published a poem of mine on 3 December that reflected a new kind of cynicism. At the beginning of 1929 I had felt that nothing mattered but the high-flown Muses, whether of history, song, the dance, poetry or drama. By the end of 1929 we were all beginning to think small, think slump. My 'Ode to the Muses' was a revolt against aestheticism at a time of economic depression.

> Shut up your singing
> Ain't got a sou,
> Take your little monkey-faces
> Back to the Zoo.
> Take your barrel-organs
> Back to the mews
> (And let's have a nibble at the peas in your shoes.)

The line in brackets was a reference to the well-off who pretended to suffer.

The point was put more seriously next year by Christopher Hobhouse, one of Balliol's brightest stars. Even before the Wall Street crash there had been a growing feeling in conventional organs like the *Isis* that young

Oxford was unbalanced and extreme, and therefore unpopular. 'We are potential devotees of the Red Flag or Green Carnation,' wrote the *Isis* on 31 October 1929, denouncing Marx and Wilde as equally obnoxious. But on 21 June 1930, in the *Cherwell*, it appeared that Hobhouse was seeing off a whole decade – the decade in which such flags and flowers had flourished.

For twelve years [he wrote] Oxford has been described as post-war, and that is now at an end. The tatty 'twenties have gone the way of the naughty 'nineties. We must settle down to the 'thirties now, and they have already shown us what to expect. Precocious, enterprising, confident, strenuous, versatile, uninspiring. The Union will come into its own, there will be empty tables at the George.

The tragedy was that 'post-war' was so soon to become 'pre-war' again, a war in which Hobhouse himself was to be killed.

The politics of party, as I have said, did not yet concern me. But in March I found myself for the first time attending a Union presidential debate as the guest of its secretary, my clever friend Kenneth Diplock, who had had the idea of writing his report for the *Isis* around my visit. Admittedly he imagined us in the parts of an uncle and niece, he wise and long-suffering, I impulsive and naïve, as indeed we were. But at least his niece Elizabeth was beginning to take notice. Kenneth's Union Report was entitled 'Candidates for Elizabeth', the competing candidates being Quintin Hogg, son of the Lord Chancellor Viscount Hailsham and himself to be Lord Chancellor twice; Henry Phelps Brown, to become a professor of Economics; Michael Stewart, a future Foreign Secretary in a Labour Cabinet; and B. J. M. MacKenna. The subject for debate was that eternal mind-twister, the death penalty.

We listened to Mr Phelps Brown reciting his prose poem on Capital Punishment [wrote my Uncle Kenneth]. Elizabeth was profoundly moved. 'Uncle,' she said, 'are we not inhuman monsters about these criminals? I *do* think Brown is attractive.' Quintin Hogg prevented her from enlarging upon the more superficial attractions of Phelps Brown. 'Uncle,' she murmured when Hogg had finished, 'are we not inhuman monsters for not hanging these criminals? I did like Hogg's speech, it was almost inspiring, but if I were his mother – and I wish I were – I should persuade him to make a joke.' As for Mr B. J. M. MacKenna, 'Is not he attractive with his lovely voice? – Listen to that now. . . . I wonder who is going to be President this time. I think Mr MacKenna is going to.' 'Why?' asked I with interest, seizing my chance to get a word in. 'Why, because he made the best speech, of course,' bubbled Elizabeth. I turned away with a cynical smile. Elizabeth has much to learn about the Union.

That at least was true. I had much to learn. Three months later I was learning some more about the Union, this time as a guest of the President, Quintin Hogg, on the occasion of his celebrated father's visit to Oxford for the summer debate. Quintin had arranged a magnificent dinner beforehand, for which the chef at Christ Church (Quintin's college) created a remarkable iced pudding in the shape and likeness of the Lord Chancellor's face: chubby, pink and white, beaming. I sat on his left. He did not seem to share my enthusiasm for the iced pudding but was persuaded to tell some funny stories about the bar. On this occasion a number of women were present and after dinner there was a move to sign the Union visitors' book; but a move by the men only. I could see no reason why, having eaten with them, I should not sign with them. So, ignoring all dissuasion, I signed. Several years later I had the chance to look again at the Union's visitors' book for 1929. My name had been erased.

Two days after the Presidential Debate I dined with Maurice Bowra, who had assembled a cross-section of the old and new order. Representing the old were Patrick Balfour and Bob Boothby. I described them as 'a ghoul who writes all the scandal columns for the *Sketch*, and an enormous MP named Boothby'. These were two of the old-timers about whom Maurice would tell heroic or deflationary stories to us, the next generation, at his dinner-parties. The new order was represented by the brilliant Rosamond Lehmann, a university graduate and also triumphantly a woman. Today I would credit her *Dusty Answer* with having had a considerable hand in changing the position of women at Oxford and Cambridge. They became not quite so invisible.

The change was, of course, also due to the general move away in 1929–30 from male aestheticism of the *carpe diem* type towards a wave of concern about the future which swept right across the board. If men were all to go down, so to say, there was really no reason why women should not be allowed to join the sinking ship.

In a book called *Woman on Woman* to which I contributed in 1971, I described this change at Oxford in terms of left-wing politicians ousting apolitical aesthetes.

The ivory tower of aestheticism [I wrote] could not stand up to the buffets of the economic blizzard which began to blow in 1929. As my older contemporaries left and the younger generation came up, politics began to oust poetry. If I had had to take a refresher course in order to qualify for élite male society, it would have been on Karl Marx not Oscar Wilde.

Thinking it over today, I feel that the change really went much deeper than I suggested above. Not from Wilde to Marx, but from an academic arcadia to something nearer to the real world in which politics and women were inevitably included. The gradual inclusion of women can be illustrated from the university magazines. In December 1928, for instance, the *Isis* had been rude about the *Fritillary* in a column called 'Eve', saying that it existed for the sole purpose of showing off its all-female contributors' 'precocious cleverness'. A mere fifteen months later the *Cherwell*, rival of the *Isis*, had a regular column called '*Revue Feminine*', in which the doings of the women's colleges were agreeably if patronizingly reported. Eve had burst into the Garden of Eden with a vengeance when this sort of gossip could be retailed: 'That clever Miss Lyman Brown – who is one of the most talented of our young contributors – and dear old Eleanor Watts gave such a jolly cocktail-party on Saturday. Miss Harman was there too, with both hands full, as she jokingly put it, so that Lady Margaret Hall was well represented.'

Three months passed and the *Isis* responded to the new style by reneging on its Philistine and anti-women past and choosing for its 'Isis Idol' of 11 June 1930 neither a President of the Union nor of the Athletic Club, nor even a President of the OUDS, as had been their immemorial custom, but from among the 'precocious' Fritillarians themselves. My own 'Isis Idol' was written in a tone so portentous as to verge on the satirical. Nevertheless, I was pleased. A semi-apologetic preface by the editor for idolizing 'a woman' was followed by a run-through of Harley Street and Headington School, finally landing me 'as a scholar of Lady Margaret Hall, a well-known women's college'.

It ended by reserving a future place for me among 'female worthies': 'May she live long in the great traditions of British women, aim high, and keep her powder dry.' One can imagine today's editor cutting off this lush encomium long before the end with the laconic words: 'Enough wimin. Ed.'

I persuaded myself that my last year was entirely devoted to work. An absurd incident, however, that I described in part to my mother, showed that the social whirligig had not been entirely abandoned. I still dined once a week at the George restaurant with Hamish St Clair Erskine, an exquisite and witty companion who liked entertaining me with highly coloured glimpses into social life outside Oxford. The conversation I best recall was about Nancy Mitford. After a sketch of the eccentric Mitford parents, Lord and Lady Redesdale – today notorious through Nancy's *Love in a Cold Climate* – Hamish launched into a touching eulogy of Nancy herself. 'She's the most wonderful, courageous girl. Beautiful, really

June 11th, 1930   THE ISIS   7

No. 748.

Miss ELIZABETH HARMAN,
Lady Margaret Hall.

[*It is almost without precedent for a woman to be Idol; but Miss Harman appears herself to be almost without precedent. Her career in this University has entitled her to such honour as we can give.*—ED.]

Springing from a well-known ophthalmologist's, poet's and lay-preacher's wife on August 30, 1906, Elizabeth Harman, prominent and pre-eminent in mentality and physique, had poetry, piety and scholarship in her blood and Patmore in the nursery. That well-known personal sympathy which she has so successfully and charmingly cultivated must have had its origin in witnessing in her childhood the versatility of her humane parents. The talents latent but suspected in a child of such birth were laid bare and proved not only in the admiring drawing-room and familiar circle, but publicly at the Frances Holland School, Baker Street, where she first paraded her cognitive and other faculties, and later, both in the classroom and on the hockey field, at Headington Girls' School. The darling of the School, she won all the prizes without discrimination, and finally descended into Oxford as a scholar of Lady Margaret Hall, a well-known women's college.

There in the remote splendour of her salons she indulged the multitude of discerning admirers in tea with her conversation, to describe which would be by failure to disappoint all those who know her and to confuse the ignorance of the less fortunate. But her activities were more than social. Beside her devout scholarship, her brave swimming for the college may appear carnal; but her collegiate activity has not been limited to the study and the bath. In the year 1928, Miss Harman produced the Lady Margaret Hall play, a Chinese comedy, and very funny it was, too. In the University at large she has had no need to make herself known, as the deepening of acquaintance with her confirms the favour of a first impression. Were we even to enumerate her multifarious activities in the University life, her essays in paid and unpaid journalism, her illumination of the English Club, her bright poetry and large sympathy, in the enumeration we could not add to her justified popularity or illustrate a character dependent upon its personal qualities and merits by the description of the recognition which they have been given.

Artistic, beautiful, cultured, decorative, enigmatic, fashionable, girlish, sometimes even headstrong, she has in her 4 years at Oxford exhausted all gift and receipt of entertainment, mistressed the philosophers, assimilated picturesqueness and precision from Herodotus and Thucydides, wooed and won those Nine Apollonian Beauties, and been wooed but not won by many more Apollos: though wit has from time to time offended against her, wit has always been her best defence, and the taste her friends have shown in having her for friend has been reflected in her taste in friends. She has confuted the dictum of Pericles, and if in full womanhood she fulfils the wide promise of her brilliant maidenhood as truly

[Owing to the machinations of a rival organisation, the portrait of our Idol must be postponed until next week.]

beautiful, dark curls, blue eyes, height and slimness and so funny, even about her dreadful poverty. She can't afford to buy *anything*. She makes all her own clothes on a sewing-machine in her sisters' nursery and yet she always looks the best-dressed girl in the room.' No wonder Nancy was to imagine for a time that he was in love with her.

After this outpouring Hamish Erskine and I joined up with some other friends at the George and finally they all took me back at eleven o'clock to Lady Margaret Hall, where we stood around talking and laughing in the road for my extra quarter of an hour, before dispersing, I into the porter's lodge, they back in their taxi to the continuation of a gay evening.

Next morning I was sent for by the Principal, Miss Grier. A long face. 'Miss Harman, I am perturbed by what I hear of your behaviour. So much noise outside the college. . . . A fourth year student, too. This is not the first time. The college may have to reconsider your future. . . .' I was dismissed and wrote home in exasperation: 'Everyone is expecting me to be sent down at any moment. I am rather afraid that now I really am a credit to the Old Coll some trivial touch really will send me shooting.'

The 'trivial touch' was in this case a habit on the part of two Lady Margaret Hall dons of themselves visiting the George for a cosy meal together. I had spotted them dining there on the same night as Hamish and me and guessed they had reported me for my part in the 'noise'. But I sympathized with the Principal's obsessive feelings about what she considered dangerous drunkenness. Her father, one heard, had run a small home for alcoholics and she had seen too many ruined lives to take her girls' parties lightly.

Nothing more was heard of my being sent down. All the same I was aggrieved, having already limited most of my outings to the vacations. I continued to my mother: 'I even refused a fine party of Frank Packenham's [*sic*] including the Bowra & the Cecil; a gesture which meant a final *adieu* to the sprightliness of Oxford.' In the vacation I can remember only one party that might have disturbed my work, at least for an afternoon.

Osbert Lancaster and I one day paid a call on Mrs Rosa Lewis, celebrated proprietress of the Cavendish Hotel in Mayfair. I had never been there before and wistfully imagined it to be an exciting den of vice. My immediate impression was of intense silence and everywhere chintz – chintz-covered sofas, chintz armchairs, chintz window curtains, thick chintz veils drawn across discreet chintzy boudoirs. It was not the 'chintzy chintzy cheeriness' that John Betjeman had written about in 'Leamington Spa', but chintz of a quietness that seemed sinister. Rosa gave us a delicious tea and then said, 'What about some champagne?' A waiter brought a bottle. Rosa charmingly asked me to come again some day and I returned elated to the subdued pleasures of Harley Street.

Next afternoon I was sitting with Father in the consulting-room, which he used as a sitting-room when most of the family were away. The telephone rang. He answered it and turned round on his doctor's swivel chair towards me. 'Betty,' he began gruffly (he had not even yet begun calling me Elizabeth). 'Betty, there's a Mrs Lewis asking to speak to you. She wants you to help her with a tea-party or something.' Aghast, I seized the telephone, still enough in awe of my father's omniscience to imagine that he knew, if not all about Rosa Lewis, enough to expose me as a harlot. I cut short poor Rosa's kind invitation to a mixed tea-party and wisely she never tried again. For years I liked to think that I had had a narrow escape from the white slave traffic.

Meanwhile at Oxford my passion for the classics was reaching a climax. Apart from Maurice Bowra, there was a lecturer on inscriptions named Hugh Last, whose dark Mediterranean appearance and reputed indulgence in peacock dinners gave me the idea of studying inscriptions at Rome after I had gone down. This consuming interest inspired a peculiar short story in *Cherwell* entitled, 'The Visions of an Antiquarian'.

I was fortunate in having the two most brilliant classical scholars of my year for friends. Denys Page and Quintin Hogg were both at Christ Church. Neither indulged in banquets at the George – too extravagant – but the highbrow tea-party with Denys and Quintin as joint hosts had a very special flavour. Both the Chancellor's Prize for Latin Verse and the Gaisford Prize for Greek Verse – a pair of blue ribands – had been won by Denys, and after he had read his verses aloud in the Sheldonian Theatre he sent me a copy of each. My copy of the Greek poem carried the dedicatory words, 'From himself to Elizabeth: *Namque tu solebas meas casa aliquid putare nugas.*' I could still manage to translate this dedication fifty-seven years later: 'For you used to think my nonsense was something important.' But the Greek inscription in the Latin poem completely baffled me and I have had to enlist Quintin's help. (Denys, alas, is no longer alive.) Quintin replied, 'I think Denys must have had at the back of his mind Plato: Theatetus 201 D. "You have given me many happy dreams. Here, in return, is a dream of my own." But Allah', added Quintin, 'is all knowing.' Denys's Latin poem was covered in pencilled commentaries to which I wrote critical 'anti-commentaries'; for example, 'All cribbed from Virgilian pessimism', on which Denys further commented, 'O gē kai theoi! *Verg*il please.' I would like to reply yet again: 'O earth and gods! how agreeably nostalgic does a Platonic love-affair sound today, conducted in two dead languages.'

The urgency of classics did not drive out my incipient interest in politics and Naomi Mitchison became a more and more seductive influence. At thirty-three she was writing her longest and finest novel, *The Corn King and the Spring Queen*. It was an intensely moving story of the ancient worlds of Sparta and Egypt, in which King Cleomenes attempted in vain to create 'New Times'; just as Naomi's socialist friends were to aim at and miss their 'New Times' in 1931 – the year her book was published. The copy which Naomi presented me with contained a mysterious dedication: 'To my original Metrotimé'. After I had read the novel I saw exactly how Naomi pictured me while up at Oxford. The portrait was not altogether reassuring. Metrotimé, a slave in Ptolemy's court, was the girlfriend of his mistress: 'an incredibly innocent-looking Ionian girl. . . . Her great accomplishment was the discovery and reading aloud in the calmest possible voice of all the most indecent books in Alexandria.' She would give 'fairy giggles' while reading; her mind was 'ironic and critical', 'unsentimental'. Yet in spite of all this she possessed a statue of a Mother and Child from a Temple of Isis. It was clever of Naomi to imagine the Mother and Child syndrome, for as far as I knew I had no interest in families or in Isis – except the magazine.

My ideas on philosophy, which I studied with zest at Oxford for two and a half years, were never quite what was intended by the academic pundits. They were purely literary. I was lucky in having for my tutor Geoffrey Muir of Merton College, not only because he rounded off each tutorial with a glass of sherry but also because he was excellent on his subject, sensible and clear. My head, however, was full of such romantic writings as Collingwood's *Speculum Mentis* and F. H. Bradley's *Appearance and Reality*. Bradley wrote somewhere that most of us hardly *thought* at all during our waking lives but were in a perpetual state halfway between dreaming and real thought. I can only retort that it was partly Bradley's own way of writing which made us 'think' like that. I would spend hours dreamily trying to define reality. The nearest I ever got – or felt I had got – to the problem was in the middle of writing an essay, when I suddenly had a revelation on Language. Language was the enemy. Language broke up truth, gave an abstract of truth, not truth itself. As long as we had to play about with language and know reality through words, reality would elude us.

As my finals approached, delightful intellectual vapourings gave way to a wild, last-minute rush to fill the frightening gaps in my learning. I inflicted on my mother an account of one of my mad dreams. 'I dreamt last night that Schools [finals] took the form of a dramatic competition. Only one first class would be awarded, to the best dramatization of Aristotle's philosophy. I led off by doing a Graeco-Christian Crucifixion scene at

Marble Arch, which ended with myself descending from the Cross, i.e. the middle arch. My tutor, a stout Presbyterian, was much impressed, for who else had discovered that Aristotle, Christ and myself were identical?'

Mr and Mrs Fordyce, a learned couple who both taught classics, he at Balliol, she at Lady Margaret Hall, invited me to tea. They were kind but austere and I was glad I had put on no lipstick. 'You need polishing up,' they agreed, and sent me for my last term to G. H. Stevenson of University College for what was really a crash course on the whole of Roman history. Hope Stevenson lived with his wife Phoebe, an Oxford City Councillor, at 10 Chadlington Road, roughly halfway between Lady Margaret Hall and Mrs Haldane's. I boarded with them, occupying the room vacated by their daughter Helen who was at Wycombe Abbey School. Again the Fates seemed to know what they were about, for 10 Chadlington Road was next door to my future home, where four of our children were to be born, while Helen was to marry as his second wife my cousin Michael Hope.

The Fordyces held out an alluring prospect – provided I got a first. There was every chance of obtaining a research grant, probably abroad, and Maurice Bowra sent me 'a most practical letter' suggesting a subject in Roman history. I might even be a don, I told my parents – 'of course as the pinnacle of ambition'.

At the last moment, in fact during the very weekend before Schools began, I developed a sudden crazy obsession. What was the difference between the Right and the Good? I didn't know. And something told me that this would be a key question in one of my philosophy papers. In anguish I besought dear old Hope Stevenson to find a don somewhere who could tell me. Miraculously Hope discovered John Mabbott of St John's, who most obligingly instructed me in all the idiosyncrasies of the Right and the Good throughout a dreamlike Sunday afternoon. I need not add that no questions whatever on the difference between them appeared in any of my papers.

I awoke on the dread morning of the first paper in a state of exhaustion, having lain sleepless and panicking until the dawn chorus broke. How lucky to be bird-brained, I thought. Nevertheless, I enjoyed the arduous week of written papers more than I ought to have. 'All the translation was utterly hellish', I wrote to my parents, ' – I liked almost all the other papers far too much & so scribbled off an entangled chaos which will not compare favourably with the slick & perfect productions of A.1 high-grade-efficiency Wykehamists.'

It was during one of the 'utterly hellish' translation papers, however, that the intense atmosphere dissolved for a moment. I had bet Quintin Hogg £1 that he would not leave the examination hall after only *one* hour, when *two* hours were allowed. The view of his fellow examinees was that, in accepting the bet, Quintin would either find it necessary to stay the full two hours and so lose his £1 or win his £1 and lose his first. There was a breathless hush as the large black hands of the clock reached the end of the first hour and a solitary figure rose from his desk, handed in his papers and left the hall – with a jaunty nod to me on the way. Of course he won his bet *and* his first.

With the end of written examinations, my life suddenly changed course. Disappointment and tragedy struck, the first not unexpected, the second out of the blue; but at the very same time I was assailed by such flights of new ideas that it seemed as if the prospects I had dwelt on so eagerly only a month before had never been more than fantasies.

My viva was scheduled for 19 July, the final result to be announced on the 25th. Meanwhile the last week of the academic year provoked a spate of valedictions. Two pages of 'Cherwellian School Notes' included a long '*Ave Atque Vale!*'

Several of the assistant masters are unfortunately leaving us this term as well as the usual amount of boys. Notable amongst the former is *Mr Lancaster* who has for five happy years taught drawing and arithmetic. . . . Though some of us may think him eccentric, we have all come to love him. . . . On the distaff side, our ever popular matron, *Miss Harman*, whose sweetness and charm have endeared her to generations of Cherwellians, is unfortunately leaving us. . . .

Armorel Heron-Allen and I decided to give an immense farewell cocktail-party at the Randolph Hotel for our friends. It was quite a roll-call of the future, as described by me to Michael Hope, then in America.

All the boys, e.g. Hamish [Erskine], Osbert, Harry d'Avigdor-Goldsmid, had had so many parties before that they were drunk & silent, sitting in little muddy heaps on the floor. But there were a lot of distinguished visitors to Oxford & some healthy-looking friends of Armorel.

Among the latter I remember Jack Wolfenden (of the 1960s Wolfenden Report on Homosexuality); Christopher Hawkes, who was to marry the famous archeologist Jacquetta; and the Narishkins, who taught Russian to some and the balalaika to others, especially Armorel. My visitors included John Aldridge, the future Royal Academician, John Maud (the future Lord Redcliffe-Maud), Patrick Balfour, Cecil Beaton, and Pearl and Maurice Green, already married.

Maurice Bowra came in his canonicals [I continued, without explaining that he was now a Proctor or guardian of the University's morals] – a great triumph, considering that he had refused Hamish's party the week before. He refused & drank nine cocktails & then went off to dine with the Bishop of Worcester.

I also remember Randolph's cousin Johnnie Churchill being there; Johnnie had painted a wonderful *trompe-l'oeil* mural of the interior of a basilica on the walls of his room at Pembroke College. Contrary to the hopes of *Cherwell*, the authorities blotted out this genuine work of art as soon as he had gone down. I concluded with a few words about my own plans:

I tried to bully Roy [Harrod] into visiting me in London, but he is fundamentally hardworking, & gives very small change in return for one's sacks & sacks of Alcmeonid gold. . . .

Tomorrow we all go down to Croyde [the Nettlefold 'Holiday House' in Devon] – Val, John Harman, me, John Aldridge, Harry, Pat de Laszlo & Armorel. My God, what will happen?

I can't think what made me put in that last sentence – Pat and Armorel were unofficially engaged so perhaps I expected a 'Holiday House' wedding – but those sudden violent words could not have been more appropriate in the circumstances. Armorel set out to drive Patrick to Croyde in her treasured second-hand car. The coveted first in Zoology was safely under her belt. Just outside Salisbury the car lost one of its front wheels and catapulted over a hedge into a field. Pat was picked up with a broken collar-bone, Armorel was dead.

For Patrick the blow was shattering. His father, the portrait painter Philip de Laszlo, sent him to America for a while but it was something like ten years before he completely recovered and married. His wife's beauty – she was a daughter of Sir Hamar Greenwood – immediately reminded me of Armorel's.

On me the effect was numbing. I felt I would come to life again only if I could discuss the whole affair with Armorel herself. Her gentle dark-eyed mother sent me a pair of Armorel's jade ear-rings, which I still wear; her father set up a science scholarship at Lady Margaret Hall in her memory, for which one of the judges had to be 'A Woman of the World'. The college appointed me as the first of the breed, and I enjoyed serving with learned men and women from the lab world. After the war the panel all realized that 'women of the world' and 'women of the labs' were no longer two separate species. My post on the panel was abolished. In Armorel's day – she died at twenty-two – her mixture of glamour and chic with devotion to retorts and test tubes had been unique.

There was no consolation for the heart in the beautifully illuminated card her father sent to his and Armorel's friends. A quotation from the stoic Seneca, it runs, in a translation supplied to me by Quintin:

What comfort, therefore, have we against these losses? This, surely, that we must remember them even after they are lost, and that we must not suffer to fall out of our minds the joy that we have had from them, even though we have them no more. What we have may be snatched from us. But what we have had is ours for ever. Ungrateful indeed is he who, having lost something, does not acknowledge his debt of gratitude for that which he has once possessed.

At the end of our macabre visit to 'Holiday House', I was still a week or so from my viva. I had intended to shut myself up at Lynchfield and plunge into revision. Again I had one of my hunches: that I would be vivaed in Roman history and the career of the brothers Gracchi. This oh so worthy period of the Roman republic had bored me excessively, particularly because it was a framework for that impossible female, the 'Mother of the Gracchi', whom of all women I least wished to resemble. I had therefore not answered a single question in my written paper on this period. It was odds-on that the examiners would make straight for this gap. Nevertheless I could not bring myself to settle down seriously to my books, and when a sympathetic and romantically beautiful friend called Hugh Christopher Holme (he had patronized Osbert Lancaster's exhibition in 1929) invited me to stay with him and his family in Buckinghamshire, I gladly accepted. I turned my back on the Gracchi, mother, sons and all, and took a few peeps at Plato. Otherwise no revision. What did it matter anyway? Armorel had got a first and where was she now?

Unfortunately my hunch about the Gracchi, unlike my earlier hunch about the Right and the Good, proved correct. I was vivaed on the Republican brothers for forty minutes in a genuine attempt by the examiners to enable me to raise myself from the second into the first class. One of them had told his mother, who had told her lodger from Lady Margaret Hall, who had told me, that I need have no worries over my Greek and Roman history papers. Yet when the moment came to amplify what I had written I was able to add not one cubit to my stature. I suffered an experience similar to that so feelingly described by my friend Esmond Warner after his own viva. 'The examiners began politely,' recalled Esmond to me. 'Mr Warner, we would like you to enlarge upon the interesting points you have made about the position of slaves under Roman law.' They then read out what he had written. He stared in amazement and admiration. Had he really been the author of such full, such knowledgeable arguments? The very idea of *adding* to them! In fact, not only could he not add to a word he had written but he had totally forgotten within the month everything that he once knew. That was my own predicament exactly.

I was dancing with Harry at Somerhill on his twenty-first birthday when a telegram was brought on to the dance floor and handed to me. I had been given a second.

Harry was very sympathetic and I had forty-eight letters of condolence, though one from Maurice Bowra was not among them. I gave the news to Michael Hope in America, taking care not to make it sound too gloomy, since he too had missed a first after a forty-minute grilling.

108 Harley Street, W.1. 2. VIII.30

Darling, we are nothing if not soul-mates! I missed the bloody thing *just*. There was a weak patch in my knowledge of the Gracchi which I intended to do at Croyde. But I didn't: and was vivaed on it for 40 minutes. Result, 2nd. Anyway I got alpha/beta in Greek and Roman history, beta++ in both Philosophies & beta+ in Logic (!!) beta− in Ancient History [my 'best' subject]. As for the Translations etc. the highest was beta− and the rest sought their natural level which was about gamma, delta, ēta!

My letter to Michael ended with news of Christine Willans, as most of my letters to him did.

Christine came in to see me at ten o'clock last night. [She was training to be an inspector of property and was very funny about the exact number of gallons of water required to flush a loo.] We talked a good bit about you, but I was most enthralled by her hair which had just been washed and looked like a newly opened horse-chestnut. There ought to have been white patches for anxiety & to finish the simile. . . .

Despite my long letter, the details of my degree were already becoming a vast unreality. An incident had taken place in June, soon after Schools finished, that had suddenly thrown a totally new light on the future. I had not yet got around to formulating in my mind exactly what it amounted to. I knew in my bones, however, that as a result of this incident and its sequel everything was going to be different.

I was sitting in my room at 10 Chadlington Road when Hope Stevenson came in. 'Someone to see you.' I ran downstairs and there at the open front door was Frank Pakenham. My first impression was repeated, of an extraordinary pink and white complexion combined with classical curls, Graeco-Roman features and a far from classically tailored suit of untidy clothes. A taxi was ticking over at the garden gate. He must have kept it ticking there for at least twenty minutes, a habit that I was soon to discover could be extended to last if necessary for an hour. Indeed a legend grew up that he had once kept a taxi waiting for a whole day.

Frank had had a dream the night before in which he had an urgent compulsion to revisit Oxford and call on me. Omitting the dream and without any other preliminaries or explanation, he invited me to stay for a week with him and his family in Ireland beginning at the end of August.

In a sense I was overwhelmed with a feeling of intense surprise, since the Sleeping Beauty whom I had awakened with a kiss on 18/19 June 1927 had fallen asleep again and slept, as far as I was concerned, for the next three years. In another sense, however, I had an overpowering but inexplicable conviction that something unalterable had been mapped for the future. Without bothering about the details, I felt like an author who is going inevitably to write a new story – that much is certain – though exactly what the story will turn out to be is not yet known. For the next two months I enjoyed the pleasant sensation of having a bit of secret capital laid up somewhere, which would keep me going until August, whatever happened in between.

While the taxi went on ticking, Frank further suggested that I should meet a brilliant friend of his named Evan Durbin, who had gone down from New College one year earlier with a second in Zoology and a first in Economics. Frank and Evan were both booked to tutor at a Workers' Educational Association summer school in Balliol College that August. Would I like to join in the fun? I was not uninterested, since Mr Fordyce, the classics tutor at Balliol, had already mentioned the WEA as a possibility during our earlier tea-party, though emphasizing his (and my) preference for research in Roman history.

Frank and I parted, he with an already large fare marked up on the meter outside, I with a sizeable assortment of hopes stirring inside. Curiously enough Frank showed no concern about whether I would get a first or not. The difference between a first and a second did not enter into his relationship with the only undergraduate at Oxford whom he had ever known.

With the death of Armorel followed by the far, far less cruel death of my first, my whole vocabulary changed. Gone in a flash was the yearning for a pinnacle of glory on which sat the exalted figure of a don; gone even the talk of inscriptions, research projects, peacock pies. They might never have been.

From 3 August I was booked to work for a week at the Balliol WEA summer school, 'under the wing of Frank Pakenham', as I put it in my letter to Michael. It would be an experimental week, enabling me to see what the Workers' Educational Association was like. 'I am giving a woman from the Potteries', I added not without irony, 'tuition in *Political Economy*. Ha!!'

7

The Engagement Is Not Announced

The Workers' Educational Association had a mythology all its own. At its heart lay a kind of paradox. Though the workers had by definition missed out on education, while the teachers were highly qualified with university degrees, there was always assumed to be a rough and ready equality between the two sides.

'Learn while you Teach' seemed to be the motto offered to us tutors at the Oxford summer school. Tutors like Frank Pakenham, who were already well versed in their subject (in his case, economics), were made to feel tiros by their pupils when it came to Life with a big L in a factory or mine. Out-of-work coalminers might spend their week at Balliol College learning about the 'Theory of Rent'; but, by God, they would keep young fellows with Oxford accents and Oxford degrees in their place when it came to the connection between 'Marginal Productivity' and unemployment.

For me, 'Learn while you Teach' was a double imperative. Far from being master of my summer-school subject, I knew virtually nothing about it. A schoolteacher from Longton, one of the North Staffordshire 'Five Towns' loosely known as The Potteries, had elected to study Rousseau's *Social Contract* during her week at Oxford. I was assigned to Leah Grocott as her tutor. Why she got me instead of one of the regular PPE tutors I never knew. Possibly because a knowledge of Plato and Aristotle was thought to make Rousseau child's play; more likely because pupil and teacher were both young women. So Miss Grocott and Miss Harman (friendship began with formalities in those days) strove for a week to unravel Rousseau's tangled idea of the 'General Will', and to apply it to conditions in North Staffordshire.

If I had a lot to learn about Rousseau, I had twice as much to learn about the workers. As children, we self-sufficient Harmans did not often play games with the village boys and girls of Detling, one traditional way of mixing up the social classes; I knew the working class well only as domestic servants. True, for a year before I went up to Oxford I was persuaded by my mother to collect for a savings scheme organized in a London slum by the Unitarian church. One day a week I would walk from Harley Street along Baker Street as far as Marylebone station and then plunge into the warren around Lisson Grove.

I would get a glimpse into a small world of extreme poverty. Pallid mothers with their hair in cotton handkerchiefs and wearing layers of overlapping rags held together with safety-pins would open their doors to me, drag back handfuls of children, fetch their savings books and either pay up their pennies or mutter guiltily, 'Call next week, Miss.' Sometimes a cat or dog would rush out between the children's legs and we would get matey chasing it down the street. Sometimes I would hear a tale of woe – sickness or unemployment – but no permanent relationships were made. They knew I was only a collecting machine. On my side there was no commitment, though for the first time I sensed the dangerous pleasure of bringing brief light to those in darkness. I realized the effect of one's pretty clothes and ladylike manners. But with my entry into the magical world of Oxford, Lisson Grove vanished into the recesses of memory. It was not recalled even by the WEA summer school. For the dynamic, high-spirited workers of North Staffs were as remote from the lumpen-proletariat of Lisson Grove as both were from me.

Not that my WEA pupils were in any way exempt from the miseries of industry under virtually free-for-all capitalism. They knew its hard, unacceptable face all too well. Halfway through my week's tutoring Leah Grocott brought along a young paintress from the Potteries to join our studies of Rousseau. Unlike Leah, Ethel was a somewhat shadowy character, perhaps because her health was not good; the skin of both her hands was afflicted by dermatitis, an industrial disease. I asked her, 'How soon will it be cured?' She looked at me sombrely, implying the answer 'Never.'

Frank Pakenham helped to fill in the picture for me by accounts of his three-year Economics class in Longton. In his eyes the star was Doris Robinson, a chair-bound cripple in constant pain who nevertheless had powers of literary, even poetic, perception that went far beyond economics. Indeed I think Doris stuck to this dour subject chiefly for the sake of the mental romance that had sprung up between her and her impressionable tutor.

In those days there were no enticing ameliorations like 'Riding for the Disabled'; Doris Robinson would as soon have thought of mounting a horse as riding on a broomstick. All she could hope for were occasional train rides in her wheelchair to one of the country seats outside the Potteries – perhaps Barlaston Hall, presented by the philanthropical Wedgwoods – for a weekend school. She had nothing to lose but her chair. Or so it seemed until, through the WEA, she won a rare scholarship to Oxford. It was, in fact, part of the workers' mythology that mind triumphed over matter, however much it was cramped and stunted by the system. And the system itself would, of course, soon be abolished. There was much optimism interwoven with hardship.

The Workers' Educational Association, whose charter I had not yet studied, seemed to me a political weapon for winning the workers their rights. If I had read the official *Aims*, I would have seen that, on the contrary, it was non-political, non-sectarian and non-vocational – a purely educational body for bringing the finest university learning to those who had left school probably at ten or twelve.

In order to prevent political bias, young Conservatives like Frank Pakenham of New College and his friend Henry Brooke of Balliol were persuaded to become tutors. They both worked in the Conservative Research Department and today both would be called 'wets'. Henry was later to carve out a somewhat hard, wooden image for himself in politics, but I knew him as a touchingly responsive friend who, after staying for a weekend, picked out for praise the size and softness of his bath towel.

Apart from Tory show-pieces, however, the majority of WEA tutors were radicals. Evan Durbin, Frank's old friend from New College days and a leading light at the summer school, was not only a socialist but intended to stand for Labour at the next election. Never have I spent a more fulfilling week. I loved the work, the workers and the odd collection of tutors: John Thomas, the eloquent Welshman who crammed the whole world diagrammatically on to his blackboard, the sultry Mr Emery who expounded D. H. Lawrence and was rumoured to have a secret life, Stuart Cartwright, the district secretary with the face of a gentle saint.

Evan Durbin had no girlfriend around, so he, Frank and I made a close trio. Evan was a natural teacher and a wonderfully human companion; deeply interested in people and a master of jokes and gossip. We argued endlessly about the working class, for whom Evan claimed to speak with an engagingly unjustified authority. 'Man, have you ever been hungry?' he had once asked Frank when both were freshmen at New College. Frank had been deeply impressed – until he discovered that Evan himself had never been hungrier than was normal for a boy at Taunton Grammar School, the son of a Methodist preacher. At the WEA summer school Frank and I encouraged Evan to speak as a realist reformer while we were content to be romanticists. 'We must support the cause of the workers', Evan would announce, 'because they are so low, so lacking.' 'No, no, we support them because they are so high, so noble,' Frank and I would clamour.

As for our courtship, if courtship it was, I was too busy and happy to notice whether it was progressing or not. Only once during that week did Frank ask a leading question: 'Do you ever want to get married?' We were walking up Broad Street towards Blackwell's, and my mind was on books. 'No; at least not yet,' I said. 'Don't you ever want to hear the sound of tiny pattering feet?' he persisted. Not recognizing this as a quotation from Frank's favourite P. G. Wodehouse, I was shocked by the apparent sentimentality. 'No,' I said again more firmly.

By the end of my visit to the WEA summer school of 1930 I was well dug in. Leah Grocott was planning to get me up to the Potteries for a series of twelve weekly lectures on literature. Another request came from Ashford in Kent to take a weekend school on 'The Financial Side of Unemployment'. I was thrilled and flattered. But how could I do it? I knew no economics.

Evan Durbin came to my rescue. 'I'll teach you the whole of economics', he said, 'over one lunch at the George!' Naturally I accepted the lunch with gratitude, but afterwards it was decided that one working lunch was not enough. I must spend one working *year* – at the London School of Economics. My heart sank a little. Back to academic learning after a week's liberated teaching? However, there was consolation in the thought that I was to visit the Pakenham home in Ireland before the London university term began.

The glitter of my first visit to Pakenham Hall will never be effaced. It was the glitter of eccentricity not luxury; but eccentricity that was intellectual, high-spirited and comical. Something of the nostalgic Oxford atmosphere seemed to have been recreated in and around this unlikely grey castle at the heart of rural Ireland – a paradise of peat bogs, low hills, lakes and ruins.

Known locally as 'The Castle', Pakenham Hall had been an Irish stronghold called Tullynally long before the English Pakenhams arrived. They came from East Anglia in the seventeenth century to settle in the middle of Westmeath and hold it on behalf of the parliamentary forces. By the eighteenth century there was an Irish peerage, Longford. In the days of Wellington, the second Earl of Longford (whose brother-in-law Wellington was) had a spacious dry moat and vast basement dug out at enormous expense. The famous Irish architect, Francis Johnston, added a vigorous sprouting of towers, turrets and battlements. When I saw it, the whole grey mass covering two acres of ground was topped by a tremendous flagstaff for the climbing of which there was a permanent reward of £20. Many cavaliers tried, none succeeded. (Our friend Commander George Martelli was to come nearest, but as he approached the top it began to shake so violently that even the navy had to retreat.)

The view from the house was of green parkland planted with islands or peninsulas of huge trees advancing into the sloping fields, blue glistening hills in the distance. These hills encircled a great lake. In the walled garden were towering yew hedges and enormous sagging Irish yews strangled with ivy, but still guarding a city of flashing glass-houses filled with peaches and grapes.

The uncontested king and queen of this fairyland were Edward and Christine Longford, Frank's brother and sister-in-law, though Edward looked more like a gigantic Tweedledum than Oberon, while Christine's clever face and curious constricted gestures could have been found at any donnish high table, rather than on Titania's throne. I was immediately drawn to Christine. Apart from her kindness and unselfishness as hostess, she had been a classical scholar at Somerville as I had been an English scholar at Lady Margaret Hall. And though we were both scholars, in another sense we were both 'commoners' in this aristocratic set-up. Christine Trew, born at Cheddar in 1900, had moved with her mother Amy to Oxford, after Captain Trew went to sea and never came back. Glad to be rid of him, the dauntless Mrs Trew opened a tea-shop and small store in Oxford, where she entertained undergraduates and watched the triumphant progress of her daughter. Christine became a close friend of Harold Acton and a constant guest of Lady Ottoline Morrell at Garsington Manor, among whose exquisite clipped yews, lawns and patios Lady Ottoline conducted the most brilliant garden-salon Oxford had ever seen. Unlike me, Christine succeeded in obtaining a part in an OUDS play; she was a lady-in-waiting in J. B. Fagan's production of *Hamlet*, the very one that I had watched as a stage-struck schoolgirl.

Edward Longford, though two years younger than Christine, had overlapped with her at Oxford; they were both reading Greats. Edward from the start shared her interest in the theatre – they were enthusiasts for the Oxford Playhouse – and soon drew her into the ambience of his Irish nationalism. The first 'sacrifice' he had made for the cause had been while a schoolboy at Eton: he had refused to join the Officers' Training Corps lest he should be called upon to take up arms against Sinn Fein. His second 'sacrifice', a more spectacular one, was made at Oxford. He opposed a Union motion condemning the 'assassins' (rather than executioners) of the British Field Marshal Sir Henry Wilson in London. Edward was seized by a mob on the way back to his college, Christ Church, who ducked him in Mercury, the lily-pool in the centre of Tom Quad, and then raided his rooms, destroying all books in which he had written his name in Irish – Eamon de Longphort. I heard later that Maurice Bowra had defended the assassination on typical grounds: 'All generals who are good diplomats', he said, 'should be murdered', presumably because they would negotiate their countries into war.

I had not seen Edward in his youthful beauty, before the fatal addiction to food overtook him. The addiction was already in the 1930s being indulged by his adoring wife; but I could note in Edward the buttercup yellow hair, large blue eyes and perfect pink complexion that were now so much more dazzlingly represented by his sisters. Julia, the youngest, a stunning blonde, was staying when I arrived and also Violet, the next sister and the only other brown-eyed, brown-haired member of the family beside Frank.

The unbounded eccentricity of the young earl (sixth in the line) turned the whole house-party into an uproarious rag. True, Frank was marked out as the conventional member of the clan and sent off with Mr White, the chauffeur, to play every day in the Cavan tennis tournament. But in the atmosphere created by Edward and Christine there was no vigorous country house 'ekker' – the word used by Frank's athletic contemporaries. Instead of exercise, Edward would sometimes take a leisurely party to fish on Lough Derravaragh. On one occasion we went round and round the lake, trying this and that piece of water, a farm-hand rowing while Edward and I fruitlessly trailed our lines. We were about to turn homeward when I decided as a last resort to try for a 'miraculous catch'. 'If there is a God,' I challenged, 'let him give me a sign, a bite!' Forthwith there was a prodigious tug at my line and Edward and I between us landed a huge pike. When we took it to the kitchen, the cook cut it open and dramatically displayed its inside stuffed with what seemed a positive shoal of little fish. I was amazed. What could this further sign mean? Surely not a collection of gods, such as were depicted on the Chinese antiques with which Edward and Christine had furnished their castle?

Edward's chief delight was to have us all pile into his large car and go touring around ruined abbeys, Celtic crosses or the abandoned homes of dim Irish peers. Our wild spirits were greatly increased by the presence as house-guest of my old friend and the Longfords' new friend, John Betjeman.

With his typical sensitivity to odd, unusual feelings in other people, John immediately detected and cultivated Edward's three remarkable enthusiasms: for theatricals, for Ireland as an independent nation and for the Irish Episcopal Church. Sometimes while on a picnic John was able to organize a celebration of all three together. I remember unpacking our lavish cold luncheon on the steps of a Celtic cross, which Edward had already saluted by raising his huge stetson hat in homage – a habit of his when passing any Celtic cross, and quite dangerous when at the wheel. After the meal was finished Edward and John converted the white cloths into surplices and conducted a service between them, which included responses and hymns sung by us all.

I must digress for a moment to describe Edward's driving, for it is primarily at the wheel that I see him in memory. Holding it in a ferocious grip, his stetson on his head and his elbows stuck out, he would sight a tiny donkey-cart at the far, far end of one of Ireland's lovely long, straight roads. His grasp would at once tighten still further, his speed accelerate and the wheel shake and wobble, while a challenge on the horn would begin the moment the distant object was sighted and continue at full blast until it was overtaken and passed. At first, of course, the donkey and its driver would hear nothing – we were too far away – and Edward would swell and go purple with rage at the sight of them still on the road. As we finally careered past, donkey and cart would have voluntarily taken to the ditch. For Lord Longford of Pakenham Hall had become an enormous Mr Toad of Toad Hall.

Hymn-singing would reach its zenith after dinner. Edward had sent for an old upright piano from the schoolroom on which he thumped out his favourite tunes from the *Church of Ireland Hymnal* while the rest of us leaned over his huge shoulders and bawled out the words. 'I loved watching his big fat fingers,' John told me years afterwards. John's favourite hymn began, 'Will your anchor hold in the storms of life?' while my favourites were, 'Let us gather at the river' and 'Dare to be a Dan-i-e-l'.

Along with Low Church enthusiasm Betjeman introduced the cult of dim Irish peers. As we swept hooting through the quiet countryside he would give lyrical and partly imaginative accounts of these derelict heroes. Charles Aloysius Trimlestown, aged seventy, was celestially happy according to John 'because he is so little known'. Or Lord Massy, equally enviable in driving a Dublin taxi. Betjeman was to keep up with the Massy fortunes and to trace a descendant who owned a grocer's shop in Leicester. 'Just the kind of man I like.' He never got to know or indeed met any of them. 'That is what I liked. I didn't like them to be well known.' We all fell in love with this prophet of dimness who of all men was least dim himself.

From being the accompanist before dinner Edward became the vocalist during dinner. His repertoire consisted of Irish patriotic songs like 'The Wearing of the Green' and 'The West's Awake'. His biographer, John Cowell, says that he sometimes side-slipped into Orange airs like the 'Protestant Boys' and 'Slitter slaughter, holy water', but I never heard this happen. I remember one lit-up evening when Edward rose from his seat in mid-song, danced round the dinner-table like a mad circus elephant, and had just mounted the groaning (literally) sideboard when Andrews, the Welsh Nonconformist butler, entered the room. He stood like the statue in *Don Giovanni* gazing at his lord and master. Suddenly the frenzied elephant caught sight of him. Silence fell abruptly. Edward signalled Andrews to help him down from the sideboard. Andrews did so and then began to clear away the plates and glasses. We all slunk out. Guests at Pakenham Hall never found the supply of drinks excessive, indeed they were known to visit the pubs in Castlepollard village before dinner, but with Edward a little went a long way.

Two other guests invited by Frank who became regulars along the field path to Castlepollard were Alastair Graham and his patron and protector, Evelyn Waugh. The two were not unalike to look at, both slight and blond. But Alastair was a pale edition of Evelyn. Whereas his expression was always amiable, Evelyn's was often satirical, menacing or even angry. Evelyn's first marriage had broken up the year before this house party and his view of the world had just been offered to the public in his second novel, *Vile Bodies*. He spoke little at meals. We all assumed he was observing, gathering material for his next book.

Evelyn was willing, however, to fabricate dramas in front of the camera. I have several photographs taken outside the nail-studded front door. In one I am fainting while Edward and John Betjeman are up to no good; in another Alastair is posing as 'A Greek Drug Fiend'; and in yet another Evelyn is attacking Edward with the circular brush used for cleaning one's boots.

Christine would watch all Edward's pranks with the look of a mother condoning her child's mischief; but when photographed herself she would droop her hands like flippers, turn in her feet and make the grimaces of a naughty child. Though she never confided her fears to me, her biographer relates that she believed herself to be repellently ugly. I imagine she exaggerated this supposed ugliness in front of the camera. She hardly ever made personal remarks, but when I was departing after this first visit she said, 'I do like your shoes. You have so many and such pretty ones.' I had assumed that because she herself always dressed uncompromisingly in Irish hand-loom woven tweeds (an industry supported by Edward) she had no interest in clothes. How wrong I was. When her first novel, *Making Conversation*, came out next year, I saw that her observation of clothes worn by undergraduettes at Oxford was accurate, malicious and witty. Martha Freke, the heroine, wears a memorably awful crocheted mauve jumper. Partly as a result of this book John Betjeman was to call Christine 'the funniest woman I ever knew'.

I rarely saw Evelyn on this visit except in the company of Alastair. But on the last night as we all trooped up to bed, he suddenly dropped behind and seized me by the arm. 'Go after Frank,' he whispered. 'Go up with him. Follow him. Go on.' Thus urged, I took Evelyn's advice, sprinted up the grand staircase, overtook Frank and joined him for the first time in his bedroom in the wing overlooking the park. There was a double bed but I did not get into it, just sat on the edge, while we conducted an ardent but chaste and anxious conversation about ourselves far into the night. I can remember only one of the nice things he said: 'Why doesn't your face fall to pieces at night like other people's?'

The plan to get me re-educated at the London School of Economics was a failure. I attended lectures sporadically, wrote history essays and benefited from tutorials with the genial H. L. Beales, but I could never get the spirit of the place. If I had known about the bizarre conjunction of Beatrice and Sidney Webb that had given it birth, I might have felt its romance. As it was, it seemed but a drab imitation of Oxford, an academic anticlimax.

Moreover, from the very beginning of the course, in September 1930, I had begun to worry about the class I would eventually be awarded. 'It's essential for you to get a first this time,' said Evan Durbin (now a lecturer at London University). 'One second is bearable but two would mean you were a second-class person.' Thus encouraged I began to panic. I turned to Frank. He merely made light of my missed first at Oxford. 'I am really relieved that you didn't get one; as I, with my poor little Modern Greats, have always a sneaking inferiority complex in the presence of a first in real Greats, and I shouldn't have been able to bear having an inferiority complex with you.'

There was also a rival attraction which was to take up more and more of my time, so that when the next summer arrived I scratched my name from the candidates' roll. What matter? I had learnt the economic jargon, 1930s style, and could give a lecture when required on 'The Financial Side of Unemployment'. I only once overreached myself and that was during an exposition in the Potteries of the May Committee's findings. I was reckless enough to use the blackboard in explaining the most intricate phases of the slump. Luckily I saw just before my audience did that my figures were not going to work out and was able to sweep them off the blackboard as if they had served their purpose.

Meanwhile my literature course in Longton had magically material-ized. It was even planned to coincide with Frank's class on economics in the same town. I wrote to my parents: 'The Potteries adore seeing their tutors getting out of buses and into trains together!' As things turned out, getting into a train together was to be of more than common importance in our lives.

The arrangement was that I would go up to the Potteries on a Thursday afternoon and spend the night with the WEA district secretary and his wife, Edmund and Maria Hobson, in their council house at Meir, the last and smallest in the string of Pottery towns. After preparing my lecture next morning, I would take the local bus to Longton, where I would give my lecture, followed by questions, discussion and distribution of books for further reading from the official 'book box'. After this I would take another bus to another of the Five Towns, Fenton, to which Frank also would have migrated from Longton, in order to have supper with his landlady, Mrs Adams, and a group of the Longton comrades. By the time I arrived supper and economic argument would have exhausted themselves and Frank and the comrades would be standing round Mrs Adams' upright piano singing 'My Bonny is over the Water' or 'On Ilkley Moor Baht 'at'. (I discovered that the last two mysterious words stood for 'without a hat'.) By about midnight Frank and I would prepare for our walk to Stoke station, to catch the 1.15 a.m. train back to London, on which two sleepers had been reserved. Once we started so late from Fenton that we had to run the last mile. My determined trot impressed Frank more than all my lectures put together.

Yet my series of twelve lectures did have a certain *réclame*. Having decided to give the Potteries the very best I could manage in the way of literary adventure, I had offered them a course on 'Modern American Drama'. The first lecture was welcomed by a startled local paper: 'What promises to be a rather remarkable series of lectures commenced last night. . . .' The reporter was careful to add that the lecturer was 'B.A. (Oxon)', which in those days was taken as a badge of sanity.

The subject was a good choice. I was able to beam the American messages on to my pupils and their problems in a way that provoked immediate response. Something for everyone – provided everyone was an underdog. In an alienated society like the Potteries, once a community of proud, prosperous craftsmen, now on the dole through no fault of their own, one could not fail to hit someone in the solar plexus. There was Eugene O'Neill's hero 'Yank' in *The Hairy Ape* asking, 'Where do I belong?' There was *The Adding Machine* where people ask, 'To whom do I belong? Who owns us?' There was *Street Scene* and *Front Page*, each showing that bewilderment was the ordinary attitude to life. 'What's the good of being alive if you can't get a little something out of life?' – lust, drink, a baby, music . . . 'Why must people always be fighting instead of just being sort of happy together?' Negro drama made a strong appeal, and I went to European drama for the effects of the industrial age on human beings. In my last lecture we scoured the universe, in the way that always stirred the WEA, for wider and deeper meanings of drama: marionettes and masques, Isadora Duncan's interpretation of the dance and D. H. Lawrence's 'Dance of the Sprouting Corn' by the Pueblo Indians. Was life a 'flawed eternity' as in Kaiser's *Gas*, or an eternity in which the ardent evangelists of the Five Towns could still believe?

My pupils were a mixed bag of Marxists, agnostics, political believers and chapel-goers. I was taken one day to see how an evangelical meeting was conducted in the Potteries. After a short period of exhortation I felt that the emotional temperature was beginning to rise. People were shouting, 'Come, come to the Penitent Form', and more and more of the 'saved' were leaving their benches to testify on the platform. Suddenly half-a-dozen *exaltés* rose in a body from the far end of the wooden bench on which I was sitting, the form tipped up like a see-saw and deposited me and my friends in a tangled heap on the floor. Someone shouted, 'I don't care if the bench tips up as long as Jesus is sitting on the other end.' Loud cries of 'Praise the Lord!'

My next course was a 'History of British Drama'. Particularly acceptable to my audience was Bernard Shaw. When he described the bloodthirstiness of the Elizabethans, pointing out that eighty per cent of ministers of the Crown met violent deaths, I brought his figures up to date, showing that only four of the (Labour) Cabinet would escape alive, to which socialist Longton responded with cheers. My class and I, in a thoroughly sceptical mood brought on by the slump and collapse of the system around us, joyfully adhered to the slogans of the 'Devil's Disciple': 'No more paths. No more straight and narrow. No more good and bad.' Yet the scepticism of the 1930s had not the depth of the post-war variety and, in fact, we were waiting ardently for a burst of faith, a new Utopia.

Meanwhile the relationship that Frank and I were constructing with one another had run into underlying difficulties, though on the surface we were both committed to it with growing enthusiasm.

Unwittingly Frank had created in me, politically speaking, something of a Frankenstein's monster. Before I met him again at Oxford that June, I had no party political interests whatever. Once introduced by him to the Workers' Educational Association, however, I found myself being swept along on a strong tide in the opposite direction to him – 'But *leftward*, look, the land is bright.' With hindsight I can see that Frank unconsciously needed friends on the Left to express the emotions which were forbidden to him as a Conservative politician; I was the female counterpart of Durbin and Gaitskell.

At the same time his social and political ambitions were well catered for in a circle of particularly sparkling and beloved friends, far removed from my Oxford orbit. He had been living in London for two or three years as a member of the Bright Young Set, some of whom had already made their début in Evelyn Waugh's *Vile Bodies*. In one sense he had been long associated with two of its leaders, Freddy Furneaux and his sister Lady Eleanor Smith. In another sense Frank and Evelyn Waugh were a couple of outsiders, drawing the social coverts together. An entry in Evelyn's diary for 26 May 1930 is an example of what Frank was later to call their 'social climbing'. 'After the theatre', wrote Evelyn, 'Frank Pakenham had a supper party at the Savoy. Eleanor, Baby, Maureen, Basil, John Betjeman, a man called Fleming and a man called Warner.'

About politics Frank was already deadly serious and intellectual while I was emotional. He had gained experience in the actual arena of conflict, being a young protégé of Lady Astor, the first woman to enter Parliament. His grandmother, the Dowager Countess of Jersey and a great Tory political hostess in her day, who had entertained my renegade great-uncle Joe Chamberlain, was now applying her acute mind to the question of a constituency for Frank. I had no political experience whatever but saw myself as a possible 'Shavian' political woman, perhaps a mixture of Saint Joan and Major Barbara.

When it came to the alleged battle between the sexes as opposed to party political warfare, the situation was reversed. I was the experienced one and Frank the novice, though like most of our contemporaries who were not actually engaged (I cannot speak of engaged couples, some of whom I think were beginning to sleep together before marriage) we were both virgins. Frank's confession to me when I woke him with a kiss at the New College ball in 1927 – 'I'd like to kiss you but I can't' – still held good. He felt himself inhibited from kissing any girls but his sisters or cousins. At first I was pleased that his second 'awakening' as well as his first should be due to me. It was several weeks before I scented danger in such an unusual relationship. And the same period was to pass before he himself realized the force of his inhibition. I loved him and needed him; he loved me and depreciated himself, suggesting that his concentration on dry economic analysis had withered his powers of expression and feeling.

After receiving a teasing letter from me just before his class in the Potteries started, he wrote:

Dear Elizabeth

This letter is 'without prejudice' (could a letter from me be anything else?) By Saturday I do not know what I shall feel like. Perhaps my analytic mind (?) will have stopped all feeling with its usual fiendish cunning. I only write to say that I have never stopped thinking about you since I saw you on Saturday and that at 10.49 a.m. Friday September 12 I can hardly bear to wait till tomorrow.

Love from
Frank.

Three weeks later I replied to another batch of self-accusations from Frank:

> To F. *Inarticulate Unreliable Incapable of Endearments.*
> Shall I examine your deep argument?
> Thesis: You do not love me.
>   I'm content.
> You, I perceive, are not.
>   Yet it is clear
> You do not, for you cannot call me Dear.
> Love does not thrive such silences among.
>
> Since when did heart require a gift of tongue?
> Of my own heart I will not judge the worse
> Though it speak only once, and then in verse.

The 'silences', if not the deep inhibitions, were gradually broken down by our Friday nights together on Stoke station and afterwards on the London express.

Our usual routine was to pass the time waiting for the train in the 'lounge' of the North Stafford Hotel after the station waiting-room had closed for the night. On 21 November the night outside seemed as cold as Ilkley Moor 'baht 'at'. But we were snugly inside the North Staffs lounge, sitting on one of the velour settees clasped in each other's arms. Suddenly the hotel manager arrived to put out the lights. 'Here, you can't do that there, not in my hotel you can't.' Driven out on to the windy platform like Adam and Eve, but conscious of a glow rather than guilt, we were still warm enough when the train came in to continue our conversation. Frank showed himself 'capable of endearments', contrary to his own analysis, and at 2.15 a.m. (my diary) proposed that we should get married. We discussed how I should meet his mother and grandmother and Mary, his closest sister (she had not been at Pakenham Hall during that summer week). Frank had already attended one family dinner at Harley Street, followed by a theatre. My pretty cousin Lola Harman, who was present, remembers two things about the party: Frank's boisterous curls and the fact that we solemnly processed into a rather hurried dinner arm-in-arm. That must have been bad enough for Frank, who was used to extremes of grandeur or informality, not this curious halfway house. Worse was to come.

Why I allowed him formally to ask Father for my hand in marriage I cannot conceive. I remember feeling apprehensive. I knew Frank was not looking forward to the interview. And it was my father's first appearance in the role of prospective father-in-law. He probably remembered his own stressful interview with Arthur Chamberlain, Katie's father, in Birmingham, which was followed so soon by his nervous breakdown. Little did he guess that this tall young man whose unruly curls added to the size of an already massive head – my father admired big heads – was as nervous as a kitten. Indeed he was about to tread a similar path to my father's. Not quite such a thorny one, it is true, but very much longer.

It was a family joke among the Pakenhams that when the divorced Henry Lamb asked their widowed mother for Pansy's hand, Lady Longford had done her best to follow protocol and enquired of Henry in reply, 'Is it a clean sheet?' Perhaps I hoped that some such dialogue would arise in my father's consulting-room; funny enough to cheer Frank up and give him something to quote afterwards. I could imagine him twisting, twisting, twisting his front curls in his left thumb and finger – a habit that lasted as long as his hair – while Father drew the red serge curtains and turned off the ceiling light to make the room look less harsh, with its sight-testing board hanging in the corner and the bookcase full of medical volumes.

When the pair of them returned together to the drawing-room where my mother and I were waiting for them, I knew that something was radically wrong. Frank looked pale and alarmed. He signalled to me that we should leave the house as soon as possible.

By tacit agreement the next move, which should have been to announce our engagement in *The Times*, was bypassed. Frank's unhappiness was so palpable but mysterious that I encouraged him to see the specialist who had treated him for headaches after he was concussed at the Oxford point-to-point in 1928. I went with him to the specialist the first time; the second time he went alone and the specialist tried hypnosis. Frank, who in any case has never been able to lie down without falling asleep, immediately passed out on the couch. When he woke up an hour had passed agreeably enough and the specialist was working away quietly at his desk.

I found it hard to understand at first what had come over him. Naturally I was worried but not in despair. Being in love brought a kind of happiness of its own. Frank's happiest moments seemed to be tinged with melancholy, while this state of never more than half-happiness seemed to be accepted by him without regret; rather with a kind of acquiescence. I celebrated the end of November with some private, unhappy verses of my own:

In Horror of Those who are Sadly Happy
or Cheerfully Resigned
Pathetic men accept depressing lives
Dog-like, with kettles banging on their flanks;
And so the fittest to survive survives
To see the unfit take his kicks with thanks.

. . .

These surface miseries heal the hearts which lack
Deep melancholy and the abyss of joy.
Resignedly they meet our best attack
With a prepared despair none can destroy.

Two things turned out to be at the bottom of the débâcle. First, the obvious feeling of being trapped. Frank says it comes at some point to all men. But in his case there was a deeper reason, peculiar to himself. He was utterly lacking in the confidence that he would make a good husband. To understand this one must go back to his childhood and youth. As the younger son in an aristocratic family, it had been drummed into him by his mother that he would not be able to afford to marry for many years, if ever. On each side of the family there was a bachelor uncle to prove the point: Major the Hon. Arthur Child-Villiers, whose elder brother Lord Jersey had married and had had children, but never Uncle Arthur; and Major the Hon. Edward Pakenham, whose elder brother Lord Longford had married and had had children, but never Uncle 'Bingo'. No doubt Frank's mother conceded that one day in the far future he would inherit a property in Sussex from his great-aunt Caroline Pakenham; then he *might* be able to marry, but not before.

Frank for long accepted this situation as an objective fact of life. Much more wounding was his mother's lack of belief or interest in him personally. She had been widowed in 1915 when her husband was killed at Gallipoli. Afflicted by arthritis from a relatively early age, she found the responsibility of bringing up six fatherless children more than she could bear. She could bring herself to show little fondness for her eldest daughter Pansy, and for her younger son Frank she felt dislike. Using the law of primogeniture as an excuse, she concentrated all her hopes and affections on her elder son Edward, spoiling him for his position, his scholarly promise at Eton and his 'golden boy' looks. (The girls were golden too but that did not count; and Frank was definitely brown.) Throughout his youth and young manhood Frank had tried to hide these things even from himself. But fifty years after her death he told the authors of a book called *The Change Makers*:

The truth is that my mother was not very cordial towards me. My elder brother she adored and always did so. I think I would have to say that I could never have satisfied my mother. So if I suffer from any kind of neurosis, it is largely because I was unable to live up to her expectations.... Someone might explain my character in this way.

That he was oppressed by his failure to satisfy her is shown in a letter written from prep school, aged twelve. He had just sat the Eton entrance examination and felt that his place, Remove, must have disappointed her, even though he would be the youngest boy in the school and had taken the highest form open to an Oppidan (non-scholar). 'I'm sorry I didn't do better,' he wrote to her; and then added, 'I'm sending you a photograph which I got out of a paper of an enormous Austrian. Isn't he terrific?' The motive for the photograph was clear, even if it involved a touch of sympathetic magic. For the sight of this 'terrific' Austrian sent to Lady Longford by her son might suggest to her a novel association of ideas: that Frank himself was just a little bit 'terrific' after all.

Now he was twice the age he had been when he wrote that letter to his mother – just on twenty-four against twelve. But psychologically the child was father to the man. And he was still saying to the woman in his life, 'I'm sorry I didn't do better....' It was for me to send that terrific Austrian, once and for all, back into the past where he belonged. His function was no longer necessary.

8

A Year to Arrive
· *1930–1* ·

Frank wrote me a long, ambivalent letter on 5 December 1930, his twenty-fifth birthday. He was staying in Oxford for the night at the Gridiron Club.

Elizabeth

I can't compose my thoughts or separate myself from the atmosphere here (undergraduate-shooting-fishing) sufficiently to explain myself properly. My mind has ever since we last met been filled not only by questions but by desires connected with you. To deal with them fully and clearly would be to become too Durbinesque. At the risk of being too like myself, I will just indicate them as I ramble on.

One side of Frank was indeed 'Durbinesque', enjoying all the pleasures of accurate analysis and theory. He and Evan would even think of forming a new society limited to two members and called The Theorists. However, having banished this method from his letter, Frank proceeded to indicate his state of mind by describing a party given at the home of Peter Fleming's mother in Chelsea.

'His mother', explained Frank, 'was once painted by John or De Laszlo or Orpen or Sargeant or at any rate by a hand other than my own.' Frank went on to tabulate his conversations, slowly getting to the point of the letter:

With David I talked about you, Baby [Jungman], Diana Cavendish, Eleanor Smith, Maurice and again of you. Also of Maureen . . . she has been very kind and you know I rather like her. With John Maud about his fiancée and then about Maurice. With Roy about the possibility of getting married and about the Prof. With Prof about women in general (especially titled women and wives of statesmen dead and living) and about Freddy. With Freddy about Mrs Sitwell and about Roy. With Maurice about women and Pakenham and about John

Maud. With myself I communed on the subject that has since the last few weeks become starred. I have at any rate got over all fits of nerves though they have been succeeded by some modest nervousness about the state of your sympathies.

Freddy Birkenhead, added Frank, had left last night for Gibraltar.

Freddy will be away for nearly two weeks, so I told him that I meant to propose –

as if Frank had not already proposed ten days ago –

and he said that if this turned out all right he must insist on being best man. I thought this rather sweet, don't you?

Looking back, I think this letter pretty depressing. But at any rate it is put down 'just as it comes'. I do want to be married to you, Elizabeth.

Love

Frank

There was one sentence in this letter that gave the keynote to the next few months. 'What a way to write,' Frank lamented. 'As though a false step would be fatal and a step in any direction likely to be a false one. Alas.'

My Christmas present from him was accompanied by an equally depressed card, written at Aspreys in Bond Street and sent with a pearl bar brooch: 'Elizabeth from Frank. *Love*, kisses and tears.' A note sent by the same post said: 'I don't think it particularly nice but I hope you will wear it.' I wore it; until one day it dropped off and was lost for ever. Perhaps not a bad omen, though I still keep the empty case. For me too the situation was poignant, but with a difference: I believed it would come right in the end.

Christmas was my last at Detling; the lease of Lynchfield was running out and my parents were moving to Crockham Hill. The unmarried Pakenhams stayed at Middleton Stoney, their cousin Lord Jersey's house in Oxfordshire, along with many other cousins. A few days after Christmas I went to Ireland with Frank for a second visit to Pakenham Hall.

This time David Cecil was there as well as John Betjeman. The emphasis was all on the theatre, literature, charades. Edward had just paid out his first big cheque to keep the Gate Theatre, Dublin, afloat and his mind was full of plays and players. One evening several members of the company came for dinner. After some high-class charades we played the Truth Game and Cathleen Delaney, the actress, was asked what seemed to me an impossibly embarrassing question: 'Who do you think is prettier,

Elizabeth or you?' With true Irish aplomb she replied: 'In England I think people would say Elizabeth, but here they might choose me. . . .' My own idea of beauty was personified by Pansy and Mary, whom I was soon to see for the first time together. I could not decide between them. Both were fair in a glittering way, but while Pansy had violet eyes and retroussé nose, Mary's eyes were aquamarine in a face of classical perfection.

The presence of David at dinner made for intense literary argument. One evening it was *War and Peace* with special reference to the character of Pierre; was he or was he not uncannily like Frank? The conventional Christmas parties we went to were transformed by Betjeman into paradises of total dimness. One local ball in particular he loved, pretending that it was the trial spin by an impoverished Irish peer before taking up a post as master of ceremonies in a Swiss tourist resort.

A visit to his Irish home, as always, raised Frank's spirits. Writing on 6 January 1931 from The Manor House, Hackney, where his uncle Arthur Villiers ran a large boys' club in East London, he talked of having hunted at Middleton, finished *Wuthering Heights* and *The Mill on the Floss* and begun *Middlemarch* (the books set him by me). 'Pakenham has to me also added new memories (and new hopes?).'

The 'new hopes', which I shared, seemed to have prompted me to ask a question about money, for his letter ended with a question from him: 'When you say that we might have a talk "about Finance", do you mean "about a Financial book" or "about how we two are to make both ends meet"?' I meant the latter. I had half accepted the hereditary view already drummed into Frank that we would not have enough to live on if we did ever marry. And yet the situation could surely not be quite so bad? Frank had lost most of his unearned income while learning to be a stockbroker with Buckmaster & Moore during the nadir of the slump; but he still had about £300 a year. Add to this £500 from the Conservative Research Department, about £100 from the Workers' Educational Association, my £300 unearned income and £85 from the WEA. Total: over £1,000 a year between us. With prices so low, it seemed enough to live on.

Frank's reading of the Victorian women novelists was undertaken in return for my reading Mrs Humphry Ward's *Robert Elsmere*. He had been deeply moved by this Victorian story of a clergyman who lost his faith. It had caused a stir when it was published in the 1880s. Why did Frank want me to read it? Certainly not because he was losing his own religious faith. His Christianity was as conventional and firm as mine was decayed since Oxford. He always said his prayers. I believe it was the actual theme of losing one's faith – any faith – that made such an appeal. After all, the young clergyman who could not accept the four gospels had much in

Above left: My father as a civilian doctor in the Boer War. He invented a saddle that eliminated sores, for which he was awarded £5 by the Colonial Secretary, his future uncle by marriage.

Above right: My mother with John and Betty, as I was then called, 1909

Left: John and I at the seaside, 1910

Prize-giving at Headington School, Oxford. Lady Barrett, the distinguished visitor, may have remembered that she brought me into the world, fourteen years before.

Aged eighteen, 1925

At Oxford with cloche hat and tasselled cane, 1928

At Davos, 1928 Christmas vacation. Standing: left to right, John, Michael Hope, Elizabeth (as I was now called); sitting: Barbara James, Alan Napier, Valerie Nettlefold, Armorel Heron-Allen, Vyvyan Holland, Gabriel Carritt.

Lady Margaret Hall Dramatic Society presents *The Yellow Jacket*, 1928. Centre: Armorel in peacock headdress; I am directly above her, Betty Lyman Brown sitting right front.

Hugh Gaitskell

'Isis Idol', wearing my sub fusc (dark dress) for 'Schools', 1930

Left: Dressed up for the Stevensons in their garden before a Commem. ball, 1930
Below: Maurice Bowra at Pakenham with my sister Kitty on his left and me on his right. Only Kitty could really hit the ball.

Houseparty at Somerhill, 1930 Back row: left to right, 2nd. Randolph Churchill, 3rd. Mrs D'Avigdor-Goldsmid, 7th. Osmund D'Avigdor-Goldsmid; middle row: 1st. Christopher Hobhouse, 3rd. Clarice Goldsmid (later Lady Kaldor), 4th. me, 5th. Jackie D'Avigdor-Goldsmid; front row: 1st. Ros Fisher, 2nd. Patrick Balfour (later Lord Kinross), 3rd. Diana Churchill, 4th. Johnnie Churchill, 5th. Harry D'Avigdor-Goldsmid, 6th. Tony Goldsmid.

Pakenham Hall, 1930: Evelyn Waugh assaults Edward Longford with the boot brush

At the same houseparty, with Alastair Graham, Evelyn Waugh and John Betjeman

Engagement of Frank Pakenham and Elizabeth Harman, June 1931

Wedding at St Margaret's, Westminster, 3 November 1931. Bridesmaids: Valerie Nettlefold and Kitty Harman, Joan Villiers and Dorothy Chamberlain, Imogen Rhys and Katherine Vane, Julia Pakenham and Christina Chamberlain (hidden), Violet Pakenham and Marian Beesly, Mary Pakenham and Lola Harman (hidden).

Family party at my parents' house, Larksfield, 1935: left to right, Thomas, Donald
McLachlan, Antonia, Frank, my sister Kitty McLachlan, Andrew McLachlan, John Harman

Next year at Brancaster: left to right, George Martelli, Thomas, Esmond Warner,
Antonia, Frank, Ann Martelli, Brian Martelli

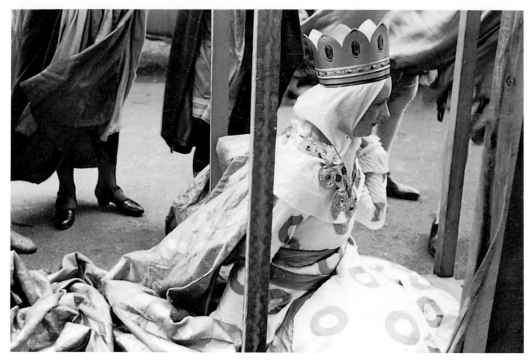

In my litter as Queen Philippa at the Birmingham Pageant, 1938

Zita and Dick Crossman with Naomi
Mitchison, 1935

Private Frank Pakenham, 1939

common with the young politician who was beginning to doubt the gospel according to Bonar Law and Baldwin.

If there were already rumblings in the depths of Frank's conservatism, his interest in the Research Department was active and growing. In the new year he had been made secretary of an important new committee on Economy. 'It means the *free hand.* So I shall enjoy myself.' The only way that I also could 'enjoy myself' was to have work as absorbing as Frank's in an orbit of my own. I therefore decided to reverse my commitments and commute from Stoke-on-Trent to London instead of vice versa. My base would be the Hobsons' heartwarming home, where I would work and sleep except for one tutorial a week at the London School of Economics. This new plan had many unexpected results.

The working-class ethos of Stoke became my own. I saw with their eyes, ate with their appetites, sensed life with their antennae. Incidentally, eating their food meant that I put on weight. Fruit and lean meat were far too expensive for most households. Maria Hobson could concoct delicious fish in batter, but we all had to fill up with platefuls of bread and potatoes. By the end of my six months' stay I weighed ten stone, and on running into my old beau Hamish Erskine in London one day I was greeted with mock horror: 'Oh, my *dear.* You look like a cook!'

Stoke became as much a part of me in 1931 as Oxford had been for the past four years. My programme of lectures increased. I devised one called 'Should the Wisest Govern?' – an attempt to lure the Potteries into studying Plato. My Longton class was bounding ahead in literary appreciation. I remember a train journey to a one-day school at Barlaston Hall when I lent my copy of *The Forsyte Saga* to a fresh-faced seventeen-year-old porter on Stoke station named Eric Tams. That was the end of Eric. He talked to no one nor answered when spoken to but read, read, read Galsworthy as he had never read a book before. Indeed he never *had* read a novel before. (He was to become WEA secretary of the whole area.)

Because I was always around, I was seized on to do voluntary research on the Social Democratic Federation, a left-wing political group. This meant my studying reports and interviewing all kinds of workers including the secretaries of trade unions, teachers and city councillors. 'This whole business fills me with enthusiasm,' I wrote home. 'Visiting the schools, especially the Mixed Infants, is my favourite part.' This seems to be the first time I showed interest in small children.

By the end of February I was feeling pretty bellicose about the economic situation.

Firms are shutting down more & more factories; there is going to be a wage dispute in the pottery industry on top of cotton & railways. It's fierce winter up here – snowing again – & people are going mad for want of work. They all agree – workers & workless – that they'll see the present economic system busted before they agree to a reduction in wages.

I felt it was time I went down a coalmine and saw for myself. Ted Hobson arranged it for me. No protective clothing, no helmet for this visitor, such as Queen Elizabeth II was to wear when she descended her mine after the war. As the lift doors clanged shut and the winding machinery went into operation I confess to having felt qualms. It was darker than I expected and the drop seemed to go on for ever. I had plenty of time to remember an incident in my childhood when an outside food lift filled with blue-rimmed nursery china and gingerbread cake, which brought up our meals from the basement kitchen to our top floor, broke down and went crashing to the bottom. At last I was at the coalface:

Not being an adept at the frog's walk which the miners cultivate, I felt very old and stiff, especially when crawling 20 yards on hands & knees along a conveyor bristling with lumps of coal. The flying dust gave me a stye in my eye – but it was an impressive and exciting experience.

One morning Ted Hobson and I were walking past the local cemetery. He told me the story of a friend of his, one of the 'cards' in whom the Potteries abounded. Old Jim was coughing his lungs out by the cemetery wall and Ted condoled with him. 'There's many a poor fellow lying in there', retorted Jim, 'as 'd be *glad* to have my cough.' Ted then suggested that I should accompany the district nurse on one of her rounds – not a special occasion, just an ordinary visit. I leapt at the chance to *see* sociology for a change; though I wondered how the patients would react to a strange visitor. I need not have worried. The majority were so indignant at their housing conditions – we were shown a staircase with a large hole in it and a bedroom floor with a cavity through which one could view the living-room below – that they were only too glad of a sympathetic audience. The rest were too apathetic to care.

There was one family scene in particular that reminded me of an etching by Gustave Doré of London's slums in the last century. A mother had given birth in a corner of the living-room the day before and the midwife had had to bath the baby in an empty food can, there being no other suitable utensil. (The tin can was to serve me as an illustration in many subsequent political speeches.) Mother and child were enthroned on a pile of rags. In another corner of the room was another pile of rags and three babies of one, two and three years old whimpering and snuggling among them. They were all feverish, said the nurse. The rest of the family lay about listlessly or crouched in the shadows, not well enough to go to school. Such dire poverty, said my companion, was not unusual in the slump, in the North.

I realized to my delight that Ted was grooming me for a political mission. That evening or soon after, two delegates came to 1 South Walk, Meir, the Hobsons' home, and asked me to let my name go forward as Labour candidate for Stone in the forthcoming general election. I would have the unanimous support of their branch. Stone was a mainly rural area and its Labour strength, such as it was, lay in the branches nearest the adjoining industrial area. I found the delegates, a Mr and Mrs Price, most appealing, with ideas for redesigning pottery on William Morris lines, as well as for reforming the workers' lives. Though I was not in the end adopted for the constituency, my short experience as a branch candidate embedded me deeper in Labour politics. It also had an effect on my relations with Frank.

Both Frank and Evan Durbin expected a general election to come perhaps in April 1931, certainly later in that year. Ramsay MacDonald's Labour Government, elected on a minority vote in 1929 not long before the Wall Street crash, was now being battered from all sides, whether by the Tory bankers of the City of London or the socialist unemployed in Stoke-on-Trent. A debating team from the Oxford Labour Club had recently visited a team of our WEA students in Stoke. The motion, expressing 'profound dissatisfaction with the present [Labour] Government's policy', was carried amidst stormy applause and cries of 'Socialism! Socialism! Socialism!'

Hugh Gaitskell and Evan Durbin were to stand for Labour in the neighbouring Medway towns of Chatham and Gillingham; but there was a problem for Frank, if not two problems. With his faith in Conservative economics impaired but by no means replaced by socialist beliefs, should he stand, and if so, where? 'I suppose in the most hopeless seat possible,' he wrote to me – I being the second problem.

Frank had been genuinely excited at my invitation to go forward for Labour in Stone. He offered to help me financially but added, 'I hope that won't annoy you.' At the same time he was passionately absorbed in the work of his 'Economy' committee for the Conservative Research Department. Every letter contained some reference to it. There was the time when Professor Lionel Robbins came to give evidence, accompanied by Evan Durbin looking like the socialist intellectual he was, in old grey flannel trousers. 'Even Lionel felt bound to remonstrate,' reported Frank.

'Durb, true to his promise, did not speak a single word throughout the two hours' enquiry, though he occasionally grinned at me in a superior yet intimate way.' Frank went on to describe 'Durb' as 'omniscient and all-psychological-powerful' in his eyes. 'It will be interesting to see what will happen if you and he happen to disagree on a question of policy.' We never did – except once, over Frank's entering the House of Lords, when Evan's policy, not mine, was rightly adopted.

Naturally Frank and I did not see eye to eye on the causes of the slump, as investigated by another of his committees. Their word was 'over-production', ours in Stoke was 'under-consumption'. That put the difference in a nutshell. But it did not get us any nearer to solving the country's problems or our own problem either.

The fact was that our wholehearted agreement to postpone the wedding indefinitely had lifted the pressure from Frank, but it also isolated me to some extent and stepped up the influence of my socialist friends. Because most of our arguments now had to be conducted by letter (we were meeting only one evening a week), they began to take on a more rigid shape. We were both articulate and nothing of our differences was lost in the writing. I in particular was becoming dogmatic. From having known the minimum about bread-and-butter politics, I suddenly felt that in one blinding flash I had come to see and understand everything. You could not be young and live for weeks in a North Staffs council house and feel anything else.

At first Frank developed a hope that he and I would divide our universe between us, I dispensing criticism in the realms of literature, he laying down the law on politics. He would even deliberately disparage his own wit and powers of expression in order not to encroach on my kingdom. And to stop me invading his. At the beginning of March, for instance, he made what he called the 'gloomy admission' that my letters were superior to his. 'Your imagination seems to give you pleasure and the result is greater pleasure for the reader. Mine (such as it is) fatigues me unutterably and it is lucky if any reader bites very deep into its fruit.' He compared himself to Peter Fleming who would surely be editor of the *Spectator* in a few years.

I was wondering only yesterday when talking to Peter why it was that I had such good ideas and yet was so ultimately sterile. People like Peter and you seem to draw inspiration from inside yourselves. When I make a good remark it is because something someone has said has suggested something good to me. But nothing I say myself ever suggests anything good to me, so I soon come to a stop.

In the weekly diary he wrote for me, Frank had noted in February that he had come upon 'Roy Harrod parodying me to Seymour Berry', eldest son of Lord Camrose, the newspaper proprietor. 'The parody consisted entirely of long pauses!' Frank's letter proceeded:

Writers like you (this time I won't add Peter) seem to get carried away. Still, perhaps Prof Lindemann is lower on the scale even than I am. And he hasn't got you to cure him, as you have begun to cure me of other forms of sterility.

While I was plying Frank with *Middlemarch*, the Prof had made him read a book on physics. The Prof's artistic taste was execrable. His rooms at Christ Church were hung with enormous oil paintings of kittens entangled in skeins of wool and fleshly pre-war *mädchen*.

I can't find any fault in you [Frank continued] except your attitude to my attitude to the kind of parties I like. I think you are rather hard on me sometimes about it. I admit it's worthy of nothing better than a callow, weak, vain and snobbish hobbledehoy, but you know by now that that's what half of me is.

As if to give me one more chance to approve of his attitude to parties, he went on to describe the latest:

I got on rather well when I was asked to meet Charlie Chaplin last night. I got sandwiched behind a door along with Charlie Chaplin, the Duke of York, the Duchess of York and Bill Astor. Everyone was embarrassed since no one had been introduced except Bill, whose eyes glittered with pleasure. . . .

But if Frank had willingly handed over the literary world to me and Peter Fleming, with the possible addition of my friend Goronwy Rees to make a triumvirate, he refused to abdicate on politics.

It was on the meaning of Conservatism that we had our sharpest (written) exchanges. Frank was usually too tired after a day's work at the Conservative Office in Great Queen Street to tackle the question as a whole, but we managed to have quite a set-to on the rather eclectic subject of 'rule'. After many conversations with Ted Hobson I had become convinced that paternalism was no good to the workers. Men of good will from all classes could back them up, but it was the workers' own efforts – *their* organizations, *their* clubs, *their* political party – which alone would win the day.

Frank happened to be suffering from what he thought was rheumatism in his back when this tirade arrived. Did I not see, he asked, that if the people could achieve everything *for themselves*, his own *raison d'être* as a politician – a member of the governing class – would disappear?

You seem to me not to realize the importance of *rule* in life. I believe in authority. [That sentence was crossed out.] I look upon it as a fortunate accident that men living in society require co-ordination . . . correction and guidance. The accident is fortunate in that it gives the opportunity for rulers to arise. If all men were perfect, it would be very difficult for the 'Men born to be Kings', even minor Kings, to serve a useful purpose and their special talents not to be lost to the world.

I agree that independence in the last resort is essential for the development of human character. The solution is a compromise. 'Representative institutions' seems as good a way as any other of giving it effect. But I can't and won't believe that the only object of the one who intends to be a politician all his life should be to *represent* others.

The truth was that in my new independent way of life at Stoke I was not in the mood to accept 'correction' or 'guidance' even from 'minor Kings'. Our abortive engagement had brought me as near as I have ever got to a series of sex skirmishes. They were not part of a declared 'sex war' but neither were they flirtatious fencing. I had stayed with Naomi Mitchison for the second time in Scotland and her influence was increasing. She did not wear a wedding-ring, 'on feminist grounds', as she said. I also stayed with her for a spring weekend on Bledlow Ridge, when she was enduring 'the deep heartache' of a love-affair that was coming to an end. I tried to comfort her and said, 'Listen to the larks.' Scores of them were rising in spirals from the ridge. Naomi made a face. 'I hate the sound. It's like a little screw.'

I had felt a touch of bitterness myself when answering the last letter from Michael Hope before he left America for home. He had got engaged to Christine, my great friend at Lady Margaret Hall and Naomi's cousin, but there had been no letter of congratulations from me. Writing at the end of January from Stoke, which I described to Michael as 'a lovely loathly place', I now explained why:

The reason I didn't write to you was because I *couldn't*. . . . When you emerged together in the Times I was feeling so personally sore & worried about Life & Things (Marriage I suppose) that I simply couldn't face seeing my bitterness on paper. Nor could you have done. But now it's all right. And I feel more than ever devoted to you & Christine. It isn't quite so selfish as it sounds, because as a matter of fact . . . Frank & I are by no means out of the wood. But I've at last had the courage to clear an open space & enjoy myself temporarily. . . .

I ended the letter with a summary of my situation and Frank's:

We are both reluctant triflers in a way. Still, I'm quite deeply in love with him, so you & I are keeping step in a way – though as far as marriage goes, I'm still on the first lap of the tortoise race.

Stoke, of course, was my 'open space' in the entanglements of 'the wood'. The letters and dialogues that Frank and I exchanged on the subject of sexual equality tended only to make the thickets thicker. The best to be hoped for was that the arguments would peter out through the pressure of our respective work.

February 17th Elizabeth darling, I meant to draw an elaborate analysis of the ideal form of intellectual relationship between men and women. But you won't be perhaps sorry to hear that you have missed it for the present (though you may get it in conversation on Friday).

February 18th [after the reception of a 'brilliant' expostulatory letter from me] What right have I to say that I could never treat you as an intellectual equal? Not that I ever actually said quite that, though I think you thought I did. . . .

He then went on to credit me with 'a better memory, more imagination, more originality I think, much more eloquence and of course most of the aesthetic perceptions (nearly all of which I obviously lack)'. He argued that in some sense he was fonder of my career than of his own, citing his immense pleasure at my being on the candidates' list for Stone.

What does all this come to? Not very much. I admit your indictment. I admit that I have two ways of behaving to you.

He meant the way of deferring to me and the way of dogmatizing or dictating to me.

But I have also a third I haven't mentioned. I would labour for your success, if you would accept my help and tell me of your ambitions. The fault is yours, Elizabeth, that my third attitude is so seldom allowed to appear. Partly because you are too proud to accept help, partly because *you hide yourself from me.*

After this offer and appeal he could not resist returning yet again to his longed-for solution of a division of spheres between us. In literature and painting he would 'of course' defer to me:

What you don't realize is that I know a great deal about politics. My views may be terribly dull and even inconsistent, but if one treated English politics in its widest aspects as a technical subject, I have the wide knowledge that one would expect of an experienced if stupid technician.

You think that you have a right to be treated as an intellectual equal in our discussions. Well so you have, as the superior possibly, but not as someone with an equal knowledge of the subject yet.

Some of my confused feelings on love, the relations of the sexes and indeed the course of civilization were to emerge in yet another attempt at creative writing. When I was researching this book I discovered a complete writing-pad ('Ben Jonson Bond – Equally good for gold, steel or quill pens. 10½d.') with all its forty-seven pages covered by the script of a play in my handwriting called 'The Absolute and the Absolutely-not or The Egg and the Ego'. Its theme was order, dogmatism and clear-cut distinctions versus a possible new world of indeterminate being, where even the sexes will not be completely distinct and everything will be ultimately united by merging into its opposite and producing something new. But when the egg is hatched on the altar of Hermes and Aphrodite, the Priest – an absolute dogmatist – kills the emergent life. 'I was afraid of it. It was the horrible uncertainty. Nothing would have been one way or the other any more.'

Frank's sudden illness put a stop to all this. It began on 8 March after his usual Friday visit to Stoke, with what he thought was again rheumatism in his back – 'not agony you know darling but just continual discomfort such as I imagine my mother suffers without complaint in her rather easier moments'. The 'rheumatism', however, turned into bronchial pneumonia and pleurisy. At first his mother felt unable to have him nursed at Peverel Court, despite there being a butler who spoilt 'Mr Frank', not to mention a full complement of other staff. So he retired to his digs in Halsey Street, where I visited him every afternoon. I used to read Tennyson aloud, knowing that he would be asleep before the Lady of Shalott had taken the forbidden look at Sir Lancelot. By 20 March, as he still had a temperature, his mother took him in and his grandmother, Lady Jersey, came over from Middleton to cheer him with stories of the Duke of Marlborough. 'I *adore* and admire her tremendously, more and more,' he wrote. He also thanked me: 'You have been an angel. But for you I should not be alive.' As soon as he could use his brain again he proposed to write an anonymous attack on Baldwin – 'pure vitriol of course but of rather an academic kind I hope'.

At the end of March he was in a nursing home, where streams of visitors arrived: Basil Dufferin and Freddy Birkenhead, Peter Fleming, John Betjeman. He was convalescing in an atmosphere of champagne at the Metropole Hotel, Brighton, in mid April, where he saw Sir Oswald Mosley orating on the pier. Mosley was said to be 'gugga' as a result of his founding the New Party, but the hotel manager described him to Frank as 'devilishly attractive'. I had got myself introduced to Lady Cynthia Mosley, Sir Oswald's wife, one Sunday evening in Stoke after a political meeting. I was under the impression that she was still its *Labour* member of Parliament. 'Unfortunately I offered my services to the wrong person,' I wrote home. 'For that very Sunday evening the papers were whispering of Sir Oswald's resignation and on Monday, shouting. The Mosleys are very sick at Stoke's firm refusal to follow in their wild goose chase.'

Among Frank's other visitors to the Metropole were Maureen Guinness (who was soon to marry Basil Dufferin, with Frank as best man), Esmond Warner and Evelyn Waugh. A few months later Evelyn was to stimulate Frank with a recital of his own achievements. 'Evelyn has finished his travel book', wrote Frank to me, 'and is getting on with a novel which he thinks is going to be the best anyone has ever dreamt of writing. The further it goes the better he thinks it gets, so that there really must be something rather successful about it.' The new novel was *Black Mischief.*

While Frank was in Brighton I took a ten-day holiday in Italy with Mary Pakenham and David Cecil. Our host was Leslie Hartley, future author of *The Go-Between* and other delights, who owned a flat on a canal with a private gondola and gondolier. I found Leslie then and always the personification of benevolence. David and I travelled out together by wagon-lit. I sketched his face – easy to get a likeness, since his hereditary 'Cecil' features also had an unmistakable stamp of their own – while he read an immensely long letter from Rachel MacCarthy, daughter of Desmond MacCarthy, the brilliant literary critic. David read aloud to me certain descriptive passages which we both agreed had a Wordsworthian beauty. It was evident that Rachel loved him and I shall always believe that that letter of hers brought about their blissfully happy marriage.

It was my first visit to Venice. I remember that halcyon afternoon when we floated on the lagoon in Leslie's gondola and David read aloud to us *The Eve of St Mark*. He was as it were taking the place of Keats' 'fair maid' who, in the poem, read the legend to herself from an ancient book. To the surprise of everyone, David included, the poem finally landed us in the same place as the maid:

> . . . At length her constant eyelids come
> Upon the fervent martyrdom;
> Then lastly to his holy shrine,
> Exalt amid the tapers' shine
> At Venice.

Dear David

by Elizabeth Harme

Sketch I made of David Cecil in the train to Venice, April 1931

After trips to Bologna and Ravenna, where I fell in love with Byzantine lambs, Mary and I went off to Rome for a few days. Again my first visit. Roman Rome meant everything to me, medieval Rome nothing. Maria and I – she said she did not care for the name Mary and I have always called her Maria – were closely linked by our devotion to Frank, and also by two unexpected connections. Cecily Hacon, a girl at Headington School whose double I was said to be, was Maria's great friend in the Pakenhams' Oxfordshire home of North Aston; and for one term Maria herself was at boarding-school with Armorel, who she agreed was 'different'. I learnt a lot about life at North Aston from Maria, who had studied art in Oxford and was now continuing in Chelsea. Everything about her, especially the very faint lisp with which her delectable stories were told, reminded me of Frank, to my great satisfaction; while I, she said, was so totally unlike him that we were sure to be very happy if we ever married.

The comrades at Stoke had taken it for granted that we were going to marry and presented us at the end of the session with cruets, an early-morning tea-set and fruit bowls. Ted and Maria Hobson were equally sure; in the summer, when Frank visited me in Stoke, they vacated their double bed and put us into it. We placed the bolster, like a sword of Damocles, between us, and though it was not a total barrier, it did manage to remind us that we must 'wait till marriage'.

Meanwhile my Socialism and his Conservatism apparently continued on their highly divergent paths. On 8 May I spoke on behalf of the Labour candidate at the Stroud by-election. The bright red leaflets advertising our meeting made even me, in my state of social *saeva indignatio*, smile. The two 'famous supporting speakers' they announced were Mr O. G. Willey, candidate for West Birmingham, and Miss Elizabeth Harman '(of London)'. Since the year was 1931, our standard-bearer was soundly beaten.

Soon afterwards I spent a political weekend at Easton Lodge, the luxury home of Edward VII's mistress, Daisy, Countess of Warwick, which she lent to left-wing socialists after her social conscience awoke and began giving her trouble. The contrast between the furnishings of Easton Lodge and us sandalled socialists was bizarre. I shared my second strange double bed of the year with a nice girl called Pease, daughter of a former secretary of the Fabian Society. It was a four-poster, decked with frills and pink satin bows. The kidney-shaped dressing-table, on which Miss Pease put nothing but a brush and comb and I the minimum of make-up, was elaborately swathed in muslin. Downstairs Douglas and Margaret Cole told us, from behind banks of hothouse blooms, that we should never get socialism until we had abolished the entire Civil Service as well, of course, as the idle rich.

Towards the end of May, Frank described his visit to Sir William Beveridge, Director of the London School of Economics, and Mrs Mair, the lady whom Beveridge afterwards married. Mrs Mair, Frank wrote, 'spent most of the week-end advising me against early marriage . . .'. Hugh Dalton was there, the Labour politician whose father had been one of Queen Victoria's canons; he tried to extract information about the Conservative Research Department. The letter ended: 'We *must* manage Commem, darling.'

On the day of the Balliol Commem ball Frank and I at last announced our engagement. It seemed as inevitable now as the postponement had seemed before. David and Rachel were in the party, which was a very jolly one. That did not stop Frank being overpowered by sleep at midnight. I suddenly felt that as an 'engaged' girl I must stick to him. So together we crept into an empty bed in one of the absent student's rooms and both fell asleep instantly. In the morning the scout burst in and shouted at us in the words of the station hotel manager at Stoke: 'Get out of here. You can't do that there here, you can't.'

As far as I was concerned, our engagement slipped by with hardly a hiccup. One weekend in August we quarrelled about politics. The Labour Government was about to collapse and Frank hoped that the 'tenderness' engendered in me by his illness would not collapse with it. 'However, all will be well after 26 October,' he wrote, the 27th being the day we had fixed for our wedding. By the end of August our socialist wrangle had reached stalemate. Frank admitted respect for my Labour feelings. 'All my nobler self feels it too,' he wrote, but concluded, 'If I was less *closed* and more responsive generally, I might throw over everything for it, but as I am, darling, you know it wouldn't last.'

Frank thought my mother 'sweet' and her arrangements for my trousseau most generous. There was only one jolt when she helped me buy bath towels from Gaylor & Pope in Marylebone High Street, where the customers' payments ran in little round boxes along railway lines above the counters to the lady at the terminal, who put in the customers' change and sent the little boxes whizzing back. While waiting for our box, my mother hopefully asked, 'Does Frank like a *very* rough bath towel?' 'Certainly not,' said Frank when I put the question to him. 'The softer the better.' He began to feel nervous again at the picture conjured up of a *very* rough, manly man.

My father went down well with his mother, who liked tall men.

My own introduction into Frank's Bright Young Set might have caused me alarm, had I known what was going on in one area beneath the surface. The only hint came when Frank and I, Maureen Dufferin, Baby Jungman and another girl were travelling by taxi to Bryanston Square for a party. Frank decided to be dropped off at Marble Arch. After he left I sensed for a brief moment that the conversation was deliberately gathering itself together over my head and I was being excluded. The feeling passed as suddenly as it had come. And though I was indeed an Oxford interloper, snatching away one of their brightest young things, Frank's set were never anything but warm and welcoming to me, once the step was irrevocable. In return I learned to speak their language – 'pith' for everything good and nice, 'path' for everything nasty. I may have begun by being 'path' myself, but I had worked my way to 'pith' before the wedding.

Yet Evelyn Waugh's *Letters*, published in 1980, make it clear that he was leading some kind of opposition to our marriage. In July 1931 he described to my friend Nancy Mitford a party given by Mrs Beatrice Guinness (known as 'Gloomy Beatrice', 'Gloomy Guinness' or just 'Gloomy'), mother of Baby Jungman by her first husband:

Gloomy Beatrice gave a great banquet for Harman & all the people were frightening ones just eight years older than Harman you know the sort I mean & she said 'I'm sure Miss Harman knows *nobody* here' & led her round like royalty & afterwards said 'Well, we haven't time to make *real* friends yet have we.' And Baby wasn't at that party so I thought it was all right.

– meaning that he hoped Baby rejected me and my designs on Frank –

but Harman met Baby at Lady Howard de Walden's and there she made such bad blood about David & Wanda & Baby that now Baby thinks she's a sweet girl. Mary Pakenham is offering 5 to 1 on the wedding & not finding many takers. I pretend to have schemes [to stop the wedding] but I haven't any really I just trust in GOD.

GOD in this case was on the side of the small battalions. And Evelyn's story of Wanda Baillie-Hamilton was a red herring. I once saw Wanda across the Ritz but never met her or knew her except as a socialite name; nor did Baby feel the least jealousy of her and David Cecil, knowing well that David was courting Rachel. It was generous of 'Gloomy Guinness' to introduce me around, since she was a little in love with Frank herself and Frank had been more than a little in love with Baby. Luckily I did not suspect Evelyn's change of front, regarding him as an ally ever since he urged me to follow Frank that first Christmas at Pakenham. Evelyn's war (undeclared by him and unsuspected by me) was not to be terminated for fifteen years.

In July Frank and I went for the night to visit his great-aunt Caroline Pakenham, whose heir he was. I had paid my last visit to Lynchfield. This was my first to Bernhurst. Aunt Caroline was eighty-nine. When Frank came into the drawing-room her niece and companion, Edie Ward, said brightly, 'Here's Frank. You know Frank, Ant Caroline.' (Miss Ward's home was in California.) 'Have you had a nice day with the scouts, dear?' asked Aunt Caroline. In her eyes Frank was still seven years old. At dinner there was no question of her accepting me. We had just started when she suddenly laid down her knife and fork, and turning to Edie said loudly and menacingly, 'Who is that woman? I didn't invite her here.' For the rest of dinner there were skirmishes between an angry Aunt Caroline, who kept taking out her false teeth, and Edie and the butler who kept putting them in again. They did it so deftly, whirling her chair round to face the wall while the operation proceeded, that for some time I did not realize what was up.

It sounds a macabre visit. But the magic of Bernhurst began to work on that first day and has never ceased during the fifty-five years that have followed.

Pakenham Hall again in August. Frank and I were travelling on the mail train from Euston and Frank wrote: 'I never get into that train without some sort of thrill, even when alone, so it ought to be lovely.' It was. My sister Kitty, Maurice Bowra, Evelyn Waugh and I played tennis together. We were all about the same height but Kitty was the only one who could hit the ball. Uncle Eddie, the poet and writer (Lord Dunsany), came over for lunch one day and conducted a literary seminar with Maurice, David Cecil and the rest of us. Accidentally the maestro referred to Tolstoy's novel as 'Peace and War'. This put Maurice in a quandary. A few minutes later he took the deferential way out and also referred to 'Peace and War'. '*War and Peace*, not *Peace and War*,' thundered Uncle Eddie. 'They always said Oxford was no good, and now I see they're right.' The Pakenham children loved him, calling him Lord 'Insany', a title which endeared him to John Betjeman. This time on the last evening everyone had to perform either with a song or a speech. John Betjeman recited 'Mumbo Jumbo, God of the Congo' by Vachel Lindsay and had us all beating time with plates and glasses. Maurice's song went back to the Great War:

> Send out the Army and the Navy,
> Send out the ships upon the sea,
> Send out my brother, my sister and my mother,
> But for Gawd's sake don't send me.

David sang in a plaintive voice:

> My mother's an apple-pie maker,
> My father he fiddles for gin,
> My sister walks streets for her living –
> Good God!
> How the money rolls in!

To his usual Irish assortment of songs Edward now contributed a Polish patriotic song in Polish, and Christine something picked up from a drunk in a Dublin street beginning:

> It's Mick McGilligan's daughter Mary Ann
> She's the arms and shoulders on her like a man.

Both Henry Lamb and Rachel MacCarthy sang French songs, Henry about a knife-grinder who seduced the women of the house. The Misses Harman sang 'Drink to me only with thine Eyes' as a duet. Maria remembers that she, Pansy and Frank 'certainly did *not* sing – though doubtless Frank made some speeches. When conversation flagged everyone sang "One more river to cross".'

The shadow of the election was falling over Frank and me. Stanley Baldwin announced the date: 27 October, our supposed wedding date. We postponed the wedding for a week, to 3 November. Up to the actual announcement of the election Frank still had thoughts of standing as a Conservative. I must have asked him whether he would want me to sit on his platform, for he wrote: 'As regards standing for Parliament, I will do whatever pleases you. As long as you wanted me to get in, longed for me to get in, I mean, I shouldn't care what platform you did or didn't appear on.' This knot was cut by urgent requests for help from Frank's Tory friends who were already standing, Alan Lennox-Boyd (later Lord Boyd) and Lady Astor. He decided to campaign if possible for both and was titillated by a piece of gossip passed on to him by Alan and to me by Frank on 12 October: 'By the way, darling, he [Alan] was staying with Winston Churchill last weekend and Winston said to him, "I hear that young Pakenham is likely to turn Socialist soon." Winston Churchill doesn't know me so it's publicity of a sort, isn't it? I was very pleased, I must say.' Frank had a secret admiration for Churchill, though his mother abhorred him as the architect of Gallipoli.

During the week before the election Frank and I were working away against each other's respective parties. Frank was granted leave from his office to dash down to Plymouth on Nancy Astor's behalf. 'I spoke at four meetings', he wrote, 'and got good at the end. I hope you spoke marvellously.' It was in King's Norton, Birmingham, that I was supporting Dick Mitchison as Labour candidate. Frank wished that Naomi had been standing instead. 'I would give a lot to see her in Parliament,' he told me. I spoke enthusiastically for Dick; and Tom Baxter, his agent, prevailed upon Naomi to wear her wedding-ring for Dick's sake. But even this sacrifice could not save King's Norton, or indeed any area of Birmingham, from the Labour holocaust of 1931.

On the evening of polling day Frank went to a Bloomsbury party where he questioned Lytton Strachey on his political opinions.

'Whom did you vote for?' Frank asked.

'I voted for Edgar Wallace,' replied Strachey in his squeaky voice.

'I suppose because you thought he was such a good writer?'

'No,' squeaked Strachey, 'I thought he was a very bad writer. I thought he was such a good politician.'

I was taken to hear the election results at Selfridges by Frank's uncle Arthur Villiers, a director of Barings Bank as well as founder of the Eton Manor Boys' Club at Hackney Wick. I had been to a party at the club shortly before, when a tug-of-war between the East Enders and the Visitors resulted in our titled anchor-girl being practically cut in half by the rope which had been inadvertently slip-knotted round her waist.

At Selfridges everyone except me was bubbling with relief as well as champagne. Never in living memory had socialists been so decisively thrashed. As Arthur Villiers escorted me through the jubilant throng, a fellow banker came up to him.

'Great day, Arthur! Great day, what?'

Arthur glanced sideways at me and replied very quietly: 'It depends which side you're on.'

His friend stared as if at a madman and moved hastily away. There was only one side at Selfridges that day.

Since 1915 Arthur Villiers had been Frank's surrogate father. I always loved him for his quizzical and original mind. He never said what one expected.

On the evening of 2 November a note arrived from Frank:

My darling, Just a line to tell you that I love you and to say how I am looking forward to being married to you. Your loving loving Frank.

Later, when I was researching *Victoria R.I.* I was to be reminded of this note. She wrote to Prince Albert before *their* wedding:

Dearest, – . . . How are you today, and have you slept well? I have rested very well, and feel very comfortable today. . . . Send one word when you, my most dearly loved bridegroom, will be ready. Thy ever-faithful,
    Victoria R.

Our wedding-day arrived in a whirlwind of flying autumn leaves and white tulle. At one moment I thought my veil would be snatched from my head and come to roost in the trees of Parliament Square like a mad white bird. Otherwise proceedings were in almost every way conventional: my dress of cream satin with love-knots, wreath of orange blossom, bouquet of roses and lilies of the valley; the church St Margaret's, Westminster; the order of service in Gothic lettering; no address; the hymn, 'O Perfect Love'; the march, Mendelssohn; the reception in Grosvenor House, Park Lane.

However, there were two or three unusual features. I had chosen as many as twelve bridesmaids, all sisters or cousins, in a rainbow mixture of velvet jackets worn over their white satin dresses. Freddy Birkenhead elevated the part of best man to one of refined artistry, combining comedy with wit: he and Frank arrived at the church somewhat late (luckily I was later) having found themselves at first inside the adjacent Westminster Abbey. When they noticed the dearth of congregation, Freddy said to Frank consolingly, 'People don't go to weddings much these days.' At the reception his speech presented Frank as an endearing prince of eccentrics, who might *seem* to be correctly dressed in a tailcoat with white carnation but whose socks were probably odd and trousers held up with safety-pins.

There was a strong Chamberlain contingent at the wedding, beginning with Canon Carnegie who officiated at St Margaret's. He was the second husband of my great-aunt Mary Chamberlain, Uncle Joe's third wife. Frank forgot to pay him the £5 generally contributed to the church after such an event, and so we never dared attend the subsequent get-togethers for young married couples to which Canon Carnegie kindly invited us.

But despite the strong Chamberlain representation, the head of Frank's office, my cousin Neville Chamberlain, was not present, nor did he permit Frank's colleagues from the Research Department to attend the reception. This, despite the fact that his wife, my spirited cousin Annie (sister of Horace Cole, the famous Irish joker), was present and their daughter Dorothy was one of the bridesmaids. I can only imagine that Cousin Neville had heard the same rumour about 'young Pakenham' becoming a socialist as had reached the ears of Winston Churchill, and thought it best not to embroil himself too deeply with a young man of such curious fancies.

Our honeymoon was to be in Ireland. When we arrived at Euston to catch the mail train, the steward had no sleepers booked under the name of Pakenham. We wandered disconsolately up and down the platform – would our first night be spent packed like eggs in a box? – until we found a reservation for 'Mr and Mrs Buckingham'. I had discovered early on that my new name was not an easy one to hear on the telephone.

When we arrived at Liverpool in a November gale, covered in confetti and enquiring for the Irish ferry, the sympathetic ticket collector took one pitying look at us and said, 'Don't go to Ireland. Go to Blackpool. Just down the coast. There's a train leaving now. Blackpool will just suit you.'

9

First Times
· *1931–4* ·

Our marriage got off to a rough start. All the aunts, uncles and cousins who wrote to thank my mother for the wedding reception agreed in hoping that we would not spend our first night crossing the notoriously savage Irish Sea. Cousin Fred Bellamy was kind enough to add: 'Elizabeth is an all-round "topper". . . .' But it was Frank who showed himself the 'topper' on that wild Tuesday night. For the first time in his life he was not seasick, though we were tossed and rolled about unmercifully, our boat depositing us two hours late in Dublin so that we missed the connection to Mullingar.

We had intended to spend the Wednesday motoring to Connemara, our honeymoon choice. But exhaustion set in. We decided to spend the first day and night at Pakenham Hall. It was the wrong decision. Pakenham had always been associated for both of us with a full house, and for me with the noise of jolly parties – someone to pluck the ancient harp in the hall, strum on the piano, sing songs, make speeches, recite poetry. I wrote to my mother from Ireland after receiving a letter from her:

It's marvellous to know you enjoyed the wedding as much as we did, but I don't suppose you felt as dreary & depressed on Wednesday night as we gradually became, despite our first manly efforts to conceal it. Pakenham was really the *worst* place in the world to stop at. Though it looks lovely in the autumn it is incredibly melancholy – so vast & solitary & decaying.

I went on to quote a poem my mother had taught me in childhood:

> The trees are Indian princes now
> But soon will turn to ghosts.

We seemed already to see the ghosts behind the gold.

But the feeling of the empty house [I continued] which always before had been overflowing, was even worse.

135

Nor was sex the elixir and panacea it was to become, despite the fact that Dr Helena Wright (a world-famous gynaecologist who lived well into her nineties) had prepared both Frank and me for our first experience. However, as soon as we got to Connemara, I concluded to my mother, our honeymoon became 'perfect'.

I was writing to her from the Renvyle Hotel on the west coast of Ireland, recently built and opened as a commercial venture by the Irish wit Oliver St John Gogarty. For our three days at Renvyle we were able to enjoy all the characteristics of an Irish autumn in the west: flashes of sunshine over intense green grass, heather and white boulders; flying storms over the sea, great banks of seaweed as bright as the beech trees that were still laden with golden boughs.

I was not quite so pleased with the west sociologically as I was with it aesthetically. While walking along the shore we dropped in on a cabin where an ancient crone crouched over a turf fire. I asked her a friendly question. She stared at me blankly. Then Frank tried. Immediately she became alert seeming to understand him and replied with a smile in language, however, that baffled both of us. I had another try. She ignored me but again spoke – to the *man* in her sights.

We had one other typical encounter when driving from Connemara to Dunsany Castle, Meath, our next and last stop. By the side of one of the straight roads we came upon a wagon with a wheel off. We pulled up and asked the disconsolate couple inside whether we could do anything to help. They kept us talking pleasantly for half an hour while we made suggestions and they politely turned them down. Then a second wagon turned up bringing a spare wheel. Our couple smiled engagingly and said, 'Well, thanks for your company.' Edward's chauffeur, Mr White, originally from Birmingham, who had been lent to us with Edward's car, was not too happy at the waste of time. But the Irish conviviality gave us a warm feeling on our hitherto solitary honeymoon.

Dunsany proved to be a blessing in every way and I learnt a great deal in those four days about Frank's brilliant and eccentric uncle and his self-effacing and saintly aunt. They were a devoted couple, calling each other 'Pony' and 'Mink', but Uncle Eddie issued commands to Aunt Beatrice as if he were the driver and she the horse. 'Beatrice, fetch me a new quill. Beatrice, wash these paint brushes.' (He was always writing, painting or modelling when I knew him.) I saw the river beside which they had stood together when they too were on honeymoon. The story went that she said, for something to say, 'I wonder how deep it is?' 'If you really want to know', he replied, 'you'd better go in and see' – and he gave her a push. I saw the rock salt on their dinner-table and heard him denounce table salt as if it were poison. I saw his dogs, all with long waving tails whatever their breed and heard him declare docked tails an abomination. I ate their excellent kippers and listened to him accusing the whole restaurant world of selling fakes. 'Don't touch them, Elizabeth. They're *dyed* not *smoked*.'

It was now a week since our marriage and that absurd fate overtook me which every bride was supposed to avoid by herself settling the wedding day. We had originally fixed on 27 October as I have said; in my diary for that date were written the anticipatory words, 'Wedding. I marry Frank after all'; but they were followed by a curt 'No!' The difference between 27 October and 3 November made hay of my calculations. While staying at Dunsany I was stricken with pain far worse than childbirth, so severe that Aunt Beatrice in alarm sent for her Irish doctor. After he had given me painkillers and sedatives, I enquired: 'Is there any way of stopping this ghastly performance? I've had it every month since I was in my teens but this has been the worst go of all. Would a baby do the trick?' He looked wise. 'Very likely.' 'Good,' I said, 'this time next month I shall be pregnant.' And I was.

The agonizing condition was known as dysmenorrhoea in the little medical diaries my father used to give me, a suitably unattractive name. The strange thing was that though my parents were both doctors, professional advice to relieve me was never sought. They were very sympathetic, but as I rolled about and howled they seemed to accept the situation as if it were indeed the 'Curse of Eve'.

We returned home on 12 November to 'Stairways', our cottage in the village of Stone, near Aylesbury, Buckinghamshire. Its descriptive name was contributed by Frank's mother and it was she who made it available to us for a first home. Stairways had been two semidetached cottages on Lady Longford's estate, now thrown into one for us. The little house had two staircases, one at each end, so that they seemed to be the main features of the building. Maria reported to me Lady Longford's ideas for its name: 'Mama suggests the cot should be called "Scala" or "Escaliers" pronounced with a broad British accent, or even "Stairways". I thought the distemper looked all right,' added Maria, ' – no need to panic.' And she appended a sketch of a distemperer painting our tiny dining-room in a dignified shade of terracotta.

We had room to entertain up to four house-guests, and to this end we started off by employing a married couple: Bill, a sandy-haired Glaswegian, to drive the car (neither of us could drive) and wait at table, Jessie to cook. They were supposed to share the cleaning but Bill relinquished that privilege to his wife. He spent a great deal of his time in the village pub, his favourite motto being, 'Set a thief to catch a thief'; which meant that he would look after our interests by stopping others from robbing us. We also had a single basement room on the Embankment in London, where we stayed once or twice a week, and I was away two days and a night lecturing, so that Bill had little to do. We were, in fact, absurdly overstaffed, as so many people were in those days.

One of our first guests at Stairways was Lady Birkenhead, mother of Freddy. Evelyn Waugh, with unusual benevolence, reported that she had found Stairways 'very comfortable'. Frank's uncle Arthur Villiers, however, had a low opinion of both our first homes. He predicted that we would be drowned in our beds on the Embankment (there was no Thames Barrier) and compared Stairways to some battered HQ behind the lines in war-torn Flanders.

My standby in Stone was Peverel, the Victorian mansion opposite, in which lived Lady Longford and my sisters-in-law, Violet and Julia (the latter when not up for the Oxford term at Somerville). 'Peverel of the Peak', as it was inevitably called despite there being no peaks in the Vale of Aylesbury, provided me with the companionship that I might have lacked as a country wife. I admired Lady Longford for her courage in defying arthritis by circling her estate in a Baby Austin; otherwise the arthritis would have conquered her by making her virtually immobile. I always see her in memory wearing a grey cardigan and long, long skirt (she was tall), her eyes pale, her hair faded gold, not grey, for she was only fifty-five. My getting on well with her made Frank very happy, since he thought his mother perfect and was not consciously aware till much later that she had been far from thinking the same about him.

She sent a touching note of thanks to my mother for returning the family veil of Brussels lace lent to me for the wedding. It was pencilled unsteadily on a visiting card:

Elizabeth's name must certainly be added. She made much the most effective use of it [the veil] I ever saw. It came just as I was starting [from Rutland Gate, her London house, for Peverel], quite reluctant to go as we have been doing nothing but discuss the wedding ever since.

I was guilty of one gaucherie in my relations with her. Feeling that to call her 'Lady Longford' did not properly convey my affection, I decided to consult Frank about addressing her in my next letter as 'Mama'. He said I could try. I tried; but a letter came back signed 'M. Longford'. In those days I should never have dreamt of calling her by her name, Mary, in the way that my daughters-in-law all call me Elizabeth. There was no obvious solution. Sheila Birkenhead, Freddy's wife, was to solve the problem by addressing her mother-in-law jocularly as 'Lady B.'.

I suppose in a way Lady L. kept me at arm's length, partly because of her deteriorating health. Her reserve I did not find chilling since my own family were singularly undemonstrative. What I liked was her advice, especially on our 'garden', a double pocket-handkerchief of grass separated by an unkempt privet hedge. On 'our' side of the hedge was one damson tree, on Bill's side, nothing. I discussed flower and shrub catalogues with Lady L., giving her great pleasure one day by ignorantly pronouncing cotoneaster as 'cotton Easter'.

It was Violet who made outdoor life at Stairways human. We would meet every day when she was not being a deb or hunting on Frank's formidable horse, Balaam, and proceed to wreck and remake the little garden together. On the first day of our labours I found that the telephone had gone dead. We had been busy with wire-cutters clearing the privet hedge, as it turned out, of our own telephone line.

Violet was 'five out of six' in her family and future author of the book of that name. From her and Maria (future author of *Brought Up and Brought Out*) I learned something about the hazards of deb life, never having been one myself, and much about Frank's youth which he himself either could not or would not remember. How he had made Maria laugh when she was in tears as a child by saying over and over, very quickly, the word 'Sugar, sugar, sugar . . .'. How Mama had tried to improve him during the school holidays: if she came into the nursery and found him lying on the window-seat playing with the blind-cord, she would say, 'Frank, why don't you get a book?' If she came in and found him reading, she would say, 'Frank, why don't you go out and get some fresh air?'

I learnt a great deal about their grandmother Lady Jersey, whose biography Violet was to write. She had been a distinguished Victorian political hostess. Living through the Second World War to the age of ninety-six, she showed only one sign of failing memory: as at the Crimea, *Russia* was the enemy. Incidentally I always called her 'Grandmama'.

Most of our visitors to Stairways came from the ranks of our unmarried contemporaries, for though Frank and I were both twenty-five on our wedding day, we were among the first of our circle to get married. In four years Esmond Warner, a friend of Frank's since Eton and future father of Marina Warner the writer, stayed with us fifteen times. Son of Plum Warner, the great cricketer, Esmond was good at everything and a Crockford-class bridge player. One weekend he brought a friend of his to stay for some serious sessions of bridge. Frank and I foolishly agreed to play together against the pros for a shilling a hundred. We were amazed to discover how much one could lose to experts even when one held the best cards. At golf Esmond's skill and good humour were occasionally defeated by his hot temper. We took him to play at Frilford Heath near

Oxford on a day when he had bought himself a very expensive new driver. His first shot sent the ball into a thick clump of gorse. In a fury Esmond hurled his new club after it. It was never seen again.

Another frequent visitor was John Betjeman. The first time he came in February 1932 he found that his predecessor, Naomi Mitchison, had written her name in the Visitors' Book and added the female sign ♀. John immediately put the female sign against his own name too. But when he came again in April we had invited our friend Penelope Chetwode to meet him. (I always thought this was their first encounter but I am told that they had already met in the offices of the *Architectural Review*.) John put the male sign ♂ after his name this time. I took it as a good omen. On the Monday morning going back to London with Penelope in the train, I asked her what she thought of John. 'Oh, I like him so much. I specially like his *pale green* complexion.'

Penelope had sent a telegram to announce the time of her arrival. The Post Office had difficulties with her name and the telegram was signed 'Pinloon'. We both loved the name and it stuck. There was indeed a touch of brilliant eccentricity about her, as well as other endearing qualities. She ran a gang of her fellow debs for the purpose of completing their education and giving them instruction in the Dravidian art of India. She was a born leader. Only once did Frank and I fall foul of her high standards. We were staying with her family at Grove End Road, formerly the palatial establishment of the artist Alma Tadema. We went out to lunch inadvertently leaving the gas fire on in our bedroom. Penelope was even more shocked than angry. 'Such carelessness. You might have burnt this lovely, irreplaceable monument to the ground!' Frank had known Penelope since she was a child, her brother Roger having been his best friend at Eton. We were to watch her over the years change from the conventionally brought up only daughter of a British Field Marshal and Commander-in-Chief of the Indian Army, into one of those intrepid female travellers who appears in every century – Lady Hester Stanhope, Lady Anne Blunt, Mary Kingsley, Isabella Bird.

Hugh Gaitskell stayed with us once, Evan Durbin nine times. On his first visit he forgot to bring his wallet and arrived at Marylebone station with no money. Kitty had to give him the fare, Evan explaining cheerfully that she was thereby doing something to rectify the unjust division of wealth between Capital and Labour. My sister Kitty had never thought of herself as a capitalist but Evan was certainly Labour.

By January 1932 I was beginning to feel awful. I had morning and evening sickness, and the smell of our new distemper at Stairways made me feel sick in the middle of the day too. Early in February I visited Dr Helena

Wright in Welbeck Street, who confirmed that a baby was present but said, surprisingly, that it must have a cradle before as well as after it was born. This 'cradle' turned out to be a vulcanite contraption to keep it the right way up until it was big enough to maintain itself in position. At present it was 'retroverted' and likely to miscarry. (My babies were all 'cradled' before birth. Oddly, I have always thought of myself as being lucky enough to have had perfectly normal pregnancies, forgetting that but for Dr Wright I might have lost my first child.)

When Frank heard the news he wrote from the Conservative Research Department: 'I am glad the doctor felt "Little Winnie"; it seems to bring her a lot nearer.' We referred to our first unborn as Little Winnie until in April I acquired a wire-haired terrier to which I gave the same name, so that at five months Winnie the baby silently changed into Winnie the puppy. (Why did we give our first unborn such a belittling name? Little Winnie, when it might have been Portia or Nefertiti or Elizabeth Fry? My daughter Rachel rightly called her first, 'Little Wonder'.)

Naomi Mitchison has related how two events could be counted on to step up her creative activity: an unhappy love affair and pregnancy. I have had no unhappy love affairs since marriage, which is perhaps why my play about the Absolute and the Absolutely-Not was my last work of fiction. Pregnancy, however, has been my state even more often than Naomi's, but it always had the opposite effect on me. I became ruminative or was endlessly knitting. Unfortunately I lived in the reign of Truby King – temporary king of the baby books and mothercraft – who insisted on all baby clothes being strictly utilitarian and hideously plain – no trimmings or fussy ribbons, such as might strangle the infant. So I concentrated on knitting which could at least be pretty, and on swimming which at least made me feel light.

In May there was a bizarre interlude. Despite my size – I was six months gone – I found myself in a court dress being presented to King George V and Queen Mary at Buckingham Palace. Frank's mother had informed me that it was correct to be presented again after marriage; I had never been a deb, so this was my first experience. I had obediently put my name down soon after the wedding. Pregnancy seemed to be no bar, for everyone hopefully said, 'Nothing shows with the first baby.' How wrong they were.

I took a lesson in curtsying when I found that my balance was not too sure, and sallied out on the day with my cousin Drusilla Hyndson (*née* Chamberlain) in a huge hired car with the required three white feathers on our heads and a backgammon board between us. The game was needed to pass the interminable hours circling in a long queue of cars round the Queen Victoria statue and up and down the Mall, waiting for the royal gates to be flung open. Crowds gathered for the traditional event: it being extremely hot, we kept the windows down and occasionally a face from the crowd would poke inside and take an appraising look.

At last the circling came to an end and we were lined up with our sponsors (in our case, Aunt Helen Chamberlain) outside the Throne Room. When the moment came to make my much-rehearsed curtsy I was torn between the need to look at the floor so that I could judge my distance and save myself from toppling over and a desire to stare long and intently at my sovereigns. Curiosity won; I gazed at the King who was royally immobile and then at the Queen who looked, I thought, severe; then I started to rise. But I had gone down too far and stayed down too long. I swayed and tottered; saw a kindly lord-in-waiting step forward to my aid and somehow straightened up in time to set sail for the refreshment salon next door.

Arthur Villiers cut out a press photograph of Drusilla and me absorbed in our backgammon and sent it to me with his own caption: 'Socialettes at play' – a wry joke about my socialist beliefs.

We had booked Dr Chadburn for the birth, on the advice of Henry Lamb whom I asked to suggest a woman gynaecologist. He had known her during his own early medical days. Frank paid her £100, which was a princely sum for that era; our good friend and doctor, Joe (afterwards Lord) Stone, charged less than a third of that amount for delivering our last child fifteen years later. Frank's aunt Cynthia Slessor (widow of his uncle Lord Jersey and now married to Ronnie Slessor) offered us her London house at 48 Sussex Gardens for the birth. There was no attempt to make me have my first baby in hospital, as would be the case now, and indeed I was to have every one of my children at home – the last when I was forty-one – which would certainly be frowned upon today. The only excess on the side of caution was to send me up to hot London from cooler Stairways twelve days before the supposed birth date, 20 August. Hot was hardly the word for London in that August of 1932: the thermometer rose to ninety-nine degrees Fahrenheit in the shade on the 22nd – and, of course, no baby. I had read enough books on childbirth to be more curious than alarmed about the experience, but I did not realize how madly a first baby can hang fire. I filled up the infinitely tedious waiting time by visiting London's parks and gardens; my brother John (by now almost a fully-fledged doctor) sat me down on the thinly grassed earth at Kew which I was surprised and pleased to find still cool to the touch. At last on the 26th, four days before my own twenty-sixth birthday, I went into labour.

Frank chose and was allowed to stay for the whole drama, not nearly such a common paternal ordeal then as it is now. During most of the seven hours' first stage we paced up and down Aunt Cynthia's bedroom, dividing the patterned carpet into the counties of Ireland which had to be crossed and recrossed in journeys from South to North and back again. The future of Ireland and its disastrous partition into the Free State and Ulster were almost as much in my mind as Frank's. For the final stage Dr Chadburn urged me on like a rowing coach shouting from the bank, 'Push! Push!' instead of 'Pull! Pull!' (This was Frank's indignant simile.) As a new idea in delivery (Scandinavian I think) she had me on my back instead of in the usual position on the side. Owing to this unfortunate experiment the coach could not see what the boat was up to and our daughter suddenly tore her way into the world at 2.45 a.m. on Saturday 27 August, with whirlwind speed, so quickly indeed that chloroform could not be administered. The coach triumphantly held up our joint prize, whose kicks and screams made me feel that our roles had been reversed – she had just given birth to a limp me instead of I to her. She looked like a miniature pugilist.

I immediately rang up Maria, who was sick with emotion as I with after-pains. She was my first visitor and we temporarily named the baby Gandhi, since mild jaundice had given her a sunny Indian glow. Later on Frank and I chose the name Antonía, with the accent on the i, from Willa Cather's novel *My Antonía*. Luckily we did not insist on this pronunciation, since the English version proved difficult enough for ordinary people in those days, and she was often called Antonio. Lovely flowers came from relations and friends and the monthly nurse got cross about finding vases for them all (prearranged flowers in baskets were not yet the thing, except from very grand shops) but crosser still when Desmond Ryan, my Oxford friend, brought me peaches in brandy. She was very particular about what nursing mothers ate, ruling out almost every fruit (acid), vegetable (loosening) and alcohol ('Baby simply *hates* it').

My father visited me when Antonia was four days old. He greatly approved of her broad brow and blonde hair arranged in a neat quartering on the top of her head, which meant that it would be curly – but he did not altogether approve of her sex.

'A man needs a son,' he said ruminatively.

'But, Father, you had *me* first,' I protested, furious at the insult to myself and my beautiful Antonia. He gave a slight smile and repeated, 'A man needs a son.'

We took Antonia and nurse for a visit to Clandeboye, the Dufferins' home near Belfast. Caroline Blackwood, their elder daughter, was a year old. Antonia and Caroline spent a fortnight together in the Clandeboye nurseries, two babies destined to marry famous writers, Harold Pinter and Robert Lowell, and to be acclaimed writers themselves. Meanwhile, Randolph Churchill was a fellow-guest with us downstairs. At lunch he began teasing Frank about the politics of Edward Longford.

'Your brother's a Sinn Feiner, Frank, a traitor to his country. How do you answer that?'

Frank sat silent, refusing to be drawn. Randolph repeated the charge until Frank was goaded into action.

'If you say that again, Randolph, I shall ask you a question you won't like.'

Randolph repeated it yet again: 'Longford's no patriot, he's a Sinn Feiner.'

Frank said, 'Randolph, what did your grandfather die of?' It was not so widely known in those days that Lord Randolph Churchill had died of syphilis. Poor Randolph crumpled.

'Frank, I thought you were my friend, I never thought you would say such a thing to me.' It was typical of Randolph, whom we both liked greatly despite everything, to insult an old friend out of sheer mischief and then suffer surprise and shock when his victim replied in kind.

Though Frank was still not a socialist, his services to the Conservative Research Department inevitably came to an end. He turned to journalism, first as a leader writer on the *Daily Mail*, where he showed some aptitude for writing succinctly on subjects about which he knew nothing by producing a paragraph on 'The Return of the Hobble Skirt'. From the *Mail* he moved on to the *Spectator*, where he assisted Peter Fleming, the literary editor, the editor being Wilson Harris. I remember Harris for giving a dinner-party in his tiny London garden and wearing a crimson cummerbund. In those days outdoor meals and decorative men's wear were both rarities.

Peter's plan for himself and Frank on the *Spectator* was that Frank should hold the fort while he, Peter, was exploring the Amazon, in return for which Frank would become literary editor and Peter editor in place of Wilson Harris, when Peter returned. However, he returned to find Harris still in place and Frank nowhere. There had been a journalistic mission by Frank which left Harris as disappointed as Frank was abashed.

The *News of the World* had carried a piece on 'Drunkenness at Eton' and Frank, as an Etonian member of the *Spectator*'s staff, was sent to interview Dr Alington, Frank's old headmaster and still very much in charge. Frank opened up his mission by trying to pretend that he was out to expose the scandalous rumours, but Alington was not to be deceived. 'If it is your purpose, my dear Frank, to blackguard your old school, you and I must part company.' Frank crawled home, his one chance of a scoop gone.

Soon he parted company from the *Spectator*. Fortunately a far more appropriate job had come his way. After a short time as lecturer at the London School of Economics he was appointed in 1932 a part-time lecturer on Politics at Christ Church, the college where his brother Edward had been ducked.

At the same time his passionate involvement with Ireland was, if possible, growing. I was beginning to share it, largely through visits to the place which I saw as the centre of present Irish history – Glendalough House in County Wicklow. It was from 'Glan', as its owners always affectionately called it, that Erskine Childers had been arrested and taken off to face a Free State firing squad in 1922 at the time of the Civil War. The house belonged to Robert Barton, first cousin of Childers. They were both Anglo-Irishmen, Bob having been educated at Rugby and Christ Church, while Erskine, author of *The Riddle of the Sands*, was a cousin of Gladstone's Chancellor and had served with the British forces in the Boer War and the Great War. Erskine's American widow, Mollie, was given a home at Glan by Bob; she was crippled. Sometimes Mollie's mother, Mrs Osgood, was present on a visit from America. Glendalough with its saints and its lakes and its luxuriant woods was a place of superlative beauty, but it was the atmosphere of the house that enthralled me. The house itself was no great thing. It looked as if it had not been furnished since Victorian days; it smelt of peat like all Irish houses; it had cups of tea to offer at all hours; it provided a sustaining and delicious high tea at seven o'clock. The real thing about it was Erskine's ghost.

I must have heard the story of his death twenty times if I heard it once. When the Free State soldiers came for him, he was carrying a small revolver given to him by Michael Collins, which was contrary to the new weapons law. Mollie, with her pain-stricken eyes and fluffy hair like a halo, was now venerated as Erskine's relict. Whatever she said went. When Mrs Osgood was there too, the mixture of Irish and American emotion developed an intensity that I found extraordinary and irresistible. In the ever-present ghost of Erskine Childers I had my first intoxicating encounter with a hero.

Eleven years before we arrived, Bob Barton had been a member of the Irish delegation which negotiated the Treaty of 1921 with Britain. It was repudiated by the Republicans led by de Valera. The outcome was confirmation of the partition of Ireland, establishment of the Free State (it lasted until 1949) and the outbreak of civil war. Paradoxically, Bob had signed the Treaty against his dominant cousin Erskine's advice. 'Don't sign,' said Erskine, who was there in London as Secretary of the Delegation. 'Mollie says don't.' That was too much even for Bob. What did Mollie, an American, know about the intricacies of Irish conflict? So

Bob signed. Later, however, he returned to his former allegiance, that is, to Childers and de Valera. And later still he decided to give his papers on the Treaty and the Civil War to Frank. As an Irishman with an English mother he felt that Frank, of all men, would do the subject justice.

From this absorbing commitment grew many new friendships for both of us. We met Moya Llewellyn-Davies, whose idol had been Michael Collins, in romantic Furry Park, Raheny, outside Dublin. While she was telling Frank about past assignations with Collins, her nineteen-year-old son Richard would take me on his favourite walk round Howth, where between the cliffs and the sea we would recite to each other Macaulay's *Lays of Ancient Rome.*

Frank and I went south to see the spot where Mick Collins was ambushed and killed in a fight between the Free Staters, of whom he was leader, and the Republicans – a dismal enough stretch of road I thought – and in London we met Lady Lavery, another of Collins' charmers and known to the Irish public for her exquisite face on their banknotes. She reminded me of a snowdrop: fragile and transparent but at the same time tough. Curiously enough it was through 'F.E.' and the Birkenhead family at Charlton that Frank had first become involved in the history of these crucial – and disastrous – Anglo-Irish decisions. The actual idea of the book had first been mooted by F.E.'s elder daughter, Eleanor Smith. Herself a best-selling romantic novelist, she introduced Frank to Jonathan Cape, the book's publisher.

During the Treaty negotiations, F.E. had grown to admire Collins; they were both big physical men in the prime of life. After the fatal gun fight, F.E. obtained a portrait of the dead warrior which he hung on the staircase at Charlton. Frank would see it every time he went up to his bedroom when staying for the weekend, and so would I after our marriage.

Yet Frank – and I following him – managed throughout his researches to remain apart from the Civil War feuds though fiercely devoted to the Ireland that both sides, Free Staters and Republicans, claimed to represent. One is reminded of the question addressed to Winston Churchill, 'Which side were you on in the Spanish Civil War?' and his reply, 'Both sides.'

Ireland was the only political problem – or rather, political answer – on which I accepted without question the judgement of Frank's head and heart. At the same time it was a minority cause and perceptibly drew him nearer to my way of thinking on English politics.

Charlton was the focus of social glamour for us while we lived at Stairways – though Clandeboye, the Dufferins' home, ran it close.

Frank had been Basil Dufferin's best man at his marriage to Maureen

Guinness, and Maureen was one of Antonia's godmothers. They both stayed frequently at Stairways. The first time, not realizing the diminutive size of the establishment, Maureen had brought twenty pairs of high-heeled shoes (her famous 'pinnacles') in her luggage which Jessie unpacked and ranged triumphantly the whole way round the skirting-boards of their tiny bedroom. Basil demanded some refreshments in the middle of the night, but the cupboard was bare. 'But you surely have a ham somewhere, at least. . . .' Our larder was a wire cage hanging on the cottage wall and it contained not even a ham.

Our visits to Clandeboye were a dizzy round of games and 'fun-and-games': fishing in the long lake (my fish seemed to be always 'feeding on the bottom'); shooting and picnic lunches in the folly called Helen's Tower of which Harold Nicolson has written; golf, when an unaffluent and unskilful guest, having lost £100, was bet next day by the generous Basil 100 to 1 in pounds that he would not sink a two-foot putt, which, of course, in his panic he failed to do; bridge or paper-games after dinner, often enlivened by the pranks of Edward (Lord) Stanley. One evening Ed switched off the lights and when they went on again it was found that a very serious lady from Durham who knitted all day and night for the unemployed was bound hand and foot in a vast web of her own wool.

The ethos of Charlton was totally different, a unique mixture of informality and 'gracious living', of strenuous sport, learning and intellectual discussion, all these ingredients being dependent on the remarkable Smith family itself, of which F.E. was the head. Margaret Countess of Birkenhead, his wife, another of Antonia's godmothers and mother of Freddy, was the daughter of Henry Furneaux, a renowned Tacitean scholar whose work I had studied while at Oxford. F.E. once amazed the secretary of the local golf club by saying to him, 'My wife's father was a Tacitean scholar so formidable that even Tacitus himself would hardly have dared to do battle with him.' Prodigiously alive and alert (she lived to be over ninety), Margaret made funny stories about her unforgettable husband even funnier. (Another reason for wishing that Frank and I had married earlier was that I would have met the great F.E.; he died in 1930.) She was a fine amateur singer and went one day to the Warneford Asylum in Oxford to entertain the mental patients. 'When in full flight,' she narrated, 'I suddenly noticed that the whole of the front row had their fingers firmly stuck in their ears. And when I sat down at the end of the song, there was my husband beside me, not consoling me for my humiliation but saying in an audible whisper, "You see, they're not so mad after all. . . ." '

The Smiths were the most argumentative family I have known, except for my own. Eleanor and Pamela (the younger daughter, later Lady

Hartwell) would challenge Freddy, or the four of them would indulge in a verbal free-for-all, supported or attacked by whatever friends were present: Aidan Crawley, Vyvyan Holland or Baby Jungman. Eleanor had a Romanian protégé named Mircea, whom Frank invited, out of fondness for Eleanor, to play in his Aylesbury rugger team. Other players were Dick Crossman and Patrick Gordon-Walker from Oxford, and Frank Owen, the *Daily Express* journalist. Eleanor assured Frank that Mircea knew the rules and had captained Romania in rugger. However, though a charming man, it turned out that he was a boxing champion. His idea of rugger was to punch his opponents as hard and as often as possible. He was beckoned off the field by Eleanor after knocking out the ref and just before the local constable arrived to put him under arrest.

Charlton was a pretty old house with many small rooms, floors on different levels and a lovely, spacious library. Despite the company's distinction, Charlton never seemed to lose touch with the village of that name in which it was situated. For though its view to the east was of a sloping garden, yew hedges, trees, tennis-courts, a natural pond in which we swam and woods rising again beyond the water, on the west side was the village street. All the rooms on that side, including the dining-room, looked straight out on to the road. I have never known a house that was so secluded and self-contained and yet so open to the world. And this dual quality seemed to me characteristic of the family who lived in it, giving them a special fascination.

Freddy Birkenhead stayed with us at Stairways both before and after his marriage to Sheila Berry. The first time he came he seems to have felt the need for a dash of colour in the plain little place and so signed the Visitors' Book as 'Birkenhead – Chief Falconer of Cornwall'. John Betjeman commented, 'Jolly good joke', which foxed future visitors who never could decide whether Lord Birkenhead's claim was true or false. Sheila's brother Michael Berry stayed too, with Freddy's sister Pamela whom he married – a brother and sister marrying a sister and brother. Betjeman's name appears in the book with Edmund Blunden, the poet, and Robert Byron, the travel writer; Evelyn Waugh's with Father Martin D'Arcy and Dorothy Lygon whose home, Madresfield, was to be the model for Brideshead.

Evelyn as usual greeted me with the words, 'How's the hockey?' I realized this was to be taken as an insult, implying that I was a female 'hearty'. (In fact it was not my imaginary hockey that he disliked but my birth. He wrote to Lady Dorothy Lygon in 1932 about 'poor Frank Pakenham who married beneath him and the Hon. Mrs P. who married above herself'.) I liked him too much to speculate about his motive. Next day he took us all to lunch at the Spread Eagle in Thame, a pub where I had spent many candle-lit evenings in my Oxford days, translating the menus which were handwritten in ancient Greek. Mine host, John Fothergill, would entertain us by moving from table to table praising his wines and helping his clients to finish their bottles. Evelyn allowed no such attentions. On the way home he honoured me with a curious confidence. Pointing to a particularly nasty damp ditch he said, 'That's the kind of ditch where I used to spend the night when I was teaching prep school boys.' '*Spend the night?*' I asked, incredulous. 'In the ditch every night with my motor bicycle on top of me. Too drunk on pub beer to know where I was till morning.' Incidentally, Evelyn was an excellent narrator. Not so emphatic a style as Maurice Bowra's, in fact rather abrupt and detached, but with the same undertone of menace that would suddenly change into a high whine of complaint or a confiding smile.

Thirteen days before Antonia was a year old her brother Thomas was born, on Monday morning, 14 August, at Stairways. (The gap between my brother John and myself was very much the same, I being twenty days short of my first birthday when John arrived.) I had decided that Thomas's birth should be a reversion to old-fashioned methods and as painless as possible: our local doctor to deliver the baby with chloroform when necessary, and the confinement to be in my own bed. The night before, Ronnie Shaw-Kennedy had been staying. Again it was an oppressive heat-wave. Violet came over from Peverel and we all went down to our small local river. Frank, who at that time could not swim, sat on the bank with Antonia in her sun-bonnet. (When Ronnie came a year later to stay, after we had moved to Oxford, I asked Antonia if she remembered him. 'Yes, a big black mess.') Violet and I swam. We were interrupted by anguished cries from a group of village boys bathing near-by. One of them came running. At first we could not understand what he was saying. Then we saw that he had lost his teeth and at last made out that he wanted us to dive for them in the weedy depths. Violet and I regretfully decided we could not risk our lives, not to mention that of the unborn child, in a fruitless search for snappers in a bundle of weed.

I had been assured that the second birth was always much easier than the first. And this proved true in every way. I wanted a son this time and had no doubt one was on the way: during labour four magpies suddenly landed in the Peverel paddock opposite. 'One for sorrow, two for joy, three for a girl, four for a boy.' I had been better prepared for morning sickness and worried less about my own diet and the baby's health. When Antonia was on the way I had given up smoking and alcohol and consumed quantities of lettuce and white of egg. Three or four times during the first few weeks after her arrival I had a nightmare that she was lying on the end of my bed and I was about to kick her off it; I would shoot up into a sitting position, back throbbing as if my kidneys were doing a fandango inside me. None of this ever recurred.

Thomas's birth took only four hours, and no stitches. He was a very dark nine-pounder, and when I saw my cousin Neville Chamberlain soon afterwards I said, 'Our son looks like you.' 'It's a very strong strain,' he said kindly. In a month or two, however, it turned out that the narrow forehead, beaky nose and slightly underhung jaw were all due to the 'moulding' during birth. Thomas began to develop a broad forehead and strong chin and to look like his father, though darker. In fact both Antonia and Thomas were the opposite to chinless wonders. I complimented Antonia at two years old on the big chin she was getting, to which she replied, 'Yes and I shall soon be getting a beard.' At three she was not always so pleased with her appearance – which was that of a golden curly-haired Florentine angel. 'I'm so unhappy,' she moaned dramatically one day, 'I've got such an ugerly mouth'; and when I misguidedly speculated on the chance of her vivid blue eyes changing to grey, she said resignedly, 'I'm afraid they will. I'm afraid they'll turn to pink.'

Antonia had shown signs of precocity before Thomas's birth – we called her our 'Wonder Child' – but this event hastened her development. At eleven months she walked, and a month before that had learned to make a 'dare'. Her game was to sit under our damson tree at Stairways and try to eat one of the tiny unripe fruit. Looking at me challengingly she would at first hold it an inch away from her mouth. 'No, no Antonia.' Like lightning she would pop it into her mouth and then snatch it out again before I could get to her, repeating the performance several times. The same with pebbles. She was clever enough to disguise her jealousy – if that was what it was – of the new baby as concern for his welfare. One day he was crying in his cot but with a curiously subdued wail. I went in to investigate. Antonia, now eighteen months old, was standing by the cot with a Mona Lisa smile on her face. She had buried her brother in toys; soft toys, hard toys, light toys, heavy toys. Was it to comfort him, to silence him or just to – bury him? I shall never know.

Lady Longford lived just long enough to attend Thomas's christening in Hartwell church, connected with Louis XVIII during his exile in England. As Thomas was held yelling over the baptismal font, a robin that had come into the building with the christening party burst into rapturous song. The baby stopped crying. Twenty years later Thomas saw in an Oxford newspaper that the little church was to be demolished. He drove over to Hartwell and rescued the carved parapet of the organ loft and a stone finial from a lorry was about to dump them with the rest of the rubbish. Today they are both at Bernhurst.

I like to think that Lady Longford was pleased at the birth of her first grandson. She probably felt he was the wrong colour, being dark instead of a radiant blond like Edward. But there seemed no reason at that date why Edward and Christine should not have an heir. They had been married six years. In November Lady Longford died at Rutland Gate. Next day the family assembled there for the reading of the will. All except Edward were sitting around talking in low voices when suddenly the door was flung open and Edward stood in the doorway, feet apart and arms raised in a theatrical gesture. 'There are two wills,' he announced in a distinctly Irish accent, 'and by evening every one of ye will be at each other's throats!' Luckily only one was signed so there were no family dramas.

Our last period at Stairways, from 1933 to 1934, was less enjoyable than before, owing to the end of Peverel as a family home. However, we paid many weekend visits to other houses, Cliveden and Taplow Court, Petworth, Firle and Hatfield. We were talking to Lady Astor at Cliveden when the butler approached Frank gravely and handed him a telephone message on a silver tray. It was from Stairways to say that the bailiffs were in; some unpaid Oxford bill from student days. Frank had to interrupt our weekend by a dash back home; and when he returned after settling this 'little local difficulty' we agreed that, if one had to be visited by bailiffs, no moment could be better than during a visit to the glories and grandeurs of Cliveden.

Lady Astor was nearly always polite to me though in principle she did not like her young men getting married. Once married she thought the wives should at least be occupied with children. One day at teatime she began denouncing contemporary wives for not having families. 'Look at you, Elizabeth, what good are you? I've had *six* children. What are you doing?' I rose unsteadily to my feet, revealing that I was pregnant. She laughed heartily. I was grateful to her for giving me the opportunity to see T. E. Lawrence at tea, when he was in the RAF and just before his fatal motor-cycle accident. But he made no impression except by his small size and reticence. Heroes should be seen on television when their height is irrelevant. Frank had a more vivid recollection of a very voluble G. B. Shaw at Cliveden. He would read his latest play aloud to the assembled company and find himself continually choked with his own mirth. Or there would be J. L. Garvin, editor of the *Observer*, sage of the newspaper world and author of the official life of Joseph Chamberlain. He was one of Cliveden's great talkers, Frank part of his audience.

Garvin: When I was a boy there was a thing called sense of shame. These things are dead today.

A woman guest: Oh, Mr Garvin, aren't you rather a pessimist?

Garvin: Pessimism and optimism – I am above all isms; I'm above all that.

Walter Elliot MP was another great talker and also something of a scientist. Frank once heard him describe the fourteen different types of aluminium, and to me at breakfast he offered the opinion: 'The hydroelectric plant is the national status symbol of the twentieth century.'

On a Saturday night Brendan Bracken MP described his visits earlier that day to 'Winston, Max and Esmond' and, having finished with the press lords, how he had called on 'L.G.' 'I said to L.G., "Get out of Distillers and get out of them quick." ' (It was Saturday afternoon and the Stock Exchange was shut, so L.G. could not have got out.)

Petworth in West Sussex, with its wonderful Grinling Gibbons carvings and Turner paintings, was the first place where I saw food served on gold plates. Yet the atmosphere was curiously austere. There were notices on many of the priceless carpets telling visitors not to walk on them, and other notices on the dressing-table mirrors stating that the servants were paid a just wage and did not require tips. I was not to see such notices again until we stayed with the Master of Balliol, when I found that his wife Mrs Lindsay also declared her servants to require no tipping, being adequately paid. This link between the Lindsays of Balliol and the Wyndhams of Petworth pleased me greatly. Evelyn Waugh and Patrick Balfour, who boasted of doing a round of the dressing-tables before leaving house parties, would not have enjoyed staying with either of them.

In Lady Desborough at Taplow I was meeting a famous Edwardian beauty, wit and member of the Souls. I had not realized the total self-confidence of a true *grande dame* until I witnessed, through the library window, a little incident on the lawn outside. White-bearded Lord D'Abernon, ex-ambassador and once known as the handsomest man in England, was walking up and down on the grass arm in arm with Lady Desborough. Suddenly he tripped, fell flat on his face and brought down Lady Desborough with him. Not a sound was uttered. They both quietly righted themselves, linked arms again and continued their tottering stroll as if nothing had happened.

I got on well with the eccentrically knowledgeable Lord Desborough. A legendary athlete, he had three subjects of conversation: sport, wildfowl and bimetallism. I could follow him on the last two and was given a magnificent bird book as a reward. He had once swum Niagara, taken a rowboat across the Channel, played cricket for Harrow, rowed for Oxford and when, in middle age, he had shown a sceptical friend the scene of his exploit at the Niagara Falls, he had there and then done the swim again. Now, as an old man, he was apt to fall into athletic attitudes in the midst of conversation: fly fishing, boxing, rowing. While booming like a bittern for my benefit, a favourite parlour trick, he would suddenly stop short and exclaim, 'On guard!'. I would realize that standing beside me was a champion fencer, rapier at the ready. He never explained his sudden miming but smiled confidentially when it was completed.

Hatfield was the most memorable experience, partly because of all our friends I was fondest of David Cecil. The Marquess of Salisbury of that date was his father. I was already becoming interested in comparisons between Victorian and modern life-styles, and the two things I remember most vividly about that first visit to Hatfield were both eloquent of the last century. When we came upstairs to change for dinner I found in my bedroom, in front of the blazing coal fire, a large oblong hole in the Turkey carpet into which was sunk a splendid bath filled from copper cans. Never have I enjoyed a hot bath so much. It reminded me of my childhood when first my brother Roger, then Michael, would be bathed in an enamel tub before our nursery fire.

Early next day there were family prayers in the private chapel. (I had not visited a family that kept up this Victorian custom since John and I stayed with our 'Harman' aunt Nell Parker-Gray in Rushmills, Northampton. It was not a very happy memory, for during prayers the death of our common cousin Hugh Barnes in the Great War was solemnly announced. There was a stunned silence. John and I, aged eight and seven, responded to the unbearable tension by bursting into hysterical giggles.) Hatfield prayers were all picturesque decorum. The whole family and staff were gathered together, maids on one side of the aisle, manservants on the other. The maids wore pretty little mob caps, and one was presented to me to wear for the duration of the service.

And, of course, there were always wonderful summer visits to Pakenham Hall. The first time I took Antonia and Thomas they were babies of two and one. The old gardener looked at them and then said to their nanny: 'Tell Mrs Pakenham that if she wants either of those children to look like her, she must have another one.' This was my first experience of an Irish bull. It was also Anthony Powell's first experience of Pakenham. I invited him to stay, having met him twice in London and decided he would add the right kind of sparkle. After we left, Tony stayed on, met the young, high-spirited Violet and married her.

Christine Longford's biographer, John Cowell, was told by her that in 1934 she and Edward had three great wishes: to see Ireland free from coast to coast, to visit China and to produce at least three children to carry on the line. None of the three wishes was to be granted. The last of them may have been inspired by Christine's first sight of Thomas. If it was, she was never to show him anything but auntly affection.

We were always visiting Oxford, for our destiny was lying more and more in that direction. I was again on excellent terms with the principal of my old college, Miss Grier, for I had married a man after her own heart – an economist with a first. We went to tea with the Warden of Frank's old college, H. A. L. Fisher, and the poet and writer Hilaire Belloc was there too. When Fisher asked Belloc if he would prefer Indian or China tea, Belloc replied in ringing tones, 'Wine!' 'Wine!' echoed Fisher, as if wine at teatime were the most usual thing in the world at New College. 'Fetch a carafe of wine!' (to the parlourmaid who disappeared in a whirl of white apron-strings). She was not seen again, for as she knew, and the Warden knew, there was no carafe of wine available in the Warden's lodgings.

Afterwards Fisher told a story of Belloc and himself at the Librairie Nationale in Paris. Belloc, surrounded by a great press of staff all anxious to serve him, ordered a huge pile of reference books to be assembled for him on a nearby table. After glancing into a few of them he turned to Fisher.

'I suggest we leave now for luncheon.' At the door he added, pointing to the abandoned stack of books: 'I shall not be revisiting them.'

At the beginning of 1934 Frank heard that he had been appointed to a Studentship (Fellowship) at Christ Church. He would be a full-time Politics don and his salary would be doubled – from £500 to £1,000 a year. Freddie Ayer, a brilliant young philosopher who had mastered logical positivism in Vienna and was now writing a book on it, was the rival candidate, but the college needed someone to teach politics not philosophy. For the time being Freddie became a Research Student. Later that year he published his seminal volume, *Language, Truth and Logic.* I met him shortly afterwards when the philosophical world was humming like a beehive that has been kicked.

'Freddie,' I asked, 'what comes next?' His black eyes glittered and he answered gleefully, 'There's no next. Philosophy's come to the end. Finished.'

The other Politics don at Christ Church, perhaps the most conservative of all colleges, was Patrick Gordon Walker. A friend of Lord Camrose and once history coach and tennis partner of Freddy Birkenhead, Patrick had appealed to the college as a scholar, an athlete and, it went without saying, a Conservative. But Gordon Walker had become one of the young Labour lions, along with Gaitskell and Durbin. Now the dons calculated that in Pakenham at any rate, a young man trained in the Conservative Research Department, they had a safe Tory.

IO

'Bliss was it, then'
· *1934–6* ·

The first five years in Oxford were the most political of my life. But I had to begin by setting up our new home and settling in our two children, married couple and nanny, a delightful robust girl from Devon. Our great friend Anne Martelli, with whose family we stayed in Brancaster by the sea that summer of 1934, was afterwards to declare that Nancy was *too* robust, holding Thomas under the cold bath tap if he cried. This was legend. On the other hand parents and nannies were tougher before the war than they are now. In the following year, when Brian Martelli was three and Thomas two, we would carry our offspring into the cold North Sea, their legs stinging with blown sand, despite their screams. Antonia, also three, needed no encouragement to plunge in. Today one seldom hears that most poignant of beach cries: the sound of scared children being forced to enjoy their seaside holiday.

In Oxford we had leased a stone-built house on Rose Hill, a developing area between the village of Iffley and the industrial suburb of Cowley. 'Cingaltree', called after a wych elm at the gate (we changed the spelling to Singletree), had been designed by an Oxford chemist to look as much like a superior college dwelling as possible – carved oak mantels with alcoves beneath the top shelf, parquet floors and an odd bow window in one corner of the drawing-room. On two sides thick shrubberies concealed the Rose Hill cemetery. There was no flower garden but a gravel terrace and a rough lawn sweeping down to the link road between Cowley and Iffley.

When we first took the house the view to Oxford would not have disappointed Matthew Arnold: spires, towers, college roofs, all carrying the eye westwards, with very little more than grass, trees and only a few streets of Victorian houses in the foreground to distract from the ethereal beauty beyond. In the course of a year or so the vision had faded: or rather, been killed by the building of Florence Park Estate. Not that I allowed myself to regret it, except in a general political context. For the staring, brick-red conglomeration of working-class boxes run up by a speculative builder was filled to the brim with hundreds of Labour voters. My only wish was that this shoddy mushroom growth had been instead an architect-designed housing estate built by the Oxford City Council.

Antonia was not quite two when I took her on her first walk around Rose Hill. Suddenly from the bottom of the hill she spied her new home at a distance. 'That's Antonia's house,' she said. 'Antonia lives there.'

She quickly transformed her nursery – a huge room compared with constricted Stairways, running along the top of the house – into her own domain. Her favourite sport was to race up and down it from end to end. She had discovered this pleasure aged fifteen months during a party given by Maureen Dufferin for Caroline, but was not able to indulge it at home. When Frank and I came to fetch her from the party, he caught sight of a figure in frills with blazing cheeks and flying curls tearing up and down the long room. 'That's a jolly little child,' he said. 'Yes, it's your daughter,' said Maureen with her mischievous faun-like smile.

It was at Larksfield, my parents' new home in Kent, that Antonia and Thomas had their first adventure. Aged just three and two, they were playing in the large sand-pit on a warm bank in front of the house, once the home of Octavia Hill, a founder of the National Trust. I was indoors when Antonia marched up. 'I killed a snake.' 'Where is it?' I asked, taking the news to be another of her fantasies. 'With Thomas in the sand-pit.' Thomas had a bandaged knee after a tumble and could not walk. She and I went down to the sand-pit together and there was Thomas sitting solemnly beside the body of a viper. Its head, which Antonia had severed with her little spade, was lying close by in the sand.

The large nursery at Singletree seems to have given impetus to Antonia's imaginative life. Her second favourite game was arranging her toys and the furniture in patterns all over the room. Every cushion would be placed on the floor with a symmetrical design of bricks to decorate it, every cup would have a ball in it, every jar a bead in its mouth. At the same time she invented two girl companions named Tibby and Tellow. They did everything that Frank and I did, including going on visits to London and teaching in an Oxford college called Cotton Church. One morning she was asked why she had not got up and dressed. 'Tibby and Tellow told me not to get out of bed', replied Antonia, 'or I'd get my feet cold.'

In the autumn when she was three and a quarter, the puzzling idea of death came to her with the falling of the leaves: 'Why don't dead people come alive again in the summer?' A picture of a family of cats with no father cat present was easily explained by Antonia herself: 'Where is the Father Cat? I expect he's in Oxford teaching.' For her third birthday I made her a little illustrated reading book. She learnt it by heart in a day and soon could read printed words of one syllable.

We had one other terrifying experience, beside the viper, during these early years. At Easter 1936 Antonia and Thomas were staying with Nancy in seaside lodgings at Torpoint, while Frank and I visited my parents. The telephone rang one evening. It was Nancy saying that Antonia had developed a pain in her right leg while out on her walk that afternoon, and now could not stand; the doctor said it was polio. My mother tried to console us, suggesting that we could buy a little gazebo where Antonia would lie and enjoy the spring in our garden. I felt the whole world had turned to winter. Next morning we took the train to Torquay. Antonia was lying on the double bed she shared with Nancy, Thomas in his cot. As soon as she saw us she sat up and began bouncing on the bed. Frank carried her to the London train where she lay wrapped in blankets; the same on the journey to Oxford. That evening our doctor, Raymond Greene, elder brother of Graham Greene, the novelist, called round. Nancy carried Antonia down to the drawing-room. Raymond, Frank and I were sitting in the bow window, at least twenty feet from Antonia.

'Put her down,' said Raymond. Nancy lowered her gingerly.

'Come over here, Antonia,' said Raymond. Antonia jumped to her feet and ran across the room.

The mystery of her 'polio' was never cleared up. It was to have a macabre sequel.

Meanwhile Thomas was as different as could be from his sister. Where her favourite colour was pink, his was purple; where she wanted to be the Fairy Queen or a mother when she grew up, he wanted to be a soldier. Antonia loved dolls but he hated soft toys and screamed when a teddy was given to him. Perhaps he thought they were captive animals, for when I took him to the zoo he was horrified and refused ever to go again. He stumped around the house at three with a stick chanting, 'I want to kill somepin'.' His favourite nursery rhyme was, 'There was a little man who had a little gun . . .' Amusing but down to earth, he had no taste for Antonia's dream world of gauzy fairies. The song of a blackbird at dusk prompted him to remark, "That's Dr Greene singing in his house.' Antonia would have said it was Titania. When I said goodnight to him in his cot he asked, 'When shall I wake up again?'

After moving to Oxford the children had a new nanny, Jean Birch. Her family lived in the East End of London, her father having been in the merchant navy; she was an exceptional girl, very pretty, clever and a deeply spiritual Anglo-Catholic. With her the children listened to their first Bible stories. As an agnostic with no interest in religion, I could not talk to them about 'Baby Jesus' myself but, perhaps illogically, was happy for Jean to do so. Up to her arrival, the children's only religious education had been to climb on to Frank's back while he was saying his prayers, like two little frogs, and echo a few words of his. The effect of Jean was for Antonia immediately to add a rainbow host of angels and saints to her fairyland. I used to question both children on simple facts while reading stories to them, to make sure they understood. When I began on *The Little Red Hen* I asked Thomas,

'What are hens?' wondering if he knew they were birds.

'Don't know.'

'What are the things that fly called?'

'Angels.'

Thomas's most effective parlour trick was suddenly to leap to his feet when visitors were present and shout, 'Up the rebels!' The slogan was a spin-off from Frank's book on the Irish Treaty, the rebels in question being Irish, but Thomas's slogan gave equal pleasure to our friends in the Cowley Labour Party.

The village of Cowley had been chosen by William Morris for the site of his motor works. We were told by an old colleague of Morris's, now a stalwart of the Labour Party in Cowley, the story of how he and 'Billy' Morris had started level in Oxford, Billy in a cycle shop, our friend in a stable. 'I'll stick to the 'osses,' said he. When Billy moved to motor cars, our friend was driving a horse cab. The story ended ironically with our friend getting ten shillings a week old-age pension, while Billy had become the multi-millionaire Lord Nuffield.

Another favourite story was of the wife of up-and-coming Morris applying for membership of the smart Huntercombe golf club. She was refused because of a rule that admitted the families of gentlemen only; whereupon Morris bought up the whole place, presenting it to his wife on her birthday. On anti-snob grounds we sided with the Billy Morris of this legend, but in every other way he was Oxford's Number One Capitalist Ogre. The appalling slump of the 1930s had forced thousands of Welsh miners to 'get on their bikes' and seek work in the less hopelessly depressed Midlands of England. Cowley was full of such families and at Labour Party meetings one heard more melodious Welsh voices than flat Oxfordshire ones. I attended regularly at the Women's Section, which was dominated by a Mrs Hoare (Welsh) and Mrs Uzzell (English). So attractive was Ruth Uzzell that when she stood for the Oxford Council the local Communist Party decided not to put up a candidate against her. Not only did she romp home but also won the Beautiful Ankles competition at the Singletree Labour fête.

The Morris Motor works and Pressed Steel works were riddled with communists, thanks to the movement of population during the depression. They were led by a professional agitator named Abe Lazarus, sometimes known as 'Bill Firestone' because of the successful strike he had led at the Firestone Tyre factory outside London. The atmosphere of the much later film, *I'm All Right, Jack*, was by no means that of the Oxford factories. Instead of the stultifying selfishness immortalized in that film, there was much idealism and socialist brotherhood. Instead of the parrot-cry from the shop floor, 'All out! All out!', there was intense and prolonged democratic discussion of the pros and cons of a strike. I remember the feeling of pride and exhilaration when the news came through: 'The press is out!' Abe Lazarus himself was a stirring speaker. Fair-skinned and reddish-haired, with pale blue eyes, he looked fragile; but on a platform he could produce a commanding voice and powerful gestures, particularly the trick of emphasizing a point by swinging his right arm in a wide arc as he brought the pointer finger of his right hand down into the palm of his left. For years I was able to spot a communist-trained orator by this gesture.

When I joined the Cowley Labour Party, Abe Lazarus was almost the only open communist I knew personally, for at this date it was the policy of the Oxford CP to infiltrate the Labour Party with comrades who did not necessarily carry a membership card, far less declare themselves. When that policy changed and communists were ordered to come out into the open, I was surprised to find that the chairman and treasurer of the Oxford City Labour Party were Abe's comrades, not mine. Yet Abe had a winning personality; he married a young graduate called Mabel from one of the women's colleges and in the five years before the war no couple was more popular than our friends 'Abe and Mabe'.

The communists of Cambridge University made no attempt to hide their allegiance from me when I visited some of them in 1935. The invitation was a personal one from Richard Llewelyn-Davies, who was in his last year at King's. Hunger Marchers from the North were due to arrive in Cambridge on the Saturday afternoon on their way to London. Richard invited me to march out with all the Cambridge leftists to welcome them, entertain them in a municipal hall and myself to stay the night afterwards with Lettice Ramsey, wife of Frank Ramsey, a King's don.

Richard met me at the station. When I reached his rooms, his friend Guy Burgess was there, waiting for a game of racing demon. I took him on. We played on the floor. Since Thomas's birth the year before I had become very slim and agile, and since racing demon depends chiefly on physical quickness, I was able to defeat Guy Burgess at that game at any rate. The room was pleasant: full of reproductions of modern paintings and academic books. Later Guy went off to work and Richard informed me that all communists had to get firsts. 'They are bound in honour to get firsts – for the honour of the Party.' Many of them did.

Lettice Ramsey, my hostess, has been described as 'redoubtable'. On that occasion she seemed unobtrusive, so far as a strong character can give that impression. I got the feeling that she would raise no objection to my spending the night with Richard under her roof if we so wished. That was the only sign she gave of being avant-garde. I knew her by name already as a leftist photographer whose partner, Helen Muspratt, had made a studio portrait of Antonia and Thomas in Oxford.

Richard and Guy both seemed to me good advertisements for the Cambridge left: Richard with golden hair, slanting fawn eyes and a very faint hint of Dublin in his voice. He told me that his father Crompton Llewelyn-Davies had belonged to the Apostles, a secret intellectual society at Cambridge; 'and at Dublin,' said Richard, 'we all – Moya and Sean [his mother and sister] and I – used to sit at his feet admiring him.'

My training at Oxford had taught me to recognize a homosexual when I saw one, and Guy seemed to send out the familiar signals: at ease with girls but physically neutral despite his dimples and wavy hair. His boyish charm had not yet been damaged by the double life he was to lead and when I met him again later on in Roy Harrod's rooms at Christ Church, I hardly recognized the drunken figure who declared himself to be a 'Tory – a Tory Marxist'.

At last the time came to set out for the city boundary with our banners and our slogans, to meet the Hunger Marchers. I helped carry one of the banners part of the way and was amazed at how heavy it was as it billowed in the wind. We had one short slogan which we ejaculated at odd moments to fill in a pause: 'Scholarships not battleships!' The one we used while marching went with more of a swing:

> One two three four
> What are we for?
> We're for the working class
> Down with the ruling class!

A later generation was to chant, 'Make love not war!' There was no hint of love or sex in our proceedings. Our minds were exclusively fixed on the Hunger Marchers and their predicament. Nor did I consider Soviet Russia as a mastermind behind the demonstration. When we thought of Russia at all it was as a potential ally who would put paid to Hitler's dreams of aggression.

My name had remained on the candidates' list after I had failed to be elected for Stone, and in the summer of 1935 I was invited to stand as parliamentary Labour candidate for Cheltenham. I accepted with alacrity, bought myself a bright red button-through dress with large white buttons and began nursing my first constituency. My old friend Randolph Churchill gave me a loyal if inaccurate puff in the *Sunday Dispatch*, quoted by the Cheltenham *Echo*:

An interesting personality among the new Socialist candidates is the youthful, scholarly and attractive Elizabeth Harman. At Oxford she obtained a first [*sic*] in Greats. Three years ago she married Mr Frank Pakenham, who was her contemporary at Oxford, and who was judged by his tutors to have written the most brilliant papers in the School of Modern Greats since the war.

This highly intellectual couple are, however, divided in politics. . . .

Randolph went on to praise Frank's *Peace by Ordeal*, which had just been published and widely acclaimed, and to prophesy his entry into the House of Commons, perhaps before me. For I was starting my political career 'in the salubrious, but not overwhelmingly socialistic atmosphere of Cheltenham'. This seat had only three times been contested by a socialist and the highest socialist vote ever obtained was 5,263. If I improved on that, said Randolph, I would surely be rewarded with a seat that boasted 'a smaller percentage of retired colonels than does this famous spa'.

Of course we did not expect to win; Cheltenham was the home of lost colonels. My hope was to reduce the majority of the sitting member Sir Walter Preston. While I was on a second holiday with the children at Brancaster, Frank wrote thanking me for a map I had sent him: 'I shall study your map of Cheltenham and plan secret canvassing raids (disguised, of course) to rescue from Sir Walter his most cherished areas.' Frank's raids had to be 'secret' for a while longer, since he was still a member of the Carlton Club and therefore officially a Conservative. However, his membership of the club was soon to come to a poignant end.

'My wife is a socialist candidate,' he told the club secretary in order to explain his resignation. The secretary blanched. At first he was speechless. Then he clasped Frank's hand with a look of unutterable sympathy, as if his wife had committed a despicable crime. 'If you are ever abroad and in trouble,' he managed to murmur, 'don't forget that the Carlton Club will never let you down.' The interview dissolved in a mist of unshed tears. A few minutes later Frank was saying good-bye to the club's barber. He thanked Frank for being a good customer and buying great quantities of hair oil. 'But don't buy any more,' he added by way of parting advice. 'You'll be bald in three years whatever you do.'

My policy for Cheltenham was based strictly on Labour's programme, and I believed in it whole-heartedly. The rise of Hitler chilled me to the bone. I remember, as I pushed the two babies in their pram to the rugger field in 1934, wondering if Hitler could possibly cause a war. Not if Labour's foreign policy were adopted, I assured myself: our policy being unequivocal support for the League of Nations and the inclusion of Russia as an ally. No need in that case for British 'rearmament'. The combined total of European armed strength would be such as to pre-empt even the maddest of mad-dog acts by Mussolini or Hitler.

On the home front I was ashamed to think that my two children drank in milk every week the equivalent of an unemployed worker's whole dole. There were no holidays with pay for the workers and we demanded *one* week's paid holiday a year for those in work. The House of Lords I regarded as rotten with decay (there were no life peerages or women members), comparing it to a mouthful of caries or, in my great-uncle Joe's more elegant phrase, 'ancient monuments'.

The absence of coalmines or heavy industry in or around Cheltenham meant that nationalization, in my supporters' eyes, was focused on the railway station. Let their proud 'Cheltenham Flyer' belong to the nation. There was, however, a certain piquancy in my attempts to sell nationaliza-tion of the banks as an attractive proposition. When I called on the manager of a joint-stock bank he said to me politely but firmly: 'There are x number of banks in this town and there is room for two or three. If they were all nationalized, my bank and my job would go. I shall not vote Labour.'

My egalitarian policy for education had an unexpected reception. When the boys and girls of the élitist Cheltenham College and Cheltenham Ladies' College saw my red-rosetted car they raised a tentative cheer. Not so the grammar school. I was heartily booed.

My worst hiccup occurred while canvassing in a convent to which my excellent agent, Bill Hayward, accompanied me. One of the nuns, noticing that I was not altogether comfortable in these unfamiliar surroundings, thought to put me at my ease by mentioning the one 'blessed' member of the Pakenham family: 'Poor Mary Pakenham' – or that is what I thought the nun said. I had never heard of the blessed lady and rashly began to question my potential supporter: 'Why do you call Blessed Mary Pakenham "poor"? Was it her own choice like the Poor Clares? Or did something dreadful happen to her?' The nun looked at me in astonishment.

'*Poor* Mary Pakenham,' she repeated, as if that explained everything. Then she added, 'We hold *him* in great reverence.' My agent was as foxed as I was. When I got home Frank solved the mystery for me. The only blessed one in the family had been the Hon. Charles Pakenham who left the Guards for the Church, bringing the Passionist Order to Ireland and taking the name of *Paul* Mary Pakenham. His uncle, the great Duke of Wellington, had said to him with typical common sense, 'Charles, you have been a good soldier. Now strive to be a good monk.'

By the time polling day arrived on Thursday 14 November, I had persuaded Cheltenham to listen to a distinguished series of visiting speakers. There was Naomi Mitchison, a socialist as uncompromising as anyone could wish. There was Aidan Crawley veering towards Labour. Roy Harrod confessed himself a Liberal but asked the electors to support me rather than a National Government whose economic policy was both callous and disastrous. Roy was a devoted Keynesian and was to write Keynes's official biography. My old friend the *Isis* reported strong support from the Oxford Labour Club:

The Hon. Mrs. Pakenham's candidature is unexpectedly popular in Cheltenham. Packed meetings have approved her energy and enthusiasm. Messrs Hood, Nield and Shebbeare from the Labour Club have been going over to assist the campaign: and the Government's attitude to the Miners' case, Foreign Affairs and Unemployment have been denounced with true Labour Club fire.

For the eve-of-the-poll meeting I was lucky enough to secure Dick Crossman as my star speaker. Dick was a great friend and a great enthusiast. Appointed a Philosophy don at New College, he had given a party in his rooms where everything he touched filled him with the enthusiasm of a natural explorer and discoverer of new ideas. That evening the special subjects of his lyrical praise were the capable hands of his guest, Renée Ayer (she was soon to marry Freddie) – which had enabled her to cross America on a motor-cycle – and the low backward-sloping angle of his up-to-date lavatory. I was to note the same ingenuous enthusiasm when Dick first went to London to meet a group of City businessmen. 'You know, they're really extremely interesting people,' he told me when we ran into each other in the Cornmarket, 'and radicals are wrong to ridicule them.'

The soubriquet of 'Double Crossman' had been planted on Dick by Maurice Bowra and it was never really eradicated. Its justification, such as it was, rested on Dick's mercurial and dazzling mind which led him, in argument, to leap on to a new idea before his opponents had caught up with the one before. So great was his mental agility that his enemies accused him of coming full circle in every discussion and ending by defending the position he had set out to destroy. Dick and I had attended the same philosophy lectures as students at Oxford, and I would pick out with interest his handsome features, blond hair falling untidily from a half-centre parting and powerful figure, usually seated between the equally craggy Stephen Spender and the slighter Douglas Jay, whose quizzical expression and bright brown eyes reminded me of a charming red squirrel.

I would have to admit that Dick's splendid oratory combined with the athleticism of his mind sometimes seemed to push him out on to ledges where he hung between reality and fiction. One such feat was achieved during that mass meeting at Cheltenham. Discussing the economic boom promised by the Conservatives, Dick Crossman, fellow of New College and member of the intellectual élite, perpetrated the great absurdity: 'They say there's a boom on the way. But what do booms mean to *working chaps like you and me?*' The remark was received with thunderous applause by the workers of Cheltenham and has been one of Frank's and my favourite quotes ever since.

On polling day there was much banging of dustbin lids and excitement among the chanting children of our two Labour wards – 'Vote, vote, vote for Mrs Pakenham' – and decorum at the count. Sir Walter Preston's unmarried sister, a friendly tweedy lady, had wished me 'Good hunting' on nomination day – 'I can't very well wish you good luck' – and good hunting I had had. In a straight fight Sir Walter polled 18,574 to my 7,784. Yet I had improved on the 1931 poll when the Conservative majority was 17,000 and I think our result seriously disappointed only two people: a garage proprietor on the fringe of the constituency who had backed me to win, and Miss Clarence, an ardent ex-suffragette in whose pretty, welcoming house at Charlton Kings I had lived.

Frank's uncle Lord Dunsany composed a long consoling poem on my defeat, based on Jean Ingelow's 'High Tide on the Coast of Lincolnshire' and entitled 'High Tide on the Coast of Gloucestershire', in which county Cheltenham is situated. He wrote it all out by hand with his mighty quill pen. Here is one verse:

> I sat & drank within a pub.
>   The pub closed down, I raised my eyes
> And there one thumped upon a tub,
> Soliciting the votes one buys.
>   She moved where Preston blathereth,
>   My nephew's wife Elizabeth.

Frank's other two uncles, Arthur Villiers and Walter Lord Dynevor, had both made characteristic comments on my candidature. Arthur felt sure that I could have got a better seat than one which meant withstanding 'the fiery onslaught of some retired gouty colonel'. He added that he had given the news to his mother (Frank's grandmother Lady Jersey) and sisters 'who are both accustomed to shocks!'. Uncle Walter, a diehard Conservative from Wales, wrote to Uncle Arthur, 'Elizabeth's intentions have caused a flutter. Did your friend Sir Stafford Cripps get hold of her? I shall be interested to hear from her why she is doing this. She will give you bankers a first-class financial crisis.'

The campaign was conducted on the highest level – no personal abuse – though one letter to the *Echo* signed 'National' came as light relief. 'National' protested that I had duped the people by preaching in a Unitarian pulpit on Armistice Day; also by happening to possess the same colour for my party badge as 'Flanders poppies', a name, Pakenham, that would come before Preston on the polling card and a 'semi-Conservative husband'. Yet my national appeal was deceptive for I was 'a socialist avowed and declared'.

Frank had spoken for me gallantly but had not needed to adopt much of a 'disguise'. For he had himself been deeply involved in the election, having been appointed election agent by the writer A. P. Herbert – the same amusing friend with whom I had 'conducted' the generating plant at Chiswick. Alan Herbert was persuaded by Frank to stand in Oxford as an Independent for the University seat, in order to loosen the Conservative academic stranglehold. Some academic in-fighting was involved. Prof Lindemann had tried for the Conservative nomination but was beaten by C. M. Cruttwell of Hertford, Evelyn Waugh's old college. (Evelyn entertained such an obsessional hatred for the harmless but hidebound old don, that he was to introduce a villainous character with the name of Cruttwell into his novels.) Alan Herbert's decisive victory gave enormous pleasure all round: to the ordinary academic voter who was immensely impressed by his election address, a brochure in which he gave his views trenchantly on the subjects he had studied but for things like agriculture and finance he wrote, 'I know nothing about it'; to the readers of his book *Holy Deadlock*, who realized that in A. P. H. they now had an effective champion of divorce law reform; and to Frank, who had avenged his friend the Prof and discovered his own remarkable talent for political organization – a talent that was in due course to be exerted in the far greater cause of the Beveridge Report and the Welfare State.

Frank wrote to me two days before the poll, looking forward to my return to the family. 'Perhaps you will feel a little lost without a great cause any more.' I appreciated his thought, but my career in the lecturing world was still absorbing enough to fill any gaps left by electoral defeat.

In 1934 I had delivered what was to be my last series of University Extension lectures on literary subjects. They took place in Canterbury, virtually under the shadow of the cathedral, for I spent each night with a canon's family in the precincts, the majority of my audience being white-collared workers and clergy wives. Indeed I was requested by the secretary of the class to wear my black BA gown trimmed with white rabbit fur when on the platform – 'our people like that sort of thing'. He sounded faintly apologetic, as well he might, for ten years later he was to emerge as George Wigg MP, one of the Labour Party's conspicuous left-wingers.

My subject was a loose comparison between Victorian or Edwardian and modern writers. Towards the end of my course I included an enthusiastic lecture on Joseph Conrad whose *Arrow of Gold* was among my favourite novels. It was fortunate that this was so, for sitting in the front row of the audience was the author's widow, Mrs Joseph Conrad. After the lecture was over, she came up and told me something of what it was like to be Conrad's wife during his later years. He used to suffer terribly from toothache. The only remedy was to keep on filling his mouth with cold water and rest his head on her shoulder, until he gradually drifted into sleep. When fully asleep his mouth would open and the tepid water dribble down inside her blouse. She would not move lest he should awake.

My next two courses of lectures moved firmly into the political arena. 'Makers of the Modern World' (1935) began with Churchill and later turned leftwards to the suffragettes and Lenin. Churchill's paradoxes delighted my Oxfordshire audience: one should be 'against Pacifists during the quarrel, and against the Jingoes at its close'; peacetime society required 'overwhelming force on the side of the rulers, innumerable objections to the use of any part of it'. But my class were against him when I quoted him as saying: 'The prevention of another great war should be the main preoccupation of mankind.' They did not want to consider that possibility. I tried to defend him over the Dardanelles fiasco in order that all sides should be heard. 'His real fault', I said, 'was not being able to convince his colleagues. A truly great man will create followers.' Five years later Churchill was to do just that.

Next year the village of Marcham in Berkshire heard from me about 'Europe Today', including the Soviets, Fascists, Nazis and Turks. I had just performed in my first broadcast dialogue, a series called 'The Under Thirties', with a Miss Erturkan from Ankara. Defending Atatürk, Turkey's dictator, she said, 'Poor countries cannot afford liberty.' Our dialogue taught me the difference in attentiveness between lecture and radio audiences. At one point Miss Erturkan lost her place in the scripted dialogue and began reading my part. As far as I know, absolutely no one noticed.

Meanwhile, Frank's political life had unexpectedly started up again in a dramatic way. During the Oxford summer term of 1936, posters went up in the city announcing that Sir Oswald Mosley would hold a public meeting in the Carfax Assembly Rooms on 14 May. Officially his movement was at that time called the British Union of Fascists. I remember passing a car in Broad Street whose registration number happened to be the abhorrent letters BUF. I wondered why its owner did not insist on a change. Later I was to realize that the owner may in fact have paid a lot to get it.

Since the Fascist meeting was to be in termtime, a good attendance of students was ensured, among them our incomparable friend Philip Toynbee of Christ Church. His mother, Rosalind Toynbee, was a Roman Catholic convert, but Philip had entered a youthful phase of atheism and was a card-carrying member of the Communist Party. His good looks were striking but ambiguous: the large nose, full lips, thin face and straight dark hair could belong either to a Christian ascetic or a modern Mephistopheles. His gleaming eyes and brilliantly ironic sense of humour suggested that it was the latter.

Philip's family were among the most distinguished in Oxford. Rosalind was married to the mega-historian Arnold Toynbee, but the marriage was not happy. Professor Toynbee had once come to tea with us at Singletree and when offered cucumber sandwiches had said, 'I never get things like this at home.' He cleared the plate. I guessed, rightly, that the marriage would break up.

Philip's grandparents lived on Boars Hill above Oxford, the famous Professor Gilbert Murray and his aristocratic wife Lady Mary, a Howard of Castle Howard in Yorkshire. She was a fanatical teetotaller and health food devotee. We went to lunch with them and I committed the sin of looking around for the salt. 'There's no salt,' said our observant hostess laconically. 'All the food is cooked on conservative principles and requires none.' Abashed, I noticed that every dish was served in oven-proof pottery and indeed tasted excellent, as did the fruit juices to drink. Since Lady Mary's time, conservative cookery in general has become more popular and more relaxed: there are oven-proof dishes everywhere and also salt if you want it. Her teetotallism, however, has not spread. Indeed her grandson Philip and son Basil Murray, as soon as the repressive influence of their families was removed, began to have drink problems.

Basil Murray, as well as Philip Toynbee, was to be at the Fascist meeting. We were extremely fond of him though not so intimate with him as with his nephew. Basil's second wife, Aline Craig, was the same exquisite figure from Ulster with whom the young Maurice Bowra had fallen in love. Though Philip was an open communist, his uncle Basil still represented the liberal ethos of pre-war Oxford: highly political but not necessarily committed to any party, devoted to cultural values and civilized procedures in public life. Yet he had a courageous strain of combativeness, perhaps inherited from his father and his father's Australian background.

The Carfax Assembly Rooms were packed to the doors. As an undergraduate I had danced many charlestons and black-bottoms in the long, rather narrow room that was hired out for subscription dances, concerts and political meetings. Frank and I walked up the central aisle to the fourth row, immediately behind Basil Murray. I saw no police on duty but a number of Blackshirts. In the audience, as well as people from the town, there were dons, their wives and a large group of Oxford busmen.

Oswald Mosley came on to the platform alone, as was his custom. This at once caused resentment among many of his audience, myself included. We believed that the presence of at least a chairman contributed to, if it did not guarantee, democratic proceedings.

The central figure of the Assembly Rooms wore a tight black sweater, black trousers, leather belt and an expression of haughty challenge. What a virile animal he is, I thought, and a wicked one too. From the very beginning of his speech it was obvious he was out to goad, needle and jab the socialists in his audience into a reaction both verbal and violent. 'I know you Ruskin fellows,' he taunted a group of bus-drivers present, 'with your sham Guardee accents.' It was a busman who took the cue. Suddenly in the midst of Mosley's tirade he lifted a clenched fist and shouted: 'Red Front!'

The audience burst into excited applause. Mosley gave a withering look and then fixed his celebrated black eyes – celebrated for spell-binding – for a moment on the back of the room where his Blackshirts were standing by. 'If anyone says that again,' he hectored, 'I'll have him thrown out.' The fluent angry oration continued, Mosley's deep chest expanding like a swimmer's about to take the high dive.

'Red Front!' Another heckler had time only to half-rise to his feet before the Leader was down on him with a roar: 'The next person who says "Red Front" will be thrown out – forthwith!'

Since that meeting I have always associated the word 'forthwith' with what we learnt to know as dictator-language. It was a word that brooked no delay. It got things done. No messing about with rules or laws or the delaying actions of the bourgeois liberal state. 'Into the Black Maria – forthwith!' 'Into the cells – forthwith!' 'Into the ovens – forthwith!' Though in memory that urgent word was spoken by Tom Mosley, in imagination the voice and the commands were those of Hitler.

Meanwhile the two hecklers had resumed their seats, but now a double file of uniformed Blackshirts carrying black rubber truncheons were inching their way up the hall. Each time I half-turned to look at them the space between Blackshirts and platform – and between them and Basil Murray and us in the row behind him – had perceptibly narrowed. They were closing in like the walls of an Edgar Allan Poe torture chamber. By this time everybody knew that someone had to say it again. Basil seemed to see himself as a priest-victim. He stood up and in a curiously academic voice enunciated the two magic words – words that he had probably never used before in his life – '*Red Front!*'

Mosley flashed the sign, the Blackshirts charged forward to seize Murray and suddenly there was a tremendous bang as if a bomb had exploded and the whole room was in uproar. That first bang had in fact been caused by the sudden clash of steel chair on steel chair, as the busmen seized the seats they had been occupying and smashed into the Blackshirts armed with batons and into their Fascist supporters with their own steel chairs. Within seconds a huge cloud of dust made it hard to see what was happening. The smell was so horrible that I took it to be literally the smoke of battle and the Carfax Assembly Rooms to be on fire.

Where was Frank? I had seen his back disappearing as he dived into the mêlée. There was Crossman. Up on the platform, bawling at Mosley, 'You call off your men and I'll call off mine!' But as Dick had no 'men', that idea led nowhere. Then I heard him shouting, 'All women on to the platform' – but, of course, we could not get near it.

I have no clear recollection of how the battle ended. The next thing I remember was reaching the pavement at Carfax, the crossroads at the centre of Oxford, and seeing Philip Toynbee standing inside a red telephone kiosk with the red blood streaming down his face. No doubt he was calling the *Daily Worker*.

When we got home I found that Frank was covered in bruises, with the marks of rabbit punches around his kidneys. Dr Greene ordered complete rest for a few days and forbade visitors. Frank's mind was throbbing with plans to 'break the Fascists' power in Oxford for ever'. Our friend Tommy Balogh, however, a Jewish exile from Hungary now attached to Balliol, saw the Oxford riot against a wider, more lurid sky. Standing beside Frank's bed as soon as visitors were allowed, he said in ominous, measured tones: 'It – has – begun.'

11

The Run-Up
· *1936–7* ·

Frank made a slow recovery from his beating up. It was not until five days after the Mosley meeting that Dr Greene diagnosed his continuous headache as concussion. As soon as he was up and about but only partially recovered, he made an attempt to bring the cudgel-bearing thugs to justice. At the same time, however, the police were bringing an action against Basil Murray and Bernard Floud, one of the young Oxford communists, for causing an affray. Our disgust was total.

I attended the first day of the police case with Frank in the magistrates' court behind the Town Hall and left with the strong impression that the forces of 'law and order' were on the side of the Fascist aggressors. The verdict was not delivered until the beginning of July when I had taken the children to Brancaster for their seaside holiday, leaving Frank, not yet quite well, in the care of Dr Greene for another week or so. Frank's letters to me told the picaresque story of the verdict.

The chairman of the magistrates announced a fine of two pounds for Basil Murray whom we all regarded as the victim of aggression, while Bernard Floud, the communist, was pronounced 'not guilty'. Basil's 'guilt' seemed to Frank a shocking miscarriage of justice and he rose excitedly to his feet, still feeling the effects of concussion, and shouted: 'I'd like to tell those buggers on the bench what I think of them!' The offensive noun was hardly appropriate to the chairman of the bench, who happened to be Lady Townsend, married to a professor at Christ Church.

Worse still, Frank suddenly saw among the male members of the bench one Fifoot, his inveterate enemy since some early Tory in-fighting between the Prof and Cruttwell for the University seat. Frank and Fifoot had been the respective agents for the two Conservative contenders. Not only did Fifoot have old scores to settle but he was also a proctor. Was Frank to incur the wrath of the University's legal arm? With all speed he vacated his seat in the court and fled to Balliol where the Master, Sandy Lindsay, reigned as Vice-Chancellor. By the time Fifoot was thundering at the door, Lindsay had listened to Frank's account of the scene in court. No more was heard from Fifoot.

Meanwhile, Frank's efforts to expose police collaboration with the Fascists were being pursued with difficulty. In an interview with the Chief Constable of Oxford – the Wolf to every socialist Red-Riding-Hood though his name was actually Fox – Frank was told: 'I am a servant of the Crown. I can do nothing.' So Frank sought out 'the Crown', in the person of Sir John Simon, the Home Secretary, to whom he was warmly recommended by Simon's fellow Liberal, Professor Gilbert Murray. Actually, Simon already knew Frank by sight if not by name, for they had often met on a station platform in Oxfordshire waiting for the London train, where he would address Frank genially as 'Charles' or sometimes 'Bracken'. (Charles is inexplicable, but Frank and Brendan Bracken both had mops of untidy curls.) On this occasion Frank was taken to see Simon by our friend Hugh Dalton MP, one of the Labour leaders. During the interview, Simon was 'really rather decent' though in fact he talked Frank down for half an hour. Nothing was gained from 'the Crown'. When I say 'nothing' I mean nothing in the way of a public clamp-down on the growing activity of the BUF, whose policy was to provoke communist violence and stir up anti-Semitism, especially by marches and demonstrations in the East End where socialism and Jewry were strong. But, as I shall show, the notorious Mosley meeting in Oxford was to leave almost everything changed in Frank's own political life, and so also in mine.

On 14 July 1936 Frank was writing to me in Brancaster that he had developed a 'shaking' hand and Dr Greene had 'climbed all over' him to find out why – a reference to Raymond Greene's exploits as a mountaineer. 'My oneness with you in politics', continued Frank, 'has compensated much for my rather moderate health since the Fascist meeting.' Frank's allies during the legal aftermath of political struggle had been Labour, Liberal or Communist; and though all our Tory friends were totally opposed to Fascism, we felt that the Conservatives as a party were ambivalent. Lady Astor's condolences to Frank on his beating up were the most unusual he received. 'Lady Astor accused *you*', he reported to me, 'of inciting me to beat up Mosley, and when I agreed you were partly responsible, she said it sent you up in her estimation!'

Two further events that summer were to accelerate Frank's movement to the left. The Spanish Civil War broke out. It seemed to us in Oxford to be a plain case of the democratically elected government being threatened by a military dictatorship. To compound his sins, General Franco, the Fascist leader, was accepting help from Hitler and Mussolini. Our Government's considered policy of 'non-intervention' in Spain on either side was playing into the dictators' hands. A Spanish Democratic Committee was formed in Oxford, frequent meetings were held at some of which I spoke, and money raised for the International Brigade that was soon to be fighting voluntarily in Spain. The Brigade, indeed, was not a mere matter of concussion and headaches; Basil Murray was to die in Spain and others of whom we knew, Julian Bell, John Cornford and Lewis Clive, were to be killed. The fervour of our fund-raising meetings in Oxford was so great that on one occasion our friend Henry Whitehead, a young Mathematics don at Balliol, found that he had signed an IOU for the whole of one term's salary. Naomi Mitchison's brother, Professor Jack Haldane, was our most successful visiting speaker. Himself an avowed communist, he managed to enunciate a defence of violence which momentarily convinced everyone in the hall. 'When governments become traitors, honest men become revolutionaries.' Tumultuous applause.

The third event to push Frank leftward was a letter I received in July from Tom Baxter, Labour agent for the King's Norton division of Birmingham. Tom invited me to put my name forward as Labour candidate. King's Norton was a very different proposition from Chel-tenham Spa. Heavy industry, in the shape of the Austin motor works, was increasing in the area and there was also Cadbury's famous chocolate factory at Bournville. Admittedly the Cadbury workers were not outstandingly militant; they had been described by Douglas Cole, a former socialist candidate for King's Norton, as having 'chocolate-coated souls'. The Cadbury family and their many relations included pacifists, Quakers and a tradition of liberal employment. The works themselves were advertised by a stroke of genius as 'The Factory in a Garden', thereby creating an image that was very different from the old associations of 'Brum' with grime.

There was a radical tradition among Labour candidates: Cole was moving steadily to the left before diabetes struck him down prior to the 1931 election. Dick Mitchison succeeded him. He had taken a double first at Oxford before fighting in the Great War. Together he and his wife Naomi had created a strong sense of idealism in the party. I was aware of the devotion which they had aroused when I spoke at the 1935 election for Dick, though a small minority of supporters trembled at the effect of Naomi's latest novel, *You Have Been Warned*, on the Quakers in the constituency. Victor Gollancz, essentially a left-wing publisher, had actually refused to be associated with the book, telling Naomi that it would certainly be stigmatized as 'filthy'. (In fact, I can remember one seduction by a skating instructor with sharp knees, but there was no filth.) When King's Norton failed to go Labour at Dick's second attempt, he decided to move to a 'winnable' seat. So the chocolate-coated souls were seeking re-embodiment in a new Labour representative. The agent's letter invited me to come and see him in August.

Frank's reaction to this new prospect for me was jubilant. He wrote to me, still at Brancaster, about Baxter's 'exciting' letter. 'You must accept the invitation in terms which while enthusiastic suggest that you have even better offers elsewhere.' (Today we laugh at the mixture of Gladstonian pomp and cynicism.) 'I think it is a great chance', continued Frank, 'and would love to help you do in young Cartland, the last relic of the authority of an era already in decay. I am madly thrilled about the King's Norton news. I am sure you could pull it off.'

Ronald Cartland, brother of the best-selling novelist Barbara Cartland, was the extremely popular member for King's Norton. Fair and romantic like his sister, he was also a knight in shining armour genuinely involved in the welfare of his constituents. Every girl who did not actually belong to the Labour or Liberal Parties was in love with him – and a few who did belong to the opposition. The only two faults we could find in him were, first, that he was a Conservative, and second, that he affected a personality cult by speaking on his platforms without a chairman. Not a few other young Conservatives adopted this method of speaking but Labour would not touch it, regarding it as undemocratic.

Frank's conviction that I could 'pull it off' referred to my appearance before the King's Norton selection committee. I took the train to Birmingham – all very familiar to me, through my own childhood and many more recent visits to Michael Hope and his family – and found that I had two outstanding rivals. One was Leonard Woolf, the former civil servant and expert on the Far East, who knew everything about colonialism and was now a leading pacifist. The pacifist bloc at Bournville were running him hard and felt that it was almost impudence on the part of a girl scarcely out of her twenties to put up against a man so distinguished, the husband of Virginia Woolf. The next thing I knew was that Leonard had withdrawn.

My other rival was a young man, younger than me and clearly destined to go far in the Labour movement. His father was Arthur Greenwood, the handsome Labour leader and President of the WEA. His son Anthony was equally good-looking with even more charm than his father and a stronger character. It was obvious that Tony Greenwood would pick up a 'winnable' seat without the slightest difficulty, even if it were not King's Norton.

We chatted together amiably in the ante-room until I was called in, followed by Tony, to make our decisive speeches. I can remember speaking louder and faster than usual and pumping out more confidence than I actually felt. I was called back to be told that I had been chosen. I don't believe that my speech had been all that 'decisive', for I heard afterwards that Tom Baxter, the divisional agent, and Harold Nash, secretary for the Bournville area, had both decided they wanted me.

My claim to King's Norton was twofold. Tom and Harold felt that a young woman was more likely to beat Ronnie Cartland than anyone else available. And the fact that I was half a Chamberlain by birth gave me a pull. I could claim that the old Chamberlain tradition of 'Radical Joe' – still a powerful one in Birmingham – was more truly represented by me, his great-niece, than by his son, my cousin Neville.

On wider issues, also, Frank and I were becoming known in the Labour movement, since Oxford was a city that liked to be visited. We put up Hugh and Ruth Dalton for the night on the occasion of a 'Pink Lunch Club' dinner – the club being *pink* rather than *red* in its political views, since it was mainly attended by academics. Dalton took this opportunity to expound to me the awfulness of Germany; not just the Nazis but the German people as a whole. I questioned him on this extraordinary view, a most inappropriate one for the party of international brotherhood. He gave me this answer. 'When I was an undergraduate at Cambridge I saw a lot of a German Rhodes Scholar. I noticed that he kept a small china vase on his mantelpiece which he treated with great care, even reverence. One day I could not resist asking him what was inside the vase that led him to handle it differently from any other ornament. He looked at me oddly and said: "The ashes of my grandmother." This nauseated me to such a degree that I have never been able to feel the same about the Germans since.'

Others who addressed us at the Pink Lunch Club were Bertrand Russell and, later on, Herbert Morrison, who entreated us never again to give a bob to a beggar in a London street – 'the Labour-dominated London County Council takes such care of these cases that today all beggars are imposters'.

I also attended many weekend conferences: one of them was organized by the New Fabian Research Bureau in Maidstone where I met for the first time an animated political gossip called Kingsley Martin. I thought his dark, curly hair and sharp profile fit for a Roman coin, and his reaction to a Nonconformist background seemed similar to my own. We both belonged to the agnostic left. He was the brilliant editor of the *New Statesman* and the subject of Basil Dufferin's wit. Speaking of a broadcast by some aspiring Labour publicist, Basil said scornfully, 'It's all my eye and Kingsley Martin.'

Early in September 1936 Frank and I attended a conference in Berlin to discuss democracy and peace with fellow-academics. At first in two minds whether or not to visit Hitler's Germany, we finally decided to go, while safeguarding ourselves against Nazi prying by an innocent device. We placed a Gollancz 'Left Book Club' volume, with its startling yellow and black jacket, on top of our suitcases, with one of my brown hairs laid across it. If we found the hair had been displaced we would – do what? I suppose go home immediately. However, the hair remained in place throughout our two-day visit, proving that no Nazi spy (or chambermaid) had interfered with (or dusted) our room. Our discussions downstairs in the hotel foyer degenerated into pointless propaganda for and against National Socialism. 'You English had your revolution three hundred years ago, when you cut off your king's head. All we want is to have our peaceful revolution now.'

'But Hitler's revolution will lead to war.'

'If we thought that, we'd leave the party tomorrow.'

I also remember arguing about leadership with a German professor and being appalled when he said: 'The best way to lead is not by words but by looking your followers in the eye. We have learnt to lead "eye to eye".'

On our return from Berlin Frank joined the Cowley and Iffley Labour Party. It was a red-letter day for me. He became election agent for Harry Uzzell, husband of our local orator, Ruth. Harry was as silent as Ruth was eloquent. Nevertheless we concocted a slogan for Harry that carried him to victory on 2 November 1936:

> Vote for Uzzell
> The man you can't muzzle.

To muzzle our dear old Harry would indeed have been an act of supererogation. As far as I know he did not open his mouth in the Council Chamber once.

Meanwhile, on 17 October I had been adopted for King's Norton by the party as a whole. Frank and I were now at last advancing together along the same road.

Some time near the beginning of 1936 I had been to my gynaecologist, Dr Helena Wright, for a routine check. During this visit she disclosed to me her interest in a simple scheme for sex determination. Beginning with a story of how Louis XIV approached his wife if he wanted a girl and waited for his wife to approach him if he wanted a boy, Dr Wright continued with an account of how farmers gave their cows alkaline douches when sterile. She proceeded to describe a method of sex determination based on the theory that male sperm preferred an alkaline solution and female sperm an acid one. She already had over a dozen women patients collaborating with her to test this theory. Would I be another?

My instinct, as the daughter and sister of doctors, was to welcome 'scientific' experiment. If Frank and I had another child next spring, Thomas would be three and a half, an ideal age I was taught by the books for a brother or sister to arrive. As Dr Wright had informed me that my normal condition was somewhat acid, I would have to take steps to get a brother for Thomas, whereas if I left it to nature a sister would result. Of course we both realized that Thomas himself had been a gift of 'nature', not 'steps'. If I was to take an active part in the experiment, I must go for a boy. This I did. On 1 August, in embarrassing circumstances, I discovered that our third baby was on the way. We were staying with the Duke and Duchess of Devonshire at Compton Place near Eastbourne. Suddenly in the midst of a lively rubber of bridge I realized that I was going to be sick. I fled out into the long hall. The grand staircase seemed far away. No time to reach my bedroom on the first floor. No idea where the ground-floor 'gents' was either. On the verge of despair I spotted a splendid silver salver on a gilded side-table. No cards or letters upon it. Saved!

When Frank came to bed at 4 a.m. I gave him the news. In return he told me how our endearing host had recounted to him the last hours of his father, Brigadier the 5th Lord Longford, at Gallipoli. The Duke had found himself, encouraged by Frank, telling the tale no less than three times in the course of a convivial evening. At the first telling, Longford had said to the Duke, then the Marquess of Hartington and his ADC, 'Lord Hartington, I wish you to take this message immediately to the commanding officer over there.' The Duke explained, 'Your father was very formal on these occasions.' At the second time round the atmosphere was somewhat less formal, and Longford was addressing his ADC simply as Hartington, 'Your father was never one to stand on ceremony, Frank,' said the duke. At the final telling, the climate at Gallipoli (and in Compton Place) had become totally relaxed and Frank's father addressed his ADC by the nickname of 'Harty-Boy'.

We had been entertained by Lord Hartington's equally charming brother the year before at Lismore Castle in Ireland. We were touring; night was upon us and we could just see the towers built by King John in the distance. We decided to drive up. Lord Charles Cavendish was looking through a letter he had written while a guest at Clandeboye and read the last paragraph aloud to us with some pride: 'I shall soon be home, dispensing justice to peasants and rebels – between drinks, of course.' We spent a delightful evening of conversation with Charlie – between drinks, of course – and woke to a view from the bedroom windows as perfect of its kind as any I have seen. The view was not above us but straight below. One looked down a sheer drop of over a hundred feet directly into the waters of the glorious Blackwater river, a vision of liquid amber speckled with pebbles and swaying water plants caught in its golden folds.

Two months after our visit to Compton Place and shortly before I met the King's Norton selection committee, I told Tom Baxter that I was expecting another baby. He had a baby son of his own and took my news with calm. It was only to be expected of a young female candidate whose chief political interest was in the family. It could even give me more authority, or at least mutual fellow-feeling with the mothers of King's Norton. So there were to be no difficulties about having another baby. No political difficulties, that is to say. Had I known, however, what was in store for us on the family front at the end of the year, I might have waited until Thomas was at least four years old.

Meanwhile, on 11 December I had arrived at my aunt Bertha Hope's house in Birmingham for a week of pre-Christmas speeches and festivities. It was in her drawing-room, glittering with high gloss paint in which the chandeliers were reflected, that I listened to King Edward VIII abdicating from his throne. The décor seemed appropriate to the occasion. (Actually it was Uncle Donald not Aunt Bertha who went in for the high gloss. He was great fun. From childhood onwards I connected him with something more dashing than the Chamberlains ever achieved: lavish ten-shilling tips delivered to me in his pyjamas just as I was leaving after a visit; glasses of rare yellow Chartreuse, his favourite drink, when I was a teenager.) My reaction to the Abdication broadcast was sheer incredulity. Could this really be the King speaking? To me it sounded more like the hero of a 'penny dreadful', with his uninhibited clichés about 'the woman I love'. All my Chamberlain blood repudiated this sin against austerity, against the dignity of the office.

From the Cavendish Hotel, where Frank was having a cocktail with his sister Mary, he wrote on the same date (11 December) giving me a more personal slant on the Abdication. 'The King's abdication leaves London COLD – Chips Channon and the Duff Coopers are apparently furious that Mrs Simpson has "let them down".'

For Christmas 1936 when Thomas was three and a quarter, Frank and I planned to stay *en famille* with the Lambs at Coombe Bissett. Thomas developed a sore throat and ran a temperature on the 23rd. So on Christmas Day I took Antonia to the Lambs, where she celebrated with her five-year-old cousin Henrietta. This suited the four-year-old Antonia well. She had become an ardent feminist. All horses were mares, Cinderella's coach being drawn by six white mares; and when she said her prayers on Frank's back, she prayed to 'Dada's *Mother*', not his '*Father* in Heaven'.

I returned to Oxford next day to find Thomas no better. By the 28th he could not move his left arm or turn his head. Dr Greene thought it was post-diphtheretic paralysis for which the treatment was electrical therapy. But before sending Thomas into Oxford for a course of muscular stimulation that would have proved fatal, he called in a second opinion. Dr Cooke removed Thomas instead to the Wingfield Orthopaedic Hospital near Cowley. When Frank fetched Antonia home from Coombe Bissett on the 30th, she had to wear a mask to visit Thomas like the rest of us. Dr Cooke and Dr McNair Scott at the Wingfield had diagnosed polio, in those days called infantile paralysis.

Thomas was in the Wingfield for four months. His hospital experiences must have been frustrating for he developed a temporary stammer, though his overt reactions were uninhibited. He had a minimum of three separate visitors every day: his parents and nanny Jean, often with Antonia. Each one of us, as he or she said good-bye and left him in his cot, would be lacerated by a crescendo of wails audible even from the hospital drive. But as soon as his visitor was out of earshot, we were assured, Thomas would stop crying and briskly make his regular demand: 'Push my cot up to Pam's bed' – Pam being a lovely teenage girl also in the children's polio ward. Sometimes Thomas assigned the privilege of entertaining him to another teenage girl, the daughter of a well-known historian.

I learnt a good deal about small children in hospital, especially their gallant efforts to keep in touch with active life. All the interesting objects that were mentioned in story-books I read to Thomas had to be reproduced for him on my next visit: a home-made flag, bow-and-arrow, catapult, feathered Indian head-dress, slip-knot. He became absorbed in how things worked. 'To make a rope you get some very thick string and twist it together.' 'Who told you that?' I asked. 'The gnomes told me.'

Where Thomas's polio had come from remained a mystery. There were no other cases in Oxford at the time so it may have been passed on by a carrier. (No vaccine in those days.) It was suggested that he had picked it up on 19 December from a children's Christmas party given by the Labour supporters of Cowley. I refused to accept that idea, preferring to believe he had caught it from a similar party in Christ Church, or even from Lady Jersey's 'Gran Pie' party – as Antonia called her great-grandmother's children's party featuring a bran-pie.

Thomas returned home on 8 April 1937, still a case of walking wounded. His head was held up in a steel and leather collar and his left arm supported by an aeroplane splint. Next day Abe Lazarus came to see him, and after an attempt at 'Up the rebels!', Thomas showed an admiring audience that he could stand up alone in his bath.

Antonia was overjoyed to have him back. She had missed him sorely, if only for their endless skirmishes. I think he too was overjoyed to be back with me at home again, for when I appeared one day wearing a bright new shirt, he shouted ecstatically, 'Oh, the blue, the blue! The sky, the sky!' He also had his nanny Jean and our beloved family midwife, Nurse Samways – 'Sammy', who was to bring into the world a whole new tribe of Chamberlains, Hopes and Pakenhams – to break the shock of the coming sibling event.

Paddy was born at seven minutes to midnight on 17 April. Our doctor, who happened to be celebrating his own birthday that evening, arrived too late to administer anything but good wishes and congratulations. Nor could Sammy spare time from Paddy's rapid progress into the world to open the formidable sterilized drum, a large sealed square tin with tin-opener attached, containing gauze, bandages and all the rest. Sammy called on the father to help her out. As Frank had never opened even a can of sardines in his life before, I became greatly alarmed at the prospect of him cutting off his fingers during the operation. I kept shouting out ways in which catastrophe might be prevented. But necessity was the father of prevention, and Frank came through his travail without a scratch.

'What shall we call him?' I asked Thomas on presenting him to his brother. Thomas looked at him. 'He's a bald pate.' Then he thought deeply and finally suggested 'Tom'.

'Why Tom?'

'Because it's a sort of little bother of a name.' That seemed to him to put the brothers into a true perspective. Thomas first, Tom nowhere.

Paddy had a high, narrow forehead; we joked that in time it would prove to be that of a Jesuit bishop. Dick Crossman visited us when Douglas and Peggy Jay, together with their first-born son, Peter, were staying with us. The sight of what young babies really looked like was a shock to Dick. He recoiled from the newborn Paddy. When Peter Jay, a few months older and with more hair, was introduced, Dick said, 'Ah, that's better.' For the first time I was conscious of Dick's clumsiness with people.

By the time of his christening in Christ Church (Anglican) Cathedral, Paddy had become a handsome baby. His godparents were Anne Martelli, Roy Harrod, Maurice Bowra, Naomi Mitchison, Professor Lindemann and Mrs Lindsay, wife of the Master of Balliol. None of them could really be called Anglican, though Mrs Lindsay was full of mystical insights. She once spoke at a discussion group on the way human beings should live in brotherhood. 'Think of seagulls, a host of seagulls flying round and round a huge ship. There is no one to direct, guide or control them yet their wings never touch, never clash. Why can't we be the same?'

Thomas was the only critic of his brother's christening. Nearly four years old, he listened carefully to the words of the service and observed afterwards: 'I didn't like that clergyman. He said he was going to smother an old man. . . .' I explained that baptism was intended to 'smother the old man' – meaning the devil – in Paddy. Thomas was well satisfied.

Now that Antonia and Thomas had a deeply religious nurse and one parent who at least said his prayers, their interest in God quickened. On Easter Sunday I had taken Antonia to the Cathedral. She whispered to me: 'No one knows who made God.' About the same time she asked Nurse Samways, 'Did God make my bicycle?' 'No,' replied Sammy and Thomas intervened to point out that it was made by a man in the Cowley works. Antonia: 'But God made the man who made the bicycle.' Soon afterwards Frank rushed into the room at bath-time with a towel playfully draped over his head. Antonia gave a delighted scream and said: 'First I thought it was God; then I saw it was only Dada.'

I was trying at about the same time to explain to Thomas the difference between public and private property when he found the answer for himself: 'God is public property because he belongs to all the different countries.'

Antonia's precocity as a reader became evident before she was quite five. I was telling my somewhat sceptical mother that she could read anything, and by way of demonstration handed her *The Times*. Antonia read the first leader through without a stumble; of course she did not understand the full meaning – who does? – but she knew how to pronounce all the words; words like non-intervention and constitutional. 'Why do you make her memorize that stuff?' asked my mother critically. With some difficulty I convinced her that Antonia had never seen the stuff before. For her pleasure, Antonia was reading to herself at six years old *Black Beauty*, *What Katy Did*, and E. Nesbit's *The Enchanted Castle*. Her advanced reading brought her to the thought that life might be a dream a year before the same thought had occurred to me as a child. 'Is all life a dream?' she asked. 'I think life is like a house you go into and then go out of again.'

From the age of three and a half Thomas would submit all the children's stories I read aloud to rational investigation, starting with Beatrix Potter's *Peter Rabbit*. 'Why did Mr McGregor catch Peter Rabbit's *father* and put him in a pie when he must have been able to run away much faster than Peter? We shall have to squeeze down a rabbit-hole and look in the Rabbits' Dictionary.' When Thomas was five I began reading aloud to them *The Story of Rome*. Though it became one of Antonia's favourite books, Thomas at first did not want to listen. 'Is it about people?' he asked suspiciously. 'I know too much about people already.'

If our two elder children kept our minds on the alert, it was Paddy who accidentally conferred the greatest benefit on the family. When he was four months old we all went to stay with Aunt Caroline Pakenham at Bernhurst. Frank's Uncle Bingo (Edward Michael Pakenham) lived across the road and happened to see his great-nephew sunbathing on the Bernhurst lawn. So impressed was he that he decided to leave all his worldly goods, when the time came, to Frank instead of to the childless Edward. According to another story, Bingo's mind had been changed by the sight not of a naked, sunburnt baby but of a silver bowl in the centre of the dining-table at his London club. 'Where did you get that bowl from?' he asked the club secretary. 'From Pakenham Hall. Lord Longford put it on the market.' Uncle Bingo never forgave Edward, or so the story goes; but I prefer to believe in the efficacy of Paddy's golden curls and brown eyes.

He was an extremely amenable baby, travelling with me to and from Birmingham at the back of my car. The permissive feeding instituted by Dr Spock was still far in the future and I was supposed to be bound by the rigid four-hourly system advocated by Dr Truby King. According to the King code, one's baby could be bawling its head off but if the time was not yet 6 a.m., 10 a.m., 2 p.m., 6 p.m. or 10 p.m., baby fury and distraught mother simply had to wait. Fortunately Paddy was a 'Truby King' natural, and would be lying placidly in his carrycot at the back of some hall or schoolroom, listening to his mother's oratory until the hour struck.

Indeed it was not the presence of Paddy that was beginning to make my visits to my Birmingham constituency more complex and challenging. It was the change in the political atmosphere as Hitler, once a mere tremor in the stomach, became our ever-present nightmare.

12

'It Has Begun'
· 1938–9 ·

One effect of the dictators' stepped-up menace was to drive our local Labour parties closer to the communists. We could count on them to be as anti-Hitler, anti-Mussolini and anti-Franco as we were ourselves. In my case, it meant my joining Sir Stafford Cripps' newly founded Socialist League, though Frank did not get involved. The League was designed to bind together all opposition forces against the dictators – Labour, Liberals, Communists. It was poison, however, to the pundits at Transport House, the joint HQ of the Labour Party and Trades Union Congress. These reactionary old buffers, as we then regarded them, knew from experience the insidious results on the party of communist infiltration. We did not. In Oxford we were continually sniping at the right-wing bosses of the big unions. We gave George Shepherd, general secretary of the whole Labour Party who sat enthroned at Transport House, the nickname of 'The Pope' and barracked him when he visited our city. Not surprisingly, sentence of execution was carried out against the Socialist League on 1 June. It was expelled from the Labour Party. Cripps himself was to be thrown out two years later.

Naomi Mitchison, in her autobiography, *You May Well Ask*, has described our feelings at this personal drama which took place during the annual Labour Party Conference of 1939. 'That rising growl: "Card vote, card vote!" impossible to feel brotherhood with them.' The 'rising growl' had come from the trades unionists and a show of 'cards' ensured that their block votes would totally overwhelm the constituency parties' previous show of hands. Naomi and I gave our single votes to Stafford Cripps. Indeed I hero-worshipped him.

Arthur Villiers was always a little ironical about Stafford, since he knew the Cripps family well, especially his brother Fred. In his fashionable social life, Fred was exactly the opposite to our austere, somewhat unapproachable leader and Uncle Arthur could hardly believe that Stafford belonged to the same Cripps clan. One day I had been researching for a lecture on H. H. Asquith, British Prime Minister from

1906 to 1915, and I read that he liked to hold hands with his lady friends under the carriage rug when out for a drive. That night I dreamt that Stafford Cripps and I drove through the streets of Bristol, where a Socialist League conference was taking place, in an open carriage holding hands. Clasped hands are, of course, a symbol of socialist brotherhood . . .

In a sense Frank had a more direct relationship with the communists. It was personal, through his much-admired young friend Philip Toynbee. The closest Frank got to Moscow was during a visit with Philip to Eire for the election of 1937. 'The election itself was agreed on all sides to be the quietest for years,' wrote Frank to me, and this disappointment made Philip's political ardours all the more attractive. 'Philip has been trying to persuade me (and you ultimately)', continued Frank, 'to join the Communist Party. I say, "Elizabeth decides my party allegiance. It is no good approaching *me*." But I know in my heart of hearts that we shall never join his party *as it is now*' – the CP being the spearhead of Marxist athcism.

Through Philip we met Esmond and Jessica Romilly, who were living in a house at Rotherhithe overhanging a Dickensian reach of the Thames. They have both been written about in Philip's moving book, *Friends Apart*. Esmond had founded a communist magazine and run away from his public school, Wellington. Since he was a nephew of Winston Churchill he constituted a juicy target for the press. To add defiance to insult, he made a runaway marriage with another Churchill relative, Jessica Mitford, fifth of the six famous Mitford sisters. Jessica (Decca) became a communist like Esmond, while her older sister Unity (Bobo) was to become a Nazi, mesmerized by Hitler personally. In 1938 Frank and I were to land ourselves in an awkward situation with Bobo.

We had been staying the weekend with our friend Alec Spearman, the Conservative MP, in Essex. Bobo was a fellow-guest. Everyone was nervous but excited to discover Hitler's dream-maiden among them. When Sunday evening came, Frank had to leave in order to be in Oxford at 9 a.m. for the Labour group's meeting in the Town Hall. Bobo told him she was staying the night in High Wycombe with her parents. Would he like to stay too? She would drive him to Oxford early on Monday. Bobo was not up to any of her sisters, not having the brilliance of my friend Nancy, or the beauty of Diana or Deborah (Debo); neither the brains of Decca nor the good sense of Pam ('Woman'). But there was a slow, naïve sweetness about her that made Frank unwilling to hurt her feelings. Surely the best thing was to travel with her instead of making excuses? In the event it proved a great deal better to travel with Bobo than to arrive.

Frank had been elected Labour councillor for the Cowley and Iffley ward of the Oxford City Council at a by-election in November 1937. His result showed the largest Labour majority ever achieved in an Oxford municipal election. On the drive from High Wycombe to Oxford the famous socialist councillor suddenly noticed that Miss Mitford's car was flying a swastika. Frank managed to get the car halted just before they reached the Town Hall and, with many secret blushes, slunk out into the anonymity of the street. Bobo was quite unaware of the drama she had created.

The Romillys gave us dinner in a room with river reflections on the ceiling. Julia, their baby, lay sleeping in a carrycot at the other end of the long room. The atmosphere was both funny and fervent – characteristic of the young in those days. We expected to see our world rebuilt on socialist lines within the next few years, instead of destroyed. The newness of the Romillys' baby and the dilapidated state of their old house seemed to set them apart, touchingly, from the brash materialism of the 1930s.

Next time I saw Decca was some thirty years after the war. She had come to England from the United States to say good-bye to her dying sister Nancy. The baby had died of measles in infancy, Esmond had been shot down in the RAF by the Nazis, Bobo had shot herself when she realized that her country and Hitler's were to fight each other. Decca's American husband, the communist Robert Treuhaft, did not meet his sister-in-law Diana Mosley. And Decca herself had written the last word on the Mitford dichotomy in her book, *Hons and Rebels*. In this double class Frank and I had also counted ourselves.

Stanley Baldwin's skilful handling of the Abdication crisis was his last real success as Prime Minister. It soon emerged that Britain's defences were by no means as strong as they had been represented at the general election of 1935. When challenged on his propaganda, he took refuge in an evasive reply: 'My lips are sealed.' The phrase 'sealed lips' became a familiar term of derision on the lips of his adversaries. He resigned as Prime Minister in 1937 and was replaced by Neville Chamberlain. The faint feeling of guilt that now assailed me at opposing my mother's favourite cousin only served to strengthen my political resolve. I must fight even harder to show that the betrayal of my family was justified.

Thanks to Hugh Dalton, I was invited to speak in the Birmingham Town Hall at a monster meeting demanding *collective* armed security against Hitler. I was paralysed with fright and felt too sick to eat or drink with the comrades beforehand. 'It's a good sign to be nervous,' Hugh reassured me. 'People who are not at all nervous never speak really well.'

What would great-uncle Joe Chamberlain have said to this audience, I asked myself. I thought of his many wisecracks, especially those against the idle rich whom he had compared to the lilies of the field – 'They toil not neither do they spin.' In due course my act of ancestor-worship brought inspiration, and though my speech as a whole was monotonous in tone and content, it did produce one good wisecrack: 'What sort of a government is this', I cried, 'that cannot say boo to the goose-step?'

Hugh Dalton was not the only supporter I had in high places. I made several speeches at Labour Party conferences to one of which Ernest Bevin, the right-wing trades union leader, listened favourably. Afterwards he told Frank that I ought to stand for the national executive: 'Our fellows would vote for her.' When Frank reported this remark to me, instead of being scornful of praise from the right wing I was distinctly elated. Next morning there was a ludicrous scene with a visitor to the conference.

I was packing up to leave my hotel. The time was ten minutes to twelve. I was just fastening the suspenders of my second stocking when there was a sharp rap on the bedroom door. In came the hotel manager accompanied by a tall, handsome lady, evidently in a state of extreme irritation.

'This is my bedroom,' she said angrily. 'Booked in my name. Why are you here?'

'I am within my rights,' I retorted, my temper rising. 'It's not yet twelve, I don't have to be out until twelve.' The manager, who had hitherto stood in silence looking uncomfortable, now decided to intervene.

'This is the Hon. Mrs Frank Pakenham,' he said to the angry lady, and to me, 'This is Mrs Beatrice Webb.' Immediately the dear lady became wreathed in smiles and begged me to continue putting on my stockings as slowly as I liked and to stay as long as I liked in the disputed bedroom. At the same time I was imploring her to move in *at once*, even if I had to leave barefoot.

Up to the year 1938 Frank and I had lived like most other young academic families: not uncomfortably but carefully, since Frank's salary had changed little since 1934 and now we had three children instead of two. Suddenly two of the Pakenham 'hons' left their all to the Pakenham 'rebels'. Our fortunes changed.

The Hon. Edward Michael Pakenham (Uncle Bingo) died in the spring of 1938 leaving everything to Frank. This included a furnished London house in Norfolk Street, off Park Lane, and a black tin box containing jewellery that his mother had left him. Heavy snake necklaces and bracelets, some set with amethysts and jet, became my unsocialist but treasured possessions. As if that were not enough, the Hon. Lady Pakenham (Aunt Caroline) died in the summer of that same year at the age of ninety-six, leaving to Frank Bernhurst and all it contained. More jewellery came my way: garnets and a beautiful star sapphire.

Antonia is the only one of the children who remembers Aunt Caroline well, and for her she was the authentic old witch of Grimm's fairy-tales. Huddled in the summerhouse or over the fire, she was always swathed up to the chin in black. Antonia got to know her even better through the acting chest, where I eventually deposited her wardrobe: the tiny-waisted black day dresses, best grey gown, lilac mantle, minuscule black satin slippers and parasol trimmed with black and white Chantilly lace. Her portrait presided over the former billiard-room, converted into a playroom, until the day when Paddy chipped a golf ball through her cheek.

Frank had been prepared to renounce all capital as a socialist, and now he had inherited two considerable legacies. He managed to dissipate a good deal of the second legacy on the *Town Crier*, a Birmingham Labour paper which he bought and to which he appointed Philip Toynbee as editor. The war was to dispose of much of the first. Nevertheless, these two windfalls left us with restive consciences. There was always to be a contradiction. I did not feel it when I was working in Stoke or Birmingham and at the same time visiting grand houses like Cliveden and Clandeboye. Socialist principles did not require one to diminish the quality of life by giving up one's old friends. Moreover, many of my students and political workers would come to stay with us at Stairways and Singletree. But these legacies were different. Nothing could completely resolve that contradiction. We decided to fight all the harder with our new weapons to bring about peace and a less inequitable distribution of wealth.

The *Town Crier* had a big voice but a tiny circulation. After Eden's resignation from the foreign secretaryship in protest over Mussolini's aggression in Abyssinia, it proclaimed: 'Chamberlain must go! The *Crier* will make Birmingham too hot to hold him!' It reminded me of a Cork nationalist newspaper called the *Skibbereen Eagle* which had once announced threateningly: 'The *Eagle* is keeping its eye on the British Empire.'

Not only did our Birmingham paper announce that Chamberlain must go, but we made this slogan the theme of a protest meeting in Oxford. Clement Attlee, our leader, came down by train from London and addressed a mass meeting in the Town Hall. At the end he was seized by a wildly enthusiastic crowd and borne shoulder high to Carfax and on along the Corn. The sounds of footsteps and marching feet alerted a prominent Conservative undergraduate who was dining in one of the clubs overlooking the route. He dashed into the street, adopted the slogan as his own – he was an ardent Churchillian and anti-appeaser – and soon the romantic, six-foot four figure of Hugh Fraser was leading the column that shouted 'Chamberlain must go!' This was the first time I met my future son-in-law.

Attlee was less exhilarated. Still borne aloft, more and more against his will, he kept looking at his watch and pleading, 'Please put me down. I shall miss the 9.34 to London.' As for Neville himself, with true Chamberlain phlegm he made no personal comment to Frank or me.

In Birmingham, Aunt Caroline's old grey Standard car was handed over to our friend George Tyler, an ex-miner from Nottingham who was posted to the *Crier*, and also became Frank's agent in West Birmingham, an inner city constituency for which Frank had been adopted.

We felt that Birmingham was beginning to hum. I had been chosen in the summer of 1938 to play the part of Queen Eleanor in the city's official pageant celebrating its history. My royal spouse (Michael Hope) would walk by my side while I would be carried in a litter around the field. I studied the gestures of Queen Elizabeth – her wave, her smile to the thousands of her cheering subjects – but on the day the ground was so bumpy and my bearers so brisk that I had to use both hands for clinging to the litter. No gracious waves.

I was invited to the famous Jewellers' Dinner and seated next to Harold Macmillan who was to reply for the guests. So tense was the future 'unflappable' Prime Minister that he addressed not a word to either of his dinner partners but spent the whole time correcting and re-correcting his speech in different-coloured inks.

When Frank ran into Ronald Cartland, MP for King's Norton, at the House of Commons and Cartland politely said, 'I wish they'd given your wife a better seat,' Frank replied with genuine conviction, 'She'll give you a fight and win it.' Fate decided that neither of us should fight King's Norton at the post-war general election.

Meanwhile our centre of interest swung from Birmingham back to Oxford.

Far from obeying the *Town Crier*'s call to 'go', Neville Chamberlain had brought off the Munich Pact with Hitler, after the crisis over the invasion of Czechoslovakia. Frank paid some of the Cowley unemployed out of Aunt Caroline's money to dig 'bomb-proof' trenches in Cowley's Florence Park. Afterwards the city engineer told him that the trenches had been badly dug. 'Munich made everybody nervous. All the work done during the Munich period was done badly.' Munich had divided the country into those who acclaimed Chamberlain as peacemaker and those who denounced him as appeaser. At this moment of strife the Tory MP for Oxford died and the violent feelings on both sides were concentrated in a by-election – the famous 'Munich' by-election. My old friend Quintin

Hogg was adopted by the Municheers. Who would fight for us, the anti-appeasers?

The Labour Party already had an excellent candidate in an even closer friend of ours, Patrick Gordon Walker. But when I attended the Party's executive committee I found the overwhelming feeling was against a straight Labour candidate and in favour of a Popular Front. Only thus, it was argued, would a political veto be put on Chamberlain and Hitler, and collective peace be preserved. I look back in shame to confess that this was also my own fervent opinion, and when I brought the news from the EC to Frank, he too agreed.

Poor Patrick was jettisoned. His wife Audrey wrote me a deeply reproachful letter, revealing that Patrick had worked out an original and ingenious plan for winning the constituency, now swept away in a tidal wave of disloyalty and false political propaganda. For a moment I was shaken. But these feelings in turn were obliterated by the mounting ardours of our Popular Front campaign. Everyone we knew was in it. At one extreme of the political spectrum was our dentist, an arch-reactionary who eagerly sat down with our new left-wing family doctor, in order to work out ways of defeating appeasement. Maurice Bowra was among heads of colleges who were outraged by Munich. At the other extreme was the whole Communist Party of Oxford, gathering triumphantly behind the Popular Front standard-bearer, Sandy Lindsay, Master of Balliol.

As it turned out, Lindsay was both too amateurish and too lofty to face a political orator like Quintin Hogg. The press were nonplussed by Lindsay's unconventional conferences, conducted in the college kitchen with Lindsay sitting on the kitchen table nonchalantly swinging his long legs. At the same time Lindsay himself was shocked by some of the political slogans put out by us in his name, notably our masterpiece: 'A Vote for Hogg is a Vote for Hitler.'

It is a matter of history that the alleged Hogg–Hitler vote triumphed on polling day, 27 October 1938. The Popular Front failed. A new official Labour candidate had to be adopted in time for the general election expected in 1940 at latest. There was no question of Gordon Walker being re-adopted by or indeed accepting a constituency so riddled with communism. To Frank, Oxford in any shape was perfection; as a constituency it would be incomparable. Since his boyhood it had been the city of his dreams, successes, intellectual growth, athletic prowess, visits to bookshops, runs around Christ Church meadows. When the Oxford City Labour Party adopted him as their parliamentary candidate in spring 1939 there was only one doubt in both our minds. Would Transport House allow him, a leftist, to transfer from West Birmingham and be endorsed for Oxford?

Frank went up to London and described the scene at Transport House in a letter to me:

The episode turned out quite amazingly unlike my anticipations. They dissolved in laughter much of the time. The final exchange between me and a red-faced Trade Unionist (whom I suspect of being the man who moved Cripps' expulsion) was this. *Red-Face*: 'When you go back to Oxford give your wife a kiss from me.' (Loud laughter.) *F.P.*: 'I hope you'll visit us one day and do it yourself.' (Loud and prolonged laughter.) *Red-Face*: 'I should enjoy that greatly – as there's nothing on her lips which would come off.' (Loud and prolonged and stormy laughter in the midst of which *F.P.* retired triumphant.)

I was ecstatic. I felt that my earlier, rather ludicrous success with Ernest Bevin, never followed up, might actually have helped Frank at Transport House. Already I saw myself entering Westminster along with Frank, joint architects of the New Jerusalem. I took it for granted that Oxford was more 'winnable' than Birmingham. All the more need to nurse King's Norton as effectively as Frank would nurse Oxford.

For the last two years I had lunched or supped with Harold Nash, my political agent, and his wife Elsie on the Bournville estate, when speaking in King's Norton. Their young sons Norman and Sidney paid an exchange visit to our children at Singletree, the size of our house and the novel food making them homesick instead of happy. Years later, when Ernest Bevin pronounced, 'The tragedy of the workers is the smallness of their desires,' I thought of the two little boys from Birmingham.

But now, in spring 1939, I took a house at 250 Mary Vale Road for myself and Mr White, Edward's former chauffeur, and his wife. White was a Birmingham man and glad to leave Ireland for a job in industry at home; Mrs White cooked for me when I stayed overnight. Antonia and Thomas were brought up for one week and sent to the Bournville Junior School, with interesting results. The teachers reported their writing and arithmetic to be no more than average but their general knowledge way above. Zealous partisans of their own pupils, they implied that parental pushing had given Antonia and Thomas an unfair advantage.

I had had some experience of a state junior school through teaching in one myself at Stoke-on-Trent for a week, and I wondered how my two sheltered children would fare. There had been excitement and trauma at Stoke. I had instructed my eight/nine year olds to act out 'The Pied Piper of Hamelin' while I read Browning's poem aloud to them. The boys, as rats, gladly bit some of the girls and burnt others by using the radiators, on my suggestion, as the babies' cradles. On returning to their desks the gang-leaders began putting up their hands, one after the other, 'Please

Miss, can I be excused?' I dared not say no, though so many calls of nature did seem unusual. At last the headmaster entered my classroom to report that three-quarters of my pupils were out racing around the playground.

Thomas and Antonia, however, aged five and six, were among children who had not yet entered the mutiny zone. They were struck only by the huge classes compared with their own class of eight in Oxford, and by the fact that I had not realized they needed 'milk money'. So they had no milk. The whole operation impressed Antonia as being a case of Mummy going quite mad. Not so Frank. He wrote to me stoutly: 'I am so glad that they enjoy the school – a good omen for their great working-class-leadership careers.'

By 1939 things were moving fast in Hitler's favour. When the Labour Party in Parliament voted against even a qualified form of conscription, Frank felt guilty. He joined the territorials. A genial photograph was set up by the *Oxford Mail* of Private 'Pack', alias Councillor Pakenham, offering a cigarette to one of his comrades. 'Have a fag, mate,' ran the caption. Frank has never smoked in his life. That about illustrated the reality at this stage of our defensive preparations against an enemy now recognized by the whole country to be un-negotiable. The Munich Agreement was broken – 'I told you so' from a thousand Oxford voices; Czechoslovakia was added to Hitler's Austrian bag and Albania to Mussolini's Abyssinian one.

We were staying at Bernhurst and attending a tennis party given by our neighbours Sir Edward and Lady Boyle, when the news about Albania came through. There was a tense hour while Sir Edward waited to see if he, the greatest living authority on Albania, would be sent for by our contemptible Foreign Office. At last the summons from Downing Street came; leaving us in the expert hands of his polymath schoolboy son Edward, who gave us a complete run-through of the Karageorgevic and Obrenovic dynasties in Serbia in the eighteenth and nineteenth centuries.

Frank was now a private in the Oxford and Bucks Light Infantry, which he liked to remember had distinguished itself at Waterloo. Filial piety and patriotism had impelled him into a profession for which he was quite unsuited, and misplaced socialist ideals had driven him into its ranks. Our friend John Sparrow was to follow the same course for different reasons, and later on others of our friends preferred to join the ranks. During the spiritual hell of a fortnight's camp, Frank never learnt to do his own 'spit-and-polish' – a kindly sergeant did it for him at ten bob a go – or to sleep soundly twelve to a tent, head-to-head and feet to the outside, or to pepper his prose with the four-letter words that would have made him one of the lads. When on sick leave, however, he found to his surprise that he had learnt enough to shock the local vicar at tennis by emitting a string of curses every time he missed a ball.

A typical letter from Private Pakenham, Headquarters Company 5th Battalion, expressed acute unhappiness at his predicament, his only pleasure being that his team had won the tug-of-war with him as anchor man. In every other respect he was utterly at sea.

As usual I had spent a week or so of the summer in Naomi Mitchison's house party at Carradale, Argyll. In the morning Naomi would say, 'Shall I shoot a sheep for dinner?' After dinner we would either swim in the phosphorescent sea or play paper-and-pencil games, every one of which Margaret Cole won. I remember an argument breaking out about friendship, when her husband Douglas said, 'I could never be a friend of someone I disagreed with politically.' There was a time when I had felt the same, applauding the Irish Nationalists of the 1880s for having no truck with their fellow English parliamentarians. But after eight years married to Frank, I thought of all our Tory friends and could no longer take that line. For the rest, there was something phosphorescent about the whole of that pre-war Scottish holiday. The presence of a brilliant young Cambridge scientist, 'Hank', who would join the navy if war broke out, made our holiday spirit seem not quite real. Was it possible that this 'young Apollo, golden haired' would go to sea and be drowned? He did and he was.

I knew something about the threat to Poland, having given several lectures on Danzig and the Corridor. Despite this threat and Chamberlain's guarantee of Polish integrity, I took the three children to Bernhurst for the rest of the summer, where Frank joined us after camp.

When he returned to his unit and I drove the family back to Oxford towards the middle of August, it was not to Singletree but to a splendid Elizabethan mansion called Water Eaton Manor, the home of our friends Teresa and Alec Carr-Saunders. Another Christ Church don, Frank Taylor, and his family were already installed. No act could have been more generous than the Carr-Saunders' in spontaneously offering to take in two pairs of parents, two nannies and five extra children. Our two elder children had been attending a class organized by Teresa in her house during the past term, so for them the move was scarcely an upheaval. Indeed that was our main reason for accepting Teresa's spectacular invitation. The routine in the children's schoolroom would not be interrupted whatever the tragedy that occurred in the Polish Corridor.

As for Singletree, we handed it over lock, stock and barrel to the Oxford City Council, to be used for the evacuees beginning to pour down from London. The Council paid the rent to our landlord and we provided all the furniture, linen, crockery and cutlery. It was selected as the home for a group of blind old people from the East End. I visited them and found them happy there. Later on when our blind guests were packing up to leave, I was amused to discover that the sheets on our double bed had been carefully re-marked in indelible ink, 'Cohen' instead of 'Pakenham'. 'We didn't like the idea of strangers using our sheets,' explained Mrs Cohen – the 'strangers' being the other blind couples living in the house. The only casualty was virtually the whole of our china. 'Blind people need to be familiar with the shape and position of the sink,' explained a social worker, 'in order not to hit the plates on the taps and knock off the handles and spouts.'

In the great hall at Water Eaton Manor on Sunday morning, 3 September 1939, I was sitting alone with the wireless turned on. Frank was stationed somewhere near Banbury, Teresa was at Mass and Professor Carr-Saunders preferred listening to the gloomy news in his own study. When Neville Chamberlain announced that war had been declared against Nazi Germany at 11 a.m. and might last for three years, I found myself thinking, '*Three* years? How can I endure the end of civilized life for *two* years, even for *one*?' It was not fear but a feeling of sudden imprisonment in a prospect that would be utterly constricted and negative. My little red Labour Party diary, stamped on the cover with a golden spade, pen and torch, offered a thought in prose or poetry for every day of the year 1939. Two verses from Kipling had been chosen, perhaps a full year before the event, for this date, of which this was the first:

> All the world over nursing their scars
> Sit the old fighting men broke in the wars
> Sit the old fighting men surly and grim
> Mocking the lilt of the conqueror's hymn.

I had a rare sensation of total discouragement and depression.

13

The War from Water Eaton

· 1939–41 ·

I t was impossible to be discouraged for long at Water Eaton. There was too much to do. The estate lay several miles to the north of Oxford, in the country, so that when petrol rationing came in on 16 September 1939 we had to draw up a rota for shopping. With about twenty people living in the house, it was quite an undertaking. A school rota also had to be organized, since two children and a governess needed fetching to and from Oxford every weekday. One of these children was Donald Hope, my cousin Michael's eldest son. His wife Christine had left Birmingham and come to live in Oxford when Michael joined the army. Their presence in North Oxford made all the difference to me.

The first book I read aloud to the whole class was Tolkien's *The Hobbit*. It had a powerful effect on their games. They divided themselves into 'Gollums' and 'Bellums', the Gollums being the baddies, derived from the monster in the story, while the heroic Bellums were based on their knowledge of Latin. I was teaching them two or three times a week from an original little book called *Latin with Laughter*.

These Latin lessons, elementary and sometimes frivolous though they were, satisfied my instinct to teach. When several of my former pupils later excelled in the classics, I took some pride in their achievement and felt that the proportion of Latin to laughter in my classes – perhaps only one to three – had been justified.

Teresa Carr-Saunders had begun to farm at Water Eaton before the war, but rationing and other shortages inspired her to step it up. Her energy and imagination were boundless and thanks to her schemes for producing more food, we were all prodigiously well fed during the first ten months or so of the war. Of course there were minor disasters, some of them much enjoyed by the children. The farm buildings housed a variety of animals, ranging from small black cows and pink pigs to several ponies and nine donkeys. Now and again while we sat at supper in the black-out, we would suddenly hear the thunder of hooves rounding the house, and a great concourse of escaped animals would come tearing past our windows in a high state of panic. I sometimes imagined that Comus himself must be at their head: 'The wonted roar was up amidst the woods.' With nothing to assist them but torches and our loud cheers, the valiant Teresa and her nine-year-old elder son would somehow get them back into the farmyard.

The little black cows were unfortunately prone to abortions or to giving birth to monsters, which, of course, we could not eat. Once, however, when a pig mysteriously died the vet passed it as wholesome. Teresa decided that to burn off the bristles and prepare the pig for table would enliven our two understandably gloomy Polish maids. How right she was. Regina in particular hung over the pig lovingly, crooning Polish melodies. Alas, when the pig was totally consumed, a worse melancholy settled on Regina. She ran away and was picked up on Oxford station snuggled into my camel-hair coat. The police asked me to prosecute. I refused. 'In that case,' they said, 'you can't have your coat back.' I was sorry to lose over thirty clothing coupons.

One day Teresa, having to go to London, left us in charge of a hundred newly arrived day-old chicks. 'Whatever you do, don't put their water inside their pen,' she instructed us, 'but just let them dip their beaks into it, outside.' As the day wore on and the adorable chicks won all hearts, some of the children decided to give them one little treat – a real splash in their water-trough. Teresa came home to find the majority drowned and a bedraggled half-dozen being dried out on the cistern in the airing cupboard. The survivors, when returned to their run, were picked off one by one by a visiting rat. The last to go was a lame chick whom the children identified with the little lame boy of the Pied Piper of Hamelin. But in his case lameness did not save him.

Even this tragedy could not for long depress the children. Their high spirits at Water Eaton convinced me that young children adapt themselves joyfully to community life.

The phoney war, as lived out at Water Eaton, would have been almost as happy a time for me as for the children – but for the plight of Frank. The army succeeded in turning him into a melancholy misfit. At the beginning of the war it was put to him that he would be more useful as a subaltern than a private. He bowed to authority. But his depression scarcely lifted. There was indeed one break early in October when the old life returned for a moment and Frank was given leave to visit Ireland. He saw President de Valera and reported to me:

My visit reached its climax on Friday night when I had two hours with Dev. . . . I am afraid that the censorship here (political and religious) inhibits my account of talks, but I will have a *lot* to tell you when I get back. Dev seemed terribly tired – it was heroic of him to see me at 8 o'clock – but when I repeated Winston Churchill's rude remarks about Ireland's part in the war, he perked up. . . .

Our feelings about Churchill at this date were ambivalent. His military attitude to Ireland – as a giant potential harbour either for German or British submarines – could not appeal. On the other hand he had been all along the chief British voice warning against Hitler and Munich. Moreover, we had been invited to tea by him in the summer of 1938, when we had taken Paddy as a baby to visit my parents. His home, Chartwell, was close to Crockham Hill.

To my astonishment, when we arrived he was standing dressed in a boiler suit by a half-built wall with a trowel in his hand. I never expected a public character to be found actually doing what the press said he did. Yet here was Winston doing it. As host, he discussed Ireland with Frank in a friendly way, while I talked to Clemmie, watched their daughter Sarah turning cart-wheels along the terrace and had a swim in the enervating eighty-eight-degree pool. After tea I could sense some kind of tension. It emerged that they were waiting for the report of Winston's doctor on his diet. Everyone, including Winston himself, dreaded a cut in his rations, especially of whisky. Suddenly the clouds rolled away, disclosing a landscape even sunnier than it had been before the doctor's visit. The verdict was that Winston had not been having *enough*. He must not retire to bed without a really sustaining nightcap, plus a generous plateful of sandwiches.

I already had something of the biographer's natural interest in people and their families, and the memory of this glimpse of a famous family at home was to lie at the back of all my future encounters with them.

In November 1939 I was receiving Frank's first letters from HQ, Banbury, describing his new schedule, trying to put a brave face on it. (After all, that burning hillside at Gallipoli where his father died had been incomparably worse.) The colonel had handed over to him, he told me, the welfare work and the job of starting French classes for officers and NCOs. Frank could read French but his pronunciation was Churchillian. Luckily he could not foresee how little of the war against Hitler was to be fought in France, apart from the Resistance. His aim in fact was to cater for the vast majority who were guarding aerodromes. 'This welfare work may be my salvation,' he wrote, 'as well as that of the troops.' A week later the regular route march was cancelled owing to bad weather, so Frank gave his men – nearly all privates – a lecture on European history, 1871–1914. 'When I asked them, "Hands up those who knew that Austria-Hungary existed before the Great War" – one hand went up. "What is neutrality?" – half knew.' I hoped it might seem to him a little like the dear old WEA.

It must have been just about now that Frank received a crucial letter from Evelyn Waugh. He suggested that Frank's 'salvation' lay in something beyond welfare work. Evelyn knew that Frank had for over a year been close to the Catholic Church. He himself was a convert of nine years' standing, and with the convert's shrewd grasp of the snares of brinkmanship in others, he sensed that this was the moment to give Frank a push. He deprecated further reading on Frank's part – Frank had probably read more theology than anyone but a trainee priest – and hinted that Frank's expected departure abroad to serve with the British Expeditionary Force might result in his being killed before he had translated his theological thought into action. Discussion could become a pure luxury, he wrote. This was no time for a soldier to delay.

Frank delayed no longer. He first sought out his great friend Father Martin D'Arcy, SJ, who had been his mentor for over a year. He was away in the United States, so Frank turned to the Franciscan Friary in Iffley Road, where he had been dropping in for Mass during our last year at Singletree. Within two months Father Wulfstan was ready to receive him into the Catholic Church. I knew nothing of all this.

At the beginning of January 1940 Frank heard that his regiment was off to guard the Isle of Wight. This was the moment. He got a night's leave, spent it at the Friary and left next morning a Catholic. Only then, after the event, did he break the news of his conversion to me. I was shocked and deeply distressed. How could he take such a step without telling me first? How could he enter on a course which would erect a barrier of priests between us? If I had known earlier of Father D'Arcy's part in the story I would assuredly have felt that my comparison of him with Mephistopheles in my student days was all too apt. As I railed against Frank's decision, I thought of more reasons, and ever more trivial ones, for objecting to it: notably that he would henceforth have to go to church every single Sunday of his life, thus spoiling our peaceful Sunday mornings together which, alone of the week, were not ruled by the clock. Nor did I forget to mention the much canvassed point that children, whether born Catholics or converted to Catholicism, were handicapped in their careers.

Frank was prepared for an outburst. He listened patiently to my protests. As I had not threatened to leave him and take the children with me, he knew in his heart that I would accept the inevitable. And in my heart I knew that even a rustling curtain of priests would never really separate us. It was not long before I began to realize that even the secrecy of his final step had been the lesser of two evils for both of us. If he had warned me beforehand I should have felt bound to use every weapon in my armoury to dissuade him, and might have worked myself up into saying things I did not really mean.

My hostility to the Catholic Church was partly due to sourness left over from the prejudices of childhood. But there were also more recent experiences. Before the war I had taken tickets for a 'Malthusian Ball', inspired by my gynaecologist, Dr Helena Wright, to further the cause of contraception. For the same cause I had spoken at the Oxford Union against the distinguished Catholic physician and former MP, D. W. J. O'Donovan, to whom Father D'Arcy gave his support. I was supported by the young Max Beloff and the old Bertrand Russell. Quoting a speech by Lord Salisbury against contraception, I denied his right to have any opinion on the subject. 'Lord Salisbury has not given birth to a child!' To my surprise the remark, which was intended to carry the defiant ring of truth, provoked a universal howl of laughter. Max afterwards scribbled a generous note: 'You have done more for women coming into the Society than a thousand others! In every way a triumphant maiden. Thanks a lot. M. Beloff.'

Moreover, certain things that Frank had said wrongly convinced me that he felt no real objections to my anti-Catholic stance. In 1934, for instance, he had written to me from Ireland about my absorption in George Moore's autobiography, *Hail and Farewell*. 'I *am* glad that you are having a real "George Moore" week and are stimulated by his Catholic or rather, anti-Catholic thesis.' To Frank, hostility to religion was better than indifference. To me, his remark suggested that he did not altogether disapprove of my bias. With the Spanish Civil War my bias was to become far stronger. I felt that the Church was not only *on* the wrong side, but *was* the wrong side. I began to think again in terms of Charles Kingsley's novel *Westward Ho!* that, together with Charles Reade's *The Cloister and the Hearth*, had dramatized my youthful Protestantism. Nevertheless, my most genuine feeling about religion was profound indifference. Left to myself, I never thought about it.

For Frank the brief joy of his reception was diminished not only by my protests but by his own departure from Oxford and all its intellectual associations, within reach of which he had been stationed for so many months. If the men of his company might remind him of the WEA, the Philistinism of his fellow officers was like nothing he had met before. On 11 January the Oxford and Bucks were entrained for the Isle of Wight. By way of breaking the ice in the railway carriage, Frank said, 'I wonder what books we have brought to read?' There was dead silence. Then one of his fellow subalterns said, 'Surely, when we get there we shall find *a book*?' Frank did not make himself any more acceptable by asking for Labour's paper, the *Daily Herald*, to be added to the short list of papers taken in the Mess.

For the next few days after his departure there was a strange semblance of normality in my life: tea with Evan Durbin, tea with Dick Crossman, a visit from Harold Nash, my King's Norton agent and – morning sickness. All familiar positive things. To start a baby at the beginning of a war seemed to me the most positive and therefore best possible response. I remembered the wife of the area agent in Birmingham telling me in 1939 that if there were a war she would put her head in the gas oven and her young son's too. She did no such thing. She had another baby.

Less than a week after Frank left for the wintry island came a message that he was in a London nursing home with gastric influenza. Alarmed and anxious, I hurried to visit him. He was in Manchester Street, in the centre of a web I knew so well from my childhood: Harley Street, Wimpole Street, Baker Street, Marylebone Road. But they all looked as if they had been immobilized by an eerie new ice age. Owing to fuel rationing, a thousand pipes had burst and the grave faces of the Georgian houses were veiled in cascades of icicles. Wordsworth's torrent haunted him 'like a passion'. These haunted me like symbols of a great dreariness.

Frank's many visitors cheered us both up. Among them were David Astor and his mother. Lady Astor saw at a glance that the best treatment for a physical wreck was to launch an attack on his spiritual state. 'How can you join those *Romans*, Frank?' Then she tried to rope me in as an ally. 'Come on, Elizabeth. You're still a good Protestant, aren't you?' 'No, I'm not. I'm nothing.' 'Nothin'?' This admission at least deflected her from Frank.

The savage January of 1940 saw only the beginning of the breakdown in Frank's health. He was back in the nursing home towards the end of March with a second attack of gastric influenza, and this time was attended by his old friend Dr Hampton. After I had read aloud a chapter of *Bleak House* at his request, he decided that he would never suffer from insomnia again: he was refreshed and ready for the 'further varieties of fortune'. These included 'a brief though *congenial* note from the adjutant', he wrote to me, 'saying that a Board would be arranged when he applied for it – no hurry suggested'. The Board might well result in his being invalided out of the army. His letter continued with an account of a visit from young Christopher Mayhew, a former active member of the Oxford Labour club and afterwards to become a Labour MP, finally a Liberal peer. Chris was on leave from the BEF in France when he visited Frank.

His account of a negress from a Lille brothel [wrote Frank] was absorbing. He asked whether she got more or less custom from the whites and was told, 'The

French draw no distinction. But few British have anything to do with me, due to their faulty Imperialist attitude.'

There followed for Chris the first really left-wing intellectual conversation he had had since joining the army. Frank ended by hoping for a weekend with me which I could enjoy in every way. 'How you deserve it, in the midst of your life of hectic administration' – of the children – 'and ministration' – to him.

The 'further varieties of fortune' predicted by him turned out to be a week's leave in April at Bernhurst with me and the family. Though longing for his Board with most of his heart and soul, another small part of Frank still took the work of a second lieutenant seriously. He set up a sand-table in the garage, where Thomas learnt how to take advantage of 'ground' and 'features'. All of us, plus four children from the village, were led by Second-Lieutenant Pakenham in an uphill attack on Bernhurst from the wood and long sloping field below the house. At the end of the operation our company commander had to inform us that every one of us had been killed by the defenders even before we reached the bottom of the garden. (Frank remembers a United Home Guard exercise later on in Oxford when precisely the same thing happened. At the end of a strenuous wriggle from the bottom to the top of Boars Hill, their CO announced triumphantly, 'You are all dead!')

Humiliating as Frank's 'Board' and his previous career in the army proved to be, the disaster was not without its consolations. He was not the only intellectual to fail in the test. Our friend John Betjeman was to describe to us his own appearance before a military board. When asked whether he ever had any disconcerting or unusual experiences, John had replied innocently, 'Oh, no, never. Except that occasionally I see the cornice moving round the room. . . .' He was eventually posted to Ireland as press attaché at the British embassy, where Frank was to meet him.

What Frank then regarded as his signal failure to show himself a true son of his father was later to bring him understanding of others who had temporarily failed in life; who had been brought, perhaps, before a magistrates' court instead of an army board, and sent to prison instead of back into civilian life. There were other consolations of which I did not then guess.

When I arrived back at Water Eaton Manor from Bernhurst with the children and their nanny in the car, the date was 6 May: four days before Hitler's *blitzkrieg* against Belgium and the Netherlands. The month we had just spent at Bernhurst was to be our last in Sussex until the end of the war, though this too I did not yet know. Indeed I had booked our local Hurst Green doctor to attend the birth of the baby due in August. By the time that month arrived the whole state of the country, and of our family with it, had radically changed.

The alarming 'bulge', as we were soon calling the process of breakthrough by German panzers into France, is mainly remembered by me for the war at Water Eaton between obstinate optimism and informed pessimism. We three mothers, supported by the nannies, would stolidly plough through our week's work until by Friday evening we would all be full of high spirits, ready to welcome our men for the weekend. On that day Alec Carr-Saunders would arrive from teaching economics at Cambridge, Frank Taylor from teaching French at Christ Church, and perhaps my husband on leave. Immediately the atmosphere would change. Every wireless set (not yet called radios) in the house would be turned on and Alec, who could not bear that realities should not be faced, would inform us hourly that 'the bulge' was at breaking-point. By Sunday night when the men were all off again, my spirits would be at breaking-point too. But on Monday our women's work would roll forward once more, varied for me by Latin and French teaching, and Labour Party meetings in Oxford and Birmingham. On the following Friday we would be fully restored, prepared once more for the truth.

Nature may have given women an in-built optimism that is perhaps less necessary to men. I can remember sitting in the Elizabethan hall where I had heard the declaration of war, listening now to the French Prime Minister's heart-cry – 'Only a miracle can save France – but a miracle *will* save France.' I knew perfectly well that the required miracle would not save France. Nevertheless, I had complete confidence in the future. When France was offered political unity with Britain I felt elated: this must be the beginning of world government in which the Labour Party and I so fervently believed. When France declined the offer, I did not feel like a 'deflated soufflé' as Churchill's private secretary, Jock Colville, vividly described himself in his diary. I simply felt sure that Churchill would think of something else. I remember meeting Frank's undergraduate friend Nicko Henderson in the Cornmarket on the first day of Dunkirk. Nicko explained the prospects with grim realism. 'Only a miracle can save the BEF.' I was not surprised when the miracle took place. Another of the miracles that saved Britain was Churchill's broadcasts: they appealed to our optimism and spoke also to our questionings and doubts. They had a way of re-echoing rhythmically in the mind and could almost be sung. 'We will fight them on the beaches . . . Te rum pom pom.' On my midnight drives back from King's Norton they went well with the other songs I hummed to myself: 'Drink to me only' and 'Clementine'.

(No car radios then; no heating either. One had to do something to keep the spirits up.)

France fell and the Battle of Britain began. It seemed impossible that our fate was about to be sealed – one way or the other – in such glorious weather. 'The time is out of joint,' I quoted, feeling that the weather of the phoney war should have been transferred to the Blitz. When nothing was doing, Water Eaton had been savaged until its water supply froze and its fields looked, said Alec, like Arctic wastes of reindeer moss. When everything was happening, we carried our picnics to the peaceful river bank and ate them under an immutably blue sky filled with larks and swallows.

By June the legend of Britain 'standing alone' had entered our island story. The phrase 'The Island' became popular and now referred to Britain as a whole instead of, as formerly, to the Isle of Wight. Our imaginations oscillated between seeing ourselves as a beleaguered garrison threatened from the skies and an impregnable fortress guarded by the seas. With the first image in mind, the Local Defence Volunteers were formed. Thanks to Churchill's good taste, their name was changed to the Home Guard. And thanks to the Home Guard, Frank found a speedy means of assuaging his guilt by continuing to render military service. Hardly had he resigned his commission before he was raising the South Company of the Oxford Home Guard, his second-in-command being a Great War veteran, Maurice Bowra.

Frank felt no scruples about rejoicing in the formation of the Home Guard. I felt no scruples about rejoicing in his release from the army proper, especially when I learnt that his unfortunate battalion of the Oxford and Bucks Light Infantry had won glory in France at the cost of tragic casualties. He would almost certainly have died had he been with them. I began to feel a bit more like the generation of 1914 when I learnt that Ronnie Cartland had been killed with the BEF and Michael Hope's brother shot down and killed in the RAF. Our great friend Aidan Crawley, another fighter pilot, had been shot down and incarcerated in Germany as a prisoner of war. (I always thought of Aidan while filing books for prisoners in the various *Stalags* later in the war, with their pink, white or blue cards for camps and subjects. 'If Camp is not on Camp List it *must* be blue.' I hoped Aidan's was not blue.) I had driven Aidan to Abingdon airport, taking Thomas along. We had waved him off in his plane, Thomas delighted by the noise and rush of air from the propellers, I with the gloomiest forebodings. Indeed I began to have superstitious fears every time I met one of Frank's former pupils in the street. Was he too doomed?

Frank himself was shot in the foot by one of his own men who inadvertently discharged his last cartridge into the Abingdon Road, 'just to make sure the gun was unloaded'. In a flash Frank and his two other fellow-officers were writhing and cursing on the ground, their legs full of metal that had ricocheted off the stones. Frank was unlucky enough to have a piece of his sock sewn into the wound, which began to suppurate – but lucky that the poison was arrested just in time to save his foot from amputation.

With Frank now serving in Oxford and the children ready to quit the governess stage in their schooling, it was obvious that we must return to city life, in a home of our own. This was the more necessary since we could no longer look forward to holidays together at Bernhurst. Owing to the invasion scare, families living within a certain distance of the coast – we were less than thirteen miles from Hastings – had to make a choice: either they stayed put or left for good. Our back-and-forth visits to a danger zone were no longer to be allowed. So we stored all Aunt Caroline's furniture in Tunbridge Wells and relinquished the house to the Government. We heard afterwards that an air-raid siren was installed on its roof, while German prisoners of war, parachutists who had baled out in the Battle of Britain, were interviewed in the drawing-room below. At least one of them was kept on at Bernhurst to do agricultural work, and after the war he came back to show his former 'prison' to his family.

The best thing about the loss of Bernhurst 'for the duration' (hideous phrase) was the evacuation of Mrs Pope to Oxford. She had been Aunt Caroline's housekeeper and our cook-housekeeper when we visited Bernhurst. Sussex-bred, dark, stout and utterly devoted, she was in fact the perfect example of the 'old retainer'. When she arrived with all her belongings in Oxford, I felt how lucky I was to inherit such a treasure at such a time – worth a million black boxes stuffed with Pakenham garnets, amethysts and sapphires. To the children 'Popie' was a surrogate Granny Longford. She and I spent our first night at 8 Chadlington Road, our new home in North Oxford, on 9 July, getting it ready for the family. The blind Londoners had quit Singletree, so there was the furniture from Singletree to arrange and new crockery to buy. We were a short walk from Lady Margaret Hall and next door to 10 Chadlington Road, where I had boarded in my last university term. It was a nostalgic sensation to smell the Stevensons' wistaria (second flowering) over the wall, on the other side of which I had once sat revising Aristotle and Plato.

In a sense I had come home. The architecture of this late Victorian villa was no doubt unprepossessing, but its ugliness was of a kind I could accept. I learnt years later that 8 Chadlington Road had been chosen out of the whole of Oxford by the great-niece of Josephine Butler, famous

Chadlington Road, Oxford, by John Betjeman

social worker, as the ideal house in which to retire. The change from Water Eaton was immense.

The Elizabethan house had a powerful atmosphere, perhaps even a ghost. One could no more imagine a ghost taking up residence in Chadlington Road than a Nazi spy-ring. One Friday night at Water Eaton the Carr-Saunders' nanny said to me: 'I didn't know Mr Pakenham would be home on leave this weekend.' 'No, I don't expect him, why do you ask?' 'Well, I saw him going upstairs to your top floor. It was rather dark, but I saw his back in khaki, disappearing round the bend in the stairs.' Of course, there had been no Frank. But there was a legend about an officer in the Great War who had shot himself in the attic and sometimes returned to haunt it.

At Water Eaton we had been isolated and almost diminished in the huge grey stone manor, with its high mullioned windows through which little sun penetrated, standing in acres of empty green fields. We were now surrounded by neighbours. To the north ran Linton Road where the Broadley family lived. At the bottom of our plot, at right angles to us, lay old Mrs Haldane's large and fertile vegetable garden, bounded on the east by the river Cherwell. Beyond our other wall were the Dragon School playing fields and headmaster's house. The distant sound of ball on cricket bat will always recall to me summer afternoons in the war.

There was only one thing wrong with North Oxford. Though flat and lush, it was the Conservative Party's 'White Highlands'.

The North Ward of Oxford in which we now lived had never boasted of a Labour representative on the council. Yet there were famous names among its members – Layard, Spooner, Gillet, Medawar. For a time our meetings were held in the home of Jean and Peter Medawar, the latter a greatly distinguished scientist and future OM. Another future OM could be relied on to support the left, Dorothy Hodgkin, the great crystallographer. Our most crowded ward meeting was the one addressed by a notoriously eccentric philosophy don on the subject of 'Why I am a socialist'. He was said sometimes to crawl about his room on all fours while giving a tutorial and once, in a burst of philosophic excitement, to have suddenly sprung at the mantelshelf and wrenched the whole thing away from the wall. Though not actually wishing for Jean's house to be damaged, the large gathering did expect some fireworks. Unfortunately the poor man had no idea why he was a socialist and gave a talk of extreme incoherence.

I had wanted a girl for my next baby, so that Antonia should have a sister and we would have two of each sex. Therefore I took no 'steps' but left the result to nature. Dr Wright's theory worked again, for Judith Elizabeth was born at 1.5 a.m. on the anniversary of Thomas's seventh birthday, 14 August 1940. We all rejoiced, Thomas taking special credit to himself. At birth Judith looked pink and placid, for the only time in her life bearing a distinct resemblance to Queen Victoria. She had arrived plumb into the Battle of Britain. I felt that for safety's sake the new baby must sleep on the ground floor, and as I intended to nurse her for the first nine months, Frank and I also moved downstairs. I found a splendid hidey-hole for her carrycot which at least made me feel that she was secure: a revolving mahogany hatch of the purest 'North Oxford' design, shaped like a half coconut and constructed so that the traditional scullery maid who put in the dishes from the kitchen could serve unseen.

One night I was awakened by a distant but unmistakable sound – church bells. Knowing this to be the signal that 'it' – the Nazi invasion by parachute – had begun, I desperately tried to wake Frank. 'Frank, Frank,' shaking him furiously, 'church bells! Listen. Wake up. . . .' Grunt. 'Shall I drive you to the Home Guard?' Another grunt. At last I got him half awake. 'Go to sleep,' he mumbled. 'You're dreaming. . . .' And nothing that I said or did could squeeze another sound out of him.

Did some profound instinct make him realize that it was a mistake, a false alarm? I never knew how many, if any, of Frank's men turned up at his HQ in Isis Street, for not a word about that phantom invasion scare was ever breathed throughout the war. Only long years afterwards did I read, with a thrill of self-justification, that I had indeed heard the sinister chime of church bells ringing at Oxford in the summer of 1940, while Frank slept peacefully in our double bed and Judith in her hatch.

At about a month old, Judith went through two more Battle of Britain scares. I had taken Popie to the shops in North Parade, leaving Antonia in charge. Suddenly the baleful ululation of an air-raid siren began. We dashed home to find Antonia sitting in the cellar with the baby in her arms and surrounded by her excited siblings. Her blue eyes stared out, large and round with a mixture of defiance and alarm. It would have made a perfect subject for a Victorian *genre* picture – 'Sisters in a Shelter' or 'Civilians at War'.

Judith came 'under fire' (literally) soon afterwards. This time there was real peril, in fact a near miss. The four children and I were in the garden after tea, Thomas in the summerhouse where he was engrossed in chemical experiments, I in knitting. Outside on the lawn Antonia played with her dolls, Paddy swung in the chestnut tree, Judith lay in her pram. Beyond the lawn was our back hedge and kitchen garden divided by a fence from Mrs Haldane's vegetables and the slow-flowing summer Cherwell. (Sometimes I used to watch Robin Dundas, an idiosyncratic Ancient History don at Christ Church and cousin of the Haldanes, lying prone on his side weeding her asparagus bed. It was said that in order to enjoy both the physical delight of his daily cold tub and the moral satisfaction of saving water, he had filled up his bath in January 1940 and not emptied it again until May.) Above the river and the row of back gardens an intricate formation of swifts whistled and dived in their innocent battle of Britain.

Suddenly the peace was broken by an ear-splitting roar that grew and grew like the widening crack of doom until the blunt profile of a giant bomber nosed its way over our fence, its belly and tail flaming like Halley's comet. Would it clear our hedge and the other hedges of numbers 10, 12, 14 Chadlington Road? I snatched Judith from her pram and shooed the three other children up the little grass hill towards the verandah. We had just about reached the loggia leading to the nursery when there was a brilliant flash as if Lucifer himself had arrived on the scene, followed instantaneously by an almighty explosion. The doomed bomber had crashed on the cottage of Mrs Haldane's cowman at the junction of

Chadlington Road and Linton Road, killing the cowman, his wife and children.

One of my most absurd experiences of the war was something I dreamt while the Battle of Britain was at its height. In my dream I had fallen asleep in the year 1940 and slept like Rip Van Winkle for twenty years. I awoke to find that there had been many changes in my family and in that of my sister Kitty. Suddenly it occurred to me that I did not know how the war had ended. I turned to Kitty's husband, Donald McLachlan, and asked casually, 'Who won?' He replied with equal nonchalance, 'They did.'

The war never came directly to Oxford. True, I once woke up to hear bombs dropping in the direction of Hinksey. Again I felt that this was 'it' at last, 'it' being the expected 'Baedeker raid' on Oxford. Hitler's so-called Baedeker raids had already led him to bomb Bath and other centres of loveliness and learning. (I heard after the war that some of our bomber pilots had tried to get the spire of Cologne Cathedral.) We all supposed that a city like Oxford would get a specially vicious dose of frightfulness. I leapt out of bed, was sick and listened for the siren. Two of the children had measles and were sleeping in my room. Frank was away. Should I carry them down to the cellar or wait for whatever came next?

There was no next. The noise turned out to have come from a stray German plane jettisoning its unused bomb-load before making for home. The experience merely showed me what a coward I was.

Because no Baedeker bombs fell on Oxford, a new legend arose to explain the omission. Hitler, we were told, had reserved our city to be his future civilian headquarters. The legend was embellished by some unlikely details that included poor old Cruttwell, Evelyn Waugh's former enemy at Hertford College. Cruttwell, it was said, having been appointed by Hitler as his liaison officer on the culture front, had naturally designated his own university as the one to be preserved.

Even if we ourselves were never bombed, we were able to feel passionately for the people of Coventry and Birmingham. Every clear night, it seemed at the same hour, we would hear the invisible fleet of Nazi bombers making its way to the industrial Midlands. I would stand in the quiet garden listening to the hum as it approached and then receded northwards. It was so high overhead, so utterly disembodied yet loud enough to be placed in space, that I remember it as the most sinister sound I have ever heard. Napoleon's distant troops winding down the hillside before the Battle of Waterloo had had the same effect of the 'supernatural'. I thought of my friends in Birmingham. It seemed impossible that one should be able to hear their approaching fate so clearly and yet do nothing about it. I felt more frustrated than a savage shooting arrows at the unseen monster swallowing the sun. At least the savage was doing something.

Excitement was added to frustration next year, 1941, when the children and I watched, night after night, the distant flak over Falmouth. I had taken them to Portscatho in South Cornwall for a summer holiday, while Frank was in Ireland. I could not even describe to him the spectacular firework displays for fear that the censor should destroy my daily letters. (A postcard to him from Antonia, aged nine, was censored, we never knew for what treasonable revelations.) My letter to Frank merely observed: 'I have several times been interrupted – I leave you to guess by what. In the end it got too good, so I took Antonia and Thomas to see it out of the dining-room window which faces the right way. They were absolutely thrilled, and what they couldn't see they imagined.' Antonia was reading *Prester John* by Buchan and writing a 'Lay of Lucifer', so her imagination was already aflame.

I continued: 'I feel so well by the sea, as I always do, but seeing what I see every day, I feel rather too closely in touch with your sea-journey back – but I don't know which day it is, so I can't focus my thoughts – perhaps a good thing.' Frank took occasional liberties with the censor, once writing to me: 'The boat was very late in – no danger reported but a lot of zig-zagging (get this, Censor? ZIG-ZAGGING).' His writing was so illegible that I doubt if the censor made much sense of it. Anyway the letter was passed by 'Examiner 920'.

By 1941 my life was zig-zagging forward like the Irish ferry between opposite points, while Frank's was advancing in a totally new direction.

14

North Oxford at War
· 1941–4 ·

After the Battle of Britain had been won, the war entered a new phase. My own new phase was polarized between two extremes: a more conventional domestic life in Oxford than I had hitherto known; and a more unconventional, even rebellious, political life in Birmingham.

The Dragon School, on whose doorstep we now lived, was among the largest and best private prep schools in the country. Part day, part boarding, it had been founded by 'Skipper' Lynam and was now carried on by his brother 'Hum'. It possessed peculiar excellencies to which there were no rivals; though Summerfields, also an Oxford prep school, would have laid claim to equal or superior scholarship. Harold Macmillan had been a Summerfields boy; Hugh Gaitskell and John Betjeman, Dragons.

Frank and I did not have to argue about what school to choose for Antonia and Thomas. At eight she was a Dragon and at seven and a half Thomas had joined her. Among their Dragon friends were the Hopes, the Martellis, and Richard and Felicity Wilding; two future politicians, Charles Williams and Rodney Elton (now both peers, one Labour, the other Conservative); and two future writers, Andrew Sinclair and Sally (Bentlif) Sampson. The diplomatic service would be represented by Peter Jay, Robert Wade-Gery and Tim Raison.

For me there was the new absorbing experience of being a 'Dragon parent', intensified by living next door to the arena. I call it an 'arena' because competitiveness throughout the school was rampant – among pupils, masters, parents and with other prep schools for major scholarships to public schools. Parents worked hard for the privilege of sending their children to the Dragon. They were said to have got good or bad marks for *their* homework. I remember especially the triumph of one particular mother who received congratulations on having 'won' the school Speech Prize three years running.

At the same time the atmosphere of the school was extraordinarily informal. Masters were known by their first names; boys wore shorts or boiler suits, blazers but no caps. As a result many of them found the transition to the discipline of public school hard to bear. But for *clever* boys and girls – and I underline this qualification – the mixture of forcing and informality made the Dragon School a memorable paradise – a relaxed, untidy hothouse.

I mention 'boys *and girls*' because during the war, at any rate, the ratio was about 10 to 1: 400 boys to 40 girls, of whom Antonia was one in 1940–44 and Judith one in 1945–7. They were spoilt to some extent, being given a classical education that few girls' schools could offer, star female parts in Shakespeare or Gilbert and Sullivan, and an option to play rugger or not as they pleased. Antonia was a dashing wing three-quarter. Judith, when asked by me if she would like to play football, replied: 'I don't mind running about on the field as long as I don't have to go near the ball.' The girls were all expected to do well at everything and when they fulfilled the school's expectations (as they generally did) were lavishly praised. A good example of this high-pitched applause was furnished by Antonia's first two school reports written by the headmaster: 'Capital! Quite an acquisition to the school!' 'Just the sort for a She-Dragon.'

The effect of a school that laid great emphasis on marks and 'places' was not to standardize Antonia's imagination, certainly not to iron out her literary precocity. During her first term (aged eight) I found a torn fragment from one of her highly imitative prose romances:

She looked at me and looked again; and ever searching was her look, as if she wished to say something, something that would have been dearer to me than words – she wished to say her passions, her love, that true love, that love that once had rent my heart, that had left its utmost secrecy to her merciful regard.

And I loved her.

As the war developed, Antonia's writings became more topical. In 1943 I was presented by her with a sonnet on Churchill's birthday. Thomas's interest in the war was from the beginning both romantic and technical. At six he was reproaching me for not teaching my children 'the melodies of life'; but after the bomber's crash so close to us he exclaimed, 'Mummy, you are so brave!' 'Why?' 'Because you bear the merciless threats of life.' All this was mostly verbal facility. What really meant much to him was being taken to see a Junker 88 and making innumerable model Spitfires out of construction kits. He would stage complicated formations with toy soldiers and balsa wood, afterwards photographing them so skilfully that I thought at first they were pictures of real battle scenes. He intended to be a professor in due course 'and a designer of planes in my spare time'. Frank and I were constantly entreated to take him with us to political meetings. His moment of qualified glory arrived when the German general von Thoma surrendered in the Western Desert. Thomas's nickname in the family being 'Thoma', he did not know whether to be proud or ashamed of his sudden notoriety.

His practical ingenuity was more evident at home, while school brought out his volubility and delight in argument. His first report from the Dragon School headmaster found him 'too talkative'. Next year the head admitted that, 'We are well satisfied and I think Thomas is also.' In the following year, at ten years old, he was beginning to shine at classics. 'His best work', the form master reported, 'bears the hallmark of the scholar "pur sang".'

At five Paddy began learning Latin with me at a great pace; otherwise his prowess was mainly physical. Nicknamed Carnera (the boxer), he swam there and back across the broad, cold Cherwell and took a hammer to a stucco ornament on the terrace at Chadlington Road, smashing it to pieces. For this event I suggested Frank should spank him, thus creating a paradox in our views of the boys' upbringing.

Before we had any children, I was strongly against any form of corporal punishment. I had reached this decision partly because of the disagreements among those who advocated it. Bernard Shaw, for instance, argued that a blow was only excusable when delivered in hot blood; others denounced all such angry reprisals, entreating the furious parents to wait till quite calm before administering 'a firm deliberate slap'. Neither process appealed to me, while Frank felt that some form of corporal punishment would probably be necessary. After our children were born, I tried to creep out of my dilemma by calling upon Frank to be the heavy father. Frank, however, now felt equally strongly that for a man weighing eleven and a half stone to hit a child weighing five and a half was inhuman. As a result, I would tend to follow G. B. Shaw with an exasperated smack. Paddy was to say that 'Mummy's hand was worse than the back of Dada's brush!' – in fact he laughed at both.

All the children had a passion for words that sometimes led them into curious usages and malapropisms. Judith at two wanted to thank me for some favour and exclaimed lyrically, 'Oh, you beautiful virgin!' At ten Antonia described the perpetrators of Shakespearian soliloquies as 'soloquislings'.

In one of my letters to Frank written in 1941 I asked him whether I was not too strict a parent. He replied that our friend Nicko Henderson thought they were well brought up – spirited, natural and unaffected. This for the moment reassured me. But later they were to nickname me, affectionately I admit, 'Mummy Ogre'.

When Judith was only a year old I found myself with the baby-itch again.

There was obviously no point in trying to direct the course of nature, since I had two of each sex. As I expected and hoped, a girl, Rachel, was born at 6.10 p.m. on 11 May 1942. She arrived in a hurry before my doctor or midwife got there, but the district nurse gave me the gas-and-air machine. I now felt I had experienced every available form of normal childbirth, from no anaesthetics at all (Paddy) to semi-consciousness (Antonia and Rachel) to a real knock-out (Thomas and Judith). Neither 'natural childbirth' nor the 'epidural' had yet been invented.

Rachel was extremely good-tempered and therefore popular with the family, being cast for a classic domestic role among her more assertive siblings. She hardly ever screamed and if she did would banish herself from the room, returning a few seconds later all smiles. Thomas was particularly devoted to her, asking anxiously when she was only two months old and he nine years, 'Do you think Rachel would miss me if I died now?'

Frank professed to have discovered an interest in babies that he had not felt with any of our other children. The week before Rachel was born he wrote to me wondering why this was so. 'Partly perhaps because I am fundamentally much more interested in children of all ages than I was – no doubt through having studied and loved ours. When Antonia was a baby I was hardly interested in children at all, but that is quite changed now.' After her birth he wrote, 'I am so glad I saw Rachel born – it seems to join you and me and her together. . . . After all, apart from that District Nurse whose historical reality I found it hard to believe in – I was the only person present when you sent her forth.'

As the babies accumulated I felt myself becoming more and more the conventional mother: longer spells at home, occasional visits to parents or friends, a fortnight's seaside holiday in August. Wartime landladies were perhaps more welcoming to large families of children than they were in peacetime, since they liked handling large bunches of ration books. Railway journeys were more of a hazard. At three months, Rachel was being nursed of course by me. The train was packed – no chance to get along the corridor when her feeding-time arrived. In any case we filled up a whole carriage, except for a young clergyman and his daughter. I thought this was a bit of luck. He of all people would not be shocked by a madonna-and-child act. I was wrong. Throughout Rachel's feed he kept his eyes closed and held up a newspaper in front of his daughter's face.

Life in Oxford would not have been as agreeable as it was but for the circle of friends who remained there permanently or paid visits. At the risk of introducing the bane of biography – a list of proper names – I recall the stimulating presence of Billa and Roy Harrod, Arthur and Cecily Goodhart (he was Master of University College), the Durbins, Isaiah

Berlin, Alan and Margaret Taylor and Solly and Joan Zuckerman. Anne Martelli, with three boys, was in the country and Christine Hope, with three boys, in Oxford; both their husbands away at the war. Christine took a characteristically strong line about that odious colour khaki, and when Michael came home on leave she would always flaunt the only colour that made khaki look bearable – scarlet.

Through the arrival of Rachel I also made a new, incomparable friend. In the same month, May 1942, was born Charlotte Fawcett, now Charlotte Johnson, the painter. Her mother Bice (pronounced Beechy, a shortening of Beatrice in Italian) had come to live in Oxford while James, her father, was serving in the navy. Bice and I would push our almost twin daughters around the Parks in their prams and in the summer holidays take our families together to Cornwall or Devon. Through her father, the distinguished scholar Professor Lowe, Bice had some Russian blood and the smooth brown hair, pale skin and slanting hazel eyes that went with it. She would spring over the wet sands and into the sea like the ballerina she had trained to be.

At one of the many wartime discussion groups founded to keep culture afloat, we met for the first time Gerald Berners, musician and author of *Far from the Madding War*, and Gay Margesson, the golden girl who was to marry Martin Charteris, the future Queen's private secretary.

The subject of Tolstoy and Art provoked a delightfully acerbic discussion and inspired Frank to plan with me a joint 'short but penetrating life of Tolstoy, concentrating on his relation to Soviet life'. Like several other 'joint works', including an economic history of Ireland, it was never written. Another group, this time a psychological one, was founded by Gay and her mother Francie Margesson. At what proved to be the final meeting our lecturer, a refugee psychiatrist, handed round coloured pictures that we had to identify. One was of a pear-shaped object. No one wanted to be the first to name it. At last our lecturer said in a voice of infinite contempt: 'Surely you can all see that it is a womb. . . .' She pronounced it to rhyme with bomb, except the final b was sounded. After that she decided our group was too thick and inhibited to continue.

Meanwhile, Frank's working life and my political life were going through some surprising changes.

For reasons unknown, Sir William Beveridge decided in 1941 to select Frank as his personal assistant on his two famous reports made for the Coalition Government. The first was set up by Ernest Bevin, Minister of Labour, to enquire into the 'Use of Skilled Man-Power in the Services'. The second, initiated by Arthur Greenwood, Lord Privy Seal, became known as 'The Beveridge Report', an enquiry into 'Social Insurance and

Allied Services'. Though Frank's work for Beveridge meant his being away in London for the whole of every week, I was lucky to have him most weekends; also to know that he was in no danger except from air raids and was at last doing work that we both considered invaluable. I looked forward to his daily letters (we did not telephone in those days) with their pungent accounts of wartime life in London.

Frank was sharing a room in Charlotte Street let to him and Nicko Henderson by Mary St John Hutchinson, the only belle of Bloomsbury who was both beautiful and smart. (Frank had begun by staying in an hotel whose address was 'Heartowest, Leicester Square', but soon discovered that it was too lively at night and too deadly in the morning – in fact, a brothel.) After an air raid in the area of Charlotte Street, Frank overheard a conversation in the local barber's shop.

1st Young Man: I never heard a thing – I slept right through it.
2nd Young Man: *She* must have been good.
1st Young Man: There wasn't a she at all.
2nd Young Man: All alone for once? I suppose you thought you could get a bit of sleep for a change. Wait till I catch Rommel. I shall kill him. I'll torture him – shoot him in the stomach. Takes a week to die that way. *Marvellous.*

Almost as brutal were the exchanges between Mr Little of the Amalgamated Electricians Union, an assessor on Beveridge's committee, and Sir Charles Craven, head of the armaments firm, Vickers Armstrong.

Craven: Have you heard of a gentleman called Ananias, Mr Little? [apropos of the Triton disaster]
Little: I have that, Sir Charles.
Craven: And where would you say he was now, Mr Little?
Little: He's sitting opposite me, Charlie!

Another snatch of dialogue was between Little and Sir Thomas Inskip, the unsuccessful Minister of Defence who was about to lose his job.

Inskip: Well, you've just about slaughtered me, Mr Little, if that's any satisfaction to you.
Little: It isn't any, Sir Thomas. I wouldn't be happy until I got you nailed up in your coffin and buried so deep that there was no chance of your coming back to life.
Inskip: That's a rather brutal way to deal with me, Mr Little.
Little: It's the only way to deal with a public *danger*, Sir Thomas.

Beveridge interviewing an employer on industrial insurance was hardly less sharp:

Beveridge: There's no real reason, is there, for distinguishing between the man who is run over by a lorry inside the works and the man who is run down outside?

Employer: No reason – from the point of view of the man – no.

Beveridge: Well, we're hardly concerned with the point of view of the *lorry*, are we – um – um. (No laughter for once from the chairman's sycophantic associates.)

Frank's attachment to Beveridge was unshakeable, though he could be difficult. He would return to work after a brief holiday and forget to greet his staff. 'No acolyte ever worshipped as Beveridge does at the altar of his own work,' wrote Frank to me.

One great friend whom Frank ardently wished to espouse Beveridge's cause was David Astor. In 1942 David was working in Combined Operations and was later to see gallant service with the Resistance. Before the war he had been on the *Observer*, which his family owned. When Frank appealed for support on the Beveridge Report, David agreed but felt bound to express the introspective self-distrust that often assailed idealistic youth during the war years.

Dear Frank,

In case you should misplace any reliance on me, I should explain that I have no steady political convictions and little knowledge; that I picked journalism because I was too lazy to pick any other profession or trade; that in place of culture I have a mild dilettantish curiosity; . . . that I am not serious, or determined, or strong, or effective, or anything of that sort; . . . that apart from the above points I am absolutely OK.

He certainly was. The letter ended, 'See you soon. And reserve Beveridge for Thursday 24th September.'

The epoch-making Beveridge Report – recognized as such by the public because it showed how to 'abolish want' – was published at the end of 1942. As Beveridge's personal assistant, Frank organized the whole of the publicity. Amazingly successful, he revealed a gift that took everyone, including me, by surprise but which was to be used after the war in many other causes. On one Sunday morning, however, Frank's instinct for the impact of the Report failed him.

I had accompanied him to St Aloysius' church in Oxford – the first Roman Catholic Mass I had ever attended. We reached the sermon without mishap. Then disaster struck. The priest, who had begun reasonably enough with a warning against man-made Utopias, gradually worked himself into a flaming denunciation of those who put their trust in Beveridge. That went for me. I felt there was no place for me in such a church.

It was during the Beveridge period that Frank's brother Edward Longford made him a staggering and totally unexpected offer from Ireland. Frank wrote to me: 'He offered me *Pakenham* provided I paid for the furniture. . . . It would of course be a life-interest for me only to pass to Thomas at my death. I do wonder what you think – I am strongly tempted to accept – though not with the idea of living there during the war.'

Next day Frank wrote again to say that he was going down with Penelope Betjeman and her mother to Pakenham in Penelope's car 'to give the old place a thorough though scarcely technical inspection'. Would it be possible to accept Edward's offer? 'I am sure you can guess I am mad keen to, though of course it is *all-important* to know what YOU think.' Edward was not making the offer in order to get Pakenham demolished, but 'with the idea of keeping the old place together'. Frank promised to write in much greater detail when he had been through 'the somewhat confused figures of the estate(!)'.

I was torn between my devotion to Ireland, which had been born ten years ago and was still as strong as ever, and our numerous and complicated commitments in England. I could not see how it would be possible to combine a full family life, an active political career *and* the life of an Anglo-Irish chatelaine in Westmeath. By the time Frank had returned from Ireland, I had decided to pull up my roots in England and start again over there, if that was what he wanted. Perhaps some day he would be elected Taoiseach . . . I remember standing under a large portrait of some of the 'Bloomsburys' by Duncan Grant that hung in our drawing-room – it belonged to my brother Michael for whom I was keeping it until he returned from the war – and thought how remote they looked, as if living in a world where it was never necessary to make agonizing decisions.

In the end, having made the *gran rifiuto*, I was let off. There was no transfer or sale and Edward continued being domiciled between Dublin and Pakenham to the end of his days. The whole episode, indeed, remained wrapped in some confusion, like the figures of the estate.

The curious non-event of Pakenham Hall had been preceded by the very real loss of Uncle Bingo's house in London, bequeathed to Frank in

1938. Word came from the agents for this Norfolk Street mansion that it was being vandalized by intruders who were using it for immoral purposes during the Blitz. We must either install a married couple and pay them to caretake for the duration, or sell. This time there was no agonizing choice. We could not afford the extra outlay, nor did we think of trying to borrow the money from a bank. Suppose the house were bombed and the caretakers killed? The further idea that it might survive and be worth a vast sum after the war, never entered our heads. 'Property deals' were not part of the mental apparatus of socialists in the 1940s. So we sold it for the offered price of £1,000. I was as thankful to shake off Norfolk Street as I would be relieved not to take on Pakenham Hall.

The early stages of war had served only to inflame my socialist enthusiasm. My King's Norton party and I were continually baiting Head Office on one or other of the topical left-wing issues. First it was the new editor of the *Daily Herald.* I drafted a motion to be presented at Annual Conference: 'Conference calls upon the National Executive to give a full report on the circumstances of the recent change and to see to it that the editor of Labour's paper is always and necessarily an avowed socialist.' My words seemed suitably menacing to impress the delegates.

More ominous was my objection, backed by King's Norton, to Head Office's interpretation of the 'Political Truce'. This truce had been negotiated between all the major parties and was to last for the duration. No doubt it was necessary in order to preserve the wartime coalition government. I did not see, however, why my party and I should not state our political views, even if we did not contest the by-election caused by the death of Ronald Cartland MP on active service. I therefore drafted and published a leaflet to this effect.

A jet of anger from Head Office. The National Agent informed me icily: 'The truce is only a reality if political controversy ceases during the war.' I retorted that our job was to work for the post-war era, when Labour would again be an independent party, not part of a coalition. In vain I argued the case for propaganda and preparation for post-war social reform. We were expelled from the Labour Party in 1941. I was to attend the next Annual Conference seated not on the floor of the chamber among my fellow Labour candidates, each with one vote, but voteless, in the visitors' gallery. Fortunately there was no other by-election in King's Norton during the war and eventually we were forgiven. I remained a hero of the activists for a year or so. Then a new controversy arose of a more personal kind.

My party in Birmingham had behaved with indulgence toward the births of our children. Judith, having brought the number to four, two of each, was assumed to be the full stop to Mrs Pakenham's family. But Rachel? More difficult to explain her. I think most of my friends concluded that she was an accident. I imagined them saying, 'People who don't make mistakes don't make anything' – a favourite quotation in the Labour movement.

But number six? By the summer of 1943 number six was on the way. I did not want them to think that this was another accident, since my addiction to motherhood was now a part of me that I could not deny. Indeed, with three girls and two boys, I had made the decision early in 1943 that it was time to even up the family again – and Dr Helena Wright's theory and practice were called into play.

That summer there were rumbles of criticism in a section of the King's Norton party about my coming 'happy' event. What guarantee had they that this would be the last and that I would not end like the Old Woman Who Lived in a Shoe? In the nursery rhyme the Old Woman had so many children that 'she didn't know what to do'. Why should I do better? How could I fit in enough campaigning to win the seat after the war, let alone represent their interests in Parliament? In August my devoted agent, Harold Nash, together with two or three other influential members of the party, came to Oxford from Birmingham to draw up a plan for dealing with the hostile criticism. At the forthcoming Executive Committee called to discuss my position, I promised to say everything they suggested: everything short of guaranteeing never to have another baby after this one.

On 1 October, just four weeks before the baby was due, I drove to Birmingham for my crucial speech. Those who wished for a change of candidate were led by Stanley Evans, later the Labour MP for nearby Wolverhampton in the Black Country. He was to become known for his post-war diatribes against the policy he called 'featherbedding the farmers'. Now in 1943 he was equally opposed to 'featherbedding' me. However, he made a restrained speech, though definitely inviting me to retire. Then it was my turn to reply. The atmosphere was somewhat torpid. 'Give it them strong,' whispered Harold in my ear. 'They need to be roused. Give them all you've got.' Thanks to Harold Nash I hit the right note. A vote of confidence was proposed and carried. I drove home still the Labour candidate for the King's Norton division of Birmingham.

On 3 November 1943 – the twelfth anniversary of our wedding day – Michael Aidan was born. For the first time there was no Frank present, since he was somewhere up North with Beveridge, assisting in a new enquiry on 'Full Employment'. He sent a jubilant telegram and signed on Beveridge as a godfather. When Francis Hope, the five-year-old son of Michael and Christine, heard the news of our Michael's birth he expressed what may have been a general view: 'What, *another* Pakenham?'

And when Solly Zuckerman came to lunch with us he remembers Frank saying as he opened the front door, 'Come in quickly or they'll all fall out.'

Hardly more than two months after Michael's birth I was to take one of the major decisions of my life.

He was our sixth child and, as with all my last three babies, I decided to nurse him for the full nine or ten months. The physical strain added to prolonged attacks of sinusitis and migraine, plus the need to collect suitable Christmas presents in wartime conditions for an extended family, suddenly made me think again about King's Norton.

We were in the middle of the greatest war in history. We knew we would win. America was in. We were shouting for a Second Front in Europe to support Russia. Even so the end was not in sight. Though I was allowed extra petrol for my journeys to and from Birmingham, the journeys themselves were becoming more unpleasant. They were lonely. No one in the car but myself and a baby on the back seat. The baby was company but also an added responsibility. What would happen if the car broke down in the middle of the night? I began to imagine things. On foggy winter nights the long road between Birmingham and Oxford could be a *via dolorosa* indeed. On one horrible occasion my windscreen had become so frozen over that I had to drive the whole way home with the glass wound fully open in order to see at all. I arrived home still able to see but not to feel with any of my fingers or toes. Was I to begin all this again in January 1944?

These were only material considerations, partly due no doubt to the physical reactions after childbirth. Once I got through the winter, most of these thoughts would surely dissolve with the Birmingham fogs. But there were mental fogs too, drifting around in my head and obscuring my judgement, blanketing my resolution. Or were they not fogs but facts? When the post-war general election came at last, was it certain that Frank would win Oxford? Harold Nash's brilliant organization of an enthusiastic party made me confident that King's Norton would be won. Oxford's winnability depended on an adjustment in the city boundaries. At present the two main industrial areas, Cowley and Headington, were excluded from the city, their many thousands of Labour votes being 'lost' in the rural division of South Oxfordshire. Suppose the new boundaries were not drawn till *after* the election? Frank might well be defeated in Oxford City while I was victorious in Birmingham. In that case, as I put it to myself, I would be sent up to Westminster with a mandate to set the Thames on fire, while Frank stayed behind to keep the home fires burning and look after the children.

The children. In wartime especially, was I not a mother first and politician afterwards? Jean, the children's highly efficient nanny, had left to join the Wrens. Though Popie's daughter Alice, an insurance clerk, had come from Bernhurst to live with us and work in Oxford, while Alice's cousin May, a dressmaker, had taken Jean's place, there was no longer anyone specifically trained to look after children.

Even if I continued successfully to shuttle between King's Norton and Oxford while the war lasted, what about afterwards? Quite apart from Frank's presence or absence from Westminster, would I be capable of doing justice both to our six children and the thousands of my constituents? My philosophy had always been that in normal circumstances a woman could do both – run a family and a career. But if there were ever a doubt, I had been equally certain that the family came first.

An ultimate, private doubt had been sown in my mind by the crucial meeting held in King's Norton the month before Michael's birth. Notwithstanding the vote of confidence, there were some who did not want me, who wanted a new candidate. Perhaps after all they were right. The next Executive Committee was due on 9 January 1944. I sent poor Harold, who had worked so hard for me, an unwelcome Christmas present in the form of a letter of resignation.

When Christmas Day arrived we went through the usual ceremonies, Frank dressing up as Father Christmas and crashing down on the kitchen lino, ostensibly through the weight of presents in his sack. (The kitchen had long ago become our family living-room because of its warm stove, but Frank's first crash as Father Christmas had been an accident due to the lino's slipperiness. The crash proved so popular, however, that it was repeated every year during the war and for forty years afterwards – it is now traditional in our family.)

At the end of that most exhausting Christmas Day I put down Michael in his cot and fell asleep while climbing into my own bed, a thing I had never done before and have never done since. In the light of exhaustion, 9 January 1944, my resignation date, seemed a day to be welcomed.

My speech to the comrades was piano. Like Napoleon at Waterloo, I had piles, but unlike him congested sinuses as well and did not feel in top campaigning form, though well up to a dignified retreat. The members present had read my letter of resignation. I told them I would not recapitulate my arguments, except in answering questions. They might wonder why I had resigned after the whole matter had apparently been settled at a meeting three months earlier. 'That meeting', I explained, 'had set up in me a train of thought. . . .' Why had I decided to resign *now* – so soon? To give them plenty of time to choose another candidate. I concluded by assuring them all that our six years of work together had not been a waste; not for them, not for me. I still think that was true. The meeting ended by taking on all the nuances of a final parting: poignancy and regret, tranquillity and relief. Yet I had not in my own mind answered the two most important questions. Did I ever intend to stand for Parliament again? Or to have another child? Like many wartime decisions, mine was made for the moment, not for all time. But it was to have a lasting effect.

Two days after my resignation the pain in my face was so bad that I had to get on my bike and visit the ear, nose and throat surgeon. He punctured and drained my antrum there and then. I felt altogether drained.

15

An End and a Beginning
· 1944–6 ·

My diary for 1944 opened on 5 January with the words: 'Antonia and Thomas to Father Favell.' This entry was to be a better signpost to the events of the next two years than the one that came four days later – 'King's Norton Resignation'.

Father Favell was a tall, striking Anglo-Catholic priest who swept about Walton Street, South Oxford, in a long black soutane on his way to and from the church of St Paul's. His sensitive charm seemed to me typical of what the Puseyites of the Oxford Movement must have possessed. St Paul's was a severe-looking basilica, with a long flight of stone steps and high pillared portico preparing one for a forbidding interior. Instead, Father Favell had filled it with the complete apparatus of High Church ritual – candles, crucifixes, incense, the reserved Host and, in his own person, celibacy.

And how did my two elder children find themselves at St Paul's? The short answer was: on the advice of my friend Muriel Williams, one of the Christ Church wives. They were being prepared for their first communion together with her son Charles, Thomas's friend at the Dragon School, and her daughter Pattice. To me High Church piety had become more attractive than Low Church simplicity. This was not always so.

On the day of Judith's birth in 1940 I had said to Frank in an access of affection, '*You* can have her' – meaning that she should be our first baby to be baptized a Catholic. Next day I changed my mind, after getting to know my new enchanting acquisition better. I refused to make a sacrifice of her, as I still saw it, to Romish superstition, so she was baptized into the safety of North Oxford Protestantism. Baptism still represented for me nothing but the conventional 'christening party' attended by one's friends, some of whom would be given the accolade of 'godparents'. In Judith's case we invited Penelope Betjeman, Christine Hope, Esmond Warner and my brother Roger Chamberlain Harman.

It was through the death of Roger in the following year that I took a short step in a new direction. Some time before the war broke out Roger had developed a tumour on the brain. I remember saying to my mother, 'If I had to choose between peace and Roger's life, I would choose his life.' She agreed, thus showing that, as Arnold Bennett wrote, 'There are no public worries. There are only private worries.' My concern was at first not so much for him as for my mother. But when I visited him at an Oxford hospital on his way to Mount Vernon where he was to die, I was suddenly overwhelmed with grief for him personally.

It began when he showed me some advertisements for farms. 'I intend to buy this one . . . or perhaps that one . . . when I am better.' (He had tried to do farming when invalided out of the army.) Yet he could hardly see the pictures because of double vision. As I came into the room he had said, with a brave attempt at a joke, 'I'm lucky. I can see *two* of your face!' We talked of this and that, of his future, all optimistically, nothing truthfully. He must have known that he was not going to live, but I, who knew it too, neither had the heart nor the faith to talk to him about realities – what are called 'The Last Things'. I gave myself two excuses: one, that he might still have been clinging to a shred of hope which, by speaking out, I would be cruelly taking away; the other, that my own beliefs were too immature and indefinite to help someone *in extremis*.

After his death I began by feeling the usual guilt at failure, increased by what seemed the pathos of his unfulfilled life. Looking back, I realized that I knew him less well now than when he had been a boy of twelve at Lynchfield. I remembered the sturdy thatched hut that he and his younger brother Michael had built under the trees, adding to it every holiday with bricks wheeled away from a disued chalk-pit and yew boughs cut from the wood. They had named it 'Prodden House', a shortening of the word 'Prodendum' which they fondly thought had something to do with progress. They had even produced the 'Prodden House Magazine' year after year, recording the life of the house and the plans of its builders. Feasts were held, guests invited, and we all toppled off our stools after drinking to Roger's future progress in dandelion wine.

Where was that progress now? A good degree at Cambridge; rowing for his college. But at thirty he was unmarried and had never been intensely loved, as far as I knew, by anyone except his mother. What did it all amount to? Or was that the wrong question to ask?

At Christmas 1941 I tried to make amends for my own unfulfilled relationship with him during the last days by writing a poem on his death and sending it to my father. The poem was vague and noncommittal; indeed I had chosen the medium of verse in which to express my feelings because poetry could hint at things without having to analyse them. At the end of each line one is not asked to say, 'Yes, I meant just *that*.'

In Memoriam: R.C.H.
He saw the harvest stand
 On Cotswold hills: he met
The challenge of the land,
 Garnered the grain he set.
The end is not yet.

. . .

Earth, with its hills and sky
 Has paid the spirit's debt.
Here is no last good-bye,
 No lingering regret.
The end is not yet.

Ambiguous as it was, my poem perhaps left room for some kind of afterlife; though hardly for a personal God.

My next hesitating steps were taken in the dimness of the hall at 8 Chadlington Road. Places had to be found for Frank's books when we moved from Singletree, his 'study' having been made into our bedroom during the Blitz. So I assigned him a tall bookcase in the hall and filled it with his volumes on politics and economics, except for the bottom shelf, which was on floor level. To this dark, not easily accessible nether region I relegated his religious books, naming it the 'Chamber of Horrors'.

For several years I studiously avoided its contents. Then one day a new volume found its way into the place reserved for 'horrors', a volume that I decided to read. This was *True Humanism* by Jacques Maritain; for me, as it proved, a seminal experience. The great French scholar showed that Catholicism and the reforming left were far from incompatible; indeed 'Humanism' was no longer to be regarded as synonymous with an atheism that saw man as the measure of all things, but with a faith that centred itself on God. If Jacques Maritain and his Russian-Jewish wife Raïssa, both trained in scientific disciplines, could believe this, who was I to be the messenger to my family of stultifying doubt? It was through Maritain that my worst demon was exorcized: dislike of the Catholic Church for its part in the Spanish Civil War. Even though I found Maritain dense reading and probably understood only one sentence in five, he convinced me that all belief, all hope, all truth were not to be judged by the events of two particular years in Catalonia and Madrid.

My discovery of Maritain was followed up by 'discovery' of the New Testament, in the sense that I read all four Gospels right through for the first time. My impression was twofold: that but for the Gospel of John we should never have guessed that Jesus *was God*, rather than the Son of God; and that the uncongenial picture (at least to me) of 'Gentle Jesus meek and mild' was a myth. I gloried in the indignant extrusion of the moneylenders from the temple, imagining the scene taking place in Cowley or King's Norton, to the loud cheers of the comrades.

Prayer was my next obstacle. I tried it out on the nights when Frank was in London, feeling unaccountably shy about flopping down on my knees anywhere except in church. I had plenty of opportunities for intercession-ary prayer in 1944, as it happened to be a year of illness in our family. Paddy had an attack of earache, bearing it so stoically that I did not realize until his temperature soared that it was due to an infected mastoid. Before the emergency operation the surgeon told us that if Paddy had been a soldier, instead of a seven year old, he would have been treated with penicillin instead of the knife. But at present the miracle drug was not available for civilians. Therefore it would be a week before we would know if our gifted, boisterous son was to survive. No difficulty about falling on one's knees during that week.

And Frank was suddenly struck down with acute lumbago. Towards the end of August we were travelling by train to stay with Nicko Henderson. On arrival at the station, Frank opened the carriage door and literally fell out on the platform. I became a little better at prayer.

The thought of his mother and her terrible arthritis was always a shadow at the back of my mind. Could it be that the climate of Oxfordshire (where she too had lived) was bad for all forms of rheumatism? Yet the expert Professor Ryle, at one of the numerous wartime Brains Trusts organized for charity, had insisted in answer to that very question: 'No climate is bad for rheumatism.' Two years later we were to move to London and then Sussex, but the lumbago did not move with us. Was it climate or prayer?

I myself had had a miscarriage of twins, so my doctor said, in July 1944, to my great surprise and grief. I had not weaned Michael nor recommenced the menstrual cycle, which should have meant, according to church teaching, that I was 'safe'. To have been pregnant, and not to know it, and then to lose it – lose them – was too much. All the fault of the Church. My anger with the Church showed how near I was to devotion and trust.

Notwithstanding this setback to faith, I was now accompanying Antonia and Thomas to St Paul's church on Sundays, taking with me Judith and Rachel. Shortly before the third anniversary of my brother Roger's death, I felt strong enough in my religious convictions to write to my mother when his birthday came round on 12 August.

Dearest Mother,

I felt so sorry for you on Roger's birthday knowing what a sad day it would be for you. And now you tell me how sad it was indeed. . . . Life is relatively short, & we are all going to lose people we love most. It is essential to find a philosophy of life & death, in order to bear these sufferings. I think Mary Clive [my sister-in-law Maria who married Meysey Clive], when Meysey was killed, first made me realize that actual *time* on earth is not the only way of reckoning. She said she had had more happiness & fulfilment in her three years with Meysey than many people have in a life-time.

Of course it seems terrible & wrong when a child dies before his parents. Frank & I were both racked with imaginings when Paddy had his mastoid operation. Soon after Roger died and I began to feel it was time to decide about the great questions of death & life – & in war-time one is absolutely impelled to do so. Now I firmly believe in immortality, even in some kind of personal reunion, though I suppose with our finite minds we can never quite conceive exactly how it can be. But the great thing is – that it will be.

Love Betty

I signed my childish name to show my continuing bond with Roger and the past.

By the autumn of 1944 Father Favell was giving me instruction. In December I was received into the Anglican Church at St Paul's and next day confirmed at Christ Church Cathedral by the Bishop of Oxford. That Christmas I attended my first Midnight Mass. Like other converts I was deeply moved by the hour, the darkness, the gleams of coloured light, the bursts of chanting in Latin, in fact the whole English–Roman ritual; more moved than I had been since the Nonconformist Thanksgiving service at the Austin Friars on Armistice Day 1918.

My diary for January 1945 opened with a list of Father Favell's times for hearing Confessions.

That year was to be the end of so many things. The end of the war. The end, apparently, of Frank's ambitions to be an MP. The rather glorious end of Thomas's last full year at the Dragon School. The end of what was to be my brief stop-over in the Anglican Church.

VE Day made little impression, unique celebration though it was, perhaps because I had conjunctivitis so badly (my father cured it by telephone, probably his last act as a doctor) that I could hardly see the huge bonfire in the Dragon School yard, to which spectacle we were all invited. For me, the war went out with a whimper. Far better than VE

Day do I remember the dropping of the metaphorical bombshell between VE Day and VJ Day – the announcement of the atomic discovery which would lead to who knew what real bombs of unexampled horror. Frank was away. I was sitting alone, reading, when I turned on the wireless for the evening news. For the first time in my life I had a strong presentiment about the future: that a brilliant scientific discovery would bring a balance of evil to the human race. In my old days with the North Staffs WEA, the pros and cons of modern scientific invention were a favourite subject for debate. We would put up the blessed electric iron and gas cooker against the accursed bomber plane and tank. But the debatable results of the atom bomb were on a different scale and overwhelmed me with their implications.

However, the second most significant general election of the century had recently taken place, with results that absorbed my thoughts. The first, held in 1906, the year of my birth, had been won by the Liberals. The third, to be held in 1979, would be won by the Conservatives. The election of 1945, halfway between the other two landslides, became an avalanche of victories for Labour in its *annus mirabilis*.

During the three weeks of hard but not bitter campaigning in Oxford, there was only one incident that revealed something of the political emotions that separated the two major candidates, both old friends. Quintin Hogg, the Conservative, had the kindly idea of calling on Frank, the Labour candidate, and shaking hands just before the battle proper began. He chose a moment, perhaps purposely, when the whole Pakenham family was sitting around the table at tea. Frank introduced Quintin. Then he turned to Paddy, the eldest of the children present. 'Get another cup for Mr Hogg, Paddy.' But loyalty forbade Paddy to sustain the enemy with anything, even a cup of tea. 'No, I will *not*,' he shouted in his victory tones. Someone else fetched the cup and Quintin praised the Labour loyalist, turning Paddy's bellow of outrage into his own characteristic shout of laughter. Years later, Quintin's son Douglas was to bait me from the gallery of the Oxford Town Hall while I was orating on the platform. I realized that old family scores had been equitably settled.

As a family, the best thing we managed on Frank's behalf was to drive through the town centre and up and down Iffley Road in a pony-cart decorated with Labour posters and a cluster of ornamental children: Judith, Rachel and Michael. Though our equipage attracted the minimum of attention from the voters – I well knew how voters had a way of detaching themselves from pony-traps set to snare them – the press were delighted and gave us a good spread in the *Oxford Mail*.

It must be admitted that my own guesses about the election result were the precise opposite to the truth. I expected Frank's long connection with the county where his family had lived for many years, together with his political work on the city council and elsewhere, his service in the Home Guard, his popularity in a wider world due to his publicity for the Beveridge Report – these things alone caused me to expect a Labour victory in Oxford. My only doubts focused on the Oxford boundaries, which still had not been re-drawn to include Headington and Cowley; and on Sir William Beveridge himself who, ungratefully as I thought, gave his support to the Liberal candidate instead of to Frank, to whom he owed so much. These doubts were removed by the news, leaked between polling day and the count three weeks later, that the Services' vote was overwhelmingly Labour.

Nationally, however, the reports of Churchill's quasi-royal progresses through the country convinced me that the grand old bulldog had not been giving his V-signs in vain.

Unlike me, my old friend Ted Hobson, who had retired from North Staffordshire to Kent, made a spectacularly close prediction of the result, putting it in a sealed envelope on the eve of the poll and winning much money from Tory acquaintances. But even his guess fell short of the tremendous reality. Labour's landslide victory, announced on 26 and 27 July, consoled both Frank and me for his personal defeat by 2,800 votes. At the same time, the surge into Parliament of so many of our contemporaries and friends – Hugh Gaitskell, Douglas Jay, Evan Durbin, Patrick Gordon Walker, Aidan Crawley, Dick Crossman – made us feel forlorn, left out in the cold.

The atmosphere changed, as so often, with a visit from Evan Durbin. He and his wife Marjorie, from their house in North Oxford, had been our main source of Labour gossip and speculation – and of convivial meals at weekends – throughout the war. Evan worked in Attlee's office. With him we discussed Herbert Morrison's attempts to oust Clem Attlee as party leader, culminating in his plan to summon a meeting of the parliamentary party as soon as the election results were out. The parliamentary party would then, presumably, vote Morrison into the leadership in place of Clem. The 'plot' was foiled. As official Labour leader in the wartime Coalition, Attlee was rightly sent for by the King to Buckingham Palace on 27 July and asked to form the first majority Labour Government of the century. With our long-held conviction that a majority Labour Government would enact not only the Beveridge Report but also the nationalization of the major public services, it was bitter indeed to be excluded from this building of the New Jerusalem – I by electoral resignation, Frank by electoral defeat. Great was our interest, therefore, when Evan Durbin intimated that Attlee wished to include Frank in his Government, but in the House of Lords.

Frank's urge to serve Attlee was a strong one. Personally he admired the unobtrusive but determined little Major of the Great War who was so firmly involved in the social reclamation of London's East End. By his close connection with the social and educational work of Toynbee Hall and the WEA, Attlee had a special appeal for Frank and me. Moreover, he came of a strong but varied Christian background. Though Attlee himself declared tersely of Christianity, 'I believe in the ethics but not the mumbo-jumbo,' his elder brother believed in the 'mumbo-jumbo' to the extent of ministering to a High Anglican church in Oxford and christening our daughter Rachel, while his niece Peggy Attlee was, like her husband, a Roman Catholic and a socialist, and would be godmother to our seventh child.

Moreover, Attlee seemed to appreciate Frank's potential as a leader of the Labour movement more, at any rate, than Morrison did. I remembered a dialogue between Morrison and Pamela Churchill, reported to me in one of Frank's letters from London during the war. Ann O'Neill (later Rothermere and then Fleming) was giving a dinner-party. Morrison sat next to Pamela, Randolph's wife, with Frank on the other side of the table. Pamela described her conversation to Frank afterwards.

Morrison: Here I am from the lower classes joining the upper classes. He [looking at Frank] is a member of the upper classes who has joined the lower classes. That always causes trouble.
Pamela: Who for?
Morrison: For him of course.
Pamela: Why?
Morrison: Because he gets keener on the party than the party is on itself!

Frank and I had all along been aware of the intellectual's problems in the Labour movement. After the party conference of 1942 he wrote to me:

I am clear that every intellectual in the Labour movement has hitherto fallen into one of two traps. He has either become a mere servant (. . . even Sam, [Gaitskell's name as an undergraduate] etc. are well on the way to it). That is to say, they bend their intellect to the level of what Huxley would call 'unregenerate men and women', *or* they remain themselves but slip off the main ladder and function at the margin like Leslie Rowse, Kingsley Martin etc.

I too had experienced the problem in a different way. Writing messages to the voters of Birmingham had been virtually my only literary outlet during the war. I put everything I had into these messages, trying to make them pungent, stirring, non-platitudinous, in short, 'different'. Alas, they did not satisfy my expert agent, Harold Nash, who knew what his members wanted, or rather, were used to. He ruthlessly scrapped my purple passages, preferring what Ernie Bevin was to call, 'clich, clich, clich'. Frank wrote consolingly, 'Even the best of the workers are curiously bad judges of literature'; but I recognized once and for all that party political propaganda can no longer be the nursery for literature. The days of Swift and Disraeli were passed.

The question of Frank's immediate decision – yes or no to Attlee's forthcoming offer – was discussed by him and me as we walked round and round the Dragon School cricket ground. Term was over. The place was empty. It was a calm summer evening. The swifts flew over the fields and river, whistling as usual, but not now reminding me of dive bombers. What I had to share in taking was a peacetime decision that would change the lives of ourselves and our family irrevocably.

One way, Frank would no doubt return to academic life as a teacher of Politics at Christ Church. That way, we would remain a sheltered Oxford family encapsulated in the University's protective shell, cut off from whatever was going to happen in the new world outside. Of course he could wait for a winnable by-election, but that was a bird-in-the-bush that might never drop into his hand.

The other way, he would accept a peerage, join the Government as a political lord-in-waiting, the lowest form of ministerial life, and perhaps eventually reach the Cabinet as Leader of the House of Lords. I confess that my heart did not thrill to this prospect.

It was the House of Commons that to me meant reality and romance. I had lectured endlessly on the grand old men who had operated there and the even grander women who had tried to breach its walls but failed. In a sense I too had failed because I was a woman, and I wanted Frank, my *alter ego*, to succeed. Unprepossessing though I found the central lobby of the House of Commons, decked out as it was with huge marble tailcoats and togas swathing the limbs of Victorian patriarchs, it still gave me a lift of excitement to think that a Gladstone, an O'Connell, a Keir Hardie had trodden these tessellated floors. The House of Lords I had never set eyes on, merely demanded its abolition in my Cheltenham campaign.

Moreover, by becoming a peer, would not Frank be throwing away his chance of the highest positions in the state? As a peer he would never be Prime Minister, Foreign Secretary or Chancellor of the Exchequer.

Evan Durbin, however, had urged on me that two apparently undeniable facts made Frank more suited to the Lords than the Commons: he would inevitably inherit a peerage when his brother

Edward died; and as a Roman Catholic would never be Prime Minister. (Both these arguments were true of 1945; neither was to apply forty years later. By then the 'Wedgwood Benn' Bill had made it possible to renounce peerages, while Shirley Williams MP had shown that her Roman Catholicism would not be the reason why she slipped, if slip she did, from the top of the greasy pole.)

When we walked home from the Dragon cricket ground the shadows had lengthened and the swifts gone to bed. I knew that I was going to remain unconvinced but that Evan Durbin's arguments would prevail. As indeed they did. In retrospect I can see that Evan was right. The House of Lords would give Frank a better platform than the Commons for his essentially Christian-socialist, but sometimes unorthodox, views. Ever since our days at Singletree, these views had included more humane understanding of the prison population; they were later to embrace help for the victims of crime, non-persecution of sexual deviants; later still, support of black communities and 'Women's Liberation' but not of abortion on demand; sympathy with the Greenham Common women as individuals, their sufferings and sacrifices, but detestation of the Soviets as a system, their materialism and aggression. Some of these beliefs were to seem to some of our friends contradictory. At any rate, the House of Lords is an arena more suited than the Commons to inter-party causes and appendices to party programmes.

At the heart of these perplexities had lain the character of Frank himself. *Five Lives* was the title he would choose for the second volume of his autobiography, and certainly his character was many-faceted. Born the second son of an Irish peer, on his mother's side he was descended from the Jerseys, whose family name was Child-Villiers, and on his father's side from another Villiers, Barbara, mistress of King Charles II. His grandfather, the seventh Earl of Jersey, was a descendant of that notorious Lady Jersey who for a time captured the heart and bed of the Prince Regent. Her eldest Jersey grandson was to marry a daughter of the British Prime Minister, Sir Robert Peel, so that from this side of the family Frank had inherited the blood of two extremely adventurous women and one notably sober man.

Margaret Countess of Jersey, Frank's clever grandmother, having been eager to give him an easy entrée into right-wing politics, had in fact produced a much more valuable gift in the person of her younger son, Frank's uncle Arthur Child-Villiers. A most unusual man, Arthur had avoided the customary ways in which the younger sons of British aristocrats earned their living and served their country: namely, by entering the army, navy or church. With a good brain for finance, like his

Child (banking) forebears, he made money in Baring's Bank and gave service through the boys' club he founded. This would have been a quite usual syndrome for the upper middle or professional classes – Attlee in the Toynbee Hall Settlement – but not for the aristocracy. Lord Shaftesburys were rare. But thanks to Arthur Villiers, when Frank quitted the Conservative high road it seemed natural that he should combine his new career with social as well as political service to the deprived.

Frank's prison visiting had begun soon after we went to live in Oxford. I well remember giving breakfast at Singletree to a working-class prisoner and his family on the morning of his release from Oxford gaol. We celebrated with Liebfraumilch in tall glasses with long pale green stems. Though grateful for the kind intention, our friends did not know what to make of this finicky liquor.

Singletree was soon on the tramps' circuit. One winter evening I opened the front door to a tramp fainting from hunger and cold. I brought him hot, thick soup. He was disgusted; he wanted spirits and a coat. Frank looked at him more closely. 'Wasn't it you I gave my coat to a few weeks ago?' 'Oh, *that* thing,' scoffed the tramp, ' – if you can call it a coat. I gave it away, wouldn't be seen dead in it.' Our tramp had a point but had also missed one. Frank's inborn untidiness (his father, though colonel of the Life Guards, was the despair of his batman) was no handicap among our new associates. In the land of the sockless, the man in odd socks is king. (Thomas, among our children, has inherited this trait and sometimes gets up in socks that don't match.)

Frank's lack of interest in appearances and possessions gradually earned him a halo for eccentricity. This was kept polished by his own activities and also by the face and figure that providence had given him. The intellectual's high domed forehead, the dark, curly, monklike tonsure (he is more brown than grey at eighty), the aristocratically curved nose, round gold spectacles, spade chin and commanding height – these all made life easy for the caricaturist. And Frank was eventually to give them an ideal subject to caricature: his crusade against pornography. The last football game he played (for charity, at the age of sixty-five) involved his being photographed with a team of Bunny Girls – at their invitation.

Frank's crusade was launched by him purely as a duty. No desire of his. Far from being a cover for his own smutty-mindedness, as some critics suggested – just as our eight children were once said to be a cover-up for his own homosexuality – porn was distasteful, utterly boring to him. Neither of us had read a word of it until the campaign opened, and Frank was profoundly thankful not to have to read another line after it closed. Though an exceptionally amusing after-dinner speaker, his wit depended not at all on dirty stories.

Caricature I drew of Frank for 'Mencap', 1983

His passion for sport harked back to captaining his football team at school. At eighty he was still to be a jogger, one of his most prized gifts being a bright yellow anorak with two red reflectors sewn to the back by Thomas, so that Frank could jog in the dark without being run over.

In the home his casual side made him a desperate loser of latchkeys, razors, clothes, library books; but this was more than balanced for me by exemplary patience in all domestic crises. Never a complaint about food, drink, cold or indeed any creature comforts. There was not a dull moment in his company. He would relate to me every incident in his day, whether he had spent it as politician, banker, publisher or social worker. Nor did he ever forget to ask me, 'What have *you* done today?' Over the years we built up a store of private jokes and catch-phrases that kept conversation light-footed: 'He would, wouldn't he?', 'Stormy applause rising to an ovation', 'Or else . . .', 'Kiss me, Harry', 'Wipe that smile off your face', 'Good Lord'.

Those last two words were Frank's habitual comment on any remark of mine to which he had not actually been attending but which he felt required an answer. His formula was rarely appropriate. For instance, 'I see the bank rate's unchanged.' 'Good Lord.'

I thought of our family as pleasantly dug in at Oxford. But already the two eldest children were on the move. Antonia, having gone to the Godolphin School, Salisbury, had completed her first year at boarding-school. Now just thirteen, she presented me with the curious but engaging contradictions of our first teenager. When I visited her at school she had asked me to bring her cakes, sweets, jam – and the poems of Cecil Day Lewis. At home she was somewhat disdainful towards Thomas and Paddy, trying to forget that she had ever scampered up the rugger field with a muddy ball clasped in her arms. At the same time she got rid of her precious dolls, distributing them between Judith and Rachel. Literature was all that mattered.

Thomas had won the Dragon School speech prize with a defence of Soviet Russia. In the Eton scholarship he had come twelfth on the list, having done 'badly', I heard, in some subjects but shown a 'spark' in others. While waiting to know whether there would be a place for him there (Frank's old school) in 1946, we decided to send him to Belvedere, the famous Jesuit college in Dublin, for at least one term. Frank had already taken him to see the college in January 1945. We all knew about its reputation as the scene of an annual hell-fire sermon, luridly described by James Joyce in his *Portrait of the Artist as a Young Man*. I had no fears for Thomas's equilibrium even if submitted to ordeal by sermon. Unlike Antonia, he had never been afraid of the dark or, as far as I knew, of the flames of hell. And Frank was determined to pass on his own bi-national affiliations – English and Irish – to his eldest son, with their well-known heritage of doubled richness but divided commitment. After all, on a lower plane, Thomas would one day inherit Edward's estate and Frank felt he owed one term of his son's education to Ireland.

After the preliminary visit to Belvedere, Thomas was allowed to imbibe the lighter spirit of Dunsany Castle. On this occasion Uncle Eddie happened to be calling down his own brand of hell-fire upon cocktails, rather than table salt or dyed kippers. 'I'm far more anti-cocktail', he thundered, 'than I'm anti-Hitler. Hitler is simply the poison that creeps into the vacuum of British weakness.'

If Antonia and Thomas were being encouraged to stand on their own feet (Thomas was also now a boarder, at the Dragon), the rest of the family were leaving childhood too fast for my liking. Judith was a wistful five year old with brown eyes and bouncing curls; our friend Pamela Berry once said of her, 'She's so pretty she'll marry a duke,' a prophesy that has so far not been fulfilled. When asked at three what she wanted to be when grown up, she had replied, 'I want to walk far far away over the hills, without you, Mummy, and then come back again.' If that is what a poet does, Judith was to have her wish.

Michael was now two, the only blue-eyed child since Antonia and in every sense my blue-eyed boy. Nevertheless, he had long ago left behind that period of babyhood that I loved best of all: the age of about four months, when you only had to look into the cot to get a smile and make a silly noise to get a laugh. Rachel wanted another sister. Three weeks after the end of the war in Europe I realized that another baby had begun. Because I had taken no 'steps' I expected it to be a girl.

This intimation of a new life in the offing was followed in a fortnight by the end of an old one. My father died suddenly in the middle of the election campaign. Quintin Hogg made a special point of condoling with us.

I was indeed sad, far sadder than I could ever have imagined I would be, twenty years earlier. He was seventy-six and old age and failing health had brought increased geniality instead of crustiness. Three years before his death I realized that he was making real efforts to win my affection, a thing he had not thought of doing while I was young. On my thirty-sixth birthday, for instance, he told me of a compliment paid to me in infancy that he had never mentioned before. My nurse was wheeling me in my pram along Harley Street when a woman stopped her and said, 'That's a first-class breed of infant!' (On second thoughts, I fear that he may have taken the compliment to himself.) I had also come to admire his versatility. Not so much his books and poems (his discovery that poems no longer needed rhymes gave him rather too much encouragement) as his practical ingenuity. The wartime slogan, 'Make Do and Mend', might have been invented for him. He mended a marble statue in his garden, broken into ten pieces by frost. 'I used as cement', he wrote to me, 'the thick remnant of a tin of enamel paint. That I found dried as hard as iron.' When one of my mother's wartime chickens sickened and had to be killed, he whipped out his dissecting knife and did an autopsy, discovering patches of tubercle on lungs and liver.

Two years before my father's death Frank also had experienced the change in him. He wrote to me from London:

I had breakfast this morning with – guess who – your father! He was *charming* – a different man I can't help saying from the ogre (?) of Crockham Hill. I saw at once how popular a man he is likely to be when he is laying himself out to be pleasant.

He was sweet about you and thought Thomas 'very thoughtful' and was very confident about his neck and health. He is now 'my favourite man'.

This letter prepared me for certain things in my father's obituary notice which otherwise I could hardly have believed. 'He will long be remembered as a public-spirited man of great versatility and charm, a cheerful philosopher and the best of friends.' I could well understand the reference to his 'eminent service in promoting the care of the eyesight of the population' to whom 'the nation owes a debt of gratitude' – but *cheerful* and *charming* . . . !

A few months before his death he had talked despondently to me about his health. 'If it were not for leaving Mother, I would not want to live on.' She told me afterwards that on his last day their doctor had pressed her to send him into hospital. 'Saline injections are his only chance.' She bitterly regretted her compliance. As the ambulance men carried him away, he looked back with an expression of infinite sorrow at her and his home as if to say – he could no longer speak – 'I shall never see you again.' He died that evening. The story made a profound impression on me. I decided that if ever I were in charge of a dying person I would do my utmost to let them die at home. At the same time I made Frank promise to do his best to outlast me. The Hospice movement was still in the future.

My father's death had two unexpected results. He left a great deal more money than any of us had thought likely. It was very nice. But why had he stinted us so obsessively in our childhood, when a somewhat gayer life-style would have been appreciated even more than his legacies could be now? I made another silent vow: to try to overcome some of my inherited Puritanism when dealing with my own family. I was to be almost as old as Father before I managed to make any considerable dent in that austere emotional legacy.

The second result of his death was to make me suddenly aware that nothing now stood between me and the Catholic Church. Frank's reception into the Church had drawn an unusually critical letter from my gentle mother, echoing the view about priests and the disadvantages to our children which I myself had held. Imagining that my father must disapprove even more than she did, I decided not even to think about following Frank into the Church while Father was alive. In this I was probably wrong.

I had not at that date read the revealing letters on religion which passed between my parents during their courtship. From these it emerges that organized religion meant far more to him than it did to my mother, who in this was a thorough Chamberlain. I have never known him happier than when he was invited to be a representative of the Nonconformists at the

Coronation of King George VI and Queen Elizabeth. He processed up the Abbey, enthralled by the beauty of the ritual, affected only with pleasure at the presence of other denominations, Roman Catholics among them. Afterwards he bought the two blue velvet chairs on which he and my mother had sat in splendour.

It occurred to me later that I would have done better to fight my way straight into the Catholic Church while my father was still alive, instead of spending a year, however happily, in my halfway house. I might then have engaged in philosophic discussion with him that in turn could have rubbed off on my mother. As it was, she sadly admitted to me after his death that she did not 'at present have any sustaining belief in personal survival'. Perhaps 'blissful' reunion with the spirit of the Creator – that was the most she could hope for. I felt I had somehow failed her, just as I had failed Roger, through not trying to resolve my own various states of half-belief earlier.

However, I made some amends to my family on the earthly plane by introducing my bachelor brother John, now out of khaki and thirty-eight years old, to a romantic auburn-haired young lawyer we had met politically in Oxford, named Anna Spicer. The scene was the Victory Ball held at the Town Hall. David and Rachel Cecil joined our party, their amusing presence helping to conceal my serious designs. Anna duly conquered John and they married with the happiest results: among them my acquisition of four nieces, all destined to be successful lawyers and the third to sit on Labour's front opposition bench as Harriet Harman MP.

The Victory Ball was followed by the first post-war Christmas. Paddy, at eight, decided to celebrate with his first – and last – poem. 'When Christmas comes we all rejoyce / Hurrah! Hurrah! Hurrah!!! / O there are lots of things for choice / After War! War! War!!!.' It was intended to be sung, tunelessly, but very loud.

Soon after my father's death there was a note in my diary that I would attend Blackfriars church in St Giles on a Sunday in September. A white-robed Dominican was celebrating, the acclaimed scholar and friend of all Catholic intellectuals in Oxford, the Revd Gervase Mathew. He was a cousin of the Robert Mathew whom I had met long ago in Grenoble. Gervase was as unusual, not to say eccentric, as many holy men turn out to be. He lectured at Balliol on Byzantine art and was also an authority on medieval English poetry and history. He belonged when I first knew him to another Oxford 'set', mainly of High Anglicans who inhabited a distinctive literary-cum-religious world of their own: C. S. Lewis, the author of literary parables for adults and children; Charles Williams, a mystical novelist; and J. R. R. Tolkien, who was not quite yet

'Lord' of the Rings but making his way there. Gervase was at his best lecturing to large groups, such as Catholic societies in London or Hellenic travellers gathered around the Tholos at Delphi. Then his oratory, which was intrinsically no great shakes, could rely for effect on the enormous variety and accuracy of his knowledge; all poured out with an intensity and suppressed excitement that was gradually communicated to his audience. In private instruction he was deeply thoughtful and subject to long pauses. These would terminate in a breathless rush of words, broken now and then by what Penelope Betjeman called his 'holy whistle'.

The year 1946 opened with me receiving instruction from Gervase two or three times a week. At the end of January Frank expressed his pleasure tactfully in a letter written from London, where he was again working: 'I mustn't disclose to you just *how* interested I am in your talks with Gervase.' Frank had always deliberately refrained from pushing or even nudging me toward the Church, though often urged by his Catholic friends to do so. Indeed he fell into disgrace with some of them for allowing me and the children to carry on so long outside the pale. But he knew me better than to bring pressure. Had he begun to argue, I should have replied in kind and probably progressed backward. For argument feeds on itself, maintaining and enhancing its own partisanship.

As it happened, it was Frank's isolated position in the family that finally drove me to the feet of Father Gervase Mathew. Frank, Paddy, Judith, Rachel and I, the girls gay in their home-made red velvet coats and fur-trimmed bonnets, would set off together on Sunday mornings. In Banbury Road we would separate, Frank alone turning to the right for St Aloysius, all the rest of us turning left for St Paul's. Moved by compassion Paddy would occasionally turn right with his father. I could not help seeing that this was not the way to conduct family life.

When I finally decided 'to convert' – to use the pleasant Victorian form of words – Frank explained my situation to the Anglican Bishop of Oxford who had confirmed me, and thanked him for all he had done for us both. With great humanity the Bishop wrote to me: 'I am certain that you are doing the only wise and right thing. . . . Whilst a family that has no religion is the worst thing of all, a family of divided allegiances is in itself unnatural. . . . So I rejoice that you are both to walk along the same path (with, I hope, the children too) even though it's not the same as mine.'

My discussions with Gervase were going along swimmingly in their unconventional way. Doctrine was taken as read. I had gone through it with Father Favell, having studied fairly systematically in the two years before that. 'Father Favell', said Gervase, 'is not a "Priest" in the medieval Latin sense of the word but in every other sense.' We had a little trouble over the purposes of marriage and contraception, but here there was some give and take. Gervase admitted that his own parents became somewhat estranged after they slept in separate rooms to avoid the conception of another child; I admitted that the 'safe period' had worked perfectly with me, ever since my miscarriage in 1944.

Another source of trouble was the Roman priesthood and, of course, the 'Black Popes', whom all potential converts feel bound to trot out. Gervase saw the priesthood as a system of pipes, some lead, some copper, some silver, along which the priestly power flows. The value or otherwise of the pipes makes no difference to the purity of the water.

I found all Gervase's images vivid and relevant. The Catholic faith, he told me, had been regarded by Catholics in two different ways, one right and one wrong. The wrong way (that of 'poor girls brought up in convents') is to think of it as a small white room in which you come and switch on the light, whereupon everything is immediately dazzlingly clear. The right way is to think of Catholicism as a huge dim room lit only by firelight. (Here I think Gervase's and my upbringing on Plato's *Republic*, with its famous image of the firelit cave, helped both of us.) As the firelight flickers certain things in the room become visible and then fade away again, brightening the next moment. But there are many, many things in the recesses and corners of the room which we never see at all. Catholic faith is still a 'Mystery' even after reception into the Church.

Transubstantiation, or the changing of the bread and wine into the body and blood of Christ – the doctrine which above all my father had ridiculed to us children – no longer seemed a stumbling-block. I knew that if the consecrated bread and wine were analysed they would still be materially bread and wine. Yet they would *really* have changed. In the same way I believed that the sacrament of marriage made Frank and me *really* one, though we would not need analysis to show that we remained two people. I remembered a letter Frank had written to me the year before, while staying with an old friend. 'Marriage is a full-time job,' our friend had said. 'You have to work at it.' 'I didn't see it that way,' wrote Frank. 'I see it as you being with me and I with you for ever and ever.' Later: 'I do understand that verse in St John a little better now, about "I in you, and you in me." I never did before.'

Though Gervase and I never talked politics, I knew that his views were left wing enough to save me from any trouble with the Spanish Civil War.

He did not use expressions like 'Our Lord' or 'Our Lady', both of which turned my Unitarian stomach, but always spoke of 'Christ' and 'Mary'. I had some difficulties at first with the Virgin, especially when my friend Anne Martelli, a born Catholic, advised me to try praying to her for special favours. 'It seems easier and less presumptuous', she said, 'to approach her rather than the Almighty direct.' I simply could not understand such personalization, which sounded to me like going to the private secretary instead of the minister.

Strangely enough, it was the dogma of the Assumption of Our Lady, declared soon after my conversion, that helped me as much as it hindered some others. I liked the idea of the Virgin's *bodily* assumption into Heaven, which seemed to glorify the body instead of debasing it, as the Manichaeans and Jansenists had done. I also welcomed the compliment to womanhood.

Catherine Rose Pakenham was born on the last day of February 1946, in a flurry of snow. I chose her name because of Cathy in *Wuthering Heights*. Though the name was not spelt the same way as my mother's and sister's, they were both pleased, Kitty writing that two such romantic names made her wish for another daughter herself. (She had another son, with the romantic name of Alastair.) The first of our children to be born a Catholic, Catherine was baptized in St Aloysius church. Evelyn Waugh, her male godparent, presented her with a golden knife, fork and spoon and me with a memorable letter. For in the same church, a few weeks later, I myself was received, or, to use again the language of Cardinal Newman's day, I made my submission to Rome.

I was confirmed at the London Oratory not long afterwards by Archbishop David Mathew, the brother of Gervase. I had brought along no sponsor, not realizing that such a thing was required. What to do? David gazed expectantly into the dim cavities of the vast edifice. Would the Lord produce for us what we needed in one of these thickets, as he had for Abraham? In a distant chapel David spied a kneeling figure. He beckoned her over. It was Rosalind Toynbee, mother of our great friend Philip but a representative of a brand of rigid Catholicism to which I had always been particularly allergic. My 'submission' was complete.

Though Evelyn's letter has already been printed in the first volume of Frank's autobiography, *Born to Believe* (1953), it must have a place here, if only for the effect on me of its prose.

Dearest Elizabeth . . .

Please let me join the Saints and Angels in their chorus of welcome. . . . I do not think anyone outside the Church can ever understand the meaning of the Household of the Faith – the supernatural unity in love that exists behind the superficial wrangles. You are certain to find disappointments as you get to know Catholics as one of themselves – the curious contradictions and frustrations in the flow of grace, and disagreements in matters which up to now you have thought essentials. But the love within the community is enormously strong and unemotional. It is a fragment of that love that I send you today.

Evelyn

After reading his message of love, I realized that Evelyn was speaking of agape rather than eros, a distinction that Father D'Arcy had drawn between spiritual and sexual love in his book, *The Mind and Heart of Love*. All the same, I felt that something had changed in our personal relationship. 'How's the hockey?', for instance, and other insulting remarks from Evelyn, I never had to cope with again. Three months after Catherine's birth he was writing to Maurice Bowra, 'I looked up effete. It means primarily "having given birth". . . . Lady Pakenham is the archetype of effeteness rather than E. Sackville-West, it seems.' In the following year he wrote to Nancy Mitford: 'Lady Pakenham is my great new friend.' I had at last been received, and not only into the Church.

At the same time a new symmetry had been woven into the pattern of my marriage. It was ten years since Frank's political conversion had carried him into my camp. Now my religious conversion had carried me into his. The old suffragette jibe – 'Husband and wife are one, and that one is the husband' – had never applied in our family, inequality in marriage being unthinkable to Frank. But now equality seemed part of the visible pattern.

The appearance of balance or 'tit-for-tat' in conversions satisfied and even amused some of our friends, who might not have been able to explain either conversion on its own. I myself knew that the symmetry had always been there, as it must be in every true marriage. But that aspect had been like a treasured carpet hanging on the wall. Now it had been taken down, for us to walk on and use every day of our lives.

16

A Post-War Family
· 1945–8 ·

The post-war medicine which all of us were asked to drink was 'the mixture as before' – the mixture offered after all 'righteous' wars: a combination of exhilaration, idealism and sense of liberation watered down by nervous exhaustion, continued hardship at home and unexpected troubles abroad.

Frank had conveyed to me the ambivalent political atmosphere of London. As he was not at first in the Government, he shared only a fraction of the euphoria that inspired Labour Cabinet Ministers like Hartley Shawcross – 'We are the masters' – or Hugh Dalton – 'We shall be in power for the next twenty years.' Frank's first post-war job was personal assistant to Arthur Greenwood, the Lord Privy Seal. This seemed less creative than being personal assistant to William Beveridge. But at least Arthur had wit and a good memory and would supply Frank with anecdotes and dialogues that Frank passed on to me, languishing in Oxford. There was the dialogue between Arthur Greenwood and Jimmy Thomas, both Labour leaders up to the crisis election of 1931, when Jimmy remained a prosperous Cabinet Minister in the National Government, but Arthur lost his seat.

Jimmy: It's a ——, Arthur.
Arthur: It is that, Jimmy.
Jimmy: Some of our fellows must be pretty hard up.
Arthur: They are that, Jimmy.
Jimmy (opening his note-case): Here's £5, Arthur. See what you can do with it.
Arthur (sorrowfully shaking his head at this offer of tainted gold, Jimmy being regarded as a traitor to the Labour movement for joining *them*): I don't want to hurt your feelings, but I'm afraid they wouldn't touch it.
Jimmy (very much hurt): It's a ——, Arthur.
Arthur: It is that, Jimmy.

It was Hugh Dalton who had got Frank his temporary post with Arthur

Greenwood. One day Frank told Arthur that Dalton had got a parliamentary private secretary called Durbin, 'a great friend of mine'. 'Oh yes,' said Arthur, 'I know him well. Such a nice chap. Awful pity that his health is so bad. His heart you know. . . .' Frank said that perhaps Arthur was thinking of Hugh Gaitskell. 'Oh, I know him too,' he said. 'He's another nice chap. *His* heart's bad also. Funny thing,' added Arthur with a good-natured chuckle, '*all* the Dalton boys have got bad hearts.'

Frank strongly denied that Arthur was 'an old drunk', as Ellen Wilkinson MP had said, though he did seem to speak 'through a haze of distant benevolence'. Nevertheless, no drink appeared in his office; and as one who was inducted early into the ways of toping statesmen, Frank regarded that as the crucial test.

I was thrilled to hear that Frank had made a speech in Greenwood's constituency, Wakefield, that went over 'BIG big big'. His letter ended with his usual favourite mixture of fervour and farce. 'But if I try to say more than that I love you more than I could ever have believed that I or anyone could ever have loved anyone I shall miss the post (I had begun quite a good Spoonerism – Piss the most!).'

Touches of post-war anti-climax had entered even into Parliament. In March Frank was dining with Aidan Crawley MP, home from his prison camp and married to Virginia Cowles. Esmond Rothermere, owner of the *Daily Mail* and London *Evening News*, was also present.

Esmond says that the *one* topic of conversation among Conservative politicians is Winston's abdication or the reverse. They are desperately keen for him to go, but all absolutely *terrified* of him physically and longing for someone like Esmond to suggest his withdrawal. Apparently he rang up from America to say 'I'm feeling fine, I'm feeling immensely invigorated and rejuvenated. I feel ten years younger.' As they all hoped he was feeling ten years older, their hearts went down into their boots.

If the defeated Tories had their troubles, so did many others. In September 1945 I had taken the children to Bude, Cornwall, for their seaside holiday. 'Living in London is very depressing just now,' Frank wrote to me, 'with no firm base to return to and in any case most people in London are rather "low".' His own lack of a 'firm base' in London had led him one night to share a bed with Auberon Herbert at the Cavendish Hotel. Auberon, Evelyn Waugh's brother-in-law, had just served for two and a half years as a private in the Polish Army. He came in at 1 a.m. in a 'low state' and insisted on sharing a bottle of champagne with Frank and then writing and posting a long letter to Ernest Bevin, Labour Foreign Secretary, before going to sleep. His letter asked for an interview, stressing the pain felt by a Dulverton man (Auberon) that a Somerset lad from the next village (Bevin) should have got on so well in life.

As for the other elements who were feeling 'low' in post-war London, it appeared that many of them were located in Hampstead. Frank was informed that the 'Hampstead Colony' missed the war very much, especially former dons who had worked in Information or Intelligence. One brilliant Oxford historian now suffered from neuroses that passed all previous records. He could not even be asked whether he meant to return to his college for the autumn term, but insisted on filing the *Evening Standard* and reading aloud from 1940 back numbers at breakfast, in order to 'restore a sense of reality'.

It was to this Hampstead 'colony' or 'set' that, a year later, I considered moving.

I was beginning to feel restive. Perhaps the simple reason why I wanted to leave Oxford was that I had lived there on and off since I was fourteen: school, university, family home. It was time for a change. But in formulating my wish to move, I assembled a number of other more cogent reasons with which to interest Frank.

On the material level, the house was getting too small for the five adults and seven children now living in it, especially the older children and me. I had no room of my own. 'The vital reform seems to me', wrote Frank in answer to my complaint that I was bearing an unfair share of the family burden, 'that *you* should have a room (the drawing-room presumably) which the children should not be allowed to enter without special permission. I don't in the least mind surrendering the dining-room [which he used at weekends] to them as long as I don't have to get their permission to enter it!'

Beyond the house, however, the life of Oxford itself somehow seemed inadequate. Many of my closest friends – the Hopes, Gordon Walkers, Fawcetts, Durbins, Zuckermans – had left or were leaving to return to peacetime activities. Even during the war, moreover, I had felt a subdued resentment at the University's essentially male aura. There were as yet, and for years, no mixed colleges for students, no women members of the Union, no women appointed to teaching posts and so with dining rights at the vast majority of Oxford colleges. It was the thought of those masculine dining-tables – High Tables – that had irritated me during the war: tables supplied from excellent cellars and kitchens filled with *eatable* eatables, while we wives made do with what our Mrs Pope called 'bits and pieces'. She was the mistress of the bit and piece, which usually amounted to a hot-pot of root vegetables.

Over against Oxford, in my imagination, stood political London where

Labour was governing and women were at least sitting around the table at 10 Downing Street; perhaps not in large numbers – one in fact, Ellen Wilkinson – but that surely was only a beginning.

In post-war Oxford I really had not enough to do, apart from the children's homework. The Dragon School was still an intellectual stimulus. I was asked to give away the school prizes in 1946 and tried to tell the old Greek conundrum of Achilles and the tortoise but I was rusty and got it wrong. Paddy, to whom I presented a form prize, did not mind my making a verbal hash. What he did mind, desperately, was my standing on the platform in a brand new hat (the war was over, after all) decorated with bobbing cherries. 'Mummy, I didn't know where to look.' I had never been ashamed of my parents, but here I was, making my son ashamed of me.

Now that Frank was a peer, Lord Pakenham, his parliamentary candidature had, of course, lapsed. No one had been selected in his place at Oxford for whom I could work, and I myself no longer had a constituency of my own. My only new, semi-political activity was to sit on the local Rent Tribunal, a country-wide Labour invention for protecting the tenant against the greedy landlord, and very occasionally vice versa. I would also give the occasional lecture on heartfelt problems like 'Women's place in the New Britain'.

I loved reading Frank's accounts of his social life in London, particularly among the politicians, civil servants and journalists – but how I longed to be there too. An evening at the Gargoyle night-club, for instance, when Frank, Philip Toynbee, Aidan Crawley and Dick Crossman had, surprisingly, discussed theology. Dick admitted that Catholic theology was the only possible system and that he had always respected and been interested in theology since writing his own book, *Plato Today*. But he cried despairingly that he could attach no meaning to statements about a personal God and (what was equally hopeless) an infinite number of meanings to the statement that Christ '*rose* from the dead'. There was comic relief, wrote Frank, when Dick, hard pressed by Philip, announced that he also had great respect for the Soviet system.

Philip: What do you respect?
Dick (seriously): Their propaganda.
Philip: Don't you respect the Nazi propaganda just as much?
Dick: Yes, I respect the Germans and Russians for the same things.

Personally I was becoming more than happy with the Catholic system. But discussing theology in an Oxford presbytery seemed less exciting than in a London night-club.

Judith's christening at Oxford, 1940. Back row: left to right, Dominic Harrod, Billa Harrod, Frank, Christine Hope, Penelope Betjeman, Judith with me, Roger Harman, Maurice Bowra, Frank's cousin Margaret Vane; front row: Thomas, Donald Hope, Antonia, Robin Hope, Francis Hope, Paddy.

Michael, Judith and I canvassing for Frank, the Labour candidate at Oxford, 1945

Frank as Minister for the British Zone of Germany, 1947, his forehead still scarred by his jump

James Callaghan and I at the Labour Party Conference, 1947

Frank plays *L'Attaque* with Michael, Paddy, Rachel and Judith, while I umpire, 1947

At Bodiam Castle, near Bernhurst, 1952. Back row: Klothilde Hammelrath (sister of our *au pair*), Catherine, Michael; front row: Kevin, Archbishop David Mathew, Father Gervase Mathew.

Labour candidate for Oxford at the general election, 1950, canvassing in my red mac.

My Party workers, general election, 1950: left to right, Mrs Pope, Antonia, Judith, Kevin, Catherine, Michael, Rachel, my agent, behind him May Munday (nanny)

At Hastings, 1952: left to right, Kevin, Charlotte Fawcett, Michael, Uncle Eddie (Lord Dunsany), Sarah Fawcett, Catherine

Hellenic cruise, 1955, in front of S.Sophia: left to right, Juliet Smith, Nicky Berry, Sheila Birkenhead, Pamela Berry (later Lady Hartwell), Adrian Berry, our guide, Paddy

Left: After the Garden Party
at Buckingham Palace, with
T. S. Eliot, Mrs Valerie Eliot
and Anne-Pauline Hall, 1957
Below: Rachel, Catherine and
I on the way to Judith's
wedding, 1962

I watch Wellington and his staff through field-glasses at the battle of Vittoria: an imaginary scene painted on a tray by Mary Clive, 1965

Exploring the battlefield of Salamanca, October 1965, with Valerian Douro (later 8th Duke of Wellington), Nicko Henderson and Diana Douro

Catherine's fancy-dress party at Strawberry Hill for her twenty-first birthday, 1967. With her are Frank and I as Prince Albert and Queen Victoria.

At the Foyles literary luncheon for 'The Pakenhams: A Family of Authors', June 1969

Golden Wedding, 1981. Back row: left to right, Robert, Flora, Arthur, Mary, Rebecca, Benjamin, Damian, Richard, Natasha, Lindsay, Maria, Miranda, Orlando; 3rd row: Michael, Ruth, Kevin Pakenham, Valerie, Frank, Harold, Kevin Billington, Alec; 2nd row: Eliza, Mimi with Alex, Paddy, Thomas, me, Antonia, Rachel with Caspar, Nathaniel, Judith, Guy; front row: Harry, Fred, Rose, Tom, Chloe, Kate, Ned. Caspar and Alex have just been separated after a skirmish.

Left: Frank and I at Bernhurst in the year of our Golden Wedding, 1981

Below: Party for Frank's eightieth birthday, 5 December 1985. Standing: left to right, Irving, Judith, Paddy, Anita, Kevin Billington, Harold, Clare, Valerie, Thomas, Michael; sitting: Mimi, Rachel, Frank and I, Antonia, Kevin Pakenham.

I had at last discovered in myself a feeling of warmth towards the Church. Even after my conversion I had still thought of the Church as 'them' rather than 'us'. I believed, but I did not love. The change was coming. When I read Evelyn Waugh's *Edmund Campion*, his biography of the Jesuit martyr, my feelings were deeply stirred. For the first time I knew positively that I had changed sides since *Westward Ho!*. I was on the side of Campion, not his enemies. (Of course, cruelty and persecution were the real enemies of the human race, whether practised by the Tudors or the Inquisition; but this was not the point I was arguing with myself.)

Two new Catholic friends of mine, Douglas and Mia Woodruff, further linked my historical sympathies to Catholicism by telling me that they had saved from demolition the house in which Campion had been captured and carried to his execution. The remarkable Woodruffs were later to live nearby at Marcham Priory; he a writer and editor of *The Tablet*, she a social worker of genius. Douglas was the first person to explain my interest in theology, an interest that continued to puzzle me a good deal. 'Theology used to be called the Queen of the Sciences,' he said.

In practical terms, I had a tragic but triumphant experience of what Catholic theology could mean very soon after my reception. A master at the Dragon School, Ted Mack, had become a close friend of the family. He had made Rachel a solid wooden dolls' pram when factory-made prams were hard to come by; he had organized a bicycling and bird-watching holiday in Breconshire for Antonia, Thomas and me in spring 1945, when we had sighted fifty-eight different species of bird, from the dipper to the red kite. (I was amazed to find, thirty years later, that the omnipresent scavenger of India was the same bird that in Wales had become a rare and threatened species.)

In spring 1946 Ted was dying of cancer. Frank and I visited him at his sister's home. I talked a bit about the Happy Valley in Wales, which led us on to the other valley he was now entering. I did not feel shy as I had with my brother Roger. When I told the children at lunch that their friend Ted had died in his sleep, Paddy and Judith immediately began putting puzzled questions – 'How?' 'Why?' Rachel intervened to say in her calm voice: 'He died because he was very ill. And when he was having his rest [she meant the afternoon nap of young children] he just died.' My own thoughts were again of Roger, and of how much more my newly acquired religion had enabled me to do for my friend Ted than I had been able to do for my brother.

The day after Ted's death my brother John and Anna Spicer were married. The processions of death and life, marching so close together and yet so unutterably separated, at last made sense to me. In my youth I had accepted Tennyson's ironical celebration of these things, believing that fatalism and hedonism were the best that human beings could do about them:

> Fill the cup and fill the can:
> Have a rouse before the morn:
> Every moment dies a man,
> Every moment one is born.

Now I felt able to celebrate both processions with wreaths of golden marigolds, as in India. And next day, 11 May, was Rachel's fourth birthday.

A third procession was formed by our children going to the altar for 'conditional' baptism, and confirmation as Catholics if they were old enough. Antonia was fervent. Of her own accord she decided to move from the Godolphin School to a Catholic convent, St Mary's at Ascot, where she was received in November 1946. She wrote to me from school next year:

I think that the longer one has attended the Mass, the more one loves it and the more it grows upon one.

She was referring to the Latin Mass.

. . . I often wonder [she continued] why there was ever a Reformation, because I can't see why people should ever have wanted to break away from the Church. I feel like rushing out into the streets and just telling all the crowd what utter fools they are not to be Catholics. If only Granny [my mother] would let you have a good long talk to her, surely you would convert her in a minute, because she must *want* to do the right thing.

A touching, enthusiastic begging of the question, 'What *is* the right thing?' But we were not mad enough to raise doubts again, at this moment, in Antonia's fourteen-year-old mind.

Judith, Rachel and Michael were received in St Edward the Confessor's church, Golders Green, for the long-meditated move to London had at length taken place.

The final push had come at the end of several shifts in Frank's political fortunes.

After serving Arthur Greenwood he had been appointed a political lord-in-waiting; not the kindly animal whose duty it was to look after Their Majesties at Buckingham Palace, but the fierce creature who was expected to lay about him on each and every issue in the House of Lords. Our friend Lord Gage was to tell us something about the first type of lord-in-waiting, a post which he himself had held. His duty at the end of each day was to escort King George and Queen Elizabeth into their lift and watch them glide upwards to the bedroom floor above. As they finally disappeared, George Gage and his companion lord-in-waiting would turn to each other and burst into peals of laughter. 'It was not disrespect or anything like that,' he explained. 'Just that the sight of two pairs of shoes slowly ascending into heaven seemed irresistibly comic.'

Of course, the mainly political nature of Frank's duties did not mean that we saw nothing of court life. We were invited to the first state banquet given at the Palace after the war, in honour of the long-suffering Queen Juliana of the Netherlands. Neither Frank nor I behaved ourselves as impeccably as we learnt to do with experience. Frank lost his head when about to bow to His Majesty and genuflected instead. I had not been able to find a single pair of long white gloves in the Oxford shops, and anyway had used up my last clothing coupons on a new dress. I arrived gloveless, to the obvious displeasure of old Queen Mary, who was among the royal guests. 'You live in *Oxford*, I believe?' she said to me, intimating that Oxford was a place where one did without not only gloves but most other social amenities, including good manners. Then she signalled urgently to her lady-in-waiting to take me away and bring up someone else, preferably someone wearing very very long white kid gloves. I consoled myself with the memory of Frances Cornford's poem in the *Weekend Book*, 'To a Fat Lady Seen from the Train':

> O fat white woman whom nobody loves,
> Why do you walk through the fields in gloves . . .
> Missing so much and so much?

Not that the Palace was exactly a field, though we saw one unexpectedly rural sight at our first post-war Buckingham Palace garden party. Down by the lake – or rather, *in* the lake – stood a male figure perfectly dressed as to the upper half but wearing waders on his feet. He was equipped with field-glasses, and his top hat, containing a notebook, lay on the bank. It was Peter Fleming, the explorer and author of *Brazilian Adventure*, checking up on the surviving varieties of rare royal duck. I found it delightful that he should be thus employed, despite the rival attractions of a pavilion full of iced coffee and cakes, and two bands dealing smartly with Gilbert and Sullivan operas.

As a political lord-in-waiting, Frank's job was to speak for the Government whenever required. Since he had no specific department it was a valuable way of learning about the whole business of government. He also learnt how to speak. Lord Jowitt, the Chancellor, told him always to present a Bill by pointing out its weaknesses himself, thus pre-empting the Opposition. He once introduced the legislation for nationalizing steel with the words: 'My Lords, I hate this Bill.' Frank's leader, Lord Addison, gave him two good rules for their lordships' House: 'Don't go over twenty minutes. Sit down as soon as you've got the House with you.' To make him sit down Addison used to kick him on the back of the calf. An ex-premier of Canada, Viscount Bennett, also weighed in with some advice on gestures: 'Your speaking is improving fast, but you wave your arms about a lot and as they are long arms it looks rather funny.' Frank could not help pointing out in return, 'with enormous deference', that his helpful critic 'always spoke the entire time with his hands folded over his paunch'. I myself had apparently made an invaluable comment on Frank's style after attending a lecture on currency that he had given as long ago as our Stoke days: 'You were utterly and absolutely out of touch with your audience. They didn't understand a word you were saying.'

By dint of continuous speaking, Frank was soon to become an effective debater, witty, lucid and responsive to the feelings of the House. In the spring of 1946 Clement Attlee promoted his forty-year-old political lord-in-waiting, first to the post of Under-Secretary for War and then to be Chancellor of the Duchy of Lancaster and Minister in charge of Germany.

I realized immediately in the midst of my rejoicing that with Frank shuttling between London and Germany he would have even less time than at present to spend in Chadlington Road. Moreover, our already inadequate house in Chadlington Road was about to shrink yet again. A new member of the family was on the way.

Driven by the appalling winter of 1947, I had decided that one luxurious night of warmth in London would be very nice. I chose the Dorchester Hotel in Park Lane. Labour had lost some sympathy, not only because of the weather, but because of the Ministry of Fuel and Power's attitude towards it. Emanuel Shinwell, the minister, brusquely dismissed the weather as 'an imponderable', while his under-secretary, our friend Hugh Gaitskell, advised the country to keep within their fuel ration by cutting down on washing. ('I never find a lot of baths necessary.') Our children had made an igloo of snow on the front lawn in January which was to stand until March. A centrally heated hotel, if only for one night, and the start of a new baby – a boy this time, making it four of each – seemed good ideas for dispersing gloom.

Breakfast at the Dorchester proved a fiasco. I telephoned for it in our room. Two tall waiters appeared pushing between them a large trolley draped with a white embroidered tablecloth on which lay a lordly dish. My mouth watered. Bacon and eggs at least, and perhaps kidneys and sausages also, heaped together in succulent profusion beneath the silver dome. A pre-war breakfast, in fact. The foremost waiter lifted the great lid with a flourish. Underneath sat two miserable mushrooms each on a tiny round of toast about the size of a pre-decimal penny.

At any rate the other object of the exercise had not failed. By the end of March, with the freeze and thaw both over, Dr Helena Wright was able to confirm that Kevin was on the way. After so much experience in deciding which sex to have, I felt no doubt that the new baby would be Kevin.

When it came to the actual uprooting, I found it more difficult to leave Oxford than I had expected. Indeed I thought for a time that I had found a compromise solution, at least to the problem of space. I went to see Cumnor Manor, a splendid Regency house a few miles outside Oxford. Another substantial building went with it which the agent said could be let to students. On his advice we offered £9,500.

Cumnor Manor stood on the site of the Elizabethan house where Lord Leicester's lover, Amy Robsart, had fallen down stairs and broken her neck. When I first looked at the polished Regency staircase now installed, I felt that I might well do the same thing. But Antonia thrilled to the thought of living in a Walter Scott novel. When our bid was accepted we were all enchanted – until we were gazumped by a director of the Pressed Steel works with an offer of £12,000.

Fate seemed to point to London. I found a neo-Georgian, Lutyens-type house with an annexe, large garden and tennis-court, for £14,000 in the Hampstead Garden Suburb. We moved in on 25 July 1947.

It was all so pretty. The view of Hampstead Heath from our garden, with distant cricketers deployed on a small square of green, looked like a hand-painted Victorian print. We had a square lawn and a concealed garden gate opening on to a short cut to Golders Green. Several of the windows were shaped like portholes, which John Betjeman told us was characteristic of the Lutyens-type architect who had designed our new home. When London was wrapped in a thick yellowy-brown fog like an overripe banana skin, the sun shone clear and golden on the Garden Suburb. On the day of our arrival Paddy happily got lost on the tube which he discovered he could explore from end to end and around and around for the price of one short journey.

Yet somehow no one really liked 10 Linnell Drive. Perhaps it was the twenty-minute walk to Golders Green tube station, anathema to our older children. Or it may have been the long journey to South Kensington, where most of Antonia's friends lived and where she was to attend the French Lycée for a term.

Meanwhile, I found my fellow-suburbans a great deal more agreeable than their habitat.

The Catholic church of St Edward the Confessor attracted the large number of Catholic families from the Suburb, among them the Kents. When I had to find a partner for Antonia at a Catholic dance, I wrote to her at school: 'I will see if Mrs Kent will lend us Bruce for the evening.' Years later Bruce Kent, by now a priest and secretary of the Campaign for Nuclear Disarmament, was reminded by Frank of this suburban episode. He wrote back: 'If Mrs Kent had lent you Bruce for Antonia, I might have been calling you Father today instead of you calling me Father.'

Evelyn Waugh was invited to address the Catholic community of St Edward's and stayed with us for the occasion. Surprised that a writer of such eminence should spend his time with a relatively obscure gathering, I questioned him on his lecture programme. 'It's my Lenten penance,' he replied. 'I have made a resolution to accept every invitation I receive for the next forty days.' I knew that the lecture would be a hair shirt for the good people of Golders Green as well as for Evelyn, having heard him address the more famous Newman Society in Oxford. His theme was 'The Church's Return to the Catacombs'. Such was the horror of the modern pagan world, he urged, that all good Catholics should cut themselves off from it indefinitely. 'For how long? Twenty years?' asked an astonished questioner. 'A hundred years if necessary,' replied the implacable Evelyn. To several questioners he answered with one word only. 'Surely Mr Waugh would make an exception for the Church's various apostolates?' '*No.*' 'Does Mr Waugh really mean that we should think only of saving our own souls?' '*Yes.*' And Evelyn's manner suggested that they would be lucky if they succeeded. He tempered his blasts somewhat to the shorn lambs of Golders Green, but even so he shocked most of the do-gooders present. As a member of the do-gooders brigade myself, I cross-questioned him afterwards about the application of his Catacomb philosophy to his personal life. 'I should like *all* my children to enter religious orders,' he announced firmly. 'All the girls nuns, all the boys priests.' Then he hesitated. 'I might make a partial exception for my eldest son,' he said in his formal way. (His eldest son Auberon was Frank's godson.) 'I might have the letters A. W. branded on his buttocks, so that the family name would be preserved if the Church were ever to emerge from the Catacombs.'

St Edward's was a large, light, clean-cut modern church in the Gothic style which only once struck a spark out of me. I had gone to Confession, never my favourite sacrament. Penelope Betjeman, who became a

Catholic in March 1948, used to discuss with me the difficulties of Confession. Often one almost wished one had committed some grave sin in order to liven up the proceedings. One Saturday, soon after our eighth child was born, I entered the box with a rather blank mind. Suddenly I had an idea. 'Father, what is the Church's teaching about the size of families? Do you think Catholic mothers should be prepared to have as many children as God sends them?' Our dear old parish priest must have heard this one often before. 'How many children have you got, my child?' he began cautiously. 'Eight, Father.' There was a slight pause. Then he spoke again with evident relief. 'Well then, there is nothing to worry about. I have rarely come across a family with more than sixteen.' So I was halfway there.

Our move to London was nicely timed to take place just before our August holiday, and well before the run-up to Kevin's birth. I took the four elder children by car to Waterville in Kerry, while the three younger ones had a good time with their nanny's family in Buckingham. The car broke down twice on the long journey, first the fan belt and then the left front-wheel suspension. We had to ride into Fishguard with the luggage and all four children piled up in one corner to keep the car on the road. After visiting the Cork museum while the car was being repaired, we started for the West in a thunderstorm, kissing the Blarney Stone on the way. Kerry was magical, though the fishermen of Waterville deplored the fortnight of unblinking sun. Judith learnt to swim at Derrynane in a crystal sea. It was sprinkled with islets and ruined chapels where both Antonia and I decided to be buried.

Derrynane House, the home of the nationalist leader Dan O'Connell, was now lived in for free by two maiden ladies, his distant relatives, on condition that they showed the public over the house at any time of day or night. We found out afterwards that we had taken away their fifth attempt to drink their afternoon tea.

The Skellig Rock, twelve miles out in the Atlantic towards America, gave me an indescribable sense of melancholy, followed by panic. The steep summit had been the home of hermits some twelve centuries ago, living innocently in their beehive huts until Viking pirates landed on the rock, slaughtered them all and sailed away again. In 1947 it was inhabited by nothing but goats and a lighthouse. After our picnic lunch the four children suddenly took to their heels, as if driven by the god Pan himself, and tore at breakneck speed down the narrow precipitous path towards the foaming sea far far below. Imagining them unable to stop themselves on the slippery rock-platform and plunging like lemmings into the waves, I tried at first to chase them, feebly shouting 'Stop. Stop.' But I was seven months gone and overloaded. I decided to leave the four to their fate and make sure of bringing back at least one child intact from Ireland.

An awful return journey on the ferry rounded off our perfect holiday. We had somehow been booked on a cattle-boat that stank to heaven. Judith was deeply touched when I sprinkled a whole bottle of perfume – Californian Poppy, an early birthday present from Thomas to me – all over her bunk. The mixture of bullock and poppy was appalling, but not quite as hideous as untreated bullock.

Kevin John Toussaint was born in the Garden Suburb on 1 November 1947. I was forty-one. During the birth I came to in time to hear the doctor say, 'My God, it's a face presentation!' But luckily the charming little face was not damaged. Kevin's third name marked the fact that it was All Saints' Day and was also my tribute to Toussaint L'Ouverture, the black Caribbean liberator born on 1 November c.1746 who had died a prisoner of Napoleon in France. At Kevin's christening, Simon Elwes, the painter, one of his godparents, suddenly snatched him up and ran off with him towards the end of the church. I chased after them thinking that poor Simon had gone mad and was staging a kidnap. I found them at last in a side chapel, Kevin lying in his frothy family christening robe, spread out like whipped cream on the top of the altar, being dedicated to Our Lady.

Unlike the other children, Kevin was born with a fine light thatch, two or three hairs of which grew under his chin and would later be called by him 'my bard'. I was delighted with his flowing curls, which I allowed to grow until the morning I was out with him for a walk and two children stopped us to say, 'Isn't she pretty?' I hurried him home and did a thorough Samson job on his curls. Next day I stopped two more children and asked them confidently, 'Boy or girl? Which is it?' Confidently they replied, 'A girl.'

Like Antonia, Kevin turned out to be the type of child who needs imaginary companions in early childhood. Antonia's two invented girlfriends, 'Tibby' and 'Tellow', were paralleled by Kevin's male friend, 'Donkey'. I never knew for certain whether Donkey was a man or a boy, but what I quickly realized was that he led an uncommonly enviable life. He had innumerable brothers, his parents were super people and he was a hundred years old. Whenever we passed a really magnificent house, opulent car or sumptuous shop window, Kevin would point proudly, 'Donkey lives there. That's Donkey's.'

The eldest and youngest of large families are supposed to occupy favoured positions, while it is the middle children who require support. I was puzzled at first by Antonia and Kevin alone of my children creating imaginary companions. Were they frustrated? I decided the phenomenon was probably a matter of temperament rather than status or position, though lonely only children would obviously be candidates for invented friendships. One could not generalize. An aspiring temperament might need to extrapolate its ambitions in a 'Donkey' just as much as a frustrated one.

A love of words seemed to be the chief thing that the younger children, especially the girls, had in common. Catherine, now two, established her seniority by using words and phrases that sounded adult, whatever they might mean. To her nanny: 'Don't be so sensitive.' To me: 'Why don't you clean Kevin's teeth? [He had none.] Perhaps you will when the sales begin.' Mrs Pope to Catherine: 'You shouldn't drape those ragged shawls over your new dolls' cot.' Catherine: 'It's the New Look.' She hated Punch and Judy shows (a favourite entertainment at children's parties in those unregenerate days) because Judy's face was so 'hidgybigeous'. After a visit to the zoo she said, 'When I saw the lion in his cage I trembled in my knuckles.'

Michael's speciality was inventing nonsense words like 'Waterposc' to make himself laugh. At four he could spell phonetically ('A is for APL'). At six, seeing so much literary activity going on around him, he decided to try his hand at poetry and wrote out in capitals his first poem (I was selling tickets for a Catholic ball): 'If the Pope had a rope / And hung us all / What would happen to the ball?' It was perfectly spelt and said with economy exactly what he wanted to say – as his documents written for the Foreign Office were to do thirty years later. But it did not encourage him to go further. Instead he cultivated his amazing verbal memory. I read aloud to Michael, Rachel and Judith every day, but it was Michael who always remembered the precise words of the last sentence I had read the day before. It was a great help to me in finding the place.

Rachel used words with discernment. At four: 'I like the tummy of the lettuce best.' She was a mixture of the domestic and the imaginative. Sometimes she took charge of me. 'Let me pull your coat down for you at the back, Mummy, I don't like to see you going about untidy.' She developed a great sense of the family. One weekend when Frank was away she came into my room and found me eating my breakfast alone in bed. 'Poor Mummy! You've got no Dada.' She was the only one of the girls who positively enjoyed bathing the babies and putting them to bed and consequently was imposed upon. But like Judith she immersed herself in imaginative games of 'schools', 'church', 'shops' and, of course, 'mothers and fathers'.

Judith had always been good at analogies. A lovely bunch of peonies reminded her of Rachel's cheeks and a stuck-up woman, who also stuck out behind, of a pheasant. Clouds were like smoke and the landscape, when seen from the train, full of 'jumping' trees. She showed no jealousy of Rachel except perhaps once when I told her I was going to have another baby (Michael). Judith: 'And then God will take Rachel away.' She read to Rachel at night, wrote verse plays for the children to act (one began, 'Godly wimen marry fatal men'), and introduced Rachel to the same problems of creation that had puzzled Antonia earlier:

Rachel (at four): God made that house, didn't he?
Judith: No, the builders did.
Rachel: God made them.
Judith: No, their mother did.
Judith's mother (intervening): Who made the mother?
Judith: Her mother.

I remembered what Aristotle had said about the different kinds of Causation, and suggested to Judith, who was painting a picture as she argued, 'You might as well say that the paint made your picture instead of you.' Rachel enthusiastically agreed that the paint indeed had.

Paddy had seen fit, the year before we moved from Oxford to London, to record the state of play among his siblings. He was nine years old.

Antonia is a girl rather clever when laden with responsibility. Mostly she is very nice.
Thomas is a boy keen on photography and bird-watching. On the whole he is very agreeable, a generous boy.
Judith loves her dolls and treasures them. She adores Antonia immensely because Antonia lets her play with her own very exquisite dolls.
Rachel like Judith likes her dolls very much, and often makes them dresses of wool and cotton, being skilled in the art of needlework. She is Thomas's pet and Thomas calls her his 'chubby lassie'.
Catherine a very jolly and stout young baby.
Michael is the one I like best and we are both devoted to each other. We both like playing soldiers. I usually let him win a few battles so he is not discouraged. He likes everybody and everybody likes him but he likes ME best.

Paddy was quite correct in his allocation of dolls and soldiers between the sexes. None of my girls ever played with soldiers or indeed with mechanical toys; none of my boys touched dolls or became 'skilled in the art of needlework'. Yet all kinds of toys were equally available to all of them, scattered over a chaotic nursery floor.

Antonia, as a child, had been encouraged by me to play with trains and Thomas's construction kits, since I fully believed in the feminist theory that only early training and segregation of toys gave girls their 'feminine' preferences. However, my own observation of four girls and four boys at all stages of development finally convinced me that it is not sexist but sensible to recognize girls' special interests. And, of course, there will always be a vast area of pencils and paint brushes, books and recorders, puzzles and dice games that girls and boys occupy in common.

Thomas was due in September 1946 to take his baptism of 'hell-fire' at Belvedere College, Dublin. The Advent term was traditionally the one when the Jesuit fathers put the fear of God into their new boys. Though fairly impervious to clerical imprecations and boarding with a delightful Dublin family, the McDonells, Thomas found the whole experience of being thrown into Dublin life at the age of just thirteen distinctly bizarre. Nevertheless, his term at Belvedere could claim some credit for his later commitment to Ireland.

Thomas's experiences in Ireland had a distinct effect on his parents' plans for him. We felt that to wait for a possible scholarship at Eton in 1947 would be totally unreal in the new circumstances. We were becoming a Catholic family. So we forgot Eton and sent Thomas to Ampleforth College in Yorkshire, the famous public school run by the Benedictine Order. Despite academic success, Thomas did not share Antonia's attitude towards religion, nor was he a bookworm. After being taken to St Aloysius on four Sundays running he said to me:

I always have extraordinary thoughts during the Hail Mary. After half an hour of solid prayer [before it] my mind is suddenly released. Sometimes it is extraordinary mechanical inventions. Today I thought of a series of euphemisms for masters to write on the blackboard.

He hardly opened a book during the holidays, becoming endlessly involved in making films and hot-air balloons. His first film, produced with a second-hand cine-camera, was shown in the nursery. Entitled 'Mad Dog', it won unbounded applause, the audience having been also the actors. Unfortunately when the lights went up it was found to be impossible to leave the auditorium. The winding-on machinery had silently broken down during the performance and the nursery door was blocked by a mass of writhing celluloid.

Poems would come from Antonia, typed out with her school letters. 'I have just taken Intermediate in typing,' she wrote at fourteen.

So you see I shall soon be qualified to be Dada's highly paid and confidential secretary who has the European situation at her finger tips and goes about with a mysterious smile, clothed in ropes of pearls. . . . To come down to earth, I hope I have passed.

Antonia's poems never came down to earth. Melancholy lyrics were her speciality, with titles like 'Plaintive Melody' and 'Mermaid Ditty'. But the melancholy was all romantic, as she was the first to recognize.

Judith also, though gay, spontaneous and active, expressed a vein of sadness in her poems. There was a big black cloud over her 'Poppy Field' and a hunter ready to shoot down her stag in a poem entitled 'The Fall of a King'.

If Antonia had fears, they were mainly about darkness, night and dreaming. Just before Catherine was born she sent me a message of 'good luck', a query as to whether I was still taking Anglican communion – 'it would be like having another child by your wife when you were preparing to elope with somebody else' – and enclosing a 'poemetta' dedicated to Judith, 'because it occurred to me when kissing Judith good-night that she might not wake up again'. The letter was signed 'Antonia Opheliana'.

Apart from Frank's frequent flights to Germany, we were at last seeing as much of each other as we had done before the war. Then, we had been united in frantic politicizing. Now we were enjoying some of the fruits together. When Kevin was under three weeks old we attended the wedding of Princess Elizabeth and Lieutenant Philip Mountbatten. Since Frank was a member of the Government, we had front-row seats in the central aisle. For the first time I heard that most evocative of sounds: distant cheering growing in depth and volume until it finally gathered itself into a huge, roaring wave of welcome, as the royal coach drove into Parliament Square and through the crowds around the Abbey. It would be another eight years before we read, in the official life of King George VI, about his ambivalent thoughts as he walked up the aisle with his daughter on his arm – ambivalent because he feared to lose her but longed for her to be happy. But one could have seen something of the struggle in his tense features, which the beginnings of illness were already causing to look drawn.

As for the Princess, I remembered what David Cecil had once said about royalty when I was still up at Oxford: 'Princes and princesses ought always to be young and beautiful. That is their excuse.' These two in front of us certainly passed the test.

It was quite a business getting back to Hampstead in time for Kevin's two o'clock feed. I had worse feeding trouble at a dinner given by the French Ambassador, M. Massigli, in honour of Mr and Mrs Winston Churchill.

The dinner had amused me greatly if only to hear Churchill again pronouncing French with his unblushingly English accent. He had a gift for choosing French words that sounded much the same to him in both languages, and then pronouncing them as if they were exactly the same. For instance, I remember his leaning across the table and solemnly describing Robert Schuman as 'un homme de *mark* et de *merit*'.

After dinner the ladies withdrew and the gentlemen, it seemed, would never rejoin them. I could see that Clemmie Churchill was getting as restive as I was, and so was one of the French wives. We three plotted together to break up the party by sending notes to each of our respective husbands demanding their immediate return. Clemmie gave an edge to her note by calling on Winston not to endanger the health of a nursing mother and her infant. Her message brought the hero lumbering out with a face wreathed in benevolence.

M. Massigli thought it was just one more example of the Pakenhams' eccentricity, first shown on Frank's becoming Minister for the British zone of Germany. His enthusiastic espousal of West Germany's cause had not been conducted with the constraints of conventional diplomacy. To begin with, he had jumped out of the plane on arrival without waiting for the steps to be wheeled up. As the steps were unable to wait for his jump to be completed, the two collided and Frank entered Germany with a deep gash on his forehead – perhaps a more violent version of the future Pope John Paul's kissing of a country's soil.

The incident was rightly interpreted in Germany as a symbol of Pakenham's eagerness to get started on his mission to rehabilitate the country for which he was responsible.

17

A Government Wife
· 1948–50 ·

West Germany was in an appalling state. The war had reduced it to ruins and the Allied policy of 'Dismantling' – destroying German heavy industry – prevented the country from rebuilding itself. Victor Gollancz, in spite of being a Jew or perhaps because of being a Jew, was a courageous friend of Germany. He told Frank about the case of Dr Carl Arnold, the saintly minister of North-Rhine Westphalia, who refused to accept a diet including more calories than were allotted to the ordinary German non-industrial worker. As a result he was starving himself to death.

Later on I paid one visit with Frank to Bonn, the West German capital, and could see for myself that these men, from the right-wing Adenauer to the left-wing Arnold, now in charge of prostrate Germany, were nothing to do with the Nazis and never had been. Carl Arnold, indeed, was tortured by them. I supported Frank to the hilt in his attempts to bring the iniquitous dismantling to an end. When he tried dutifully to put the policy across to intelligent German audiences, he would hear a strange sound: not shouts or boos (very much *verboten*) but the rapid shuffling of feet like thousands of angry cicadas. No action seemed to him too drastic to effect his purpose, including resignation. Indeed his great friend David Astor, now managing editor of the *Observer*, had written of Frank: 'If he is impeded he will resign.'

Many were the walks he and I took together, back and forth across Hampstead Heath Extension, discussing over and over again how to force the Foreign Office's hand – which meant Ernest Bevin's pudgy fist and, behind him, Attlee's remote but firm control. Often our discussions would end in yet another failed attempt to resign. Frank would draft an impassioned plea to Attlee to save West Germany from death by dismantling, or else . . . Attlee would send one of his terse replies, which totally ignored Frank's threats and generally ran something like this: 'My dear Frank, Thank you for writing. I have noted your points. Yours ever,

Clem.' Once Attlee gave his answer by telephone, thus offering Frank a chance to pre-empt the use of the 'retort monosyllabic' by adopting it himself. Since I was staying with my mother, Frank sent me a transcription of this dialogue. (Incidentally, I missed his letters, with their recorded dialogues – the only things I was left regretting when our wartime separations came to an end.)

Clem: Is that you, Frank?
Frank: Yes.
Clem: I've spoken to Ernie about the point you raised.
Frank: Yes.
Clem: I want you to see him.
Frank: Yes.
Clem: It's all part of a very big picture he's discussing with the Americans. It's one of a number of things.
Frank: Yes.
Clem: He's going to get in touch with you before the end of the week.
Frank: Yes – thank you very much.
Clem: Right. Good-bye.
Frank: Right [rings off].

I found Clem difficult to talk to but easy to like. He and his wife Vi came to dinner with us once in the Garden Suburb. To mark the occasion we decided to broach the last bottle of my grandfather Arthur Chamberlain's vintage port. As the port was over fifty years old, I guessed that it would need straining very carefully before being offered to the Prime Minister. The cork came out of the bottle in one piece, to my relief, but was followed by a mass of stuff like deep brown potting soil. After the soil had been drained and thrown on to our compost heap, there did not seem to be much of anything else left. With some trepidation I later offered what there was to Clem and, having given him the age and family history of the vintage, explaining that it might even have been drunk by my great-uncle 'Radical Joe' himself, I invited Clem's opinion. He sipped it. 'Seems all right.'

Vi Attlee was as confiding as Clem was laconic. She told us ladies after dinner that she had never voted Labour until she married Clem; and indeed she was always dressed with a neatness and elegance that would have been the envy of a Conservative women's conference. She also confessed to a dread of forgetting people's names when having to make official introductions, and other fears. Yet I can remember only one occasion when she showed the nervous tension that she must often have felt.

At Christmas she and Clem invited the families of ministers, staff, tenants and friends to Chequers, the Prime Minister's official residence in Buckinghamshire, for a magnificent children's party. Since many of us ministerial wives lived in Hampstead, one of our number, Peggy Jay, gallantly organized a coach to take us all to Chequers and back. Rightly assuming that there would be frequent stops on the way for children to be sick, we started in good time and in fact our crowded coach swept up to the front door of Chequers half an hour before we were invited. The driver rang the bell. The Prime Minister's wife opened the door herself and stood there, transfixed, with an expression of growing horror as she saw the mass of 'early worms' beginning to wriggle from the coach. 'You can't come in. It's only two-thirty.' But before poor Mrs Attlee could add that we were asked for *three* – as we all knew too well – Peggy had explained apologetically but firmly that the children were tired and cold and could not be driven around a frozen Buckinghamshire even for half an hour. Mrs Attlee responded courageously to the inevitable and the whole lot of us were ushered into the bedrooms where we spent as long as possible taking our children to the loos.

Frank and I were invited to the opera by the Attlees, the other members of the party being Ernest Bevin, the Foreign Secretary, and his wife Flo. Bevin was not at all well and vastly overweight, but he had a big personality to match his cumbrous form. However, much as I disliked his prejudices, especially those against the Germans ('I 'ates them') I wanted to be liked by him. It would be nice to sit next to him or Attlee in the box. When we arrived at Covent Garden we three wives were assigned, to my surprise, the three front seats while the ministers sat in a row at the back. I protested. The women couldn't have *all* the best seats. Halfway through the first act I had my explanation. Glancing behind me, I saw that all three ministers were fast asleep.

The funniest official lunch I attended was when Ernie welcomed some Dutch delegates as 'my dear old Danish friends . . .'. Frank, in his book *The Search for Peace* (1985), has described how Ernie, in response to corrective hisses from all quarters, observed good-naturedly, 'I gather they prefer to call themselves Dutch, nowadays.' Loud laughter. But before this successful emendation, I had overheard Ernie muttering to himself, 'What's it matter, they're all the same anyway.'

The most memorable official dinner to which I was invited took place at the Soviet embassy in Kensington Palace Gardens, alias 'Millionaires' Row'. A palatial, rather rambling residence, it had been the scene of an incident blown up by the press the day before when some visitors had inadvertently been locked into an area of the embassy from which they were able to escape only by climbing through a lavatory window. The accident added fictitious spice to our own visit and opportunities beforehand for dramatic exchanges in the genre of international thrillers. 'I've got a rope ladder in my handbag.' 'Right. I've got a torch and blowlamp.' 'Imagine the headlines tomorrow. "Sensation! Foreign Secretary squeezes to safety between bars." '

Our host was M. Molotov, the Soviet Ambassador. Also present were M. Vishinsky, the Foreign Secretary, two interpreters and several wives. I was astonished to see that the women were segregated at one half of the table, the men at the other. Of course, there were two key places at the table where a dominant male had to come in contact with one of the 'weaker vessels'. I was lucky enough to occupy one of these strategic *placements*: in fact I was seated next to Molotov while Mrs Bevin sat beside Vishinsky. About halfway through the dinner a discussion broke out between the men about Karl Marx. We could all see that Ernie was more than holding his own – until Molotov brought up reinforcements in the shape of Hilferding, the modern commentator on Marx. Mr Bevin ought to study Hilferding, he said. We all held our breath. Had Ernie even *heard* of Hilferding? Ponderously, but with enormous effect, our champion replied: 'I've read 'Ilferding and I find 'im *tedious.*'

After the main, male debate on Marx had abruptly subsided, I thought to carry it on through a modest intervention of my own. 'Tell me, M. Molotov,' I said, 'do students in the Soviet Union study Karl Marx today as much as they used to in the past?' Molotov gave me a stare through his pebble glasses, half basilisk, half domestic cat. The thick lenses made his brown eyes, the colour of a peat bog, look huge. Then he picked up his crystal wine glass and asked me a question apparently in reply to mine. The interpreter translated it as: 'What does Lady Pakenham think of our Georgian wines?' I felt sure that the interpreter had not been at fault. It was simply that weaker vessels at Soviet tables were not encouraged to spill their meagre intellects over subjects more controversial than drink.

Frank never did have that real talk with Ernie Bevin that Attlee had said he desired. Nor did Frank ever quite resign. For one thing, our closest friend and mentor in the Labour Party, Evan Durbin, implored him to do anything but that. 'Resignation from a Labour Government', he urged, 'is the one thing the party will never forgive. Labour is more than a political party. It is a movement. You can disagree, criticize, fight for your policy *inside* the Government; but to resign – that is to injure the whole movement, publicly, in the eyes of the world.'

Durbin was probably right about Labour Party sensitivities in 1947. Until the great victory of 1945 there had not been a Labour Government since 1931 when Ramsay MacDonald, Jimmy Thomas and others had left the party to form a Government of Betrayal – the so-called National Government. The word Resignation still had a bad smell. But in 1951, when the Labour Government itself was not smelling so sweetly, Harold Wilson and Aneurin Bevan were able to resign one year and be forgiven the next.

By then Evan Durbin was no longer with us, to see the change. He had been drowned in 1948 while on a family holiday in Cornwall. He rescued two children – one his own younger daughter – from a dangerous current around rocks, but was unable to save himself. For Frank the tragic loss of his friend at the beginning of their parliamentary careers was a severe political as well as personal blow. Evan, Hugh Gaitskell and Frank had formed one of those loose triumvirates, based on old associations, whose break-up suddenly leaves the prospect looking barer and poorer. Within two months of Evan's death there was to be another tragedy which would set in train a serious reversal in Frank's political progress.

'You can't hold down Germany with one hand and hold back Russia with the other.' These words of Frank's referred to the contradiction that had flawed Allied policy since the Cold War began in 1946. The force of these unhappy circumstances was finally to heave even the anti-German Bevin into a new political stance – the end of German dismantling, the end of German starvation, the beginning of German currency reform. But by this time Frank, with his clearly articulated mission and reiterated pleas for reconciliation with Germany, based on Christian principles, had rubbed Bevin up the wrong way once too often. Bevin's irritation with the Christian factor came through strongly when he was asked in Cabinet about Germany's desperate food situation. He replied that with Pakenham and Cripps (both Christians) to advise him, no source of supply would be ignored. It was a neat joke, even if it suggested that starry-eyed Christians were expecting manna from Heaven.

In the summer of 1948, after just a year in charge of West Germany's British zone, Frank was moved. Attlee appointed him to a full ministry for the first time, Civil Aviation. This did not stop Frank from continuing to badger Attlee and Bevin about the fate of West Germany at every opportunity. The chances of real influence, however, were to slump, not only because of his move but also owing to the tragedy already mentioned above.

An appalling civilian air disaster took place on 20 October 1948 when a plane, coming in to land at the northern airport of Prestwick, crashed in fog, killing all thirty passengers and crew of ten, including the experienced Dutch pilot. As Minister, Frank immediately ordered an enquiry into the disaster, appointing a Scottish KC to conduct it. The report was not to be presented for another nine months.

Meanwhile, Frank was not altogether comfortable in his new job. He would never have thought of himself as a natural devotee of aviation. Thanks to his traditional education at Eton, all manual skills were a closed book to him. When we first married he had been used to handing his pencils to someone else – formerly his mother's butler – to be sharpened for him. He had never learnt to change a light bulb or connect up a plug; once when I was ill he did find out how to make tea and coffee, though he would use the coffeepot for tea and the teapot for coffee, whichever came handy. The miracles of technology raised no excitement in his brain or stirred his imagination. Two years before this new post at Civil Aviation he had written to me about Attlee asking him to chair a committee on the location of British flying boats. Three exclamation marks followed this announcement, a clearly ironical comment on his own aptitude.

Nevertheless, he must have done well with the flying boats. Moreover, he was admirably suited to undertaking the task which Attlee now entrusted to him: the task of moulding Civil Aviation into an efficient public service. Possessing a head for figures and the ability to use the expertise of civil servants, he soon picked up the technical jargon as well, if only by listening carefully to a group taking him round a factory and then importantly repeating the knowledge he had just acquired to the people coming up behind. A flying boat, for instance, would pass by. 'There goes the boat,' Frank's guide would say and Frank would stop and turn round: 'there goes the boat.' He also learnt a good deal about planes from his schoolboy sons.

When the official report on the Prestwick crash was put into his hands in August 1949, he read it through quickly and came to a rapid decision. The report must be rejected. Its meticulous account of the events leading up to the crash did not tally with its own verdict: namely, that the staff at Prestwick airport were guilty of fatal error rather than the pilot. Frank's own officials in Whitehall had reached independently the same conclusion as he had. Several months of study followed. When Parliament reassembled in the autumn he confidently expected to announce the report's rejection without opposition. Unfortunately he did not prepare the author of the report for this unwelcome decision or for the reasons behind it. This 'clumsiness' (as Frank himself was to call it in his autobiography) was a bad beginning. Far worse was his failure to consult a 'senior Cabinet Minister' over a matter that was likely to become controversial. This procedure was not mandatory but was being worked out by Attlee's Government. Through inexperience, Frank ignored the consultative steps and went straight ahead.

His actions were blown up by the press not only into scandalous high-handedness and downright misjudgement (the press in general backed the report) but also into an act that was flagrantly unconstitutional. How dared Lord Pakenham set aside the report that he himself had ordered?

If the Cabinet had been unprepared for the débâcle, I myself was no better prepared. I was finishing some shopping in Oxford Street when a partly obscured poster caught my eye: '. . . NHAM ON THE CARPET'. For a moment it struck me that the end of the name was familiar and it could be PAKENHAM who had been carpeted. In fact for the moment I could think of no other name which ended that way. However, I dismissed the thought as impossible – and arrived home in the normally peaceful suburb to find to my astonishment a clamour of telephone calls, among them one from Hugh Gaitskell. Standing in for Evan Durbin, who would assuredly have advised the same thing, Hugh told me not to let Frank resign, 'quixotic though he is'.

For the next twenty-four hours we were ambushed, besieged and pounced upon in Linnell Drive by a press anxious, I felt, to drive us through their apparent hysteria into making some hysterical move of our own. But thanks to the firmness of the Government and our friends, and also to a stick-it-out reaction in himself, Frank kept his head. Forty-eight hours later it emerged that he *had* been within his constitutional rights.

The press lost interest as instantaneously as they had assumed it. I reported to Frank that Linnell Drive had suddenly 'gone dead' and I was left with some bewildered feelings about the newspaper world, which, incidentally, I was soon to know from the inside. What could be the human relationship, I asked myself, between those individual journalists who had been waylaying us and the machine that employed them? Though outrageously persistent and artificially excited, they were never rude. Yet the system within which they worked seemed to possess every vice from inaccuracy and exaggeration right through to callousness and deliberate invention. From this incident I derived my only personal experience of press harassment. It was enough to make me sympathize when it happened to others. The worst thing about it was the hunted feeling, the feeling that nowhere, not even one's own burrow, was safe.

The aftermath of the Prestwick Report was not a happy one for us. Frank's *cursus vitae*, which had been glittering, was now blotted and blotted during a critical period. Though he was justified in the event, the ideal political career, at least in its early stages, does not have to justify itself at all or run the gauntlet of public censure. His loss of influence luckily showed least in that area for which he cared most: the future of Germany. Nevertheless, it showed. The thing on which Churchill had congratulated him at a Buckingham Palace garden party – that his was the one voice speaking for 'the miseries of Germany' – was no longer quite so true. He spoke with the same voice but that voice had lost some of its authority.

There were compensations. West Germany itself was securely set on the path of reconstruction, though at the price of increasing Soviet hostility and suspicion. It was only long afterwards that I came to understand the special place which reconciliation with Germany could hold in an idealistic scheme of things, as visualized by Frank. The same instinct that later was to direct Frank – and me to a lesser extent – towards the reform and restoration of individual prisoners, had operated for a brief spell in regard to a whole country kept behind bars.

The set-back was far more serious for Frank personally. Before Prestwick, Attlee had hinted at his leadership of the House of Lords in the not-so-distant future. 'Christopher Addison won't last for ever,' he said of the then leader. Addison was in the Cabinet. So would Frank be, if and when he succeeded to the leadership. Indeed our friend Evan Durbin had used this argument in persuading Frank to accept a peerage. But Prestwick would stand between Frank and the Cabinet at a crucial moment, as we were soon to discover.

As for Civil Aviation, it turned out to be one of the nationalized industries, if a relatively minor one, that went from the red into the black, and then into substantial profit under the Minister's guidance. Occasionally the Minister's 'perks' would come the way of his family, particularly in the line of air displays and model aircraft rallies. Thomas was old enough to attend a Glider rally (flights aborted by bad weather, to my relief) and earlier to be suspected of sabotage by Soviet officials. This was when he had been taken by Frank to welcome the arrival of a Soviet minister on the tarmac. Thomas unslung his little box camera and had snapped the plane and some of its passengers who were standing around before anyone knew what was happening. Short of arresting a fourteen year old, the Russians had no answer. They wisely decided to congratulate Frank on his astuteness in sending in a schoolboy where angels feared to tread.

One of my 'perks' consisted in meeting 'personalities' at the various office cocktail-parties. Among them was Alison Munro, later to become headmistress of my granddaughters' London day-school, St Paul's; and Philip Moore, the Queen's private secretary in the 1970s and 1980s, whom I was to visit at Buckingham Palace in search of further knowledge – but not about aviation.

When Frank was moved from Germany to Aviation, M. Massigli, the French Ambassador, had made an excellent joke: 'Now Lord Pakenham

will be able to have his head *always* in the clouds' – the point being that
Frank's German policy had seemed to the French Ambassador to be
more often up in the clouds than down to earth. The final success of his
years at Aviation showed that effective policies had to be both.

Another 'perk', if I may call it that, was to meet the Duke and Duchess
of Windsor during a private visit to London. Their host, Lord Dudley,
happened to run into Frank in the House of Lords and invited him and me
to join a dinner-party in their honour at Claridge's, the presence of two
Labour people probably seeming to him a good, if unusual, idea.

'Sorry, my wife has to give a lecture that evening,' replied Frank.

'Then join us afterwards.' We did so, I having given my talk to a group
of workers in East London and being dressed accordingly: black jacket
and skirt, flat shoes; no time to change. The Claridge's party had just
reached the coffee when we were shown in. Dead silence fell among the
forty or so diamond-bespangled ladies and white-tied gentlemen as this
unexplained workaday couple suddenly appeared. A chair was squeezed
in for Frank beside the Duke and another for me beside the Duchess. And
there we remained, incongruously, until the party broke up. The
Duchess, in a straight clinging dress of black sequins, looked like a shiny
London lamppost on a rainswept night; but she had nothing of the
lamppost's hardness or unfriendliness. I shall always remember her
exquisite manners towards someone whose point must have been for her
an enigma.

We were approaching election year, 1950. In the first five years of Labour
rule we were optimistic about a second term – we had established the
Welfare State. It seemed to me the culmination of Frank's work for
Beveridge, as well as being in some way the apotheosis of countless
comrades in Stoke, Cheltenham and King's Norton. At the pinnacle of
our dreams – now realities – stood the National Health Service.

I was sitting beside Aneurin Bevan at a lunch in 1948:

'I hear you have a large family,' he said.

'Yes, eight.'

'Mine's bigger than that.' I must have looked surprised, knowing that
the Bevans had no children. With one of his lyrical Welsh laughs, he
explained: 'The whole of the National Health Service.'

His had been the political and personal skill to get the Bill through the
small Tory opposition in the Commons (not all Tories were opposed) and
the doctors outside. My own medical background caused me to rejoice
exceedingly when the doctors and Nye signed their concordat.

It was a very jolly lunch. After the coffee we stayed on still talking. In the
centre of the room stood Nye Bevan, his beautiful black-eyed wife Jennie

Lee MP, the Liberal MP Megan Lloyd George and myself, our arms round each other's shoulders, swaying slightly like a four-leaved clover in an afternoon breeze.

In 1949 an invitation came from Oxford to represent the City Labour Party at the forthcoming general election. I felt myself in a not unpleasant dilemma. On the one hand, I was deeply touched. My heart was still in Oxford. I knew the key members of the party and was particularly pleased that my having become a Catholic since the last election had not prejudiced them against me. I remembered the strained moment in the party when Frank confessed to his conversion. One member of the executive had proposed that a prospective Labour candidate who could take such a dubious step should at least submit himself to a vote of confidence. The vote went strongly in Frank's favour, supported by the chairman, a Unitarian minister who said he hated popery but hated bigotry more. Nevertheless, the experience had been a disturbing one, occurring as it did within a party that boasted no distinctions of sex, colour, class or creed. The invitation to me showed how successfully Frank had later demonstrated the reality of this boast. As Frank's peerage precluded him from standing again, I felt that this invitation was a compliment to his past work and narrow defeat, and must be accepted by me.

On the other hand, I had resigned from King's Norton nearly six years before for the sake of the family, my place being filled by a brilliant young soldier returned from the war, Raymond Blackburn. I well knew that no one was ever indispensable. They might find someone else as brilliant as Blackburn for Oxford if I declined. The only thing that had changed since my resignation as King's Norton Labour candidate in 1944 was that then I had six children and now I had eight. Or was that the only change?

The tide had been running strongly in Birmingham for Labour during the war. I had felt in my bones that we should win – as indeed Raymond did, with a majority of over 12,000. But now the ebb tide had set in. Battling against it was a tired Cabinet whose leaders would soon have been in office for ten years, including the five of the strenuous wartime coalition. The health of both Bevin and Cripps was on the point of collapse. Wartime shortages still marred the picture of peace and plenty that our Paddy had imagined at Christmas 1945.

Mrs Pope and I still kept six hateful chickens in the garden, stinking to heaven and reducing the grass to hideous excavations of bare earth, for the sake of their unrationed eggs. There was still a feeling of austerity. A cocktail-party we had given for thirty-three friends, including Gaitskells, Fawcetts, Muggeridges, Crawleys, Tony and Violet Powell, consumed no more than four bottles of sherry and two and a half of gin. It was only after our children began asking their friends to the house that we were reluctantly persuaded to add whisky and ice to the drinks' table. Life was still relatively simple. Passionately devoted to 'fair shares', if not to strict egalitarianism, Labour was determined to keep on 'controls' as long as shortages lasted. But a revolt was building up in the country which would emerge within two years as the winning Tory slogan, 'A Bonfire of Controls'.

So I had a new feeling in my bones – that I would be defeated if I stood for Oxford in 1950. The fight would be a 'propaganda' one and none the worse for that. My family would not suffer and I would discharge my political debt. In fact, I was not on the horns of a dilemma after all.

On 20 January 1950 I drove over to Oxford to start my campaign. Next day Judith, Rachel and Michael were brought to visit me by coach, followed later in the campaign by Catherine and Kevin as well. They made day trips, which were very convenient along the North Circular Road, far more so than if they had gone by train from Paddington. Nevertheless, these coach journeys were to make their own small contribution to the ambivalent effect of my family on my candidature.

On the positive side, the children enjoyed it madly, especially being photographed, though Kevin, aged three, pointed at one of the pressmen interviewing me and said, 'Pity!' I tactfully suggested he meant 'Pretty'. I loved their company, and that of Antonia who had left boarding-school and often visited Oxford before she went up to Lady Margaret Hall that October. Years later Antonia revealed that she used to joke about 'Mummy's red mac for canvassing and grey fur coat for everything else.' I had my answer: 'If I could have found a *red* fur coat I would have worn it.'

When polling day arrived the family had proved to be both my greatest personal asset and heaviest liability. Under the heading 'Unusual Candidate', my most ardent press supporter had written:

It is only a very remarkable woman who can combine being a mother to a family of eight growing children and being a parliamentary candidate at the General Election. To be a success in either role would tax the endurance of most people, but to discharge both functions superlatively calls for qualities possessed only by the very few. One of the few is Lady Pakenham. . . . She is, as far as I can gather from the records, the first woman with such a large family ever to fight a parliamentary election.

The idea of a record made a good talking-point. And some of the hard-pressed Oxford wives probably felt that, even if my family was excessive, my own experience of family problems would help me to appreciate theirs.

Another press report reflected the adverse criticisms that could and did arise on this same point:

At one of her meetings Lady Pakenham was asked if it was possible to give up looking after her family in order, if elected, to represent the City in Parliament. She replied that ever since she had been married she had managed to combine public work with her home responsibilities.

'I had two children when I stood as a candidate at Cheltenham,' she said, 'and even with more babies coming along I "nursed" the King's Norton Division of Birmingham for seven years, some of them when Birmingham was being blitzed.' She said that she had help in the home.

Of course, there was a substratum of really malicious criticism based on an assortment of anti-Catholic, anti-children and anti-feminine views mixed up together in a box labelled 'Party Political Prejudice'. The attacks began soon after Kevin's birth, fifteen months before the election. Interviewed by a newspaper under the caption 'Mother of Eight', I had joked that in the Soviet Union I would have reached the sublime status of 'Mother Champion' – reserved for those with eight children. Next day I received an anonymous letter. The educated classes, it began, should know better than to 'breed like rabbits'. Had I never heard of birth control? It was people like me who ruined people like him, forcing men who of their own choice had remained unmarried to pay for other people's huge families, the results of animal self-indulgence. He signed it 'Disgusted Bachelor'.

At the bottom of his grievance lay unplumbable depths of religious and sexual hatred. But the murk had been stirred up and brought to the surface by Labour's introduction of Family Allowances. Fought for in the past by many women's organizations covering the whole political spectrum, Family Allowances at first amounted to only a few shillings a week – but paid to the *mother*. This was the nub of 'Disgusted's' fury.

I got it again with class hatred added to the brew during the election itself. Another anonymous letter. This time the author denounced my 'snotty-nosed' children for occupying space in the coach which was required for people who could not afford to travel by rail. If my children *had* to be dragged to Oxford for my political purposes, they should be brought by train in a first-class carriage, where they could not disturb other passengers; a luxury which socialists of my type could well afford, thanks to this iniquitous Labour Government's policy of etc., etc.

Looking back on the election, I felt that it was Frank who discovered the best way to defuse such anger, when speaking for me. A typical exchange would run as follows:

Heckler: The country cannot afford over-population.
Candidate's husband: It depends on what you mean by –
Heckler: – your wife's what I mean. *Eight* children. All hers alone.
Husband: I always thought I had a hand in it . . . (Loud laughter in which the population question was for the moment drowned.)

There were four candidates involved at Oxford. Quintin Hogg was defending his seat as a leading Conservative. In nine years' time he was to lift the morale of delegates by 'ringing in the new' with a large hand-bell at a Conservative Party conference. Needless to say, he never mentioned my eight children, maintaining amicable relations throughout the campaign with his chief rival.

My candidature was supported, I was delighted to find, by the former Liberal MP, Sir Geoffrey Mander, who had held the record for the greatest number of questions asked at Question Time and was the husband of my friend Rosalie Mander. This despite there being a Liberal candidate. There was also a communist, Ernie Keeling, the young local party organizer. His candidature did not prevent me from being invited to address all the trades union branches and holding factory-gate meetings. For my advantage over Frank was that the city boundaries had been extended since his election campaign to include the new working-class areas surrounding the old city, particularly Cowley.

Both Hugh Gaitskell and Harold Wilson spoke for me. Harold was *the* up-and-coming young politician and the jokes he made in his north of England voice went over big. I remember one. 'The rate of bankruptcies has fallen under this Government. Industries and commerce are buoyant. All except the money-lenders. And we have never promised, in any of our manifestos, to put money in the usurers' pockets.'

The Wilsons and Pakenhams were neighbours in the Garden Suburb, the children going to each other's Christmas and birthday parties. Thirty years after the 1950 election Harold told me that his official driver still remembered dressing up as Santa Claus and scaring the little Pakenhams into hysterics. I can only imagine they were so used to seeing their own father in the title role that the presence of an interloper had the most sinister effect.

One of the pleasures of electioneering in the university towns is the help one gets from students. The future Sir Peter Parker – who many years later was to be a popular chairman of British Rail and whose wife, Dr Parker, was to keep Antonia's family among many others in health – organized and led my light brigade. Maurice Bowra, though he had not voted for Frank in 1945 to our considerable surprise, did support me in 1950, because of Labour's impressive build-up of the universities.

Yet with all these advantages I did slightly worse than Frank had done five years before. For I had one great disadvantage: the swing of the pendulum. Quintin beat me by just over three thousand votes.

I have a photograph taken of the three candidates (the Liberal was ill) on Nomination Day, captioned in the *Oxford Mail*, 'Three Oxford rivals take wine together in Mayor's Parlour.' The Conservative looks jubilant, the communist detached, the Labour candidate talkative. That about summed us up. But I never talked myself into believing that I would win, or indeed into thinking too much about the result. As so often in life, it had been better to travel than to arrive.

Aidan Crawley was defending his Buckinghamshire seat at this election. I had often spoken for him, when Frank and I would stay with Virginia and him at Kingsbridge, their farm near the constituency. During one of these visits I had experienced a sudden revulsion against our life in Hampstead Garden Suburb and a longing for Sussex and Bernhurst. I photographed the Crawley children sitting on a garden seat, the lawn rather rough but a marvellous sweep of cornfields in the background. Their two younger children, Harriet and Randal, were almost the same age as Catherine and Kevin. I felt Virginia was giving them a freer, more natural life in the country than I could give mine in a suburb of London. They would have rivers, real woods, ponies. They would never have to 'go walks' on pavements or 'swim', as mine did, in an inflated orange life-raft bought from surplus RAF stock.

On 24 February, the day after my defeat, Aidan's victory was announced. Frank and I drove over to celebrate with him and with a squadron of RAF helpers who had been working in the constituency for their wartime comrade. We stood on end the empty papier mâché cases that had earlier contained bottles of champagne, and played bowls with them on the drawing-room carpet, using oranges as balls. Next morning, feeling much the worse for wear, I drove Frank back to the Suburb with room for only one thought in my mind. It must be Bernhurst this year.

18

Enter the Black Art
· 1950–5 ·

'The Hampstead Set' was supposed to be a political pressure group. Young, ambitious members of the Labour Government were said to frequent Dora and Hugh Gaitskell's house every Sunday morning before lunch and drink dry sherry. (The slightly fastidious picture that these last two words presented was later to be developed by the press into Roy Jenkins's alleged love-affair with claret.)

Only occasionally did Frank and I drink Sunday morning sherry at 18 Frognal Gardens. But it was true that a surprisingly large number of the Government's younger members, ourselves included, did live in or around Hampstead. Certainly my chief anxieties about pulling up our roots again and moving from Hampstead centred around the loss of our political friends and neighbours. Apart from those whom we had known since Oxford days – Marjorie Durbin, Evan's widow, the Gordon Walkers and Jays – there were the Wilsons and Soskices, Frank Soskice to be a future Home Secretary. I guessed, rightly, that some of these families would come and visit us at Bernhurst, but the Gaitskells were different. I regarded Hugh and Dora as essentially town dwellers. Yet I felt a special bond with them which I did not want to break. Many years later, when Hugh was dead and his diaries had been published, I found that he had felt the same about us.

The test of our friendship, now of over twenty years' duration, had really come when Hugh supported me during the Oxford election of 1950. The experience struck him as 'strange'. He was speaking for me in the Oxford Union 'with Frank there as well'. Should he 'refer to our long friendship'? He was 'a little doubtful' until I referred to it first. Afterwards we all three moved on to the Randolph Hotel and 'gossiped away about Nye Bevan, among others, Hugh prophesying that Nye would be leader of the Party and therefore Prime Minister one day'. Frank was 'rather horrified' but I stood up for his 'great qualities' (perhaps thinking of that lunch with him, Jennie and Megan). 'He has every virtue,' I said, 'but Virtue.'

Hugh in his diary then became quite moved at the thought of the nice things Frank and I had said about his speech: 'One could not help feeling what a pleasure it was to have such friends in the middle of all this political struggle. So far at least there does not seem to be any sign of any strain in our friendship, I shall continue to watch this carefully.' How nice it would be to disprove the cynical saying: 'There are no friends at the top.'

I myself had no fears about 'strain' in our relationship. I simply wondered whether living fifty miles away from our Hampstead friends – and in Sussex, the most consistently Tory of English counties – might not separate me from one of the most active growing-points in the Labour Government. Frank, of course, would see them all in Parliament. Nevertheless, the arguments for returning to Bernhurst seemed the stronger, at any rate from the children's angle.

Antonia's last year in the Suburb had been a series of escapes from a base she did not enjoy: courses at the French Lycée and Courtauld Institute, followed by a brief attempt to sell hats at Fenwick's of Bond Street. The *Bangkok Post* was kind enough to say that the eldest daughter of the Minister of Civil Aviation had 'given up her job in order to devote more time to social affairs'. In fact she was sacked after a group of male acquaintances came to visit her on a Saturday morning and began playing catch with the hats. Antonia had also shown too much spirit in demanding 'Sits and Sats' for all shop-assistants; namely, seats to sit on and Saturdays off. The 'social affairs' mentioned by the *Bangkok Post* began with her presentation at Buckingham Palace to King George VI and Queen Elizabeth. The latter said to her: 'Going up to Oxford? Then you must have a good fling first.' Antonia took this as a royal command.

Thomas had hitchhiked to Rome and back for Holy Year and was all for further travel. Paddy had just attended his first dance. He picked up the prettiest girl in the room who appeared for some unaccountable reason to have no partner; she turned out to be Princess Alexandra. (Frank had had a similar experience forty years before with Princess Mary.)

For Judith, Rachel and Michael, the Golders Green convent to which they all three went had served its purpose. Judith's best friend, a Polish girl, had emigrated to South America, leaving Judith the unchallenged top of her class, but forlorn. Rachel and Michael were together in a lower form, Michael's phenomenal memory giving him an unfair advantage, while Rachel's protectiveness towards her younger brother and 'general sense of responsibility' (school report) encouraged the good nuns to load her with class duties to the detriment of her lessons. Catherine and Kevin, aged four and two, were stuffed full of visions of calves, lambs, kittens and ponies at Bernhurst. There were no animals at Linnell Drive except for

Vicky, the corgi, and some creepy white mice who were always eating each other, though grossly overfed.

My mother, Michael and I had already picnicked at Bernhurst on a spring day in 1950. The sight was discouraging. We sat on a bank of dandelions beside the overgrown drive in the shadow of the 300-year-old oak, looking across at oblongs of cement dotted over the front lawn, until lately the foundations of soldiers' Nissen huts. Three rhododendron bushes had actually survived but were hidden underneath a massive entanglement of brambles. The great oak itself had lost all its lower branches in the interests of a free passage for army lorries, while a camp kitchen had been scooped out of its massive trunk, which was now filled with half a ton of ash. No damage had been done inside the house, not even to the banisters (though the officer in charge was said to have gone off with great-uncle Frank's brass-bound travelling chest of drawers) and the War Office had kindly painted the whole house from top to bottom in deep banana yellow.

My mother said I would have great fun redesigning the garden, which I did. In spite of my design being far too elaborate, with new shrubs planted almost on top of each other, the backbone of the new garden remains intact today. One of its prettiest additions I copied from my mother's garden at Crockham Hill: long narrow paths of mown grass winding through clumps of fir. Part of the wilderness once occupied by a fruit cage and vegetables was brought to attention by four golden cypresses, planted in a square at the intersection of four herbaceous borders. I went wild over hedges, having learnt from Vita Sackville-West at neighbouring Sissinghurst that even yews shoot up in no time. I also learnt from Vita to love white flowers – and white squirrels and blackbirds, of which we occasionally bred one. The golden cypresses are now twenty feet tall and have housed generations of pearly grey doves. Their eerie wingeing cry, a cross between a whine and a whistle, is a feature of the garden in summer.

We finally moved in on 30 July 1950. Catherine and Kevin survived a complete change-over in the nursery, two nannies getting married and being replaced by the first of our au pairs, Hildegard from West Germany. 'I hope that Hildegard will teach me German', wrote Judith from her new boarding-school convent at Mayfield, 'so that I can be Dada's secretary.'

Rachel was a day-girl at Tates, a junior school in the next village run by Audrey Townsend and her husband. Here Rachel met both the daughter of Audrey and also of Arthur Gaitskell. Catherine and our butcher's clever daughter Susan were taught at Bernhurst for a year by an ex-governess who happened to live in the village. She revealed that her last pupil had eventually gone through a sex change.

Bernhurst, by D. E. Cameron, 1962

As for Michael, from having been a rather timid gentle boy in a girls' convent, he became one of the lads at the Hurst Green village school. He tried to introduce some swear words into the home, all uttered in his rich new Sussex voice. I first heard the latter when driving him to a pantomime in Robertsbridge. Seeing a group of school friends in the village street he waved to them and then bawled, 'Oi! It's Moichael!' After the first term the voice, bloodies and buggers were all reserved for school hours. His new friends became constant visitors to Bernhurst for games and charades, all behaving with perfect decorum. One of them was to marry and have a family before Michael had gone to university; another won a state scholarship and set up a thriving business. Mrs Hollis, the renowned headmistress to generations of Hurst Green children, predicted an equally bright future for Michael. She was able to boast that after the regular county test, one of her pupils had an IQ of one hundred and sixty plus.

There was one sharp pebble on my shore. In May 1951, to my surprise and sorrow, I had a sudden miscarriage. After a week in hospital I realized how lucky I had been. When I got home again Mrs Pope said sombrely, 'I never thought to see you again, after the ambulancemen carried you out feet first.' Of the children, only Rachel had returned from school in time to see her moribund mother depart. The sight of the ambulance and the sound of Mrs Pope's wails convinced her that she would never see me again. Frank wrote afterwards: 'Certainly the Bernhurst adventure, if merely *unlucky* so far, has not brought you happiness.'

I learnt at least three things from this experience, one consoling, the others sad. The many women who in the past have died of a haemorrhage probably suffered as little as I did, though I did not die. I was drifting peacefully away when my doctor, interrupted on his rounds, dashed in and gave me an injection; this brought me back to consciousness – and to pain. Comparing notes afterwards with various friends, I was amazed to find what a large proportion of women seemed to round off their families on the negative note of a miscarriage. My mother was the first to tell me that this had been her lot.

On a different note, I found myself unexpectedly depressed at the loss of this baby, despite the fact that I had always regarded Kevin as the perfect Benjamin to complete the family and had lost my philoprogenitive urge. Nevertheless, the 'miss' – my second and last – seemed an insult, an act of nihilism that must be wiped out in the only way I knew. Fortunately, Nature knew otherwise. I was lucky to sail through the 'change' without disturbances, despite warnings from Vi Attlee about the menace it was to women in public life. Drugs to control the symptoms were probably not generally available in the 1950s; at any rate I did not make enquiries, and in wintertime found even the dreaded 'hot flush' quite pleasant.

Meanwhile, life at Bernhurst continued apace. Judith's pony Swallow was joined by Rachel's Just William and later replaced by Judith's Jason; the boys all began asking for airguns or shotguns for Christmas and shot grey squirrels, pre-myxomatosis rabbits and the occasional pigeon on the wing. The girls began writing poetry about the countryside: Judith on the sad end of summer in a poem called 'Passing', Rachel on the value of golden leaves versus golden coins. Catherine at four showed her devotion by drawing 'A Garden for Rachel' in which the entire sky was covered with the letters RP repeated over and over again.

The only aspect of our new country life that did not please Frank and me was the absence of a Catholic church. We either went to a Mass in an upper room of the Rose and Crown in Burwash or at the village hall in Hurst Green. However, our postmistress, an ardent Catholic, made it clear that the Catholic community of Hurst Green expected the lord of Bernhurst to do something about a local chapel. So a field was given by

Frank behind our house, and soon the familiar process had begun of raising money to pay for the building. A striking modern chapel sprang up, semicircular, with a roof like a fan shell (some said like a garage) and beautiful crescent-shaped pews from Ireland.

I never cease to marvel at the growth of Catholicism I have seen in East Sussex. Thirty years ago the Rose and Crown; now new churches in both Burwash and Hurst Green as well as other parts of the county. We were breaking down a fierce anti-Catholic tradition that had lasted for five centuries. In the course of writing an article for an American magazine on 'Main Street: Battle', I discovered that an ancient Guy Fawkes kit still existed above one of the Battle shops, while the 'Battle Bonfire Boys' were famous for their militant Protestantism.

Distinguished Catholic heroes of the media and stage were press-ganged into opening our fêtes for nothing. Ben Lyon and his family, Max Bygraves, Eamonn Andrews, Gilbert Harding and Alec Guinness. Eamonn and his wife were rewarded next day by a gritty picnic in the Camber sand dunes; Alec arrived with an injured toe in plaster, which he wished had been amputated so that he could have had it auctioned.

Frank was just beginning to find the daily commuting by rail between Bernhurst and London somewhat trying – one hundred minutes then, seventy-five minutes now – when we suddenly heard that we had a new house in London.

In May 1951 Attlee appointed him First Lord of the Admiralty, with the picturesque 'perk' of Admiralty House to live in. Of course it was promotion. He was now judged to be 'of Cabinet rank' – but still neither in the Cabinet, nor Leader of the Lords. The dead hand of Prestwick lay almost as heavy on his career as it had lain over two years ago.

For the children and me there was a wonderful opening of new vistas in space and time. Paddy, now aged fourteen, wrote from Ampleforth College, a fortress of Tory Catholicism:

Many – many congratulations. I received your wire on Thursday evening and until Friday I was wondering what was in the offing – Fr Columba suggested it was an engagement ('Perhaps your elder sister has got engaged at Oxford – you never know what happens at Oxford – nyum – nyum – nyum'). The gloomy top-table Tories said they hoped you were resigning. But, as it turned out, you are the 1st Lord (rattling good show). . . . When the news came through, dear bovine Miles said he was glad somebody was now able to clear up the mess in Civil Aviation, and it was just bad luck on the British Navy.

Admiralty House had its forecourt off Whitehall. From our small kitchen-diner we looked across the road towards the vanished platform outside the Banqueting Hall where Charles I had been executed. Behind, we faced on to Horse Guards Parade where the children watched Trooping the Colour. The splendid room in which the Board of Admiralty had met since before Nelson's day contained the famous interior wind-vane, with its direct contact upwards to the London sky. Admirals of the Fleet had looked at it during crucial board meetings to see if the wind was changing. First Lords of the Admiralty, like Churchill, had looked at it, perhaps because of tedium. So did the Sea Lords, among them Earl Mountbatten who was fourth Sea Lord during Frank's regime and keeping a low profile; he probably looked at it a good deal. The political wind changed once rather violently during that period, when Mussadeq nationalized Persian oil – a prelude to the Suez crisis five years later.

The most fascinating historic relic in our domestic quarters at Admiralty House was the set of deep round marks in the blue Axminster carpet in our bedroom. They were made by the feet of Lady Diana Cooper's former four-poster bed. The marks extended far beyond the ends of our mahogany twin beds provided by the Office of Works. She had had a glorious carved and gilded bed designed for her by Rex Whistler when her husband Duff Cooper was First Lord, to match the celebrated 'Dolphin' furniture in the state rooms. The bed had departed with Diana; but I still enjoyed seeing its footsteps in the pile of time.

I was again living within sound of Bow Bells, as I had lived for my first twenty-five years. Bow Bells did not disturb me but Big Ben did. Most mothers of young children become light sleepers and I became almost an insomniac, waiting obsessively for that quarterly chime. Fortunately I had learnt how to deal with chimes when visiting Thomas and Paddy at Ampleforth. I had told one of my fellow parents, a doctor, that the hymn tune, 'Through the Night of Doubt and Sorrow', played in a village belfry – one more line added at each quarter until 'the Promised Land' was reached at the hour – had kept me awake all through a night of dirge and stupor. He handed me two pink pills.

When we moved in, the children were given rooms on the second floor, with small square sash windows and fresh chintz curtains. The staff were pleased to have children in the house after years without. I did not ask for any changes of furnishing downstairs. (How long would our tenure last, with Labour's minuscule majority?) But I was delighted when a Man from the Ministry came and cleaned all the upholstery on the spot. I did not think to ask what magic lotion he used, but I myself have never been able to find anything so effective.

It was enchanting to meet the admirals; one did *petit point*, another studied Kant and Hegel. Once when Thomas was two he had told me he could always recognize bus conductors from their white faces and big ears. On the same principle I learnt to recognize admirals from their sea-blue eyes.

With Frank I visited Portsmouth, marvelling at the scale of HMS *Victory*. There was just room for our party to dine where Nelson and his officers had banqueted; I felt that the berths were too small even for men to die in. At Chatham the old gardener gave me a raspberry cane for Bernhurst and pointed to his wife picking off the leaves of that self-rejuvenating garden pest, ground elder. 'It weakens them,' he said hopefully. I tried his method out in the half-cleared garden at Bernhurst but found that in the end one had to fork out every inch of white worm-like root.

The duty to entertain was a light one in Admiralty House where the naval personnel made everything easy. No one complained when, after a strenuous cocktail-party, some of the statues in the hall had to have their lipstick removed.

The grandest party we gave was in honour of the Prime Minister. Clem was asked beforehand to choose some distinguished character whom he would like to meet. His choice fell on Sir Arthur Bryant, who had published his *Age of Elegance*, dedicated to Montgomery, the year before. His kind of literary patriotism appealed to Clem.

Hugh Gaitskell, also our guest, did not enjoy the party so much. After sitting next to Lady Mountbatten, wife of the Fourth Sea Lord, he noted in his diary that he did not like her serious talk about nursing and would have preferred the subject of New York night-clubs. As for her husband, 'I feel uneasy', wrote Hugh, 'with Royal Princes who are Admirals, who are also left-wing and what Dalton calls "viewy" on public affairs.' Hugh added kindly: 'Frank and Elizabeth are evidently enormously enjoying his new job, and all the reports I hear about how he conducts himself are excellent.'

Arthur Villiers was another who had heard reports about the new First Lord. He sent on to me a letter received from one of his 'old boys' of the Eton Manor club, who was now in the navy:

I have just returned from the pier head where I proudly witnessed the arrival of the First Lord. He did very well. His bearing and manner is excellent, his keenness and attention to both officer and rating. His saluting (best Naval style which is unusual) everything very well carried out.

Of course I paved the way for him. I told the Commander all about him and assured him he was an excellent type, to which the Commander replied, 'It makes a good deal of difference to the way we receive people when we know whether or not they are the type.'

Arthur Villiers clearly doubted whether his nephew was really 'the type', for he commented dryly to me: 'I feel you must have had a hand in the First Lord's smart appearance.'

The truth was that Arthur, keenly aware of the Service traditions in both the Villiers and Pakenham families, had been greatly dashed by Frank's failed career in the army. He had suggested in 1942 that both he himself and Frank ought to be 'patrolling the fly-invested and flea-bitten darkness around Tobruk'. Frank's success as First Lord soothed Arthur's avuncular pride.

At the last party I went to in Admiralty House, in December 1951, we were guests instead of hosts. Frank's brief reign had ended when the Labour Government had fallen three months earlier. The new First Lord invited us, together with the Crawleys and Mountbattens, among an otherwise victorious crowd of Conservatives. Virginia Crawley, who knew the Mountbattens, seized me by the hand saying, 'Let's go up to Dickie and ask him about his inventions. He adores talking about them and won't be able to resist.' So we stood like two gawping schoolgirls on each side of the great man and Virginia began, 'Is it true, Dickie, that you invented a new captain's bridge? Elizabeth and I want to know.' Dickie fell into the trap – if trap it was – and gave us a full exposition of his invention's merits. But such was his enthusiasm and charm that though we may have come to jeer we stayed to praise. Years later my books were to benefit from his quite exceptional generosity and kindness in giving time and thought to other people's problems.

With the change of government, Frank was out of a job. I could see that the days of our idyll at Bernhurst were numbered also, in the sense that it could no longer be our main family base. Frank decided to return to teaching part-time in Oxford, while he also researched the 'Causes of Crime' at the Nuffield Institute in London. It was obvious that our base must now be in London, where in any case I had committee work at the Catholic Central Library and on the Paddington and St Pancras Rent Tribunal.

Neither of these occupations was intrinsically my cup of tea, but I enjoyed each for the people I worked with. On the former was Monsignor Gordon Wheeler, an inspired priest who made even the most boring decisions seem like an exciting drama. On the latter were my two co-panellists, one a Moslem, the other a Jew, whose urbane views of the world compensated me for having to study hideous exhibitions of ingenuity in dividing late-Victorian houses into mid-twentieth-century flats. I got to hate the sight of very narrow apartments with very high ceilings, half a window apiece and inflated rents.

Frank's temporary reversion to university life produced one memorable experience, which incidentally showed that old practices at post-war Christ Church died hard. He came within an inch of being beaten up, though not as a 'bloody aesthete' – the usual cause for breaking up rooms in the past – but as a bloody socialist who was teaching politics.

Frank was reading in bed when he recognized the shouts and approaching footsteps of Loders Club, a smart social club like the Bullingdon. Quickly turning off the light, he lay perfectly still. He heard loud whispering and drunken laughter outside his door. Suddenly one of their number was pushed into his bedroom.

'Go on. Get him out. Let's wreck his room.' But their emissary had made two fatal mistakes. He had not switched on the light for fear of being recognized, and once inside the room he had hesitated long enough to lose his nerve.

'Come on. What are you doing? Fetch him out.'

'He's not there.' A few thwarted growls, more drunken laughter and Loders withdrew in a body, mission unfulfilled.

I chose Chelsea for our new home, an area for me of history and mystery that was infinitely seductive, quite apart from its charming Albert Bridge over the Thames. I fell in love with this elegant Victorian suspension bridge before I realized that to cross the river over Albert Bridge was the quickest way to Bernhurst. I intended to drive the family back to Sussex for as many weekends as possible.

I found a three-storey Victorian house with a basement and paved garden at 14 Cheyne Gardens, just behind the more prestigious Cheyne Walk. Michael and Kevin managed to play cricket by chalking up wickets and bails on our back fence. We were living on the site of English history in all its startling variety: first Henry VIII's manor, where Princess Elizabeth had listened to Thomas Seymour romping with her stepmother Catherine Parr and occasionally making unwelcome advances to herself; then the poet Dante Gabriel Rossetti's long garden, with its zebu, wombat and screeching peacocks.

The schools' problem resolved itself, except for Kevin. Rachel, Catherine and Kevin all began by attending the Holy Child convent in Cavendish Square, beneath the benign shadow of Epstein's Madonna and Child. The long bus journeys, however, proved too much for Kevin at barely five, so I found myself teaching him for 'two terms' at home, under the aegis of the Parents' National Educational Union. They sent me professional programmes and I was able to flourish one of them in the face of the school inspector when he questioned the quality of Kevin's instruction. The two of us went the whole hog, performing the recommended 'singing-games' together as if we were a class of twenty. I had only one failure and that was in Nature Study. We had found a small brown chrysalis in the rockery which Kevin treasured in a matchbox until the triumphant day when he saw it was about to break open and release its precious occupant. We put it outdoors on a table in the pale sunshine and were watching the emerging moth stretching its moist, trembling wings, when – down came a sparrow and pecked off Kevin's moth under his nose. My explanation of 'nature red in tooth and claw' was given to an accompaniment of heartbroken sobs.

St Philip's prep school in Kensington was attended by Michael, now nine. His two years at Hurst Green village school had made him a prince of the three Rs, but French was gobbledegook. He proudly recited his first French sentence to the family at tea: 'Il y a daze possy nooges danz le basseen.' It was only after examining his exercise book that we realized he had been talking about there being 'poissons rouges' in the pool.

Judith was a founder member of a new Catholic day-school called More House, run by the Canonesses of St Augustine. Other founder members were Anita and Rita Auden, nieces of Wystan Auden, and Mary Rose Pollen, whose older sister Lucy had been Antonia's great friend at St Mary's, Ascot, and whose younger sister Margaret was to be Rachel's friend when she too arrived at More House. There is always a particular satisfaction in finding that the children of one's friends have become the friends of one's children. This pleasure has frequently been ours, but never more so than with the Pollens. At twenty-one Frank had thought of proposing to Daphne Baring, only to find that she was about to marry the sculptor Arthur Pollen. Daphne and Arthur were among those who brought light and grace into our Catholic world. Their son Francis was to design our church in Hurst Green while Arthur himself sculpted its four statues. Many years later, when I was researching the life of the poet and diarist Wilfrid Scawen Blunt, I made the discovery that my hero had seduced Arthur's grandmother. I felt rather guilty.

A family of eight children was not so common in the 1950s. I suppose for this reason my telephone began to ring more and more often with requests from journalists who were writing pieces on family problems like nail-biting or night terrors. Some of my interrogators took it for granted that the size of my family was a function of Catholic anti-birth-control dogma, and that therefore, as a reluctant mother, I would be struggling with problems wished upon me by the rigours of my faith. This, of course, was untrue. I had six children before I even thought about religious faith of any kind.

One day early in 1953 Frank happened to remark on my long exchanges with journalists to Eve Perrick, herself a feature writer on the

Daily Express. 'Why doesn't Elizabeth write the articles herself?' asked Eve. From this question stemmed the whole of a new life for me. It was said of Eve that she dipped her pen in vitriol, a comment on the thin skins of newspaper readers in those days. To me, after 25 March 1953, her pen seemed to be dipped in the milk of human kindness.

It was on this date that a lunch was arranged for me with Anthony Hern, then features editor of the *Express*, to discuss the possibility of my writing articles on family subjects for his paper. With the biggest circulation of any daily paper, it would offer me, if I succeeded, an incomparable platform for what I regarded as progressive views on the upbringing of children.

Tony suggested that I should write three articles which he would pass on to Lord Beaverbrook, super-active owner of Express Newspapers, for his verdict. Three weeks later Frank and I were invited for dinner and the night to Cherkley, Beaverbrook's home in Surrey. He had clearly read the articles, for he remarked on what an 'original' subject I had chosen for the first: namely, 'What do we learn from Fantasy?' – a study of children's invented friends based on my experience of Antonia's Tibby-and-Tellow and Kevin's Donkey. I was not so innocent as to think that 'originality' was the most sought-after quality in *Express* writers. Beaverbrook would surely have preferred something more popular, like 'Children and the Coronation', which was coming up that year. Nevertheless, the visit to Cherkley, went off comparatively well and I had hopes.

In fact I made one blunder that might have proved fatal, had not Beaverbrook been agreeably prejudiced in favour of the Pakenham family by the journalism of my sister-in-law Maria. Before the war, Mary Pakenham had written for Beaverbrook's *Evening Standard* with a wit that the press lord had not forgotten. The bad moment came when Beaverbrook, suddenly halting the flow of dinner-table conversation, went round the table clockwise asking each of his guests in turn, 'Who is Barry Appleby?' I was sitting on his left, so I was the first to reply, 'Never heard of him.' All the rest of his guests gave a similar answer, some contemptuously ('What a name!'), others puzzled ('Who on earth . . .?') until our host reached Barry Appleby himself, smiling heroically in a state of horrible humiliation. Beaverbrook then explained that Barry Appleby was the author of the world's most popular strip cartoon, 'The Gambols', which appeared daily in the *Express*. Had I been more worldly-wise I would have read the *Express* from front to back page before entering the Beaver's den. As it was, I and my fellow-guests were no less humiliated than the unfortunate Appleby himself. The whole episode was a good example of the mischievous, if not malicious, vein that was known to lurk in Beaverbrook.

His generosity was equally well illustrated during that first encounter. In deference to Frank and me, he showed in his private cinema after dinner a film of vaguely left-wing flavour. Next morning I was ushered into his sanctum to say good-bye. He began, 'You have a lot of children to feed and there are still shortages. Would *these* be any help?' Mystified I stared at him till he suddenly pressed a magic button in the bookcase to the left of his desk. The shelves rolled back, revealing a vast array of canned foods. It must have been the remains of the 'iron ration' that he, like the rest of us, had been urged to lay in during the war. 'Do you drive?' he continued. Then to the attendant footman he said, 'Carry out as many of these as you can and put them in the boot of Lady Pakenham's car.'

Thanks to Tony Hern's ingenuity, the title of my first article was announced before publication, *Express* readers being invited to contribute stories about the 'fantasy friends' invented by their own children. I was overwhelmed by the number and variety of stories that came rolling in. Britain was clearly the home of a huge invisible population who were always giving trouble by getting lost or sat upon in buses or tubes. Years later I learnt that these imaginary beings had even entered a royal nursery, for Princess Margaret had her fictitious friend 'Inderbombanks'.

When my weekly series on family problems – fathers, teenagers, quarrels, punishment, presents, hospitals, adoption *et al.* – was well under way, Lord Beaverbrook asked us to dinner at his flat in Arlington Street, overlooking St James's Park. Again there was the contradictory mixture of malice and kindness. In the middle of dinner he sent out Charles Wintour, then a favourite journalist on the *Standard*, to look up Peter Townsend's war record. (Peter's love for Princess Margaret and hers for him had become public knowledge since the Coronation when she was seen by journalists removing a speck of dust from his uniform. *C'est le premier* speck *qui coute*.) Beaverbrook, hostile as ever to the Royal Family, denounced the love affair, even questioning Townsend's courage as a pilot. Charles Wintour returned from his researches:

Charles: He was honoured. DSO, DFC and bar. He was wounded.
Beaver (with a snarl): In the foot?
Charles (after returning from another look in *Who's Who*): It doesn't say.

But it was the other, charming Beaverbrook who said to me as we thanked him for the party: 'You are now practising the Black Art,' meaning journalism; 'no one who once practises the Black Art can ever escape.'

I was being trained in the art by the ever-helpful Tony Hern. He taught me about the short sentence. Sentences with a maximum of ten words were not essential, contrary to the practice of Frank Owen, a brilliant

Express journalist and Liberal politician who spoilt his book on Lloyd George by rigorously applying the ten-word rule. Yet though short sentences were not essential and indeed could become as monotonous as rifle fire, sentences of fifty words or more, with dependent clauses hanging like monkeys from a tree, were equally unacceptable – unless, of course, they were written by Bernard Levin, master of the hundred-word rule.

Tony Hern also instructed me in the art of switching articles back to front, so that they began with a loosened-up, free-flowing paragraph instead of one that was still cramped and stiff. After all it is the first paragraph that counts, on the assumption that newspaper readers rarely reach the end of any one article.

And he warned me against choosing subjects that might embarrass 'our readership'. 'Don't touch on sex or religion until our readers know you very, very well.' Our readers never knew me well enough to take sex from me, and the nearest I got to religion was an article on Christmas.

Meanwhile, there was the Coronation of Queen Elizabeth II. Frank and I were invited to sit in Westminster Abbey among our peers – which was near the back of our respective stands, lords and ladies being separated. On the way to the Abbey in the cool June dawn, Frank's uncle Eddie Dunsany had kindly picked us up in his car. To my surprise he ordered his chauffeur to circle around Belgravia instead of driving direct to the Abbey. It transpired that his coronet had accidentally been left behind in Ireland and he was looking for the house of a nobleman of the same rank as himself whose occupant was abroad. At last he found one, rang the doorbell, borrowed the coronet and returned to our car in time for us all to sweep up to the Abbey in the full glory of the baronage.

Our children as well as ourselves were by now enjoying the fun of Uncle Eddie's eccentricities, for Bernhurst was not far from his English home at Shoreham. He used to kidnap people who trespassed in his woods and make them sit for their portraits as a penance. It was nothing to him to take on four of our children at chess. ('Beatrice, bring the four chessboards into the garden!') I remember one summer day when he took us to the Hastings Caves. 'Now children, get out your pencils and write your names on the walls,' he commanded them, leading off with a large D, to the astonishment of the children, who had been taught never to write their initials on anything except an exercise book. Lunch at the Queen's Hotel produced another delightful shock. Seeing a cruet containing table salt in front of him, he snatched it up and hurled it to the other side of the hotel dining-room where it smashed a mirror and several glasses.

There were no eccentricities that we could note at the Coronation, though in the past peers had stumbled over their robes and peeresses had dropped a jewel or two down the lavatory – if there was one. Frank was deeply moved by the Queen's youth and dignity, afterwards writing an article on it for the *Manchester Guardian*. I was disappointed that the shouts of the peerage, 'God save the Queen!', were not more full-throated. However, none of us had rehearsed and no one knew how loud or soft his or her voice would sound in that soaring edifice. Many years later, during a visit to the Crown Jewels, I learnt that the carpet in the Abbey had been laid, eccentrically enough, with the pile facing back-wards. When the Queen tried to drag the heavy gold metal fringe of her dress across it, the pile held her back. 'Get me started,' she whispered to the Archbishop, and with a holy pull she was off. At a reception in Buckingham Palace two days after the Coronation I saw her close to for the first time, and was surprised and impressed by her animation.

The reign of Elizabeth II was to inaugurate a new era. Labour and its seemingly pedestrian concern for dividing the cake into 'fair shares' was out of favour. It gave place to a Conservative spirit of enterprise that veered between merchant adventuring and buccaneering. Though I had added a small Catholic feminist society to those I supported – St Joan's Alliance – my political interests were beginning to express themselves more in writing than on the doorstep. And my journalism was steadily leading me towards the pleasures of writing for its own sake. Indirectly one hoped to be fighting on the side of the angels. But direct propaganda, such as I had sought to make readable in my election addresses, was becoming rare. An element of literary interest was invading Frank's life as much as mine. His *Born to Believe* was published a week before the Coronation. In the same year we asked Angus Wilson to drinks and T. S. Eliot to dinner. Tom Eliot had reached his so-called 'Establishment' phase but was, as always, shy; so we decided to balance Antonia with William Clark, a friend of both Eliot and Frank. Unluckily William did his job as intermediary all too well. Whenever Eliot opened his mouth to express an opinion or answer a question, William would intervene with the words, 'I think what Tom is trying to say is. . . .' We did not love William any the less for his well-intentioned interruptions but neither did we, at this dinner, get to know Tom any better.

Graham Greene came to lunch with us while Gervase Mathew and his historian brother David were staying with us at Bernhurst. I also talked to Graham while we were both staying with Catherine and Harry Walston near Cambridge. One such conversation sticks in my memory. Graham asked me whether I had ever read the works of Père de Caussade. No, I had not. In the most impressive way he then proceeded to explain de Caussade's doctrine of 'Submission to Divine Providence'. It was a case of accepting all the eventualities of life as God's will, in all circumstances. 'I can recommend it to you,' he said. 'You will find that it will solve many problems.'

Of course I knew Graham's writings even if I had hitherto missed out on de Caussade's. After reading the latter, I realized that while talking to Graham Greene I had been listening to the faith of a Catholic fatalist, who had desperately battled to substitute submission to Divine Providence for the game of Russian roulette. Over twenty years later Kitty Muggeridge, who with her husband Malcolm had become our nearest and dearest Sussex neighbours, set about translating de Caussade herself. There was nothing of the Russian roulette player in Kitty; she was a pure mystic who found 'submission' the most natural thing in the world. This in turn showed me that it was through mysticism that Graham Greene had made the transition from the unwilled, fatalistic bullet to the willed submission.

An Hellenic cruise in April 1955 helped to turn my thoughts from Fleet Street, especially as a newspaper strike was preventing my articles from being printed. My old world of history and the classics reasserted its dominion. I was among old friends – Sheila Birkenhead, Pam Berry, the Moynes, the Goodharts and their children, with Gervase Mathew, Mortimer Wheeler, Ronald Syme and Maurice Bowra as lecturers. I took Paddy with me, now just eighteen and equipped with a classical scholarship to Magdalen College, Oxford. Nicky Berry, Robin Furneaux and Paddy organized a debate on board SS *Aigaion*, the subject being 'Plato versus Aristotle'; Maurice answered the questions of North Oxford dames as assiduously as he attended to his friends, though he was once criticized on the ship's 'Suggestions' board for not circulating at dinner around the tables but sitting with his cronies; Mortimer Wheeler disappointed the Hellenic travellers only once, by being overcome with seasickness during a lecture in the stormy Adriatic. 'I don't believe he's even *trying*,' I overheard one keen lady say to another as the poor man bolted for the second time towards the exit.

The cruise had sent Maurice back, he told me afterwards, to 'the old boys and their books' – to the histories of Herodotus and Thucydides. It sent me home with a longing to write history myself. This was just as well. For when the newspaper strike came to an end, I found I had come to an end also. My two years of practising the black art with the *Express* were over.

19

Troubleshooter
· 1955–60 ·

My wish to write a book did not arrive out of the void. By 1955 I already had some slight experience of book publishing. It came about through Antonia. She had gone down from Oxford with a good degree in History and an even better prospect of making history into an important part of her life. In her first year she had written to me rather rebelliously, saying that she was not at all interested in the 'mind-training' aspects of the history school at Oxford but simply enjoyed reading history for its own sake. Through Frank's long-standing friendship with the publisher George Weidenfeld, Antonia was taken on to the editorial side of the firm and next year, 1954, she and George were both involved with my first book.

George persuaded me to bring out my *Express* family articles in book form under the title *Points for Parents*. With unbounded enthusiasm George envisaged an endless proliferation of family books – *More Points for Parents, Still More Points for Parents* – before the market was saturated. In fact the market was satisfied with quite a small print run of the first and only volume, though it was revised and reprinted fifteen years later.

This book introduced me to the horrors of book-signing in the early 1950s, a relatively new pastime for authors. Antonia nobly accompanied me to a bookshop in the Midlands, where we were visited by not one single customer. After an excruciating hour of fruitless waiting, the proprietor took pity on me and asked me to sign one copy – for himself.

George soon had another idea: that I should edit a collection of essays by distinguished Catholics on a variety of subjects ranging from Sex to the End of the World. We called it *Catholic Approaches*, to show that it was to some extent tentative, undogmatic. Frank delved into himself for 'The Catholic in Politics' and Father D'Arcy worked out a (to me) convincing approach to 'The Problem of Evil'. I did not quite convince even myself on my own piece about Catholic marriage, in which I argued for family planning only through the 'safe period'. Today I can no longer accept that argument. One cannot believe that one kind of contraception is natural and therefore permissible while all other kinds are unnatural. Or rather, I find that the words 'natural' and 'unnatural' are virtually meaningless in a world of blood-transfusions, kidney-machines, grafts and transplants. It is surely the motive that counts in contraception more than the method.

As editor, the aspect of *Catholic Approaches* that I enjoyed most was my correspondence with potential and actual contributors. I had the temerity to invite Evelyn Waugh to be one. Though I did not really expect him to accept, I was not prepared for the mixture of fantasy and hardheaded realism in his reply.

Piers Court, near Dursley, Glos.   3 March 1953

Dearest Elizabeth,

        I am glad to learn that you have a hobby to distract you from your Mau Mau activities.

I was a founder member and sometime chairman of a society called the Africa Bureau, whose aim was to work with African leaders to influence British public opinion towards liberal policies. Evelyn continued:

I do not know how you reconcile your cut rate terms [for contributors to *Catholic Approaches*] with your trade union principles. That is not the reason for my refusal to contribute. I simply have nothing to say on the subject. I am afraid you will find practising authors disappointing when it comes to theorizing. We leave that to Spender who can't put two words together.

Evelyn, of course, knew that Stephen Spender was a friend and hero of mine.

After that I may sound uncharitable if I say 'Try Speaight'. He will do just the article you require – only of course you will have to pay him at least £50.

Robert Speaight, another friend of ours and a Catholic, had made his name as Becket in Eliot's *Murder in the Cathedral*. Bobbie had not yet written his acclaimed biographies of Eric Gill and Teilhard de Chardin. Unfortunately we were able to offer our contributors no more than £25.

One valued contributor, Douglas Woodruff, found he could not get going on his chosen piece, 'The Uncommitted Mind' – until he had left England and committed himself to a cruise ship on the Red Sea, where the ideas flowed.

The most enigmatic and stimulating contributor was David Jones, the mystical painter and author of the poem 'Anathemata'. His piece for me, called 'Art & Sacrament: An Enquiry', made me feel differently ever after about the Cross. It was one of those rare essays, like the ones in Maritain's *Redeeming the Time*, that one only half understands but which is none the worse for that.

After six months we had not sold many copies. 'Plenty of time,' I said hopefully to Douglas; 'it's only been out six months.' '*Only*,' retorted Douglas. 'A book that hasn't sold by then never will sell. It's the first six months that count, the selling life of most books is *only* six months.'

Grave news indeed. I never forgot it. Successful publishing should be a sudden drama, not the slow-and-steady, gradual build-up I had imagined. Nevertheless, I was determined to pursue the idea of a third book, this time to be a full-scale biography – of Joseph Chamberlain.

'Radical Joe', as my great-uncle was known in his forties, 'Pushful Joe' in his sixties, epitomized my divided feelings about the Chamberlain–Birmingham connection. I admired the qualities that had brought him to fame: his energy, his Nonconformist reforming zeal, his ascendancy over a great manufacturing city, his personal impact on Parliament with, of all things, an orchid in his buttonhole rather than a tract in his baggage. I disliked the 'pushful' characteristics that had propelled him far beyond the limits of his own true base and his own native understanding, into the pitfalls of imperialism.

In the early twentieth century there had been the inevitable diaspora of Chamberlain descendants from Birmingham and the Midlands into the South of England. Something had been lost, and not only our parents' Midland accents. To be sure, Joe's sons Austen and Neville had both kept more than a toehold in Birmingham, but it was not enough to preserve the match-winning quality that had been their father's great asset. Austen, said Beaverbrook, 'always played the game and always lost it'. Pushful Joe would never have lost out in the Bahamas or let Hitler push him around as the unlucky Neville did. Yet in some ways, despite the obstinate weakness of the 'Appeasement' policy, I felt that Neville, my first cousin once removed, had been a more appealing man than my great-uncle. It was in this state of ambivalence that I decided to sort out myself as well as the Chamberlains.

My first visit was to my eighty-two-year-old cousin Hilda Chamberlain, great-uncle Joe's surviving daughter who lived in Odiham, Hampshire. It was a lovely June day. We sat in the garden for afternoon tea brought by a maid. The world of Birmingham and heavy industry might never have existed – except for one thing. About every twenty minutes there would be an extraordinary roar lasting long enough to break the thread of conversation completely. Cousin Hilda explained that they were testing aero-engines in some neighbouring works. During the three minutes of uproar Hilda would sit staring placidly at her herbaceous border, crowded with brilliance. 'I never need to have it weeded,' she said. 'I grow everything so close together that there is no room for weeds.' I tried this method at Bernhurst but succeeded only in creating a hideous jungle.

My reason for contacting Cousin Hilda was to satisfy my curiosity about 'Radical Joe's' alleged love affair with 'Radical Beatrice', the beautiful daughter of Mr Potter, a wealthy industrialist. When her love for Joe remained unrequited she married on the rebound Sidney Webb, who was to become king consort to this queen of state socialism.

Cousin Hilda could not but confirm the *amitié amoureuse* while insisting that Beatrice's harum-scarum habits had made her a totally unsuitable bride for the elegant Joe. She gave me a vivid picture of the young Beatrice driving with her in an open carriage to Regent's Park, hatless and hair flying. I used it in my book. After publication, Hilda wrote thanking me for the 'enthralling' story but saying she wished to add something to the passage about Joe and Beatrice. Her father's third wife, the American Mary Endicott, she told me, once asked her about Joe and Beatrice – had there been anything in it?

Hilda had replied: 'He could never have married a woman who rolled with Sidney on the carpet in front of the fire.' There was a touch of 'coarseness', she said, as well as physical untidiness, and Joseph Chamberlain was very 'fastidious'. He ordered his clothes from a London tailor long before he entered Parliament, always wore a monocle and orchid, and at political meetings dressed in a frock-coat or white tie and tails in the early days for evening meetings. 'I always respect my audience,' he would say. In retaliation, added Hilda, Beatrice described her supplanter, the neat and tidy Mary, as a mere 'Dresden shepherdess'.

The book that my venerable cousin was to find 'enthralling' was not the one I had intended to write. Five months after my visit to Odiham – five months spent in extensive reading around my subject – I approached Terence Maxwell who controlled the Chamberlain papers. Terry, married to my cousin Diane, Austen Chamberlain's daughter, was extremely helpful and sympathetic; but unfortunately the papers were not yet available. Locked in the strong room of a bank, they would remain inaccessible until such time as Birmingham University should be ready to receive them.

This was a blow. Writers who need access to essential sources for their research will recognize the dilemma. Give up? Or get on without them? Neither was an acceptable solution. I escaped from my dilemma by deciding to write on one episode in Chamberlain's career for which there seemed to be abundant original sources, instead of the whole life. It was one of those dramatic episodes where very much history is suddenly encapsulated in very little time: the Jameson Raid of 1895–6. An analogous episode was *The Marconi Scandal*. I note that its author, my friend Frances Donaldson, and I both started off our biographical careers with an 'episode'.

The Jameson Raid related to history in just the way I wanted. A buccaneering attempt by Cecil Rhodes to seize Johannesburg and so the whole of South Africa for the British Empire, it proved to be, in Winston Churchill's words, the beginning of 'these violent times'. My special interest in the Raid was sparked off by two writers: J. L. Garvin, the official biographer of Chamberlain, and a South African historian.

On one side, Garvin hotly repudiated the widespread rumour that Joseph Chamberlain, British Colonial Secretary, had connived at Rhodes's conspiracy involving Dr Jameson's fatal 'ride' across the South African border. Garvin cited the Committee of Inquiry's acquittal of Chamberlain as irrefutable evidence that he had not been an accomplice. The fact that Chamberlain himself sat on the Committee of Inquiry did not seem to arouse Garvin's suspicions.

On the other side, the South African writer, a woman, Jean van der Poel, denounced Rhodes's plot as a 'fiasco', Chamberlain as in it 'up to the neck' and the Committee of Inquiry as so much whitewashing – 'Lying-in-State at Westminster'. I appointed myself troubleshooter for Chamberlain. While unable to accept the unqualified verdict of 'not guilty', I could not believe that great-uncle Joe had lied deliberately and in such a way as to make several of his officials fall guys. Did he or did he not know what was going on?

As I saw it, he knew enough to turn a blind eye on the rest. Unofficially he knew too much for an acquittal; officially he knew too little for a conviction. According to Victorian lights, I summed up, he had not behaved dishonourably in denying collusion and I dwelt particularly on what my mother remembered of the night when the Raid news broke. 'We were dining with Papa at Moor Green Hall,' she told me, 'and suddenly Papa was summoned by Uncle Joe, who was dashing up to London' to try to stop the Raid, '*before he knew*', emphasized my loyal mother, '*whether it would succeed or not.*'

All these arguments, which most people today (1986) would regard as at best equivocal, did indeed make my head spin. The Raid became an obsession. I wriggled and writhed at every new discovery, whether on microfilm from South Africa or in the Colonial Office files. I had never read crime books for fear of getting hooked; but the detective element in the Raid story hooked me all right, and for full four years. Determined not to lose the element of mystery in the telling, I devised a complex structure to my book that sometimes foxed even myself when re-reading it. My plan was to preserve the suspense by narrating the story three times over at three levels: first, the façade as presented to the general public; second, the backstage revelations; third, the official Inquiry and verdict.

The result was reminiscent of my Bernhurst garden as initially planned by me after the war: far too many complicated borders and concealing hedges. I learnt at least one lesson from the entanglements of my *Jameson's Raid*: that chronology is the historian's best friend.

During this period I had enough airy spin-offs from my journalism to save me from going mad over Dr Jameson. The *News of the World* took me up as a kind of 'clean' writer for its centre pages, as opposed to the front-page dirt. 'Why a White Wedding?' would be the sort of thing they liked. By a definitely Freudian slip, I sometimes referred to the *News of the World* as the *Observer*, Frank said because I was secretly ashamed of writing for the former.

But in fact I was closely connected with the *Observer* and its editor David Astor through the Africa Bureau, that organ of the Mau Mau, as Evelyn Waugh liked to call it. I worked with David and the Bureau's heroic founder, the Revd Michael Scott, as well as other African experts, for many years, meeting outsize characters like Dr Hastings Banda of Nyasaland, Seretse Khama of Uganda and Sir Roy Welensky of Rhodesia. Seretse, his wife Ruth Williams and their two babies lunched with us in Chelsea, Ruth recalling that she had been evacuated as a child to Hurst Green during the war and taken to Bernhurst for some of her lessons.

It was partly because of my interest in the Bureau that I decided to study Chamberlain against the African background of the Raid. The fatal Raid had started a sinister chain of disasters that led in the end to all that the Africa Bureau stood against: the Anglo-Boer war leading to the war guilt of the victors, leading to South Africa's freedom to deal as she wished with her blacks, leading eventually to apartheid.

Committee meetings have never been my favourite occupation. If I happen to take the chair, my one ambition is to say at shorter and shorter intervals, 'Next question', whereas Frank has explained to me again and again that the good chairman allows the members to feel they have said every syllable of their say, even when the result of the discussion is a foregone conclusion. I remember Roy Harrod once confessing to an inordinate love for committees: 'My idea of heaven would be an eternal committee meeting.' For me that would be the first circle of hell. The only committees I have wholeheartedly enjoyed were those of the National Portrait Gallery and Victoria & Albert Museum, for their advisers were required to choose or reject actual pictures and works of art instead of arguing abstract points. And all this in the presence of experts like Helen Gardner, Jack Plumb and Anthony Powell, directed by John Pope-Hennessy, Roy Strong or John Hayes.

Nevertheless, my committee life in the 1950s flourished despite itself: a Youth Commission for the Labour Party, a Maternity and Allied Services Committee for the Ministry of Health. The latter was a revelation to me. In order, apparently, to bring down the disgraceful maternal and infant mortality rates, it was necessary for 'multipara' to be confined in hospital. How lucky I was to have had all my eight safely at home. I asked our family doctor about this. Would he have any fears that the hospitals might deprive him of all his interesting cases? 'No fears whatever,' he replied. 'Already I never do any real complications. Not even high forceps cases.' There was a grim incident when we were reminded that disaster can never be entirely eliminated. We learnt that one of our prospective witnesses, with a new plan for safer delivery, had died in childbirth.

Another spin-off from journalism, or rather from the fact that journalism made one known to the public, was work on the radio (still called 'the BBC' in the 1950s) and television. Except for the hanging about beforehand, I found myself as happy with the media as I was allergic to committee work. On committees the anchor man is the solemn polymath who knows everything and obviates the need for an encyclopaedia. In 'Any Questions', he or she was the one who could be relied on to make the jokes. Robert Boothby MP was our anchor man in our early days. I remember his only once missing fire, and that was at a charity ball for New Bridge, an ex-prisoners' society founded by Frank and some friends. Bob was asked to say a few words. With great geniality he began, 'There is no audience I like so much as a captive audience. That is why prisoners are the best audience in the world.' No laughter. The ex-prisoners present looked black as thunder.

At a later period I regarded Malcolm Muggeridge as our best anchor man in 'Any Questions'. Over the thirty years since I have known him well, he has never failed to spark off something. I take an instance at random from my diary of 1958:

September 18th: We discussed AID [artificial insemination by donor]. Malcolm thinks it is wrong but does not regard it as adultery. 'You can't very well cite a test-tube,' he said, 'and in fact you can't have adultery without what Beatrice Webb called "inter*curse*".'

The pleasure of being an 'Any Questions' panellist was increased by the company on one's journeys to the West Country. On a single occasion, however, my pleasure was less than total. I was travelling by train with Tom Driberg, an old friend, member of the Labour Party and also an Anglo-Catholic. 'Begin all your answers* to questions with the word "Well",' he advised me. 'It sounds more relaxed.' After consulting the *New Statesman* and *Spectator* and deciding on the likely questions, Tom fell asleep. Suddenly he awoke with a strangled cry and gazed with horror into the corridor. 'They . . . they . . .' he muttered. 'I thought they were after me.' Then he apologized. 'It was a very frightening dream.' I guessed that 'they' were the police, who in his dream had been about to arrest him on a homosexual charge. That look of abject terror on the face of a fellow human being, however misguided he might be, was infinitely shocking and caused me years later to welcome the Wolfenden Report.

When television came along I took part in an entertaining series, as well as the serious Brains Trusts. The series was called 'Who Said That?', a game of guessing quotations in which Gilbert Harding was our star performer. I only once saw him indulging in his notorious rudeness, and that was when he was offered the wrong kind of soda water to drink. On a dismal day I agreed to take part in a general knowledge quiz game – a team of mature highbrows (Veronica Wedgwood, Marghanita Laski and myself) versus three potential young masterminds. We were beaten hollow. Laski was not too bad, Wedgwood fair, Pakenham hopeless. Out of nine questions I got only one right – 'What is amber?' – having chanced to turn it up the night before in *Pears Encyclopaedia*. I learnt my lesson – never to attempt a quiz again.

I did not last long on the BBC Brains Trust either. On about the third week, the question was put: 'What do the panel believe is the purpose of life?' The majority of replies amounted to some form of 'self-fulfilment'. I disagreed, and with the enthusiasm of a still recent Catholic convert, suggested that every life should be lived '*ad majorem Dei gloriam*' – to the greater glory of God. My answer sank into a pool of shocked silence, as if I had used obscene language. I was not invited again. Afterwards I decided that it was Julian Huxley, our panel scientist, who had blackballed me, not out of personal spite – we got on well – but because he felt that a practising Catholic was incompatible with the enlightened self-image our Brains Trust had been trying to create.

Two paradoxical occurrences were to follow. Soon after I was dropped from the Brains Trust, a good Catholic lady reprimanded me: 'You must learn not to mention the Church in public; it does *positive harm*' – a new version, I realized, of Evelyn's Catacomb theory ('Get thee to a catacomb'). But in the next decade, to my amazement, who should write an introduction to Père Teilhard de Chardin's book on evolution, *The Phenomenon of Man*, but the great Julian Huxley himself.

The real age of the Brains Trust was during the war. Philosopher C. E. M. Joad ('It depends what you mean by . . .') made his name on the weekly broadcast from London. In order to raise money for a Forces' Comforts Fund we invited him to Oxford for a Brains Trust on which the other two panellists would be an Agony Aunt and 'Bert', Duke of Marlborough.

'I will come', replied Joad to Frank, 'provided you arrange for me to spend the night at Blenheim.' Frank was astonished. What was Joad, that world-famous agnostic-socialist, up to, trying to have truck with a palace? Nevertheless, for the sake of the Forces' comfort, Frank passed on Joad's request as tactfully as possible and received an affirmative reply from the Duke. The Brains Trust went off well. And the night at Blenheim Palace? 'How did you get on?' Frank asked Joad next morning. 'It was perfect. He behaved like a Duke. Treated me like dirt.'

I expected 1956 to be a purely domestic year for us. Antonia had become engaged to Hugh Fraser MP and they were married on 25 September in the Church of the Assumption, a little Catholic church once much favoured by foreign exiles in London. I forgot Hugh's intense Conservatism in his wit and high spirits and in the romance of his Highland ancestry – all loyalties and executions, rather like the Queen Mother's – and in any case he had had an uncle, Charles Lister, who founded the Oxford Labour Club while at Balliol and was one of the 'golden generation' to be killed in the Great War. Hugh's maternal grandfather, Lord Ribblesdale, was said to have been *the* handsomest man in England, and I thought Hugh was too, when he stood up in the aisle six feet four inches tall, in his kilt and his frills and the dirk in his stocking. Antonia wore a white organza dress and Mary Queen of Scots satin cap and pearls – a glimpse of the future – but was not attended by Judith, Rachel and Catherine as bridesmaids, to my surprise. 'I've been a member of a big family all my life,' Antonia said. 'Now I want to stand alone.'

Hugh's nephew Kim was playing the bagpipes in the street when the bridal procession emerged. We held the reception in Fishmongers' Hall. A romantic photograph of Antonia looking remarkably like Mary Stuart was taken by Cecil Beaton at the foot of Blackfriars Bridge. Frank had asked Clem Attlee to propose the toast of the bride and bridegroom. Clem did so, in a memorably short speech: 'Prettiest wedding I can remember. Good luck to them.'

My next vivid memory should have been of our Silver Wedding day on 3 November, a mere thirty-nine steps away from the Fraser marriage. But meanwhile a cloud no bigger than Nasser's hand, the hand with which he took back or seized the Suez Canal (whichever way you looked at it) had plunged us all into the fiercest crisis of the mid century.

It certainly overshadowed the evening party we gave for our friends in Chelsea. As a very old friend, we had invited Quintin Hailsham. He was now First Lord of the Admiralty, just as Frank had been five years before when the Mussadeq trouble broke out in the Gulf. Quintin arrived early and left before the party began. He was in a state of great distress. 'His' ships were at that moment, as far as we knew, still ploughing towards the scene of battle, Alexandria. He paced up and down our drawing-room. I said that in the very act of accepting a Service ministry he had automatically shouldered responsibility for casualties in a possible war. He refused to accept this as an answer to his problems. After about twenty minutes he returned to Whitehall.

Rumours were flying around regarding collusion between the Conservative Government, Israel and France – at first denied, later substantiated. Of course I believed them to be true from the word go. I was not in the thick of my researches on the Jameson Raid for nothing.

Quintin suffered in his spirit. Another Conservative close friend suffered in his spirit and also in his career. Sir Edward Boyle, Financial Secretary to the Treasury, resigned. He lived a mile from us at the other end of Hurst Green, so we saw a good deal of him. Courageous and fair-minded with a powerful brain, he won the devotion of his personal friends and his Birmingham constituency. Indeed many of us marked him out as a future prime minister – until after Suez. For a time Edward returned to the Conservative Government. Indeed Malcolm Muggeridge criticized him just over a year after Suez for being an inverted Omar Khayyam: 'He went back by the same door as out he went.' But finally Edward came to see no future for his essentially liberal attitudes in contemporary Conservative politics. He retired to academic life, as an outstandingly successful vice-chancellor of Leeds University until his premature death. His constant mixing with and personal knowledge of the students enabled him to sail through the university problems of the troubled 1960s.

One advantage of a big family is that the pressures of the outside world on the parents can never suppress the family's insistent demands. Suez may have overshadowed our Silver Wedding, but in the year following Suez my attention was firmly riveted to the arrival of my first grandchild. I had never seen the actual coming into the world of a baby, since modern methods of watching the birth of one's own child had not yet been developed. Frank was ahead of me in that respect. He had seen nearly all our children born. So naturally I accepted eagerly when Antonia asked me to be present at the birth. I was summoned from Bernhurst one Sunday afternoon and saw Rebecca born at 5.40 next morning, in the Fraser flat in Eaton Square.

The first fleeting vision of a newborn human face was something so unexpected that for a few seconds the whole world seemed to stand still. One perhaps imagined a tiny crumpled red face all puckered up in the agonizing effort to give the first cry. That was not at all the picture. Before Rebecca had drawn her first breath, her face had a statuesque beauty as if carved in marble, every feature calm and immobile in static perfection. I felt that my granddaughter was still trailing clouds of glory, but motionless clouds as if from a strange, white, wraithlike world. The pause was over in a flash. Next moment the breathless, disembodied beauty passed, little human Rebecca was screaming loudly, her face flooded with colour, and all the joyful bustle that follows the instant of birth had begun.

Frank, who had kept Hugh company in the dining-room next door, was very soon introducing himself on political platforms: 'I used to be known as Lady Pakenham's husband, now it's as Rebecca's grandfather.'

Later on we had a photograph taken of 'Four generations': my mother, myself and Antonia, all smiling at Rebecca who miraculously smiled back – at her great-grandparent's hat. Judith, however, now seventeen, declined to meet her niece except privately. 'I do not worship at crowded altars.'

She was working for her Oxford entrance, having found liberation from school at Perugia university and a wild journey around Sicily. She was in the full flight of youthful poetry writing. Nevertheless, she consented to worship, coolly, at the altar of Majesty. A 'reluctant debutante', she was one of the last to be presented before the ritual was abolished.

It was in the following year, 1958, that Frank and I were invited to dine with Queen Elizabeth II in Buckingham Palace, first at a small party, one of a series devised for the young Queen and her consort to meet 'interesting' people from all walks of life; then at a state banquet in honour of President Heuss of West Germany. After the former I wrote my impressions:

A rather low-key start on Prince Charles and inoculations, in which the Queen ended by saying in the saddest voice, 'Plague is another horrible illness.' Then we got on to her TV Christmas message. She suddenly came alive and discussed it in an amusing & vivid way. She described the rivalry between sound & sight producers (the latter only in Britain), the endless rehearsals and failures over her make-up ('The first time, my white skin & broad jaw made my face come out like a huge white plate with two dark cavities containing black boot buttons; my hair was parted in the centre, & looked like a white line down a main-road. It had to be blacked in & yellow paint daubed on my cheeks & the tip of my nose . . .'). I could tell she has a real gift for anecdote. The oddest thing she told us was that on the following Sunday at Sandringham Church instead of the usual thousand sightseers there were – ten thousand! She had become more than a Queen – a TV personality.

I went on to describe Frank's discussion with Prince Philip on the same occasion about press interference.

Frank defended the press, saying certain well-known people were glad to get good publicity, but then objected when it was inconvenient. P.P. 'Exactly who are you thinking of?' F. 'My wife. She was burgled & resented 9 press men ringing up for stories. But she's glad to get a good TV press!' An enthralling evening.

Today Frank would take a sterner view of press harassment.

The state dinner was an extremely grand affair, in no way marred by one or two untoward incidents. We began with turtle soup in gold soup plates. Suddenly from the infinitely remote distances of the gilt ceiling a dead bluebottle fell silently into the centre of my soup. I admired the scarlet-coated footman whose expression did not change when I showed it to him. As silently as the bluebottle had arrived, he stretched out his white-gloved hand and removed the plate.

When we rose to drink the loyal toast I found that Lord Airlie was standing on my dress. My alternatives were to drink the toast in a crouching position like a dwarf or to ask him to move off. I did the latter. He laughed heartily, saying that the lady on his other side had once been similarly pinned down by the Archbishop of Canterbury; everyone had thought she was drunk.

After dinner the Queen Mother talked feelingly about 'waiting for baby' – and ten days later Rebecca's sister Flora was born. Her christening took place on Frank's fifty-third birthday in the Church of the Assumption where her parents had been married, but not without a brief argument with the priest about her name. He claimed that Flora was pagan, not a saint's name. On the contrary, Flora was a genuine *Christian* name, replied our friend Father Caraman, there being two Floras in the Church's calendar. (Having won their battle for 'Flora', her parents saw no reason to give her a second name, but Flora herself was later to add the name of Elizabeth to her own.) At her sister's christening Rebecca was in my charge. Her main object was to grab the lighted votive candles. 'Gamgee, walky! Cangles!'

During these years I only stirred from London and Sussex for electioneering or television. I never went abroad, as Frank hated it. But he made one exception: to visit Nicko and Mary Henderson at their diplomatic post in Vienna. On Frank's last evening (I was staying on for a couple of days), Nicko took us to dine in the cellar-restaurant made famous by Graham Greene's *The Third Man*. I had Frank's passport with mine in my handbag and forgot to give it back to him. We put him on his sleeper, in which he would be carried home across the frontiers of various foreign territories, including the Russian zone. Or would he? The extraordinary thing was that he got through passport-less. True, he remembered certain visitations throughout the night and dreamlike voices making unreasonable demands. Each time he turned over in his bunk, grunted and went to sleep again. There was still something in being the phlegmatic Anglo-Irishman.

Nicko was our son Michael's godfather, and we were encouraged by him to think that Michael might one day be suited to the Foreign Office. His phenomenal memory had enabled him to win a scholarship to Ampleforth like his brothers. He was no highbrow; he worked hard in the term and rested very hard in the holidays. He had a tidy mind and a tidy bedroom – the latter a rarity in our family.

It was through the insistence of Catherine, now thirteen, that I consented to leave Bernhurst for a fortnight in 1959 and 1960. 'You ought to give us culture holidays,' she said. On our first culture holiday there was a veil of rain between us and Tintern Abbey but I had brought my Wordsworth in my mac and was determined to read them the Ode. As we five – four children and I – crouched under one umbrella on a sopping hillside, I wondered how to persuade them to listen to poetry. Then I saw the solution. Rachel should read it. She read beautifully and we all listened under the dripping umbrella and stared down at the ruins of Tintern in the valley below.

After this success, I made Catherine keep the diary of next year's visit to Wales. From these two experiences I learnt one secret of such holidays for children: they, the children, must create Do-it-Yourself tours. The four children took turns in choosing the culture for the day. Michael and Kevin went for the castles, Rachel and Catherine for the cathedrals.

Thomas had been working on the *Times Educational Supplement* since 1958, though his passion for education was not obsessive like his passion for travel. He and five Oxford friends had toured Greece and Yugoslavia in an old taxi, and his nine months exploring Ethiopia, 1955–6, had resulted in his first book, *The Mountains of Rasselas*. His formal education had terminated in a degree in Mods and Greats, won in the teeth of many counter-attractions. After his finals Frank and I went to Oxford for his farewell party, celebrated with Mark Girouard, Lawrence Kelly and others in his digs on the Isis above Folly Bridge. Frank was shocked to see that his eldest son's hair had turned white – 'the result of overwork', said Thomas lugubriously. Fortunately I noticed a splash of silver spray inside his ear. After dinner the room was cleared for a party by throwing the dining-table into the river, where it instantly whirled away downstream. Thomas had to swim for it.

While in Ethiopia he had received regular letters from me which, surprisingly, he preserved. They kept him in touch with home problems; indeed he was to describe me at that period as troubleshooter for the family.

Kevin's class of eight year olds had been set an essay on 'My Father: Appearance, Character, Occupation'. When it came to 'Character', Kevin wrote: 'My father is weak-minded.' After much probing I discovered that he meant Frank was gentle, not strict. Judith and Rachel, I wrote in a moment of anxiety, thought about nothing but clothes. (A few years later they were to be immersed in the world of books.) I discussed with Thomas where to get his travel articles published. The *News Chronicle* took them and Julian Huxley told me, at our Brains Trust, that 'they are the best things out of Abyssinia since Evelyn Waugh'. He also told me a strange story about Evelyn that I passed on to Thomas: 'A woman once wrote to congratulate Julian on having become a Catholic. He replied that he had not, to which she retorted, "a friend of mine tells me she was present *in person* when you and Miss Evelyn Waugh were received together into the bosom of the Church".'

In the new year of 1956 I had advised Thomas not to leave the Middle East as long as the wanderlust held him:

Once you get home, & a job & a wife & a child & a car & a desk, you will have said good-bye to wandering. I often wish I had wandered further than Stoke when I had the chance.

. . . .

People keep asking me when you are coming home, but I just say *Never* – until you arrive in 20 years time with your children & children's children, aunts, uncles & cousins: all black.

Jameson's Raid was published on 29 January 1960. There was no stampede to buy, but the generous reviewers more than made up for the cautious purchasers. There was also the bonus of unexpected anecdotes picked up on one's way to publication. I was sitting next to Lord Stansgate, father of Tony Benn, at a dinner in the Lords when he suddenly made it crystal clear why my great-uncle Joe had not married

Beatrice Webb. 'When she and Sidney got married,' said Lord Stansgate, 'she said to me: "We have decided that Sidney shall make the big decisions and I shall make the small decisions. And I shall decide which are the big decisions."'

Most of the reviewers did not feel that Chamberlain's 'honour' had been saved by his great-niece, though my attempts at salvage had been 'scholarly' and 'readable'. I was thrilled when Alan Taylor chose *Jameson* as his book of the year and when Robert Blake described my chapter on the Colonial Secretary's character as the best pen portrait of Chamberlain he knew.

My experience of research, gained from *Jameson's Raid*, was to be invaluable for my next book. I learnt how to work on private papers and in public libraries and record offices: never to enter these (especially the British Library) without having done one's homework thoroughly first. I learnt to look for the cover-up in history.

The greatest bonus of all literary work is the new friends one acquires through correspondence and discussion. During my research on the Raid I got to know the Haleys (he was editor of *The Times* and let me into their archives). William John Haley was to propound the most interesting explanation of the Queen's 'boredom', as described in my diary for 18 February 1958. 'The Queen was not bored,' said he, 'but just taking a "moment of repose" as many public figures do, later returning, like boxers, refreshed to the ring.'

I also met Robert Rhodes James through *Jameson*. He first pointed out to me that Disraeli had once described my Birmingham ancestors as the 'Shopocracy'!

I was glad that my mother lived to read my book. She celebrated her eighty-seventh birthday on 23 May 1960, and died after an active day in her garden on 10 June. She was not upset by my strictures on her uncle Joe, having crossed swords with him herself as a young medical student in London. Her first cousin, Neville Chamberlain, was the one she really liked. Criticisms of his Appeasement policy were painful to her. After all, when they were both young in Birmingham, Neville had fallen in love with her and asked her to marry him. One wonders what changes there would have been had he found his support in the steady illumination of Katie Chamberlain instead of in the fey sparkle of Annie Cole.

Two other literary ventures came my way about the same time as *Jameson* was published. Newnes, mainly the publishers of magazines, commissioned a 'Pakenham Party Book' to which all the female Pakenhams contributed one way or another, Catherine painting an alluring frontispiece of a birthday party, with considerable help from

Charlotte Fawcett. I offered the book as a present to Evelyn and Laura Waugh, who by now had six children. (I was indebted to him for a query and correction in my *Raid*.) He wrote back:

4 January 1960   *Combe Florey*

Thank you for your charming letter and the promise of your Party Book. . . . Laura has never given a children's party in her life. Pray God it does not move her to do so. . . . It was nice of you & Frank to go to [his son] Bron's party. I feared press photographers – apparently there were none and I could have gone safely.

It is very interesting that you are sending a boy [Michael] to Cambridge. I should never have conceived such a thing possible 20 years ago but now I believe it is the better place. Oxford has gone wrong. Do you know what the young call Maurice? – 'Old Tragic'.

Evelyn then went on, characteristically, to consider some other alleged failures, implying that he liked them all the better for it.

It has been a bad year for the old literary hacks – Elizabeth Bowen, John Betjeman, Leslie Hartley down & out of the race; Tony Powell & Nancy Mitford just clinging to their saddles but out of control. And now Graham Greene has written a most distressing work.

Two months later, in March, Evelyn invited us to stay.

I shall be at Downside on Wednesday in Holy Week, until Easter morning. Pius XII's new routine for the Triduum leaves appalling longueurs. Do persuade Frank to leave his bank and shrive himself there.

Frank was chairman of the National Bank. He was to spend the Triduum with Evelyn. It was said that on the occasions when Father D'Arcy spent an Easter Triduum at Combe Florey he would absolve Evelyn from his usual Lenten vow to give up alcohol. Such was the intolerably gloomy effect on Evelyn of water.

Evelyn concluded this letter to me by inviting us to stay any time within the next six months: 'I remain immovable until October for fear of the Americans.'

He was a model godfather to Catherine, sending her many of his books and giving her an occasional penance, as when she refused, at five, to sit beside him at lunch. But he was pleased that she said at the same age: 'The Holy Ghost's coming down tomorrow' – tomorrow being Whit Sunday – 'He must be very excited.' She received from Evelyn some typical advice when she wrote at sixteen asking what career she should choose. Secretary? Journalist? Doctor? He rejected them all. 'Why not be a nun?'

Three years later I was questioning him myself, as I sometimes did, on religious matters. What did he think about Pope John XXIII's recently published diary? He replied:

It was exactly what a thousand priests in search of perfection might have kept (and indeed do keep). Its chief interest was that it exploded all that air balloon about the 'Johannine Revival'. He was a good old man who got better. He had no conception of the Pandora's box which his Council would open. This comes out most clearly in the French book of anecdotes I reviewed at the same time. The best (which I can't at the moment find) when asked about that Jesuit archeologist whom the Americans admire [Père Teilhard de Chardin]: 'He is French. Why worry about such things? Teach the *Pater*, the *Ave*, the *Credo*. Basta.' That was Pope John whom the conspirators are trying to inflate into a colleague.

. . . . . .

P.S. Miss Foyle, having given a luncheon in aid of French letters has, I see, got the Cardinal to lunch with her in aid of Pope John's humble, simple, conventional book.

My other literary venture was on the *Sunday Times*. The editor, Harry Hodson, whose intelligence was subtle and incisive, summoned me to his office one day early in 1960. He proposed that I should write articles on family affairs myself and also commission them from other experts – in a ratio of about one to two. Nothing could have suited me better. Those weekly articles for the *Express* in the 1950s had been a fine training in speed and brevity but facing a 'D-Day', so to speak, every week had become a strain. Harry Hodson's idea would involve less pressure and more work with other interested people which I enjoyed.

For the second time in my life I hurried to Fenwick's of Bond Street and bought a smart black suit, appropriate, I thought, to my future desk in New Printing House Square. At the end of a constructive interview I ventured to glance around and ask, 'My desk? Where will it be?' Harry looked blank. I saw too late to save myself from appearing a fool that there was to be no desk. I was to write as usual from home and in fact I have never in my life worked in an office, an experience I would have liked to have had but am grateful for having missed.

My career on the *Sunday Times* lasted for two years without a hitch. They even put my photograph into a glossy brochure describing the paper's staff. Then in February 1962 came the beginning of my downfall. It was due to the bad timing of one of my experts' contributions. Having launched Dr Ann Dally, Claire Rayner and other notable writers, I failed to get wind of the fact that the *Observer* was contemplating a rival family column of their own, to be introduced with a fanfare by no less a guru of the nursery than the great Dr Spock himself. As ill-luck would have it, on the very first Sunday that Dr Spock appeared in the *Observer*, I invited Harry Secombe to conduct our column in the *Sunday Times*. The enthusiastic comedian had been following our articles and asked to be allowed to write a piece on the pleasures of having a second child. There was nothing wrong with the piece; but to put up Secombe against Spock, however inadvertently, was an affront to the *gravitas* of our newspaper.

I could not blame either of the Harrys. Harry Hodson let my articles run on until July. My final piece was a shorty called 'The First Job'. Then I was handed my cards.

This was to be my last long-term connection with a newspaper. I had learnt another lesson. The professional antennae necessary to a first-rate columnist were never likely to be sufficiently developed in me. It was a pity. However, I was already steeped in another enterprise – neither a shorty nor my 'first job' of its kind, but something new to me in its historic scale and human fascination: the life of Queen Victoria.

20

The Scribbling Sixties
· 1960–6 ·

There is a critical time for biographers when they are about to give birth to one book and are trying to get pregnant again with the next. I know that the metaphor does not really work, yet that is how it feels with books, at any rate when one is in full creative spate.

One hands over the finished manuscript to the publisher and perhaps nine months will pass with nothing to do but correct galley and page proofs, assemble source notes (admittedly a lengthy task since a handful of delinquent references, however carefully pinned down three years before, will always escape and produce mayhem at the last minute), collect illustrations and perhaps do one's own index. (I did my index for the *Raid* but never again.) However hard one tries to re-write the whole book at the galley stage, the publishers will prevent one. Thus there will be very many pre-publication hours in which one has nothing to do but think about what to do next.

In my case, while the *Raid* was nearing birth, I had formulated an idea for the biography I wanted to write. It must be about a historical woman, someone like Flora Shaw in the *Raid*, who became a top journalist of *The Times* but could not be categorized as a feminist. Nicko Henderson's mother, Faith, a member of the Bloomsburys who had known Flora, told me that she was 'Victorian to her fingertips, with all their strength and humbug'. I wanted a woman who was not content with the embargoes put upon Victorian females and yet found herself working successfully within the system. Florence Nightingale would have fitted well but my friend Cecil Woodham-Smith had 'done' her brilliantly already; the suffragettes were too extreme for the subtle contrasts I envisaged; the papers of Flora Shaw were not available. Suddenly my agent Graham Watson, a true man of letters, said 'Why not Queen Victoria herself?'

Why not indeed. Though I had read no full-scale assessment of her since Lytton Strachey's biography, I had a distinct remembrance of something unusual, something attractive, something critical and not easily fudged in the character displayed there. I had a suspicion that the

Queen was not such an abysmally solemn, unqualified Victorian as legend (not Strachey) portrayed. David Cecil's life of Lord Melbourne, giving many hints of the other Victoria, may have been at the back of my mind.

It was not long before I was in a fever of impatience to explore these Victorian depths, murky or clear as they might prove. There was one obstacle: the problem of 'getting inside the Royal Archives' – an absolute necessity if I was to write a worthwhile new life of this monarch.

The Royal Archives at Windsor were hedged about like a sleeping princess with ways of keeping you out. True, you did not need to be a prince of the blood or indeed blue-blooded in any way to break through, but neither could you be a student, hoping to make your name by rummaging in royal cupboards. You could not be a journalist or even a writer of learned articles but must be an author with at least one book to your credit, and this book had to be passed as satisfactory. You had to request permission to research on one complete subject, not to go snippeting around in the Archives for desultory information on this or that. Nor could two people be admitted to the Archives to work on the same subject at the same time. A biography of Queen Victoria would be the right sort of subject. Provided I was the right sort of author.

With some trepidation I sent in *Jameson's Raid* as my sole credential to Martin Charteris, at that time the Queen's assistant private secretary and a great friend. (It was Martin who had warned me of the thorn hedge around the Archives.) I wondered how my account of the Raid scandal would fare inside the Round Tower where the Archives were lodged. My attitude to the Raid had not been the official Conservative one, nor indeed was I a Conservative, but the socialist wife of a member of the Opposition front bench in the House of Lords.

Whoever Martin passed my book to was without prejudice. *Jameson's Raid* got through. I could research a new life of Queen Victoria. I was in the Archives.

How that phrase 'in the Archives' echoes in one's memory. I remember meeting Norman St John Stevas for the first time at a party and discovering that we were both fans of Queen Victoria. 'I've got a pair of HM's stockings,' boasted Norman. 'Black silk with white soles.' I countered with an original photograph of HM in her donkey-cart. Suddenly a chill thought struck me. Norman knew too much about HM.

'Are you by any chance writing a life of Queen Victoria?'

'Yes. Are you?'

'Yes.' I was appalled. Then came the saving question.

'Are you in the Archives?'

'No. Are you?'

'Yes.' That was it. Norman was prevented by me from becoming the best biographer of Queen Victoria up to date and became instead a Tory Leader of the House of Commons and wittiest of politicians.

Starting on 5 May 1960 I was to drive to and from Windsor twice a week during termtime for the next three years. There were two things that made my researches particularly rewarding, quite apart from the contents of Queen Victoria's letters and journals.

First, the stimulus to the historical imagination of working in the familiar surroundings of my subject, hearing the sounds she heard, seeing the sights she saw. I would park my car under the southern bastion of the Castle, collect my huge brass key from the lodge opposite the Round Tower and let myself into the Round Tower itself. A long climb up steep stone steps (a panting pause halfway up) would bring me to the small door leading into the series of rooms which house the Archives – one large library, several librarians' rooms and some very small reading-rooms.

The Archives' door when unlocked let out a waft of warm air carrying the nostalgic smells of gas and books. As I sat endlessly reading and note-taking in my comfortable little cell, with its square of Victorian carpet, coal fire in black-leaded grate and narrow slit window, I would half-hear a military band practising in the quadrangle below. Immediately I would think of the forty-two-year-old Queen Victoria listening, heart-broken, to the same poignant music while Albert was dying in the Blue Room nearby. Or, hearing the distant footsteps of tourists tramping past the Archives' door and onwards to the Round Tower's roof, I would think of the young Victoria and Albert scampering up to watch the flames of a fire twenty miles away in London. I was lucky enough to reach the account of Albert's death in Victoria's journal on the actual anniversary of the event, 14 December 1861. By chance the weather on that day in 1962 was exactly the same as the weather described by Victoria 101 years before: brilliant sun and sparkling frost. From the moment of Albert's typhoid onwards, I felt myself beginning to identify with her, and Frank wryly called my attention to a new concern for his own health. I could understand the contrary pulls in Queen Victoria between her family and her public life. In her, of course, it was all stepped up: she had ten times more public life than I had and one more child – her nine to my eight – though she also had more help in the home.

I must have been working nearly a year in my small room when a major improvement came about. For several days running I had heard through the partition wall a voice in continuous conversation, apparently with itself. At last I tumbled to the obvious: someone was dictating on a machine. A great hope dawned. Could it be possible that tape recorders were permitted in the Royal Archives? Hitherto I had been copying every word I needed from Queen Victoria's journals by hand. Progress had been slow. And extremely tiring.

Robin (now Sir Robert) Mackworth-Young, the Royal Librarian, promptly gave me permission and next day I bought a tape recorder – my first – and advanced upon Windsor with my fabulous new time-saving equipment. It was cumbersome and heavy but it was modern technology. It was also AC – alternating current. I switched it on and had been recording for a few minutes when I noticed a curious smell – then a plume of blue smoke: my modern technology was on fire.

In my ignorance I had failed to find out whether the Round Tower was equipped with modern AC or with the old-fashioned DC, direct current. Of course it was DC; indeed I doubt whether it had been rewired since its installation. I was lucky only to burn out my machine and not to burn down the Round Tower and all it contained.

When I last visited the Round Tower everything was changed again: no more coal fires, no more DC and no more warm drifts of gas as one unlocked the door in the echoing stone staircase.

I had one other hiccup while working at Windsor, a hiccup that Cecil Woodham-Smith was to share with me. Neither of us could sit on the uncompromisingly straight-backed chairs without getting acute lumbago. Cecil had the nerve to ask for an armchair; I bought a low camp chair designed for picnics from a Windsor shop during my lunch break, and worked comfortably with my papers spread around me on the floor and Queen Victoria's journals on my lap.

The fate of Queen Victoria's journals was a mixed one. They were preserved, but only in the sense of being copied from the originals by her daughter Princess Beatrice. Hers was an extraordinary work of filial piety. On and on the diaries flow through eighty volumes of exercise books in a placid stream of blue ink, all in the same regular, readable handwriting, without a flaw, without a blot, without mis-spelling or crossing-out. But it was also a work of filial destruction. On the orders of her mother she had removed everything that in the originals struck her as unsuitable for preservation. Hence no references in the copies I read to the more violent family storms, scarcely any references to John Brown. Considering the deep interest of what Princess Beatrice left untouched, I never cease to regret what she expurgated.

One batch of originals, however, survived the censorship of the Princess. This was the young Victoria's most touching and vivid diary of her childhood up to her marriage. Even from this account one page has been cut, as if with a knife, but happily restored. Without these original diaries we should never have guessed how stubbornly Victoria battled against the troubles of her youth, nor how desperately she needed the haven of Albert's love. It has been my constant experience that the less we are kept in the dark about the lives of Queen Victoria and her descendants, the more human and in many cases admirable they become.

For a time after her death Victoria was preserved on an absurd pedestal. Iconoclasm inevitably followed. Today, with ever more research, she is again recognized as one of our most fascinating monarchs; not a monarch in monochrome but a woman with all the contradictions and quirkiness, the delights and surprises of our own grandmothers and great-aunts.

I regard James Pope-Hennessy's *Queen Mary* as the great breakthrough in royal research. This was brought home to me on two occasions. First, James invited me to lunch with him at Chichio's in Kensington Church Street as soon as he heard I was 'in the Archives'. His generous object was to tell me about his own experiences in that privileged position and to advise me how to proceed. It amounted to a warning against sending in my manuscript chapter by chapter, as I proposed to do, for perusal at Windsor and the necessary blue pencil. 'Chapter by chapter's no good,' said James. 'They'll get a piecemeal picture not a true panorama of your book and also they'll feel bound to make *some* alterations in every chapter as they receive it.' I took James's advice, and as a result only two sentences were blue-pencilled in the whole of my 577-page book.

Second, James had pioneered outspokenness in respect of royal sex in ways that were to benefit all his successors. At one point my account of Queen Victoria's compassion towards a young German cousin who was seduced by her ducal parents' footman was queried. I was able to point out that the episode had already been published in Pope-Hennessy's *Queen Mary*.

Censorship eventually was the least of my problems. Far more serious was Queen Victoria's handwriting. This paradoxical old lady, who made such a fuss about her secretaries' writing, produced among her own innumerable letters examples of sublime illegibility. Either she failed to form her letters properly or chose pale blue ink on the same coloured blue paper, or economized by writing on both sides of paper so thin that the ink came through. My indispensable aid in handwriting crises was always Robin Mackworth-Young. He had already grasped the 'pattern' of the Queen's writing (bad writing has its pattern as well as good; one has to learn it), but even he was sometimes temporarily flummoxed by the execrable examples of the royal script I brought to him.

The key to success, he explained to me, was never to pore over an unintelligible phrase – that only made it worse – but to prop up the letter in which it featured on one's desk and take a casual glance at it every now and then. Taken unawares, so to speak, it would sooner or later yield up its secret. This method, together with my own additions (inspecting the letter upside down, sideways or in the mirror), was to stand me in good stead when I came to study the equally appalling handwriting of the Duke of Wellington.

Wellington's attitude to this failing was exactly the opposite to Queen Victoria's. Whereas she had no idea how badly she wrote in old age and would have been shocked to discover, the Duke faced his frailty with characteristically sardonic wit. When a letter he had written to one of his ministers was returned to him for decipherment, he sent it back again with the message: 'It was my duty to write that letter. It is your duty to read it!'

A minor problem was how to satisfy my visual imagination. In order to enter into another human life I have to follow as far as possible in his or her footsteps, look at the houses, gardens, scenery they knew. With Queen Victoria I was steeped in her surroundings thanks to Queen Elizabeth II's private secretary. Michael (later Lord) Adeane enabled me to see Windsor Great Park with all its 'cottages' and especially the royal mausoleum at Frogmore. This was such an intimate part of Victoria's love, faith and culture that I needed to visit it quietly and virtually alone, rather than with the public who were admitted in large numbers on one day a year. Among the crowds I might have been tempted to ridicule its Victorian appetite for intricate ornamentation; alone, I found even its excesses touching.

Helen (Lady) Adeane and I went together to Osborne House, where the beauty of Albert's *blicks* through the trees and the jollity of Victoria's little beach demonstrated to me exactly why it had become their 'dear' marine home. Part of the house was now a convalescent home for officers, and after my book was published a friend, himself a convalescent, told me of a new legend that had sprung up. He overheard one sightseer saying to another: 'See those men over there in wheelchairs? They're the illegitimate descendants of Prince Albert!'

Curiously enough, I had tea with a delightful old lady who cheerfully believed that Albert himself was illegitimate. She admitted, however, that it was only a palace rumour. She was the daughter of Lord Stamfordham, the old Queen's private secretary and the mother of Michael Adeane. A picture of Queen Victoria was painted by her very different from the usual gloomy one. The smiling old Queen would invite the palace children to take a good look at her in all her finery before she set off downstairs for a state banquet.

Thanks to Martin and Gay Charteris I explored the romance of Deeside, Balmoral and Lochnagar. One could see exactly why Victoria dragged her family up Mount Lochnagar twice a year (and why Prince Charles was to weave a fairy-tale around it for his young brothers). We stayed in the long stone cottage on Loch Muick where Victoria would retreat attended by her ladies and John Brown. It was quite clear to me that nothing peculiar could have gone on there between her and Brown without her ladies knowing.

I made a special study of Victoria's alleged involvement in psychic research, particularly in relation to John Brown's second sight and mediumistic powers. Apart from Brown's claim to second sight – by no means rare in the Highlands – I found the whole rigmarole, involving Victoria's scientific spiritualistic interests *before* Albert's death and her attempts to get in touch with him after it, as baseless as her great-great-great grandson's Ouija board and seances with the spirit of his assassinated uncle Lord Mountbatten. Queen Victoria's bit of table-turning was explained by her as something to do with 'magnetism', a semi-scientific idea that was having its transient vogue in those days. She took it not much more seriously than others have taken it at house-parties before and since, including a house-party at Pakenham Hall in 1930, when Christine Longford set out a small round table in the library and we all pressed our fingers and thumbs lightly around its edge – 'lightly, not so hard, you'll tip it over!'

I was glad that when the book came out Asa Briggs, historian of the Victorian age, told me that he agreed with my conclusion on Brown and spiritualism but added for my information: 'Even Gladstone once wrote, "one must not underrate the Psychic".'

I felt a little conscience-stricken when accepting a spiritualistic book from an elderly lady whose father claimed to have discovered the identity of Jack the Ripper and to have introduced Brown to Queen Victoria as her private medium. The lady was perfectly sincere and utterly mistaken. I had not the heart to tell her that the more she confided in me the more sceptical I became. It was the same with the College of Psychic Science (now Studies) in London. They kindly offered me a cup of tea and slice of cake along with a story about Queen Victoria's intending to present John Brown in 1883 (the year he died) with an inscribed gold watch originally given to a lady known as the best clairvoyant in Britain. As the Queen had already given Brown an inscribed gold watch (now in the possession of a professor at London University) a few years before, in gratitude for saving her from the assault of Arthur O'Connor, one of her seven would-be 'assassins', it seems unlikely that the second gold watch was more than a psychic manifestation. In any case it had recently been spirited away from the College's headquarters, so I was able to see only its empty showcase and (misspelt) label.

Before I leave the writing of *Victoria R.I.*, I would like to make one general point concerning the Royal Archives. When I began working there I noticed, not without sympathy, that the librarian treated me with considerable caution, if not suspicion. After all he was the guardian of a huge, intimate family collection. He knew nothing of me personally nor of my basic intentions. Gradually the cautious attitude was relaxed as he found, I hope, that I was a respecter of history and of my subject. Where at first I had had to ask for access to documents I needed, in the end the librarian and his staff were calling to my attention documents I did not know existed. I have no complaints, only gratitude.

When I had finished, however, and was considering the jacket for my book, I was again made aware of the special position among libraries of the Royal Archives. My obvious thought was to use a portrait of Queen Victoria. This turned out to be against the rules. In so far as a book jacket was a commercial asset, it could not draw on royal portraiture to advertise itself – that is, unless the book had been commissioned by royal command. My *Victoria R.I.* had not been so commissioned and therefore the publishers and I had to assemble some royal props – a piece of Honiton lace from the Victoria & Albert Museum and a length of Garter ribbon from Garrard & Co., the Crown Jewellers – and make them into an all too impersonal jacket. Of course my American publishers, Harper's, knew nothing of this British rule and went ahead with a splendid portrait of the Queen. In fact the rule lapsed in time for my second British impression to have a lovely Landseer portrait of the young Victoria on the jacket. Nevertheless, the discarded rule still focuses attention on a perhaps inevitable problem facing all who wish to use the Archives – their dual nature.

They are both the private records of a family – and the Royal Family at that – and also the public history of the nation in so far as the monarchy is representative. While recognizing the need for great care in the granting of access to this special archive, I wonder whether present arrangements should not some day be modified in order to create a wider but equally safe access. Perhaps a division could be made between the political and personal papers, or between past and relatively recent times, the former in each category being hived off to the British Library.

Though we who have benefited from the conditions prevalent in the Round Tower – intimacy, quietude, even cosiness – may desire no change, I cannot help feeling that scholars as a whole, as well as librarians, would welcome some rational changes.

I may add that after *Victoria R.I.* was published I received a stream of letters from students, mostly American, asking how they too could get inside the Archives. I explained the rules as lucidly as possible. They went away, I think, more than ever convinced that I had got in solely because I was, as they put it, 'a lady of title'.

Victoria R.I. was published in the autumn of 1964 to a welcoming litany from 'Whitefriar' in W. H. Smith's house magazine. Our friend Esmond Warner, then managing director of Bowes & Bowes' bookshop in Cambridge, predicted my first best-seller. I could not believe it. The *Raid* had sold about four thousand copies and the most I expected was something better than that. I said to Frank just before publication: 'After all that new material from Windsor I shall be terribly disappointed if it doesn't sell well.' It did; and it also won the James Tait Black prize for biography. Kind readers sent me mementoes of the Queen which I greatly treasured: a descendant of a sprig of myrtle from her wedding bouquet, a wooden wedge to stop her pony-trap from running away, a piece of the original Balmoral tartan, pretty souvenir mugs and plates. In a letter to Ann Fleming, Evelyn Waugh said that it was 'jolly good', an unexpected accolade from the master who had incidentally told me that no woman understood grammar.

Amid the general euphoria I was suitably humbled, however, by the reviewer who saluted me as an up-and-coming *amateur* historian. I did not care for 'amateur', which could so easily slip into amateurish. But I was honoured to be coupled with my friend and contemporary at Oxford, Veronica Wedgwood, whose work has surely made it necessary to take another look at words like 'amateur', 'professional' and 'academic'.

My publishers, Weidenfeld & Nicolson, gave me a wonderful send-off, the staff presenting me with an enormous Diamond Jubilee portrait of Queen Victoria: her life-story designed by one B. D'Israel, in which every part of her – eyes, nose, mouth, jewels, dress – was composed of the words telling her story. All this and nothing in return from me – except my book. Those were the days when the author handed over the book and that was that. No 'promotion'; no radio or television interviews. I gave talks to literary societies and luncheons but that was all. How much harder the author is made to work today. Writing the book is only the beginning.

The business of promotion, however, had already begun in America; and as I happened to be there on a visit when *Born to Succeed* (the American title) was published in January 1965, I called up Harper's and asked if they wanted me to do anything about it. To my relief they said no. I don't think they expected any more of it than I did myself, though it sold even better in the United States than at home. ('Vicky in the best-selling list for 4 months,' wrote my son Michael from the States in May. 'Mum, I'm proud of you.')

It was just as well that they said no to promotion. I was busy enough celebrating a famous British defeat in New Orleans.

The 'Sesquicentennial' of the Battle of New Orleans fell in January 1965. In other words, a century and a half ago, on 12 January 1815, the last war fought by Britain against America had been won by the latter after the British commander, General Edward Michael (Ned) Pakenham, had been slain by a cannon ball on the field of Chalmette. To celebrate the anniversary of victory, the city fathers and mothers (Martha G. Robinson in particular, a glorious matriarch who was to live to over ninety) decided to invite the 'descendants' of the opposing generals, Andrew Jackson and Pakenham, to assemble at New Orleans and renew a resolve of peace and eternal friendship between their nations. The fact that neither Jackson nor Pakenham had married and therefore had no direct descendants did not worry the organizers. There were plenty of their kith and kin in the States and across the Atlantic, and all were welcome.

The head of the Pakenham family was no longer Edward Longford, who had died suddenly of a stroke in January 1961, but Frank, now the 7th Earl. There were other changes in our family. Thomas had inherited the Pakenham estate in Ireland and had restored its original Irish name of Tullynally. As Frank's wife I had become Elizabeth Longford instead of Pakenham – a change that necessitated a decision about what name to continue writing under. *Jameson's Raid* as well as all those family articles had been written by Pakenham. But I had by no means made the name so famous that I must cling on to it; besides, Longford had fewer letters and was easier to pronounce correctly. (The 'Pak' is pronounced 'Pack' not 'Pake'.) I decided to change. Only one awkward moment ensued. A reader of my family articles who thought the author had changed and disagreed with the new author's point of view, wrote to the editor: 'When Miss Longford is married and has some children of her own she may realize that what she has just written is rubbish.'

One further change in our lives might have taken place since Edward's death, but for the tragic death two years later (January 1963) of Hugh Gaitskell. We had both looked upon Hugh as our ideal leader: an orator since his 'Fight, fight and fight again' speech, every inch a Labour democrat and known to us through an intimate friendship of over thirty years. Hugh was deeply touched and surprised to find that Frank wanted to renounce both his peerages (Pakenham and Longford) and support him as future Labour Prime Minister in the Commons. Frank had never quite lost his hope of one day working for prisoners and other outcasts as Home Secretary, despite Evelyn Waugh's remark to Ann Fleming in 1951 that he was glad Frank was not Home Secretary or we should all be murdered by sex maniacs. With Hugh's death this and other dreams faded. Frank and Elizabeth Pakenham were never to reappear.

When the invitation from New Orleans reached our family it was found that Thomas, his wife Valerie and I would have to represent Frank, who was not free to leave England. (Thomas had married Valerie McNair Scott, niece of two of our oldest friends, Sheila Birkenhead and Michael Berry, in 1964.) Another Pakenham, our third son Michael, was able to join us from Rice University, Texas, where he had won an exchange scholarship after taking his Cambridge degree.

This was my first visit to America. When we changed planes in New York for New Orleans I suddenly had a rush of entirely unexpected sentiment. To hear English – my language – spoken in this huge, overwhelming concourse of total strangers was in some way deeply moving. In fact I was indulging in a preview of precisely that sense of unity which the generous people of New Orleans would be aiming to create.

We stopped for the eight days of celebration with Martha G. Robinson and her infinitely hospitable family in stylish Audubon Place and elsewhere in 'Lovely Louisiana'. (Lovely indeed in its swaying curtains of Spanish moss but not, to English eyes, in its oil derricks rearing up like monstrous cacti from every lucky person's garden.) It was a festival of jazz and dedication. We listened to famous bands and cheered Miss America and Miss Britain at a football match. Two young men, Michael Edward (*sic*) Pakenham and Andrew Jackson Donaldson, 'direct descendants' of the warring generals, paraded the girls around the arena, changing partners when they met in the middle – a symbol of concord. One evening there was a *Son et Lumière* in Jackson Square, with Michael Edward and Andrew Jackson seated in the centre of our dais and occasionally lit up by a beam of *lumière*. We saw Ol' Man River and many homes: plantation homes, ante-bellum homes, garden homes. Martha gave us an exotic breakfast after Sunday Mass of hot grapefruit, ham and eggs on toast, and bananas in hot rum with ice cream. At the grand banquet Russell Long, son of the assassinated Huey Long, made the best crack: 'At any rate the Longs and the Pakenhams have one thing in common – if you shoot one of them ten spring up to take his place.' Public opinion was divided between those who felt gratitude to Russell for making a change from the usual speech and those who considered it in bad taste.

On the last day we celebrated peace on the battlefield with typical American ceremony and informality combined. Schoolchildren were allowed to rush up screaming for autographs at the most solemn moments; flags were raised, lowered, offered, received; wreaths laid; the ubiquitous Canadian Highlanders marched about twirling their sticks. Thomas played a manly part on the programme as 'Mr Thomas Lord

Pakingham', I as 'Lady Longhorn'. After it was over we visited the avenue of Pakenham oaks, all veiled in lichen and planted in memory of Edward Michael. The day ended with the Victory Ball of the Sons of 1812. 'I have almost created a new persona for myself,' I wrote to Frank, 'being always nice & smiling . . . it will be a treat to snarl.'

Unspeakably tired, we flew on to Mexico for a few days' rest with Anne and Christopher Fremantle, friends of mine since we were up at Oxford together. In a tiny bay a few kilometres from Acapulco I got my first feel of the tropics. While undressing by a pile of rocks I noticed tracks like bicycle tyres in the smooth sand. I wondered who would be cycling round in that remote place. When I came out of the sea I saw who. A large scaly snake was on guard, head held high, beside my clothes. As soon as he saw me he vanished into the rocks.

The Pyramids of the Sun and Moon north-west of Mexico City were finer than anything in Egypt, said Thomas, except for the sphinx. Valerie stormed the Moon despite the altitude and the fact that her first child, Anna Maria Pakenham, was on the way. As we all walked along the broad processional grass strip towards the Sun, we were conscious of faint music, intermittent and eerie. Were we hallucinating in this rarified atmosphere, where the ritual of human sacrifice might still be lingering in the air-waves? No one liked to mention what he or she heard. At last the great Sun pyramid came into view. And there, elegantly draped over the ruins, in period costumes, was a television cast and crew shooting an advertisement for Ferguson Tractors.

I flew back on 15 January 1965 to a cheerful welcome from a stream of children passing through our Chelsea flat (we had moved across the road from Cheyne Gardens when the lease expired) and a rather too touching greeting from Frank. I wrote in my diary: 'Frank seems to have been more lost than usual (winter season?) and I found him wearing an odd suit – coat charcoal grey, trousers faint stripe! The correct pair can't be found.' Frank told me that he had taken a random 'sortes' from my *Victoria R.I.* while I was away to see if it would produce a comforting message. The book opened at page 131 where the youthful Prince Albert's practical jokes and mimicry were said to be 'harmless and even popular in an entirely male society'. Poor deserted Frank.

We were never to find the perfect pattern for our family holidays. While the children were small and I took them to the English seaside, Frank would enjoy a two-day flying visit out of the statutory fourteen. But when they were older and wanted to go to Italy or France? In his own childhood Frank had subscribed to the alphabet that began, 'All Abroad's Awful, Books are Bloody'. He nobly flew out to La Gaude in the Alpes Maritimes when we stayed in that village paradise with the Fawcetts. At night there was Sputnik threading its way among the stars and a vision of Venus and Jupiter's mini moons for those who could wake up before dawn to look at through James Fawcett's telescope. But alas, when Frank flew back after only two breakfasts on the terrace, he was running a temperature from sunburn. The Anglo-Irish Pakenham complexion did not welcome the Mediterranean sun.

The procession of children to greet me on my return from America began with Catherine, who emerged from my bedroom where she was temporarily installed, warmly wrapped in my clothes – 'getting to know the parents', as she told Rachel, who came up from St Clare's, Oxford, where she was reading English. From the flat opposite came Judith, her husband Alec Kazantzis and their baby Miranda. I had been present at Miranda's birth, an anxious one. She took four hours to breathe properly but has made up for it ever since. Judith had read History at Somerville, going on an Aldermaston anti-nuclear march in her second year. She wrote for several student magazines, including Ian Hamilton's *To-Day*. One poem on 'Age' (she was eighteen) was quoted in the *Standard*:

> Rose pink lipstick once I used with care
> Until no subterfuges hide
> How crumpled is the petal.
> My mirror still
> Adores me – but the trick has grown
> Brutally to see in restaurant mirrors how
> The flower has blown.

After taking her degree, she had hesitated between television and politics, but it had become politics by the time she married Alec in 1963. She stood for a hopeless Chelsea ward; he won a ward but was defeated for Edgebaston, Birmingham, in the 1964 election. Both Roy Hattersley and I spoke for him.

I had to wait to see Kevin, who was at school at Ampleforth. He had hoped in vain to muscle in on the American trip. 'I am doing a rehabilitation of Sir Edward Pakenham for my History master,' he had written from school. 'I have succeeded in putting all the blame on a Colonel Keane and the shallowness of the Mississippi!'

When Michael was about to return from Texas, Kevin wrote: 'I am dreading seeing Michael again, not because I don't want to for any personal reason, but I have *all* his clothes & unless he has changed that facet of his character he will demand them back – I may forgive him if he really does produce a beautiful, *intelligent* American girl.' Michael did produce the beautiful, intelligent American girl, Mimi, but not for another sixteen years.

The rest of January 1965 turned out to be gloomy, if dramatically so. Patrick Gordon Walker, Labour's Foreign Secretary elect, after losing his Birmingham seat on sub-racist issues at the 1964 election, lost a London by-election on 21 January. My diary called this second defeat 'ghastly, incredible'. Solly Zuckerman, Dora Gaitskell, Nicko and Mary Henderson, Frank and I all combined to give the Gordon Walkers a consoling dinner. Patrick behaved with gallant gaiety, drinking alternately out of glasses of red and white wine while Nicko quoted a wonderful phrase of Bevin's that showed how mad life was – 'a Pandora's box full of Trojan horses'.

Winston Churchill's amazing life came to an end on 24 January – the date on which his father Lord Randolph Churchill had died exactly seventy years before. Winston had always said he would die on the same date as his father. As well as attending the memorial service in St Paul's, Frank and I went to the lying-in-state with the Cabinet and their wives. The black velvet catafalque covered with the Union Jack looked like a battleship at anchor in the icy wastes of Westminster Hall. I had last seen the 'former Naval Person' in that hall when he received his portrait by Graham Sutherland as a retiring gift from both Houses of Parliament. I was astonished by the spontaneity of his reaction, the closeness of his emotions to the surface, like a child who has been presented with the wrong birthday present. He quickly twisted his first menacing frown into an ironic grimace, looking exactly like the magnificent painting that glowered back at him. As we walked away Frank said to me: 'I first fell in love with Churchill through his writing.' I replied that his impishness in old age had won my heart.

Mary and Christopher Soames had twice asked us and the Frasers over on Boxing Day to share the dinner of sucking-pig – a family tradition that reminded me of my grandfather's banquets in Birmingham. After dinner we acted charades. A phrase in all our minds at that time was Rab Butler's description of Harold Macmillan as 'the best Prime Minister we've got'. So when Antonia, impersonating Anne Boleyn, was asked why she did not leave Henry VIII, she replied, 'He's the best husband I've got.' Winston's eyes gleamed with mischief and as we said good-bye he congratulated Antonia on her 'historic' dialogue.

For Churchill's memorial service we set off in great comfort at 9.15 a.m. in a government car and found St Paul's looking positively radiant under the television lights – instead of eerie as in the gaslight at

Wellington's funeral. The joyful impression was maintained by rollicking hymns and a very short service – no address. I was glad to see two little Churchill grandchildren in red and blue coats with black armlets only. Winston's red hair flamed splendidly in his grandchildren. Outside in deep cold and gloom with dirges playing it must have seemed much more melancholy. We sat four rows behind the Royal Family with the Jays and Croslands. De Gaulle looked very frail, almost transparent; Queen Juliana rather fine; the King of the Hellenes a handsome, young 'boyo'. For a perishing hour outside the cathedral afterwards we waited for cars. I feared for poor little Clem, sitting shrivelled up on a wooden chair on the pavement, and felt he would be the next to go. Macmillan and Avon were other fragile-looking pallbearers. (They all three survived for years, Macmillan being still alive at ninety-two in 1986.)

Soon after the manuscript of *Victoria R.I.* was handed over to the publishers, the old question had arisen: what should I do next? Graham Watson, my agent, gave me lunch and came up with a biography of Mary Queen of Scots. I could grasp the connection. Another Queen. But it has always been my aim that one biography should lead to another within a span of two centuries at most. Mary was wildly outside 'my period', which I was already beginning to see as the nineteenth century. So when I mentioned Mary to my daughter Antonia, it was doubtfully. Her reaction left no room for doubt. 'No, I must do Mary,' she cried with unalterable if instantaneous conviction. I saw immediately how right she was. She had begun making genealogical tables when she was twelve, one of which started off with Mary Stuart and ended up (through the Villiers connection) with Antonia Pakenham.

My problem remained. I mentioned it to my publisher George Weidenfeld at one of his buffet dinners. I can still recall the scene. As I passed his table to fetch my pudding from the buffet, George leapt up, throwing down his napkin like a gage. 'Elizabeth, you will do the Duke of Wellington. Antonia will do Mary. You *must* do Wellington.' It was an imaginative coup on George's part. Wellington had already featured in my 'Victoria' researches as the Queen's adoptive father and an intriguingly eccentric one. Moreover, the Duke's wife had been Catherine (Kitty) Pakenham, a shadowy figure but Frank's great-great-aunt.

Kitty, however, might prove the fatal obstacle to my new ambition. For if I were to write with any authority on her husband, I would need permission to work on the family archives. Now Gerald, 7th Duke of Wellington, her direct descendant and possessor of the papers, was a distinguished historian in his own right and well versed in the sad story of Kitty Pakenham and her duke. She had her failings but no one could say that Wellington had treated her well. Would not her great-great-niece by marriage take her side in the family saga and diminish the stature of the Great Duke?

On the other hand, Gerry Wellington was eager for a new life of his illustrious ancestor based on the extensive archives at Apsley House in Piccadilly and Stratfield Saye in Hampshire, the family's country seat. Originally Gerry had thought of my friend Philip Magnus as the ideal biographer, but Philip did not consider there was enough material to suit his special talent for grinding down a mass of new facts. So 'Cousin Elizabeth' it was, as Gerry whimsically called me.

How incredibly lucky I was. He knew almost everything, but when I sent him something original he would be as pleased as if it had been his own discovery. In any difference of opinion he would always end by saying, 'It's your book; you must decide.' As when he wished me to leave out Arthur Wellesley's visits to Harriette Wilson, the courtesan, because of the brilliant tapestry of lies she had woven in her memoirs. I convinced Gerry that it was better to take Wellington's famous line over the affair: 'Publish and be damned.'

I worked solidly for two years at Apsley House, paying frequent visits to Stratfield Saye and collecting anecdotes wherever I could. At a Buckingham Palace banquet in honour of the Chilean president I asked Dickie Mountbatten whether he had any good Wellington stories. 'Yes,' he said, with his usual instinct to be helpful. 'There was a schoolgirl who used to bid an impassioned farewell at the end of every holidays to Wellington's equestrian statue outside Apsley House. One day she said, "By the way, Papa, who is the man on his back?"'

On 18 June 1965 Frank and I flew to Brussels with Kenneth Rose ('Albany' on the *Sunday Telegraph* and twenty years later the brilliant biographer of George v) to visit the battlefield of Waterloo and attend the Drumhead Service at Hougoumont, after lunching with the ambassador and the Duke and Duchess of Kent. It was a pouring wet day, just as it had been one hundred and fifty years earlier. The dye from the soldiers' red coats ran into their white belts as before, except that no one now thought it looked like blood. The rain that fell on the umbrellas of us women sounded like gunfire and drowned the Drumhead Service's message of peace. In 1815 the rain had fallen only on the surgeons' umbrellas, since Wellington forbade his officers to carry such unmanly weapons. In 1965 Frank, as a Cabinet Minister, also took the heroic course.

At the end of my first eighteen months' research I decided to continue in Spain. Frank and I had twice visited the country a few years before. The first time was to give a double lecture in Barcelona on British democracy. This attempt to *encourager les autres* fell flat, as despite the interpreter's efforts, our audience could not understand what either of us was driving at. Our second visit was rather more successful. General Franco was said to be vetoing the import of Protestant bibles into Spain. In the cause of religious freedom we urged him to change his policy. The interview in Madrid produced one amusing moment. As I marched up the long room, at the end of which stood the General awaiting us, I sneaked a glance at the wall on my right. I was looking for three photographs which Ian Gilmour had described in a *Spectator* article as being hung to resemble Christ between the two thieves – Franco, of course, being the central figure. Sharp enough to notice my glance, Franco remarked, 'I see you are looking for the photographs. Pure invention.' So was the report about the bibles, he said. Nevertheless, we were told that after our visit the flow of Protestant bibles improved.

I now planned to go with my sister-in-law Maria and Gerry Wellington to explore the battlefields of the Peninsula. Gerry cried off – 'I don't really like battlefields and you'd run too fast up the hills for me' – but we had a wonderfully rewarding time, at first staying with our ambassador in Madrid and then exploring Ciudad Rodrigo, Salamanca and other sites in depth with Nicko and Mary Henderson and the Douros. (Nicko was minister and Valerian Douro military attaché in Madrid.) We asked a ploughman on the field of Salamanca whether he ever turned up bullets or shells from the red soil. 'No,' he said. 'All gone.' Diana Douro, however, refused to admit defeat – until, after much hot scrabbling, she unearthed only the heel of a modern shoe. Many of the more remote sites which Maria and I later visited on our own proved extremely difficult to locate and I begged the Spanish Society in London to put up plaques as the French did.

That Christmas Mary Henderson designed a witty Christmas card of 'Los Hendersons – Escuela de Velazquez'. In the background was Nicko's bookcase containing a large tome entitled 'Weidenfeld the Man. In 100 vols'.

I returned to the Hendersons in the following April and this time researched in Portugal as well on the sites of Spanish sieges. We were accompanied by charming Piru, the Spanish niece of my friend Mabél Burns. In the Portuguese village of Óbidos we had our only political brush. We asked a shopkeeper where *Wellington's* palace was. He asked us in return, 'What are you? American?' 'No, English.' Immediately he flew into a rage, and believing we had enquired after *Harold Wilson's* palace, ordered us to go home and 'tell your Mr Wilson he bad man. Mr Smith good man. Tell Mr Wilson to send Mr Smith oil.' The rescue of the Peninsula from Napoleon had been forgotten; Britain now meant only Rhodesian oil sanctions.

Five months later I felt that Wellington's world-famous Lines of Torres Vedras in Portugal had not been sufficiently grasped by me. Thanks to the generosity of the Gulbenkian Foundation, Catherine and I spent a week there, Catherine mostly shopping, I photographing in blazing heat the overgrown forts and gun emplacements under the direction of a bilingual army engineer, Colonel Baptista.

I also photographed Catherine and the Colonel in front of the victory obelisk inscribed '*Non Ultra*', Catherine in a red cotton skirt and white shirt, the Colonel perfectly dressed in tweeds as if for the grouse moors. (His late wife had been a Scot.) The sky was full of dragonflies and swallowtails, as lovely as the earth was scorched.

The good Colonel had met me at the airport expecting to find a man. He bore the shock bravely and when we departed said to me, 'At least you worked hard.' Again I had only one political brush – this time over Goa. The Colonel could not forgive us for backing the Indians against our 'oldest ally' in their rival claims to possession. I had to make a rule. No discussion of politics after the year 1815.

Catherine, at twenty, was funny, pretty and very popular. The year before she had said to me: 'I want to marry in about a year's time someone who travels a lot and is clever.' If only she had. But at any rate I was able to give her a perfect week of travel.

There had been one brief month towards the end of 1964 when it seemed possible that my life would change again, adding an exciting detour to the round of politics, writing, family. It was suggested that I should put in for the post of principal of one of the Oxford women's colleges. I was greatly flattered and drawn to it. The thought of renewing our Oxford connection on a lofty level attracted both Frank and me. All our children had left home except Kevin, either to get married, work abroad or share flat life in London with friends. Kevin was in his last year at Ampleforth, hoping to gain an entrance to New College in 1965. I liked students. I was soaked in the story of women's higher education and it would be stimulating to be involved in it again. I was by now neither an out-and-out rebel nor a total conformer, which I thought might just about suit the 1960s' ethos at Oxford.

The arguments against, however, were stronger. It would mean deserting Frank from Monday to Friday for twenty-four weeks in the year. The weekends would be a problem. From Oxford to Bernhurst was a tedious journey (no motorways then) and I could never forget the horrors of a frozen Oxfordshire hill when visiting my parents' home in Kent during the war. I had had a car full of children. Suddenly we heard shouts ahead and a group of Italian prisoners-of-war working on the road tried to wave us down. But I could not stop. We zigzagged down the hill in a wild skid narrowly missing bunches of collisioned cars until at last we hit and ascended the frozen bank. 'Get out and run!' I yelled to the children, and we all tumbled over the bank and took cover in a fallow field. Behind us a Rolls-Royce came swaying past in a dignified waltz and crashed into a van at the bottom. I did not fancy repeating this kind of thing throughout the winter.

But the main obstacle was Wellington. I was under a deep obligation – and impulse – to finish the book (the first volume as it turned out) in time to publish it on the bicentenary of Wellington's birth, 1969. I am not a quick worker or a quick reader. Added to that I hate trying to divide myself between different projects, preferring to concentrate. On an analogy of Isaiah Berlin's 'fox and hedgehog' I am not a spotted terrier who runs around with eager nose to the ground, but a black cat who walks slowly but unstoppably towards her object. Those who can divide themselves between husband and children on the one side and government and academic assignments on the other, like my friend Mary Warnock, have all my admiration and envy.

So it was the usual round after all. But unusual in a way, owing to the special interest of politics in my sixtieth year. In December 1965 all our affairs seemed to come to a longed-for head. On Christmas Eve Kevin heard he had been awarded a History scholarship to New College. Two days before, Frank had been summoned to No. 10 by Harold Wilson, who was conducting the first reshuffle of his 1964–70 Government. The press, in their charming way, had long been predicting that Frank was for the political chop – no more Cabinet meetings to attend as Leader of the House of Lords; a backbencher at sixty. (Frank's sixtieth birthday had fallen on 5 December.) Instead of that, he was invited to remain in the Cabinet as Leader of the Lords but with the added bonus of a department of his own – the Colonial Secretaryship.

Our three-year-old granddaughter Natasha Fraser was the only disappointed member of the family party that Christmas. We took the four young Frasers – Rebecca, Flora, Benjamin and Natasha (Damian was a baby and Orlando not yet born) – to the traditional Boxing Day meet at Battle. Poor Natasha kept asking, 'Granny, where's the *meat?*' But she enjoyed the Christmas Mass. 'He's a nice man,' she said, meaning the priest. 'He's giving everyone presents,' meaning the wafers.

My political life, though not directly active except at elections, was full of interesting events and people. We had a good time at Lancaster House receiving the Commonwealth at the celebration of Parliament's Seven Hundred Years. The Prime Minister was down on the programme to receive, but Harold Wilson happened to be himself receiving an honorary degree in Oxford. Several guests asked Frank: 'Have you become Prime Minister?' I noted in my diary that the Commonwealth ministers shook hands gaily but their wives were too shy to smile.

I met old Mr Herbert Wilson, Harold's father, at a No. 10 garden party. He was holding court in a basket chair in the centre of the lawn. 'He is exactly like one of the old boys I used to teach in the WEA,' I wrote in my diary. 'He had bought Morley's *Life of Gladstone* as a twenty-first birthday present to himself and said son Harold had inherited all his great qualities of unflappability from his grandfather. I asked what he, Herbert, had donated. "Interest in politics," old Herbert replied, " – if that is a good quality." '

Frank had run into Harold at the royal garden party the week before. 'I'm in the doghouse,' he told Harold, 'I've lost Elizabeth.' 'You may be in the doghouse,' said Harold, 'but Elizabeth's in the wrong tent.' I had mistakenly taken Rachel, who was with us, into the diplomatic tent. As we were leaving, Alexander Weymouth ('Bath's boy' as Evelyn would have called him) spotted Rachel and came bounding towards her, hair and beard flying. 'The moment I arrived', he told her, 'I was followed by a plain-clothes man.'

My worst experience of the doghouse at a Buckingham Palace garden party was when I was officially presenting Valerie Eliot, recently married to the poet T. S. Eliot. We were bitterly disappointed to find that 'presentation' carried no guarantee of meeting the Queen, Prince Philip or any other member of the Royal Family. In vain Frank waylaid every official he knew. 'This is our greatest living poet. *Please* present him and Mrs Eliot to someone royal. . . .' The officials did not actually reply, 'Never heard of him', but that was the unspoken message. In the end I lined up Tom and Valerie, both immaculately dressed and she looking as lovely as the Blessed Damozel, against the Palace railings, where a street photographer was persuaded to snap us.

We had taken Rachel with us to the garden party in 1965 because she was shortly to leave for America. With a degree in English and several months' training with Independent Television, she had decided to work for the American Broadcasting Company. I wrote to Rachel that I had persuaded Lew Grade to come to her farewell party in the House of Lords, so all she needed to do now was to 'make the Grade . . .'. Lew prophesied that she would 'do wonders' and anyway promised to keep an eye on her. Another male guest arrived at the party wearing a tiepin inscribed, 'Rachel Don't Go!'

I felt the same, but also exhilarated for her. (Of course I did not foresee her meeting the brilliant film director Kevin Billington there, and later marrying him.) I had written to her on her twenty-first birthday two years before, while she was still at St Clare's, Oxford: 'Darling, I feel like using Q. Victoria's favourite phrase, "He/she never caused his/her dear parents a moment of anxiety".' The Principal of St Clare's, Anne Dreydel, had told us that the essay Rachel wrote on 'My Life' as part of her entrance examination was the best she had ever read. In view of Rachel's long list of future novels, I suspect that the brilliant essay was pure fiction.

Most of the family were home for the weekend before my sixtieth birthday, 30 August 1966, which we celebrated at Bernhurst. Judith and Alec came over from nearby Glynde where they had a cottage. She had recovered from an appendicitis operation and was considering having another baby, a companion for Miranda. (Arthur was duly born next year.) With her passionate interest in words, Judith had rejoiced in her surgeon's semantics before he cut her open: 'I want there to be complete confidence between us,' he began. 'After all, your life is in my hands. One nick in the bowel, and . . . ?' Warming to his theme, he continued, 'Don't worry about your inside. It is all mine, now, all mine. Leave it to me.'

Michael, having passed into the foreign service, was away on a temporary job in Kenya. 'Life is roaring on,' he wrote in April; 'the only drawback being that so far I haven't met a single African with the exception of the lift-boys. I'm living in the Great Old Colonial Hotel, the Norfolk, where Lord Delamere used to shoot out the lamps every Saturday night and gentlemen are still requested to leave their guns with the desk-clerk.' On the back of Michael's letter Catherine had scribbled, 'Ma – taken your strapless bra – do ring tomorrow at office.' She was working for Weidenfeld.

Frank gave me an amethyst four-leaved clover in a gold bracelet, Thomas a lovely pencil and sepia-wash of eighteenth-century Chelsea by Anthony Devis. Antonia had two shining silver eggs made for me by my nephew William Phipps (married to Henrietta Lamb), one inside the other. Rachel had already given me a Russian Easter Egg dated 1850, made of bejewelled wax, and Catherine a polished wooden egg from the Mount of Olives; Judith and Alec a green glass egg-shaped paperweight containing the fully developed bust of the Victorian General Buller. Paddy, Michael and Kevin, on the other hand, worshipped the god Bacchus rather than Cybele, the egg-goddess of childbirth. They had given me wine, a crystal decanter and cork ice-box. So I had been right all along. There did seem to be some sort of gender difference.

In presenting his gift, Paddy made an eloquent speech about the evening of my life. I had to correct him. 'Not evening. Early afternoon.' And there we have left it ever since.

Epilogue

It was to be an unconscionably long 'afternoon', all of twenty years. But I have decided to finish this memoir at my sixtieth year for what seems a good reason. Whereas I kept a regular diary for most of those sixty years, it was generally a short, factual one.

In the last twenty years that has changed. I kept full diaries during my travels in Greece, Italy, Switzerland, India and Egypt, while researching the subjects of later biographies, Byron and Wilfrid Scawen Blunt. I may have acquired the habit when researching Wellington in Portugal and Spain. At any rate, my diaries for the last twenty years are much fuller. To include them would have unbalanced the book.

One later year, however, stands out from my pebbled shore, that I cannot forget or omit. This was the year 1969. Most of my pebbles have been gaily coloured, particularly when the waves of time wash over them. 1969 bade fair to be a year of unique family celebration.

Paddy, at the Bar, had married Mary Plummer the year before, and in April 1969 their eldest son Richard was born (to be followed by Guy and Harry). Moreover, such a spate of family books was either just out or about to be published during the year that Christina Foyle gave a special luncheon for the whimsically labelled 'Literary Longfords'.

Antonia led the way in May with her best-selling biography, *Mary Queen of Scots*, which won the James Tait Black prize; there was Thomas's historical *Year of Liberty*; Judith's *Women in Revolt*, published the year before; Rachel's first novel, *All Things Nice*; my *Wellington: The Years of the Sword*, which won the Yorkshire Post literary prize and, to put us all in our place, Frank's *Humility*. Kevin had founded and was editing a magazine at Oxford called *Cover*, which had the honour of publishing the year before (February 1968) the first draft of Philip Larkin's poem 'History', later published by Faber as 'Annus Mirabilis' in *High Windows* (1974). The first stanza of *Cover*'s version ran: 'Sexual intercourse began / In 1963 / (Which was rather late for me) / Between the end of the Chatterley ban / And the Beatles first L.P.' Catherine was now working on the

327

Sunday Telegraph magazine. From Michael in Poland, where he was second secretary at the embassy under Nicko Henderson, the ambassador, came a letter of congratulatory protest: 'It is in fact becoming rather ridiculous that every time I open a paper I see a member of the family smiling out of it. Are you all using the same press agent or is there an entire firm under contract?'

That August Rachel and I decided to visit Michael and the Hendersons in Warsaw. Catherine would normally have spent the weekend at Bernhurst with us, but as I was away she stayed with her friend Gina Richardson in East Anglia. Early on the Monday morning, 11 August, the car of their photographer friend Stefan, in which they were returning to work, was in collision with a lorry. All three were killed instantly.

This was an appalling black, slippery rock suddenly outcropping on my pebbled shore. I had to get over it or go round it if I were ever to reach my ocean. I think I have got over it. I am sometimes asked whether faith helped: belief in immortality and a personal resurrection. My answer is that nothing lessens the pain at the time. I remember Frank being sent for by Mrs de Valera, a devout Catholic and wife of the Irish President, soon after Catherine died. 'Tell Elizabeth', she said to him, 'that I cried every day for a year when our youngest son was killed in a riding accident. She will do the same. But now I would not have him back.'

Faith saved me from asking the terrible questions, 'Why? Why her? Why me?' I also had a growing conviction that Catherine was all right. It was a comfort to be able to do something for her, Gina and Stefan every day, if only to say a Hail Mary. A Catholic family friend, Professor Agnes Headlam-Morley, gave me unexpected strength when she presented me with a translation of Dante. I had been worried about the Catholic idea of 'years' in Purgatory, wishing that it could all be over in a timeless flash. But I stopped thinking along these unhappy lines after reading the end of the *Purgatorio*:

This mountain is always hard at the start and the higher one goes it is less difficult; therefore when going up seems to you as pleasant and easy as going down-stream in a boat, then you will be at the end of this path. . . . From the most holy waters I came forth again remade, like new plants renewed with new leaves, pure and ready to mount to the stars.

After Dante came St Thomas More's last letter to his daughter:

Pray for me, and I shall pray for you and all your friends, that we may merrily meet in Heaven.

I also liked to remember two things that Catherine had said in her last year. When a young friend, a grandson of Harold Macmillan, died suddenly, I naturally commiserated with her, but she had said, 'I don't think it's sad to die young.' And when she was in Jerusalem that Easter she went to Confession and Communion. At twenty-three she was not an indefatigable church-goer, so I expressed surprise and pleasure when she told me. She laughed and referred to the unpredictability of life. 'One never knows.'

Frank's apparent epilogue had begun the year before with his resignation from the Cabinet on a question of principle – he was for raising the school-leaving age. His funniest letters of congratulatory condolence came from Lady Diana Cooper and Lord Willis. 'My dear Frank, I am so proud of you, in spite of not being your mother,' wrote Diana. 'Well, well done. This is not written as a Tory but as an admirer of your character.' Ted Willis (Labour) wrote:

I shall miss the sight of that long bean-pole figure rising in front of me, like a spring slowly uncoiling; I shall miss the vision of your lovely blueish-tinged pate, catching the amber light from the chamber roof: I shall miss those kind thank-you notes you used to write at the end of each session, with an absolutely unintelligible bit in your own hand-writing at the bottom: I shall miss you.

After this epilogue there followed for Frank another important public chapter with which I at first disagreed. I was proved wrong. Frank took up the crusade against pornography. The *Sunday Times* reported him in Copenhagen 'Amid the Alien Porn', and taxi drivers would say to him, 'I know you're Lord Porn but what's your other name?' I objected to the crusade on anti-censorship grounds – until I read some of the hard porn that was circulating in comprehensive schools among girls of twelve. If one is against racism, sadism and sexist exploitation of women, one must be in favour of banning these cesspits that degrade the name of 'book'.

Meanwhile, my understanding of the art of biography was growing. Inspiration comes to biographers as much as to novelists but cannot be commanded by any cerebral tricks. Nevertheless, one can do something to help it breathe.

In the last twenty years I have worked out a 'writing day' for myself. I write best in the morning, though not immediately after breakfast. I use that first hour to write letters or shopping lists; even the laundry list loosens me up and gets me going with a pen. Writing out of doors suits me best, either in the Sussex garden or on the Chelsea balcony. Outdoor sounds seem to absorb the distractive parts of my brain and leave the rest free to concentrate. It may be that I have got used over the years to writing in some degree of noise indoors: children in the same room or myself on a train journey. The only place I can't perform is at a desk on a straight-backed chair.

Writing late at night seems more inspirational than it is. I seldom find the results come up to scratch when I re-read them next morning. Indeed problems that have appeared insoluble at midnight have a way of smoothly solving themselves at midday.

Structure and chronology are among the perennial problems. How to deal with the subject's personal and public life? They are, in fact, happening simultaneously, whereas in the biography there may have to be some measure of separation. Should it be separate chapters? Or separate sections within the same chapter? I have used both methods, though the former more with public male characters who tend, conveniently for the biographer, to compartmentalize their lives. Women, even public women, are more 'open plan'.

I re-read endlessly what I have written and make continuous corrections: sometimes substantial ones involving rearrangements of material, more often verbal changes. Really obstinate problems have to be solved with the help of manual labour – preferably gardening. Not in order to continue thinking but for mental refreshment. Clearing the ground for a new rosebush clears away the mental rubbish as well.

All these techniques to be developed for what? Biography. Not for the (superior) arts of fiction or history. I think biography chose me, as it chooses most of its operators. And chose me because I wanted to write in the ways it had to offer. Michael Holroyd, author of *Lytton Strachey*, has said that biography is the nearest art to the novel. It is about people and it thrives on imagination, to decipher them if not to create. I prefer to work on people who were or are *there*, as a doctor or teacher does, not so much on might-have-beens. I like to see them in my mind's eye as a novelist does, but also to see the actual letters they wrote, clothes they wore, parks they walked in. There is a special excitement in handling their possessions that seems to generate extra perceptiveness. One begins to explore the personality as if with a compass or divining rod instead of at random.

Of course one can misinterpret physical surroundings. I remember being impressed by the gaiety of the calves skipping and cavorting in Windsor Home Park. What a cheerful sight for royalty to watch from the long grey windows, I thought – until a lady-in-waiting explained that the skipping showed they had warble-fly in their ears.

I like my subject to be encapsulated in a life, as history is not. All the same, my biographies must always to some extent be a 'Life and Times of . . .'. The balance between 'Life' and 'Times', however, is one of the most difficult to achieve. A reviewer said there was not enough historical background in my first biography (*Victoria R.I.*); when I tried to repair that omission in my second (*Wellington*), another reviewer said there was too much. Can one win? Help has come, notwithstanding, from two guidelines, the first having been offered by Cecil Woodham-Smith, biographer of Florence Nightingale. 'Always keep your narrative moving.' That means, among other things, avoidance of too much argument with other historians, a pastime in which academics delight. My second rule is never to lose sight of my subject for more than a page or so. I aim at the maximum of background detail with the minimum of digression.

Another elusive question of balance concerns sympathy with one's subject. I could never write a biography of, say, Hitler, though I recognize the need for such works; perhaps the author's righteous indignation supplies the adrenalin usually produced by enthusiasm. Every self-respecting biographer tries to avoid hagiography like a plague of treacle. (I once described Queen Elizabeth II at a ball as looking 'out of this world', which my biographer daughter Antonia pointed out was 'literally hagiography'.) The difficulty is that *your* hagiography is *my* good manners. While several critics congratulated my *Elizabeth R* on not being sugary, my candid friend John Grigg, author of *Lloyd George*, said it was 'all guff and gush'. I looked up 'guff' in the *Concise Oxford Dictionary*. No such word. Then I tried the *Shorter Oxford Dictionary*. There I found 'Guff: Nonsense'. That must explain the difference between conciseness and shortness.

Perhaps the thing I am really striving for is 'empathy'. It was not an English word before 1912, but it has since been successfully reintroduced from America, via the Greek *empatheia* and German nineteenth-century psychology. While sympathy merely means fellow-feeling, empathy means 'the power of projecting one's personality into, and fully understanding, the object of contemplation'. I can only do this with someone I like. As Thomas Carlyle wrote of Mahomet in *Heroes and Hero-Worship*: 'I mean to say all the good of him I possibly can. It's a way to get at his secret.' Incidentally, the one thing that makes biography unreadable is to lecture or rebuke one's subject.

Satire, though more fun than hagiography, can be equally misleading. When I came to write *Eminent Victorian Women* I found that Lytton Strachey's satirical attitude towards Florence Nightingale in his *Eminent Victorians*, in many ways so brilliant, had led him to fudge her most interesting characteristic. God, he wrote, appeared to her as 'a glorified sanitary engineer'. A dazzling phrase, but untrue. By setting up her God in a bathroom rather than a cloud, he had blinded himself to the problem of her neurotic mysticism.

I have only once felt my empathy oozing away while in the midst of writing a biography, an alarming experience. My subject was Wilfrid Scawen Blunt, the poet and amorist. Fortunately my sympathies returned as his physical powers failed. G. M. Young, however, completely lost his empathy with Stanley Baldwin while writing his official life and produced an attack instead of a biography.

Detection is another aspect of biography that I like: both the probing into character and the weighing up of fact versus legend. A 'Catch 22' situation is often involved at the beginning of these researches. If one reads secondary sources first – other authors' books – one may be prejudiced by them before one has had time to form one's own opinion; but if one goes straight into the original sources – letters and diaries – one may not be sufficiently well equipped to detect the hidden evidence on some controversy or problem. My own solution has been to read (or re-read) *one* general account first – Strachey's *Queen Victoria*, Guedalla's *The Duke*, Marchand's *Byron* – and then dive into the primary sources.

Questions of fact or legend require exhaustive research but are sometimes solved by accident, occasionally too late, alas, for one's current book. I could not decide, for example, whether Queen Elizabeth II kept a real diary or merely a brief engagement record. After the publication of *Elizabeth R* I happened to mention this doubt during a lecture to a conference of American university women in London. One of them came up to me and said: 'I *know*. When our group was introduced to Her Majesty I asked, "Ma'am, do you keep a diary? If so, how do you find the time?" The Queen replied, "Prince Philip and Prince Charles read in bed. I write my diary. And it's a great deal more honest than anything you'll find in the media." '

My conviction that Queen Victoria never became the mistress of John Brown, her gillie, was strengthened after the publication of my *Victoria R.I.* It was reported not long ago that a man had died in Paris, aged ninety, who claimed to be Victoria's and Brown's son. If true, that would have meant the Queen's secretly bearing a tenth (bastard) child at fifty.

In the decade when I became a biographer – the 1960s – a double revolution in the art took place, the matrix being American universities. First, the availability of sources suddenly increased with the large-scale collecting of archives and the development of photocopying. As my friend Professor Phyllis Grosskurth, author of *Havelock Ellis* and *Melanie Klein*, has said, the old laborious hand copying by biographers had become almost a 'cottage industry'. Today we are in the electronic age.

Second came the distinction between narrative and analytical/

psychological biography. While I myself did not abandon 'narrative', I have learnt from the disciplines of 'in-depth' research. Forget all we ever knew about biography from the *Oxford Dictionary of Quotations*, especially Disraeli's 'Read no history; nothing but biography, for that is life without theory.' Today in certain quarters biography has become theory without life. As far as possible the life *story* is ignored; even dates of birth and death may be hard to find. There is instead a wealth of interpretation of the subject's own words, which should eventually lay bare the 'naked self', the 'inner me'. Individual lives being incoherent, there must be no attempt at continuous narrative but everything should be 'discontinuous' and open-ended.

In still safeguarding narrative, I accept the need to add to my duties as biographer 'the roles of interpreter, mediator between other writers' views, and analyst' (Grosskurth). The literary analyst will search for and find the 'great moment' (Gissing) in his or her subject's life: the moment when Queen Victoria hears a mystic voice saying, 'Still endure'; the moment when Wellington says, 'I am the King's retained servant'; the moment when Elizabeth II says, 'I must be seen to be believed.'

My chief fear for the future is that the analytic game may become too facile, too seductive. Queen Mary, for instance, said towards the end of her life, 'The one thing I regret is never having climbed over a fence.' How easy to interpret this 'in depth', seeing in it a repressed wish to get to the other side, to be ordinary, to leave royalty behind. Or the white soles to Queen Victoria's black stockings? Did she have them woven thus in response to a play upon words that haunted her unconscious? 'White soles . . . white soul . . . black soles . . . feet of clay. . . .'

Biography is too important to become a playground for fantasies, however ingenious. I believe its future is safe with the reading public, who will keep it human, not too solemn, and more or less sane.

My grandchildren and my writing must be the epilogue to this epilogue. Thomas had a six-sided glasshouse, known as the Lantern, set up at the bottom of the Bernhurst garden, so that I could work inside it if the rest of the garden had been taken over by the younger grandchildren: his and Valerie's Ned and Fred; Rachel's and Kevin's Nat, Rose, Chloe and Caspar; Michael's and Mimi's Alex and Clio; Kevin's and Ruth's Kate and Tom, his and Clare's Ben and Hermione. It was a favourite corner for me, having an ethereal view to the west and being bounded by a golden yew grown from a seedling that my mother had given me. By sunlight or moonlight, everything in this part of the garden looked more beautiful as the years went by – everything except the moon itself. I told

Judith one day that I could not feel the same about the moon since the landings. She wrote a poem on it:

> Now   here
> in the cool bottom, the moon's
>   bare golden cavities
>   hide
> US and Soviet hardware; and
> my mother says wistfully, she
> can't take pleasure in the July country
> moon, a vast hunk beyond the pine trees,
> any more – but only her unclipped golden yewtree
>   on the lawn
> facing out west, like a ship's maiden –
>
> How graceful is the golden yewtree,
> seedling of my grand mother,
> facing out west. How hard and golden
> is the July country moon, crowded
> with pickaxes, a used
> vehicle lot. I said: I forget. That
> doesn't worry me.

Occasionally the grandchildren take me over as well as the rest of the garden. When Thomas's daughter Eliza was just eleven, she sent me a poem for Christmas in which she saucily reversed our roles:

> Anyone that's sane can see
> That my granny takes after me.
> She is wise and very clever,
> Makes mistakes oh! never! never!
>
> We are beauties her and me
> Just as women should rightly be.
> So brilliant, brainy, driving genes –
> Me and my granny make a team.

Perhaps she was right and grandparents do take after their grandchildren. I hope so. However, having spent my whole life looking out at people, I had never until then wondered what the young saw when they looked in at me. Into the glasshouses where grandmothers sit knitting, reading or writing their books. Old, old women with white hair? I cannot imagine myself in that image. Except when I am actually looking in the mirror, I feel and am exactly the same person as I was sixty years ago.

On a summer evening last year I was sitting inside the Lantern deep in the writing of this book. Suddenly I began to feel that someone was looking in on me. I half turned. It was a young fox, black nose pressed against the glass like an urchin outside a sweetshop. The moment our eyes met he was off. What had he seen? Perhaps a hen on her perch. Too hard to get. What does anybody see?

Index

337